# Change and Continuity in the 2016 Elections

**John H. Aldrich**
*Duke University*

**Jamie L. Carson**
*University of Georgia*

**Brad T. Gomez**
*Florida State University*

**David W. Rohde**
*Duke University*

FOR INFORMATION:

CQ Press
An Imprint of SAGE Publications, Inc.
2455 Teller Road
Thousand Oaks, California 91320
E-mail: order@sagepub.com

SAGE Publications Ltd.
1 Oliver's Yard
55 City Road
London EC1Y 1SP
United Kingdom

SAGE Publications India Pvt. Ltd.
B 1/I 1 Mohan Cooperative Industrial Area
Mathura Road, New Delhi 110 044
India

SAGE Publications Asia-Pacific Pte. Ltd.
3 Church Street
#10-04 Samsung Hub
Singapore 049483



Printed in the United States of America

*Library of Congress Cataloging-in-Publication Data*

Names: Aldrich, John H., author.

Title: Change and continuity in the 2016 elections / John H. Aldrich, Jamie L. Carson, Brad T. Gomez, David W. Rohde.

Description: Los Angeles : SAGE/CQ PRESS, 2018. | Includes bibliographical references and index.

Identifiers: LCCN 2017042445 | ISBN 9781544320250 (pbk. : alk. paper)

Subjects: LCSH: Presidents—United States—Election—2016. | United States. Congress—Elections, 2016. | Voting—United States. | Elections—United States.

Classification: LCC JK526 2018 .A54 2018 | DDC 324.973/0932—dc23
LC record available at https://lccn.loc.gov/2017042445

This book is printed on acid-free paper.

Acquisitions Editor: Monica Eckman
Editorial Assistant: Zachary Hoskins
Production Editor: Christine Dahlin
Copy Editor: Pam Schroeder
Typesetter: C&M Digitals (P) Ltd.
Proofreader: Alison Syring
Indexer: Amy Murphy
Cover Designer: Janet Kiesel
Marketing Manager: Erica DeLuca

18 19 20 21 22 10 9 8 7 6 5 4 3 2 1

# CONTENTS

## PART II • VOTING BEHAVIOR IN THE 2016 PRESIDENTIAL ELECTION

# TABLES AND FIGURES

## Tables

## Figures

# PREFACE

On November 8, 2016, Republican Donald Trump was elected president of the United States despite losing the popular vote. Trump's Electoral College victory over the Democratic nominee, former Secretary of State Hillary Clinton, marked the first time since 2000 that the popular vote winner did not also win a majority of votes in the Electoral College. The Democrats gained two Senate seats in 2016, but this was insufficient for them to regain majority control of the upper chamber. The Democrats also gained six seats in the House of Representatives, but the Republicans maintained a sizable majority and thus control of that body.

In the short term, the reemergence of unified partisan control of government created new opportunities for a Republican majority in adopting key aspects of their political agenda. Yet with recent legislative struggles in Congress and a new president besieged by his inability to deliver on major campaign promises—somewhat unusual circumstances for a first-term president with unified government—Democrats remain cautiously optimistic about winning back control of government in the future. Democrats have now won the popular vote in six of the last seven presidential elections. The party currently draws support from a coalition of the highly educated, women, African Americans, and Latinos. The latter two groups are expected to increase as a share of the U.S. population over the next twenty years, and electoral participation among both groups has increased steadily in recent years. Yet any talk of a long-term electoral advantage for the Democrats presupposes that current voters will maintain their loyalties to the two political parties and that group allegiances will be stable over time. The past shows that this can be a tenuous assumption.

Is America in the midst of an electoral transformation? What were the sources of Trump's victory in 2016, and how do they differ from Republican coalitions of the past? Does his victory signal a long-term positive trajectory for Republicans' chances in presidential elections? And are the electoral forces at play in presidential elections similar to those that structure congressional elections? These are the sorts of questions that we seek to answer here.

## OUR ANALYSIS

In our study of the 2016 elections, we rely on a wide variety of evidence. Because the bulk of our analysis focuses on individuals' voting decisions, we rely extensively on survey evidence—four surveys in particular. In studying voter turnout, we employ the Current Population Survey (CPS) conducted by the U.S. Census Bureau. The CPS provides information on the registration and voting behavior of more than 131,000 individuals from more than 80,000 households. In examining voting patterns, we rely heavily on a survey of more than 24,500 voters interviewed as they exited the voting booths; this survey, conducted by Edison Research for a consortium of news organizations, is commonly referred to as the "pool poll." We employ pool poll data in our analysis of the 2014 congressional midterm elections as well. These data were also collected by Edison Research and reflect a combination of exit and telephone interviews with more than 19,000 voters. In studying the party loyalties of the American electorate, we also analyze data from the General Social Survey (GSS) conducted by the National Opinion Research Center at the University of Chicago, which measured party identification twenty-seven times from 1972 through 2008, usually relying on about 1,500 respondents.

Our main source of survey data is the 2016 American National Election Studies (ANES) survey based on 1,181 face-to-face and 3,090 web-based interviews conducted before the 2016 election and 1,059 face-to-face and 2,590 interviews conducted after the election, using the version of the data released for analysis on May 2, 2017. This 2016 ANES is part of an ongoing series funded mainly by the National Science Foundation. These surveys, carried out originally by a team of scholars at the University of Michigan, began with a small study of the 1948 election; the first major study was in 1952. The ANES investigative team has studied every subsequent presidential election, as well as all thirteen midterm elections from 1954 to 2002. The 2016 ANES was conducted jointly by Stanford University and the University of Michigan. In the course of our book, we use data from all thirty-one surveys conducted between 1948 and 2016.

The ANES data are available to scholars throughout the world. Although we are not responsible for the data collection, we are responsible for our analyses. The scholars and staff at the ANES are responsible for neither our analyses nor our interpretation of these data. Similarly the organizers and researchers of the CPS, GSS, and national pool poll bear no responsibility for our analyses or interpretation.

## ACKNOWLEDGMENTS

Many people assisted us with this study. We deeply appreciate the hard work of our research assistants, Ryan Williamson at the University of Georgia, Mark Dudley at Duke University, Jessica Sullivan at the North Carolina School of Science and Mathematics (serving on a mentorship program at Duke) and now at Duke, and David Macdonald and Joshua Scriven at Florida State University. Ryan assisted with the data analysis for Chapters 2, 6, 7, 8, 9, and 10; Mark provided special assistance in integrating the 2016 ANES with earlier election studies; and David assisted with the data analysis for Chapters 3, 4, and 5.

In our study of turnout, we were greatly assisted by Michael P. McDonald of the University of Florida, who for several years has provided scholars with a valuable resource on voter turnout. McDonald's website, the United States Elections

Project (http://www.electproject.org), presents detailed national- and state-level estimates of voter turnout based on both voting-age and voting-eligible population estimates.

Several years ago Russell J. Dalton of the University of California at Irvine and the late Robert W. Jackman of the University of California at Davis helped us locate information about cross-national estimates of voter turnout. Abraham Diskin of the Hebrew University of Jerusalem helped us locate turnout data for Israel and provided us with updated data for this volume. Corwin D. Smidt at Michigan State University exposed us to several recent studies on religion and politics. And we thank Gary C. Jacobson of the University of California, San Diego for sharing his data on 2016 House and Senate race types.

We are grateful for support from the Department of Political Science at Duke University, the Department of Political Science at the University of Georgia, the Political Institutions and Public Choice Program at Duke University, and the Department of Political Science at Florida State University.

At CQ Press we are grateful to Charisse Kiino and Monica Eckman for encouragement and Michael Kerns for help in the early editorial stages. We are especially grateful to them for finding reviewers who had assigned our book in the past, thereby allowing us to receive input from instructors and, indirectly, from students. The reviewers were Suzanne Chod (North Central College), Abbie Erler (Kenyon College), Alison Howard (Dominican University of California), Brad Lockerbie (East Carolina University), and Thomas R. Marshall (University of Texas Arlington). We are grateful to Christine Dahlin, our production editor; Zachary Hoskins; and Erica DeLuca for her efforts in marketing our book. Pam Schroeder did an excellent job of copyediting the manuscript.

This book continues a series of books that we began with a study of the 1980 elections. In many places we refer to our earlier books, all of which were published by CQ Press. Some of this material is available online through the CQ Voting and Elections Collection, which can be accessed through many academic and public libraries.

Like our earlier books, this one was a collective enterprise in which we divided the labor. With the volume preceding this one, however, membership in the collective changed. With David Rohde's retirement from the writing and data analysis, Jamie Carson was invited to join the authorship team. Brad Gomez had primary responsibility for the Introduction and Chapters 3, 4, and 5; John Aldrich for Chapters 1, 6, 7, and 8; and Jamie Carson for Chapters 2, 9, and 10. Aldrich, Carson, and Gomez collaborated on Chapter 11.

Finally we dedicate this book to our friend and colleague, Paul R. Abramson of Michigan State University. Paul coauthored seventeen volumes in the *Change and Continuity* series, beginning with the first volume in 1980. Although he retired from writing on this series, Paul's influence remains. We are indebted to him for his contributions to this project. Paul and his wife, Janet, lost their beloved son, Lee, in 2016 to his long, brave fight with ALS (Lou Gehrig's Disease). Lee also contributed to these volumes from time to time with assistance in gathering data. Paul, Janet, and their daughter, Heather, remain in our thoughts. Shalom, friends.

We appreciate feedback from our readers. Please contact us if you disagree with our interpretations, find factual errors, or want further clarification about our methods or our conclusions.

John H. Aldrich
Duke University
aldrich@duke.edu

Jamie L. Carson
University of Georgia
carson@uga.edu

Brad T. Gomez
Florida State University
bgomez@fsu.edu

David W. Rohde
Duke University
rohde@duke.edu

# ABOUT THE AUTHORS

**John H. Aldrich** is Pfizer-Pratt University Professor of Political Science at Duke University. He is author of *Why Parties? A Second Look* (2011) and *Before the Convention* (1980) and coeditor of *Positive Changes in Political Science* (2007), and he has also published numerous articles, chapters, and edited collections. He is past president of the Southern Political Science Association, the Midwest Political Science Association, and the American Political Science Association.

**Jamie L. Carson** is professor of political science at the University of Georgia. His research interests include congressional politics and elections, American political development, and separation of powers. He is coauthor of *Ambition, Competition, and Electoral Reform* (2013) and *Electoral Incentives in Congress* (2018) and has published articles in the *American Political Science Review*, *American Journal of Political Science*, *Journal of Politics*, and other journals.

**Brad T. Gomez** is associate professor of political science at Florida State University. His research interests focus on voting behavior and public opinion, with a particular interest in how citizens attribute responsibility for sociopolitical events. His published work has appeared in the *American Political Science Review*, *American Journal of Political Science*, *Journal of Politics*, and other journals and edited volumes.

**David W. Rohde** is Ernestine Friedl Professor of Political Science and director of the Political Institutions and Public Choice Program at Duke University. He is coeditor of *Why Not Parties?* (2008) and *Home Style and Washington Work* (1989), author of *Parties and Leaders in the Postreform House* (1991), and coauthor of *Supreme Court Decision Making* (1976).

# INTRODUCTION

Presidential elections in the United States are partly ritual, a reaffirmation of our democratic values. But they are far more than rituals. The presidency confers a great deal of power, and those powers have expanded during most of the twentieth century and into the twenty-first century. It is precisely because of these immense powers that presidential elections have at times played a major role in determining public policy and in some cases altered the course of American history.

The 1860 election, which brought Abraham Lincoln and the Republicans to power and ousted a divided Democratic Party, focused on whether slavery should be extended to the western territories. After Lincoln's election eleven southern states attempted to secede from the Union, the Civil War broke out, and, ultimately, the U.S. government abolished slavery completely. Thus an antislavery plurality—Lincoln received only 40 percent of the popular vote—set in motion a chain of events that freed some four million black Americans.

In the 1896 election Republican William McKinley defeated the Democrat and Populist William Jennings Bryan, thereby beating back the challenge of western and agricultural interests to the prevailing financial and industrial power of the East. Although Bryan mounted a strong campaign, winning 47 percent of the popular vote to McKinley's 51 percent, the election set a clear course for a policy of high tariffs and the continuation of the gold standard for American money.

Lyndon B. Johnson's 1964 landslide over Republican Barry M. Goldwater provided the clearest set of policy alternatives of any election in the twentieth century.[1] Goldwater offered "a choice, not an echo," advocating far more conservative social and economic policies than Johnson. When Johnson received 61 percent of the popular vote to Goldwater's 38 percent, he saw his victory as a mandate for his Great Society programs, the most far-reaching social legislation since World War II. The election also seemed to offer a clear choice between escalating American involvement in Vietnam and restraint. But America's involvement in Vietnam expanded after Johnson's election, leading to growing opposition to Johnson within the Democratic Party, and four years later he did not seek reelection.

Only the future can determine the ultimate importance of the 2016 election. Some scholars argue that American elections have become less important with time, and there is some truth to their arguments.[2] Yet elections do offer important choices on public policy, choices that may affect the course of governance—even if only in the short term.

Despite the continued, fifteen-year-long presence of American combat forces in Afghanistan, the 2016 presidential election focused mainly on economic issues. Nearly a decade removed from the Great Recession of 2007–2009, the U.S. economy had experienced a prolonged period of economic growth, but growth had been slow and uneven. The average annual growth rate in real GDP between 2010 and 2016 was 2.1 percent, well below the average 3.1 percent growth rate experienced during the decade before the economic collapse or the 3.2 percent growth rate experienced in the 1990s.[3] Between 2009 and 2016, corporate profits in the United States had grown by nearly 50 percent, and the Dow Jones Industrial Average signaled a bullish stock market, increasing a staggering 12,000 points over the seven-year period.[4] But these corporate gains were not always felt in the pocketbooks of average citizens. By election day 2016, the U.S. unemployment rate had declined to 4.6 percent, well below its 2009 high mark of 10 percent and similar to 2007 levels. But the number of long-term unemployed individuals was higher than pre-recession levels, and so too was labor force participation, meaning that many Americans who could not find jobs simply withdrew from the labor market.[5] Real median household income in the United States declined in four of the seven years between 2009 and 2016, and economic inequality in the United States, which has increased markedly since 1980, reached levels not seen since the 1920s.[6]

These economic issues provided the backdrop for one of the most remarkable electoral events in U.S. history—one not soon to be forgotten. For the first time ever, one of the major American parties nominated a candidate with no prior political or military experience, Donald J. Trump. Trump, the Republican Party nominee, was no stranger to the American public; the billionaire New York real estate developer had been a fixture on Americans' televisions and tabloid magazines since the early 1980s, and for fourteen seasons, he hosted a reality TV show, *The Apprentice*, on NBC. And now he was an American Silvio Berlusconi, a billionaire populist, speaking for the "common man" against the "rigged system."[7] Trump argued that America's economic woes were the product of unfair international trade deals, taxation, and illegal immigration. According to Trump, "[America's] politicians have aggressively pursued a policy of globalization—moving our jobs, our wealth, and our factories to Mexico and overseas."[8] Trump's anti-free trade message was counter to conventional Republican Party doctrine, and he promised to renegotiate America's trade deals with China and "tear up" the 1994 North American Free Trade Agreement (NAFTA) with Mexico and Canada.[9] Trump's views on taxation were more in step with his party, favoring significant reductions in corporate tax rates, a lowering of the top individual tax rate from 39.6 percent to 33 percent, and a repeal of the estate tax. Perhaps his most noted (and divisive) policy position was on the issue of immigration. Even before announcing his candidacy, Trump had warned conservatives in his party against comprehensive immigration reforms that would create a path to citizenship for illegal immigrants already in the United States: "They're taking your jobs. You better be careful."[10] Instead Trump promised, "I will build a great, great wall on our southern border. And I will have Mexico pay for that wall."[11]

For the most part Democratic Party nominee Hillary Clinton's economic positions were more in line with her party's typical positions. Clinton called for increased government spending for job training programs and community college education; the former First Lady, senator, and secretary of state argued that spending in these areas could help retrain workers who had lost jobs in manufacturing industries. Clinton's position on taxation was antithetical to Trump's, arguing that "we need to get the wealthy and the corporations to pay more for their fair share."[12] Clinton also argued that Trump's trade policy would start a trade war with China. But Clinton was forced to take a more nuanced approach to trade policy than perhaps she would have liked. For instance, as secretary of state, Clinton had originally supported America's participation in the Trans-Pacific Partnership (TPP), calling it the "gold standard" of trade agreements. But after fighting back a primary challenge from Vermont senator Bernie Sanders, a socialist and only recent affiliate of the Democratic Party, she withdrew her support from the TPP rather than risk alienating Sanders's supporters: "I oppose it now. I'll oppose it after the election, and I'll oppose it as president."[13] Clinton's position on immigration also contrasted sharply with Trump's. Clinton claimed that the U.S. border with Mexico was "the most secure border we have ever had" and that Trump's plan for a wall across the entire border was pure "fantasy."[14] And Clinton supported immigration reform efforts to provide lawful status to the children of illegal immigrants and a path to citizenship for undocumented immigrants who did not provide a security threat.

Another issue on which the candidates differed was on the future of the central legislative achievement of the Obama administration, the Affordable Care Act of 2010, commonly known as "Obamacare." The legislation marked the most significant change to the nation's health care system since the creation of Medicare and Medicaid during the 1960s. It mandated that all individuals who are not currently insured or already covered under government insurance programs buy a private health insurance policy or pay a penalty (a "tax" according to the United States Supreme Court). And to lower the costs of policies, Obamacare promoted the creation of state-level health insurance exchanges to foster competition among insurance providers and grant subsidies to low-income individuals and families to offset costs. Clinton hoped to amend the program, among other things, expanding the tax credits individuals could receive to offset out-of-pocket health expenses, increasing funding for community health centers, and increasing government control over drug price increases.[15] Trump offered few details about how he would reform the health care system other than his oft-stated pledge to "immediately repeal and replace Obamacare."

The contrast between the two candidates who squared off in the 2016 presidential election could not have been sharper, both in style and substance. On the Republican side was a highly confrontational political novice who often engaged on the political trail in both bombast and profanity, pledging to "make America great again" and claiming during his nomination acceptance speech that "I alone can fix it." On the Democratic side was the ultimate political insider, a policy wonk who had not only served a president but also had been married to one. However, for all of their differences, Trump and Clinton had one thing in common—Americans didn't seem to like either one. On the eve of the election, the Gallup Poll reported that the candidates suffered from the lowest favorability ratings recorded by the company since it starting asking the question back in 1956. According to Gallup, 52 percent of Americans viewed Clinton unfavorably, whereas a record 61 percent found Trump unfavorable.[16] Yet, despite the public's consternation, the election went on . . . just as the Constitution mandates. On November 8, 2016, Donald J. Trump was elected president of the United States, winning a comfortable Electoral College victory despite losing the popular vote to Clinton, 48.2 to 46.1 percent.

To be sure, the 2016 presidential campaign was unusual; from the rise of an unorthodox candidate to the presence of a woman at the head of a party's ticket (a historic first), and there were missing emails, stolen emails, FBI investigations (of both candidates we would learn later!), charges of Russian interference, and abhorrent conversations recorded on buses. Yes, 2016 was unusual (or, at least, one might hope)!

But none of this means that the election itself was unusual. Indeed, as we hope to show, the 2016 election is in many ways the product of electoral continuity. Although American parties have become more ideologically disparate over the past few decades, no party holds a clear advantage. The 2016 election marked only the second time since Franklin D. Roosevelt that one of the parties, the Democrats, won the popular vote in three straight elections—the Republicans did so in 1980, 1984, and 1988. But the popular vote balance was so close that it became feasible for the second-place finisher in the popular vote, Trump, to capture the Electoral College and the White House. Once considered a historical aberration, this divergence between the popular vote and electoral vote has now happened in two of the last five U.S. elections.

With the election of Republican majorities in both the House and Senate, along with Trump's victory, 2016 brought unified partisan control of government. Whereas unified government has not been the norm in modern American politics, it is important to note that the Republican majorities in both the House and Senate are relatively small. The Republicans lost six House seats in 2016, bringing their majority down to 23 seats (roughly 5 percent of the chamber). Senate Republicans also lost seats (two) in 2016 but maintain a slim, two-seat majority. Although the election outcome did advantage the Republican Party, it would be difficult to claim that the GOP now holds an electoral advantage. Indeed, with only small majorities in both houses of Congress, there is no guarantee that President Trump will be able to push through his legislative agenda with ease. The first six months of Trump's administration have borne this out. Consider Trump's campaign promise to quickly repeal and replace Obamacare. During the Obama presidency, and knowing full well that the president would veto their efforts if necessary, Republicans voted on 54 separate occasions to repeal all or part of the Affordable Care Act.[17] Yet with unified Republican control, the Congress has failed to repeal the law. In March 2017, during what should have been the new president's "honeymoon period," House Speaker Paul Ryan (R–WI) cancelled a vote to replace Obamacare (a full repeal was not in the offing to the consternation of some conservatives) because he did not have the votes.[18] Although the House would eventually pass a replacement bill in May, the Senate failed to pass a similar bill in July by one vote.[19] An apparently final attempt for the year in the Senate was pulled from consideration in September after the Republicans failed to receive commitments for at least a bare fifty-vote majority. There are prospects for major policy changes during the remainder of Trump's term, of course, particularly on issues such as tax reform, but majority status alone is not sufficient for legislative success.[20] If the Democrats are able to gain control of the House and/or Senate during the 2018 midterm election, the Trump agenda clearly would be in peril.

Is America in the midst of an electoral transformation? What were the sources of Trump's victory in 2016, and how do they differ from electoral coalitions of the past? Does his victory signal a long-term negative trajectory for Democrats' chances in presidential elections? And are these electoral forces similar to those that structure congressional elections? These are the sorts of questions that we seek to answer here.

This book continues a series of seventeen books that we began with a study of the 1980 elections. Our focus has always been both contemporary and historical. Thus we offer an extensive examination of the 2016 presidential and congressional campaigns and present a detailed analysis of individual-level voting behavior, examining those factors that lead citizens to vote as well as those that affect how they vote. We also aim to place the 2016 elections in proper historical and analytical contexts.

## CHANGE AND CONTINUITY

Elections are at once both judgments on the issues of the day and the product of long-term changes in the relationship between the political parties and voters. For example, Democrats' aspirations for an emerging electoral majority following their 2012 presidential victory were not unfounded. If one is to believe the projections of the U.S. Census Bureau, many of the social groups that have supported Democrats in recent elections, particularly Latinos, are growing as a percentage of the overall U.S. population. And turnout among these groups has increased in recent decades. So, for some Democrats, their party's future success in presidential elections over the next few decades seemed all but assured. Then Donald Trump won, and the questions became: Was 2016 the dawn of an emergent Republican majority? Had Trump realigned the American party system?[21]

It is not uncommon for winning parties to make hyperbolic claims about the "historic" nature of their victories or to assert that their win was a sign of impending electoral dominance. Indeed, in 2008, Democrats were exuberant over Obama's sizable victory over John McCain and were even more pronounced in their claims of a bright Democratic future. Some observers saw the election as restoring Democrats to their status as the majority party, which they had enjoyed between 1932 and 1968. Lanny J. Davis, a former special counsel to President Clinton, wrote following the 2008 election: "Tuesday's substantial victory by Barack Obama, together with Democratic gains in the Senate and House, appear to have accomplished a fundamental political realignment. The election is likely to create a new governing majority coalition that could dominate American politics for a generation or more."[22] Two years later the Democrats lost sixty-three seats and their majority status in the House of Representatives—the largest seat change since 1946—and six seats in the Senate, where they maintained a slim majority.[23]

In 2004, following incumbent President George W. Bush's victory over Democrat nominee, John Kerry, scholars speculated about a pro-Republican realignment. Indeed speculation about Republican dominance can be traced back to the late 1960s, when Kevin P. Phillips, in his widely read book, *The Emerging Republican Majority*, argued that the Republicans could become the majority party, mainly by winning support in the South.[24] Between 1969, when his book was published, and 1984, the Republicans won three of the four presidential elections, winning by massive landslides in 1972, when Richard M. Nixon triumphed over George S. McGovern, and in 1984, when

Ronald Reagan defeated Walter F. Mondale. In 1985 Reagan himself proclaimed that a Republican realignment was at hand. "The other side would like to believe that our victory last November was due to something other than our philosophy," he asserted. "I just hope that they keep believing that. Realignment is real."[25] Democratic victories in the 1992 and 1996 presidential elections called into question the claims of a pro-Republican realignment.

Obviously not all elections are transformative. So how is electoral change—not simply the ebbs and flows from election to election but changes in the fundamental factors that link parties and voters—to be understood?

For generations of political scientists, theories of electoral change have centered on the concept of political realignment.[26] Political scientists define *realignment* in different ways, but they are all influenced by V. O. Key, Jr., who developed a theory of "critical elections" in which "new and durable electoral groupings are formed."[27] Elections like that in 1860 in which Lincoln's victory brought the Republicans to power, in 1896 in which McKinley's victory solidified Republican dominance, and in 1932 in which the Democrats came to power under FDR are obvious candidates for such a label.

But later Key argued that partisan shifts could also take place over a series of elections—a pattern he called "secular realignment." During these periods, "shifts in the partisan balance of power" occur.[28] In this view the realignment that first brought the Republicans to power might have begun in 1856, when the Republicans displaced the Whigs as the major competitor to the Democrats and might have been consolidated by Lincoln's reelection in 1864 and Ulysses S. Grant's election in 1868. The realignment that consolidated Republican dominance in the late nineteenth century may well have begun in 1892, when Democrat Grover Cleveland won the election, but the Populist Party, headed by James D. Weaver, attracted 8.5 percent of the popular vote, winning four states and electoral votes in two others. In 1896 the Populists supported William Jennings Bryan and were co-opted by the Democrats, but the electorate shifted to the Republican Party. The pro-Republican realignment might have been consolidated by McKinley's win over Bryan in 1900 and by Theodore Roosevelt's victory in 1904.

Though the term *New Deal* was not coined until Franklin Roosevelt's campaign of 1932, the New Deal realignment may have begun with Herbert C. Hoover's triumph over Democrat Al Smith, the first Roman Catholic to be nominated by a major political party. Although badly defeated, Smith carried two New England states, Massachusetts and Rhode Island, which later became the most Democratic states in the nation.[29] As Key points out, the beginnings of a shift toward the Democrats was detectable in Smith's defeat.[30] However, the "New Deal coalition" was not created by the 1932 election but after it, and it was consolidated by Roosevelt's 1936 landslide over Alfred M. Landon and his 1940 defeat of Wendell Willkie. The New Deal coalition structured the distribution of party support within the electorate during the earliest decades of the post-World War II period, and its decline and eventual replacement are important to understanding the changes and continuities of modern electoral politics.

Past partisan realignments in the United States have had five basic characteristics. First, realignments have traditionally involved changes in the regional bases of party support. Consider, for instance, the decline of the Whig Party and rise of the Republicans. Between 1836 and 1852, the Whigs drew at least some of their electoral support from the South.[31] The last Whig candidate to be elected, Zachary Taylor in 1848, won sixty-six of his electoral votes from the fifteen slave states. In his 1860 victory Lincoln did not win a single electoral vote from the fifteen slave states. Regionalism may be less important to future electoral changes, however. Today television and other media have weakened regionalism in the United States, and politics is much more nationalized. Two-party competition has diffused throughout the country, and the issues on which the parties compete tend to be more national in scope.[32]

Second, past party realignments have involved changes in the social bases of party support. Even during a period when one party is becoming dominant, some social groups may be moving to the losing party. During the 1930s, for example, Roosevelt gained the support of industrial workers, but at the same time, he lost support among business owners and professionals.

Third, past realignments have been characterized by the mobilization of new groups into the electorate. Indeed the mobilization of new voters into the electorate can result in significant electoral volatility.[33] Between Calvin Coolidge's Republican landslide in 1924 and Roosevelt's third-term victory in 1940, turnout among the voting-age population rose from 44 percent to 59 percent. Although some long-term forces were pushing turnout upward, the sharp increase between 1924 and 1928 and again between 1932 and 1936 resulted at least in part from the mobilization of new social groups into the electorate. Ethnic groups that were predominantly Catholic were mobilized to support Al Smith in 1928, and industrial workers were mobilized to support Franklin Roosevelt in 1936.

Fourth, past realignments have occurred when new issues have divided the electorate. In the 1850s the Republican Party reformulated the controversy over slavery to form a winning coalition. By opposing the expansion of slavery into the territories, the Republicans contributed to divisions within the Democratic Party. Of course no issue since slavery has divided America as deeply, and subsequent realignments have never brought a new political party to power. But those realignments have always been based on the division of the electorate over new issues.

Last, most political scientists argue that partisan realignments occur when voters change not just their voting patterns but also the way they think about the political parties, thus creating an erosion of partisan loyalties. During the Great Depression in 1932, for example, many voters who thought of themselves as Republicans voted against Hoover. Later many of these voters returned to the Republican side, but others began to think of themselves as Democrats. Likewise, in 1936 some voters who thought of themselves as Democrats disliked FDR's policies and voted against him. Some of these defectors may have returned to the Democratic fold in subsequent elections, but others began to think of themselves as Republicans.

Not all scholars believe that the concept of realignment is useful. In 1991 Byron E. Shafer edited a volume in which several chapters questioned its utility.[34] More recently David R. Mayhew published a monograph critiquing scholarship on realignment, and his book received widespread critical acclaim.[35] Mayhew cites fifteen claims made by scholars of realignment and then tests these claims. He argues that many of these claims do not stand up to empirical scrutiny, questions the classification of several elections as "realigning," and suggests that the concept of realignment should be abandoned.

Although we agree with some of the claims made by Mayhew, we see no reason to abandon the concept completely. Some electoral changes may correspond to the critical election-realignment dynamic—a long period of stability in the party system is altered by a rapid and dramatic change, which leads to a new, long-term partisan equilibrium. Using biological evolution as a theoretical analogue, Edward G. Carmines and James A. Stimson argue that partisan realignments of this type are similar in form to the evolutionary dynamic known as cataclysmic adaptation.[36] But the authors note that biological examples of the cataclysmic adaptation dynamic are extraordinarily rare and suggest that critical election realignments are likely to be rare also.

Carmines and Stimson articulate two additional evolutionary models of partisan change. The authors argue that Key's secular realignment dynamic is consistent with the model of Darwinian gradualism. In this view electoral change does not result from a critical moment but instead is "slow, gradual, [and] incremental."[37] As noted in Key's original work, the secular realignment dynamic "operate[s] inexorably, and almost imperceptibly, election after election, to form new party alignments and to build new party groups."[38]

The third model of partisan change espoused by Carmines and Stimson is consistent with the "punctuated equilibrium" model of evolution.[39] In this dynamic process,

> the system moves from a fairly stationary steady state to a fairly dramatic rapid change; the change is manifested by a "critical moment" in the time series—a point where change is large enough to be visible and, perhaps the origin of a dynamic process. Significantly, however, the change—the dynamic growth—does not end with the critical moment; instead it continues over an extended period, albeit at [a] much slower pace.[40]

In our view the punctuated equilibrium model best captures the dynamic nature of electoral change in the United States since the 1960s.

The 1960s were a critical moment in American politics. The events of the decade were the catalysts for fundamental changes in the rules that govern political parties and the partisan sentiments that would govern voters for years to come.[41] Of particular interest is the transformative power of the issue of race. By 1960 the national Democratic Party's sponsorship of civil rights for African Americans had created a schism between the more-liberal elements of the party and white southern Democrats. But it had also allowed the party to chip away at black voters' allegiance to the Republican Party, "the party of Lincoln." The partisan loyalties of African Americans had been shaped by the Civil War, and black loyalties to the Republican Party—where and when allowed to vote—lasted through the 1932 election. By 1960 a majority of African Americans identified with the Democratic Party, but there was still a substantial minority of Republican identifiers. Between 1960 and 1964, however, African American loyalties moved sharply toward the Democrats. The civil rights demonstrations of the early 1960s and the eventual passage of the 1964 Civil Rights Act solidified the position of the Democratic Party as the party of civil rights. By late

1964 more than 70 percent of African Americans identified as Democrats, a level of loyalty that persists today. The change in partisanship among blacks and the subsequent mobilization of black voters following the passage of the 1965 Voting Rights Act provided the rapid, critical moment that disrupted the stable equilibrium created by the New Deal Coalition. And, as the punctuated equilibrium dynamic suggests, the electorate continued to change in a direction set forth by the critical era of the 1960s, but it did so at slower rate, and it continues to have ramifications for politics today.

The political events of the 1960s also had an effect on white partisanship, but the change was neither immediate nor decisive. From the mid-1960s to the mid-1970s, there was a substantial erosion in party loyalties among whites. The proportion of the white electorate who considered themselves "independent" increased noticeably. By 1978 nearly 40 percent of whites said they were either pure independents or independents who "leaned" toward one of the two parties, nearly double that found in the late 1950s and early 1960s.[42] These changes led some scholars to use the term *dealignment* to characterize American politics during the period.[43] The term was first used by Ronald Inglehart and Avram Hochstein in 1972.[44] A dealignment is a condition in which old voting patterns break down without being replaced by newer ones. Yet, beginning in the 1980s, the proportion of whites claiming to be pure independents declined as whites nationally began to lean toward the Republican Party. In the once "solid Democratic South," whites have become decidedly Republican. Voters appear to be aligned.

Despite these changes the Republicans have never emerged as the majority party among the electorate. Democrats, however, saw a growth in political loyalties between 2004 and 2012, and in 2016, the party once again emerged as the majority party among two party identifiers, albeit a small majority.[45] This is not to say that Republicans cannot win, of course; it simply means that the GOP has entered recent elections at a numerical disadvantage. Democrats' electoral gains have largely been the product of the critical events of the 1960s, which established them as the party of civil rights. As America's nonwhite population has increased—more than half of the growth in the U.S. population between 2000 and 2010 was due to an increase in the nonwhite population—and Democrats have been the beneficiaries. For instance roughly two out of every three Latino voters in the United States identify with Democratic Party, and 54 percent of Latino voters say that Democrats have more concern for them, compared to only 11 percent who say that Republicans do.[46] America's racial and ethnic minorities continue to view the Democrats' adherence to the civil rights agenda of the 1960s as providing them with a natural political home, and America's whites are increasingly more likely to side with the Republicans. In our view the 2016 elections do not represent a fundamental change in America's electoral politics. Instead the 2016 elections continue to reflect electoral alignments set in motion by a critical era that occurred nearly a half century ago.

## VOTERS AND THE ACT OF VOTING

Voting is an individual act. Indeed the national decision made on (or before) November 8, 2016, was the product of more than 230 million individual decisions.[47]

Two questions faced Americans eighteen years and older: whether to vote and, if they did, how to cast their ballots. These decisions, of course, are not made in isolation. Voters' decisions are influenced by the social, economic, and information contexts in which they live; they are influenced by the political attitudes that they have acquired throughout their lifetime; and they are influenced by the voting decisions they have made in the past.[48] Voters' decisions are also constrained by America's electoral rules and two-party system—these are the primary sources of continuity in our political system.

How voters make up their minds is one of the most thoroughly studied subjects in political science—and one of the most controversial.[49] Voting decisions can be studied from at least three theoretical perspectives.[50] The first approach is *sociological* in character and views voters primarily as members of social groups. Voters belong to primary groups of family members and peers, secondary groups such as private clubs, trade unions, and voluntary associations, and broader reference groups such as social classes and religious and ethnic groups. Understanding the political behavior of these groups is central to understanding voters, according to Paul F. Lazarsfeld, Bernard R. Berelson, and their colleagues. Social characteristics determine political preferences.[51] This perspective is still popular, although more so among sociologists than political scientists.[52]

A second approach places greater emphasis on the *psychological* (or, more aptly, attitudinal) variables that affect voting. The "socio-psychological model" of voting behavior was developed by Angus Campbell, Philip E. Converse, Warren E. Miller, and Donald E. Stokes, scholars at the University of Michigan Survey Research Center, in their classic book *The American Voter*.[53] The Michigan scholars focused on attitudes most likely to have the greatest effect on the vote just before the moment of decision, particularly attitudes toward the candidates, the parties, and the issues. An individual's party identification emerged as the most important social-psychological variable that influences voting behavior. The Michigan approach is the most prevalent among political scientists, and party identification continues to be emphasized as one of the most influential factors affecting individual vote choice, although many deemphasize its psychological underpinnings.[54]

A third approach draws heavily from the work of economists. According to this perspective, citizens weigh the costs of voting against the expected benefits when deciding whether to vote. And when deciding for whom to vote, they calculate which candidate favors policies closest to their own policy preferences. Citizens are thus viewed as rational actors who attempt to maximize their expected utility. Anthony Downs and William H. Riker helped to found this *rational choice* approach.[55] The writings of Riker, Peter C. Ordeshook, John A. Ferejohn, and Morris P. Fiorina are excellent examples of this point of view.[56]

Taken separately none of these approaches adequately explains voting behavior; taken together the approaches are largely complementary.[57] Therefore, we have chosen an eclectic approach that draws on insights from each viewpoint. Where appropriate we employ sociological variables, but we also employ social-psychological variables such as party identification and feelings of political efficacy. The rational choice approach guides our study of the way issues influence voting behavior.

## SURVEY RESEARCH SAMPLING

Because of our interest in individual-level voting behavior, our book relies heavily on surveys of the American electorate. It draws on a massive exit poll conducted by Edison Research for the National Election Pool, a consortium of six news organizations, as well as surveys conducted in people's homes by the U.S. Census Bureau, and telephone polls conducted by the Pew Research Center. But our main data source for 2016 is the 1,181 face-to-face and 3,090 web-based interviews conducted before the election and 1,059 face-to-face and 2,590 interviews conducted after the election as part of the American National Election Studies (ANES) Time Series Survey.[58] Originally conducted by The Survey Research Center (SRC) and Center for Political Studies (CPS) at the University of Michigan, the ANES surveys have been conducted using national samples in every presidential election since 1948 and in every midterm election between 1954 and 2002.[59] The 2016 ANES was conducted jointly by Stanford University and the University of Michigan, with funding by the National Science Foundation. Since 1952 the ANES surveys have measured party identification and feelings of political effectiveness. The CPS, founded in 1970, has developed valuable questions for measuring issue preferences. The ANES surveys are the best and most comprehensive for studying the issue preferences and party loyalties of the American electorate.[60]

Readers may question our reliance on the ANES surveys of just over 4,200 people when some 230 million Americans are eligible to vote. Would we have similar results if all adults eligible to vote had been surveyed?[61] The ANES uses a procedure called multistage probability sampling to select the particular individuals to be interviewed. This procedure ensures that the final sample is likely to represent the entire population of U.S. citizens of voting age, except for Americans living on military bases, in institutions, or abroad.[62]

Because of the probability procedures used to conduct the ANES surveys, we are able to estimate the likelihood that the results represent the entire population of noninstitutionalized citizens living in the United States. Although the 2016 ANES survey sampled only about one in every 55,000 voting-eligible Americans, the representativeness of a sample depends far more on the size of the sample than the size of the population being studied, provided the sample is drawn properly. With samples of this size, we can be fairly confident (to a level of .95) that the results we get will fall within three percentage points of that obtained if the entire population had been surveyed. For example, when we find that 52 percent of respondents approved of the job Barack Obama was doing as president, we can be reasonably confident that between 49.7 percent (52 – 2.3) and 54.3 percent (52 + 2.3) approved of his performance. The actual results could be less than 49.7 percent or more than 54.3 percent, but a confidence level of .95 means that the odds are nineteen to one that the entire electorate falls within this range. The range of confidence becomes somewhat larger when we look at subgroups of the electorate. For example, with subsets of about five hundred (and the results in the 50 percent range) the confidence error rises to plus or minus six percentage points. Because the likelihood of sampling error grows as our subsamples become smaller, we sometimes supplement our analysis with reports of other surveys.

Somewhat more complicated procedures are needed to determine whether the difference between two groups is likely to reflect the relationship found if the entire population were surveyed. The probability that such differences reflect real differences in the population is largely a function of the size of the groups being compared.[63] Generally speaking, when we compare the results of the 2016 sample with an earlier ANES survey, a difference of three percentage points is sufficient to be reasonably confident that the difference is real. For example, in 2008 during the final year of the George W. Bush presidency and during the onset of the "great recession," only 2 percent of respondents said that the economy had improved in the last year; in 2016, 28 percent did. Because this difference is greater than three percentage points, we can be reasonably confident that the electorate was more likely to think the national economy was improving in 2016 than they were to think it was improving back in 2008.

When we compare subgroups of the electorate sampled in 2016 (or compare those subgroups with subgroups sampled in earlier years), a larger percentage is usually necessary to conclude that differences are meaningful. For example, 35 percent of whites who did not complete high school favored Hillary Clinton; among those who graduated high school but did not continue their education, 33 percent favored Clinton. We cannot be confident this is real, however, because the subsample sizes are quite small—only seventy-seven people are in the first category, whereas there are 463 people in the latter. With subsamples of this size, we would need to see a difference of thirteen points to be confident in the results. Thankfully, the relatively large sample size that we obtained in 2016 by using the full (face-to-face and Internet) sample means that statistical confidence in our subgroup comparisons is much easier to achieve. For instance, among voters, we have 2,131 men and 2,392 women.[64] With subsamples of this size, a three-point difference is large enough to conclude that the gender difference was real. However, it is important to recognize that in previous years, our sample sizes (face-to-face only) were much smaller. Generally speaking, comparisons of men and women using data from previous ANES studies require a difference of five percentage points. Similarly it is important to be mindful of racial differences in the sample. In 2016 our full sample contains 4,563 whites (71.6%) and 598 blacks (9.4%). Thus, to be confident in racial difference, we require a spread of more than four percentage points. When using data from previous years with smaller sample sizes, a difference of at least eight percentage points is needed to conclude that differences between whites and blacks are meaningful.

This discussion represents only a ballpark guide to judging whether reported results are likely to represent the total population. Better estimates can be obtained using the formulas presented in many statistics textbooks. To make such calculations or even a rough estimate of the chances of error, the reader must know the size of the groups being compared. For that reason, we always report in our tables and figures either the number of cases on which our percentages are based or the information needed to approximate the number of cases.

## PLAN OF THE BOOK

We begin by following the chronology of the campaign itself. Chapter 1 examines the battle for the Democratic and Republican Party presidential nominations. Three major Democratic candidates and twelve major Republican candidates campaigned for the chance to square off in the general election. As is typical when no incumbent president stands for reelection, both parties featured heated contests for the nomination. In Chapter 1 we discuss the regularities in the nomination process that explain why some candidates run and others do not. We then examine the rules governing the nomination contests, and we also assess the importance of campaign finance. The dynamics of multicandidate contests and the concept of momentum to discuss nomination contests in the 1970s are covered in Chapter 1 as well.

Chapter 2 moves to the general election campaign. Because of the rules set forth by the U.S. Constitution for winning presidential elections, candidates must think about how to win enough states to gain a majority (270) of the electoral vote (538 since 1964). We examine the Electoral College strategies adopted by the campaigns. There were three presidential debates and one vice presidential debate, and we discuss their impact. Last, we turn to the end game of the campaign, the battle over turnout. We examine the "ground game" undertaken by each campaign in an effort to get out the vote, and we will examine how these strategies differ from previous presidential campaigns.

Chapter 3 turns to the actual election results, relying largely on the official election statistics. Our look at the electoral vote is followed by a discussion of the election rules, noting that the U.S. plurality vote system supports "Duverger's law." We examine the pattern of results during the eighteen postwar elections as well as those in all forty-seven elections between 1832 and 2016. We then analyze the state-by-state results, paying particular attention to regional shifts in the elections between 1980 and 2016. We focus special attention on electoral change in the postwar South because this region has been the scene of the most dramatic changes in postwar U.S. politics. Finally we study the results of the last five presidential elections to assess the electoral vote balance.

Chapter 4 analyzes what is perhaps the most important decision of all: whether to vote. We examine the dynamics of electoral participation in U.S. politics, particularly changes in turnout during the postwar period. Although turnout grew fairly consistently between 1920 (the year women were enfranchised throughout the United States) and 1960, it fell in 1964 and in each of the next four elections. We show that the decline in turnout during this period coincides with steep declines in partisan attachment and political efficacy in the electorate. As partisan attachments have increased in recent decades, turnout has risen, but it remains lower than its 1960 high. Turnout is low in the United States compared with other advanced democracies, but it is not equally low among all social groups. In Chapter 4 we examine social differences in turnout in detail, using both the 2016 ANES survey and the Current Population Survey conducted by the U.S. Census Bureau.

In Chapter 5 we examine how social forces influence the vote. The ANES surveys enable us to analyze the vote for Clinton and Trump by race, gender, region, age, education, income, union membership, and religion. The impact of these social factors has changed considerably in the postwar period as the New Deal coalition broke down and new partisan alignments emerged after the critical era of the 1960. We show that minorities—specifically blacks and Latinos—are now central to the modern Democratic coalition.

Chapter 6 examines attitudes toward both the candidates and the issues. We begin by examining voters' feelings toward the candidates before turning our attention to their appraisals of the candidates' personal traits. We then attempt to assess the extent to which voters based their votes on issue preferences. We conclude that voters' issue concerns were particularly important in determining their vote choices in 2016.

We then examine how "retrospective evaluations" influence voting decisions. Existing research suggests that many voters decide how to vote on the basis of past performance. In other words voters decide mainly on the basis of what the candidates or their parties have done in office, not what they promise to do if elected. In Chapter 7 we show that retrospective evaluations, particularly those related to the performance of the economy, were a powerful reason underlying citizens' vote decisions. Perhaps most interesting we find that just one in four American voters in 2016 thought that the country was on the right track.

In Chapter 8 we explore the impact of party loyalties on voting using the ANES data. Since the 1980s there was a substantial shift in whites' partisan loyalties—particularly in the South—toward the Republican Party. The clear advantage Democrats once held among whites dissipated. Although the 2008 election that initially brought Obama to office saw a resurgence in whites' Democratic identification, that advantage proved temporary as whites' party loyalties reverted to near parity in 2012. Remarkably the Democrats were able to reestablish an advantage in party loyalties in 2016. This is a striking (and unusual) finding, not just because the Republican won the Electoral College vote but also because Clinton won the popular vote by only a few percentage points, hardly a sweep toward the Democratic Party. We examine partisanship among whites and blacks separately, tracking change from 1952 to 2016. This analysis reveals that the patterns of change among whites and blacks have been markedly different. We also compare Latino partisanship in recent elections. Finally we take a close look at the role of party loyalties in shaping issue preferences, retrospective evaluations, and voting preferences. We find that the relationship between party identification and the vote was very strong in every U.S. election since 2000, including 2016.

In Chapters 9 and 10 we are reminded that election day 2016 featured many elections. In addition to the presidential election, there were twelve gubernatorial elections, elections for thousands of state and local offices, as well as thirty-four elections for the U.S. Senate and elections for all 435 seats in the U.S. House of Representatives.[65] We focus our analysis on the 2016 House and Senate elections, which are by far the most consequential for national public policy.

Chapter 9 examines the pattern of congressional outcomes for 2016 and brings to light those factors that affect competition in congressional elections. We review the pattern of incumbent success in House and Senate races between 1954, the first Democratic victory in their forty-year winning streak, and 2016. Despite citizens' low levels of trust in government and the large portion of voters who believed the country was heading in the wrong direction, congressional incumbents were returned to office in droves. In the House, 96.4 percent of incumbents were reelected in 2016, whereas the success rate for Senate incumbents was 93 percent—not the "anti-Washington" fervor that one might infer from the outcome at the presidential level. We examine the interplay of national and regional factors in structuring congressional election outcomes. And, of course, we give particular attention to the critical factors of candidate recruitment, incumbency, and campaign finance. Finally we speculate on the future of congressional elections and party polarization in Congress in 2018 and beyond.

Chapter 10 explores how voters make congressional voting decisions. Using the same ANES surveys we employed to study presidential voting, we examine how social factors, issues, partisan loyalties, incumbency, and retrospective evaluations of congressional and presidential performance influence voters' choices for the House and Senate. We also try to determine the existence and extent of presidential "coattails," that is, whether Democrats were more likely to be elected to Congress because of Obama's presidential victory.

Finally, in Chapter 11, we attempt to place the 2016 elections in the proper historical context. Although we examine changes and continuities in American elections over the course of the nation's history, the great advantage of our analysis is its use of high-quality surveys of the electorate over the last sixty years. This wealth of data provides extraordinary insights regarding the political preferences of the America people, how those preferences have varied with time, and how they relate to voting behavior. Thus we explore the long-term changes and continuities in the politics of American national elections.

# PART ONE

# THE 2016 PRESIDENTIAL ELECTION

CHAPTER ONE

# THE NOMINATION STRUGGLE

Presidential nomination campaigns are the contests through which the two major political parties in the United States select their presidential nominees. As they have done since 1832 (Democrats) and 1856 (Republicans), the delegates who are chosen to be seated at the national party conventions do the actual selecting. However, since about 1972, both parties have used public campaigns for popular support as a way of selecting and/or instructing most delegates to the convention on how they should vote. Many people think of these primary contests as formal elections, just like those in general elections in the fall. Whereas presidential primary elections are, indeed, run by the government, they are actually designed solely to help each political party select delegates to choose its presidential nominee, and that applies only to the roughly half of the states that use primary elections to select or instruct their delegates.[1] States that use the alternative means, caucus or convention procedures, instead of primaries (see what follows) do so without involving the government at all. Presidential nominations are thus a mixture of public and private selections, and they are conducted at the state level only, even though their ultimate outcome is to select the two major parties' nominees for the only national offices that Americans elect.

In this, America is nearly unique. In almost no other country have the leaders of the major political parties' leaders ceded so much control over candidate selection to the general public. While now and then there are primary elections run by political parties in other nations, they are rare, typically isolated to one or a few parties, and are often used only once or twice before being discarded. American nominations, on the other hand, have run this way for Democrats and Republicans since the 1970s and have become entrenched in the public's and the political leaderships' minds. It would be very difficult for a party to nominate someone the public did not support at near or actual majority levels in the primary season. The leadership has, in that sense, ceded its control over its own party to the general public.[2] In turn that has empowered the media who seek to inform the public and the many activists, supporters, and financial donors of the presidential nomination campaigns who provide the wherewithal for most candidates to have any chance of reaching the public to win their support.

The 2016 campaigns in many respects were like all of those since the 1970s, that is, in the era of the "new nomination system," as we call it. As we shall see there were perhaps a surprising number of similarities between the two campaigns of 2016 and their predecessors. Most people, however, when they speak of 2016, talk with wonder about specific and individual aspects of the campaigns regardless of the similarities to other contests. They ask "How could someone like Donald J. Trump win the Republican nomination?" and (if they disliked the outcome) "Why couldn't Republican leaders prevent his nomination?" On the Democratic side the question more often seemed to be "Why didn't Hillary R. Clinton win nomination more easily and quickly instead of appearing unable to reach out to larger numbers of Democrats?" or (if the outcome was viewed as negative) "How could the party fail to nominate someone more at the heart of the Democratic Party and end up with someone who so epitomizes the 'establishment' in this anti-establishment year?" As we will see the answers to these questions are that the two parties' campaigns largely unfolded in replication of the many and well-established continuities established since the empowering of the public and consequent loss of party leadership control over nominations. But it is the unique properties of the two winners, especially in comparison to their major party opponents, that made the two campaigns unlike previous ones and in sometimes very important ways.

In short, reforms in the late 1960s and early 1970s brought about a new form of nomination campaign, one that required public campaigning for resources and votes. The new nomination system has shaped many aspects of all contests from 1972 onward, and we examine the similarities that have endured over its more than forty-year existence. Each contest, of course, differs from all others because of the electoral context at the time (e.g., the state of the economy or of war and peace) and because the contenders themselves are different. And in the new nomination system, the rules change to some degree every four years as well. The changes in rules and the strategies that candidates adopt in light of those rules combine with the context and contenders to make each campaign unique.

## WHO RAN

A first important regularity of the nomination campaign is that when incumbents seek renomination, only a very few candidates will contest them, and perhaps no one will at all. In 1972, although President Richard M. Nixon did face two potentially credible challengers to his renomination, they were so ineffective that he was essentially uncontested. Ronald Reagan in 1984, Bill Clinton in 1996, George W. Bush in 2004, and Barack Obama in 2012 were actually unopposed. They were so, in large part, because even a moderately successful president is virtually undefeatable for renomination. Conversely Gerald R. Ford in 1976 and Jimmy Carter in 1980 each faced a most credible challenger.[3] Ford had great difficulty defeating Reagan, and Carter likewise was strongly contested by Democratic senator Edward M. Kennedy of Massachusetts.[4] Of course Obama was ineligible to run for a third term in 2016, and so there was no incumbent running in either party. President Trump may well run for reelection in 2020 or perhaps join the few incumbents who chose not to run for reelection even though eligible, such as Harry S Truman in 1952 and Lyndon B. Johnson in 1968.

The second major regularity in the nomination system concerns the contests—such as those in 2016—in which the party has no incumbent seeking renomination.

In such cases a relatively large number of candidates run for the nomination. For our purposes we count candidates as "running" if they were actively campaigning on January 1, 2016 (or entered even later, although none did this time). That definition means that there were twelve major candidates who sought the Republican Party's nomination in 2016. There were actually quite a few more in 2015—by most counts seventeen—although that means that five were sufficiently "defeated" (or at least believed their chances of winning were too remote) so that they dropped out before January 1, 2016.[5] By our counting procedure there were three Democratic candidates in 2016.[6] Thus, in this section, we will be considering fifteen major party contenders. The numbers are higher on the Republican side and lower on the Democratic side than usual but not substantially out of the ordinary in either case.

Since 1980 there have been thirteen campaigns in which there was no incumbent seeking a major party's nomination, and the number of major candidates that were in the race as the year began varied remarkably little: seven in 1980 (R); eight in 1984 (D); eight (D) and six (R) in 1988; eight in 1992 (D); eight in 1996 (R); six (R) and two (D) in 2000; nine in 2004 (D); eight in both parties' contests in 2008; eight in 2012 (R); in addition to the twelve Republicans and three Democrats in 2016. Thus most such races featured at least six candidates. Only 2000 (D) and 2016 (D) had noticeably fewer, whereas 2016 (R) had a third more candidates running than the next most crowded field (2004, D).[7] We will discuss why there were fewer candidates in those two races, but note that both had larger numbers of declared candidates before our January 1 date for counting (as did most other races).

The three candidates on the Democratic side were: Hillary Clinton, who most recently served as secretary of state in the Obama administration;[8] Bernie Sanders, senator from Vermont; and Martin O'Malley, former governor of Maryland. The large number of Republicans was somewhat unusual in that the list included three candidates who had held no previous political office experience and very unusual in that such candidates (such as Ben Carson and Carly Fiorina in 2016) generally fare poorly, whereas Trump went on to win the nomination and election. There were also three incumbent senators (Ted Cruz, TX; Marco Rubio, FL; and Rand Paul, KY), two incumbent governors (John Kasich, OH; and Chris Christie, NJ); three former governors (Jim Gilmour, VA; Jeb Bush, FL; and Mike Huckabee, AR), and a former senator (Rick Santorum, PA). See Table 1-1 for these and other details we will discuss shortly. We have so far illustrated two regularities: few or no candidates will challenge incumbents, but in most cases many candidates will seek the nomination when no incumbent is running. In this 2016 is not particularly exceptional.

A third regularity is that among the candidates who are politicians, most hold or have recently held one of the highest political offices. This regularity follows from "ambition theory," developed originally by Joseph A. Schlesinger to explain how personal ambition and the pattern and prestige of various elected offices lead candidates to emerge from those political offices that have the strongest electoral bases.[9] This base for the presidential candidates includes the offices of vice president, senator, governor, and of course, the presidency itself. Note that even with a large number of contenders, there were no sitting members of the U.S. House who chose to run for the presidential nomination in 2016. House members do not have as strong an electoral

**Table 1-1 Candidates for Nomination to the Presidency by the Democratic and Republican Parties, 2016, With Various Aspects Pertinent to Their Candidacy**

| | Name | Last Political Office | Withdrawal Date[a] | Campaign Expenditures (in Millions of Dollars)[b] | Independent Expenditures (in Millions of Dollars)[c] |
|---|---|---|---|---|---|
| Democrats | Clinton | Sec of State | None | $187 | $12 |
| | O'Malley | Gov (former) | 1-Feb | $6 | $0.40 |
| | Sanders | Sen (current) | 12-Jul | $213 | $6 |
| Republicans | Bush | Gov (former) | 20-Feb | | $87 |
| | Carson | None | 4-Mar | $6 | $5 |
| | Christie | Gov (current) | 10-Feb | $8* | $22 |
| | Cruz | Sen (current) | 3-May | $85 | $27 |
| | Fiorina | None | 10-Feb | $11 | $4 |
| | Gilmour | Gov (former) | 12-Feb | $0.40 | NA |
| | Huckabee | Gov (former) | 1-Feb | $4 | $3 |
| | Kasich | Gov (current) | 4-May | $19 | $21 |
| | Paul | Sen (current) | 3-Feb | $12 | $5 |
| | Rubio | Sen (current) | 15-Mar | $52 | $49 |
| | Santorum | Sen (former) | 3-Feb | $0.30 | $0.20 |
| | Trump | None | None | $62 | $44 |

*Source:* Compiled by authors.

[a]Information obtained from the *New York Times*, http://www.nytimes.com/2016/65/election/2016-presidential-candidate.

[b]Information obtained from the Federal Election Commission, http://www.fec.gov/disclosurep/pnational.do—and various subpages from there; accessed March 20, 2016.

[c]Information obtained from OpenSecrets,org, https://www.opensecrets.org/outside-spending/summ.php?cycle-2016&disp-C&type-P.

base from which to run for the presidency, and they may well have to abandon a safe House seat to do so. As a result few House members run, and fewer still are strong contenders. The most prominent exception to the strong electoral base of ambition theory—Trump having had no experience in politics—will be at the center of our account of the unique features of his victory.

Most candidates in 2016, as in all earlier campaigns under the new nomination system, emerged from one of the strong electoral bases. Table 1-2 presents the data for 2016 and for all campaigns from 1972 to 2016 combined. More than two-thirds of the presidential candidates had already served as president, vice president, senator, or governor; another one in eight was a member of the U.S. House. In 2016 those ratios were largely true again, although no member of the House from either party was still a candidate as 2016 opened.[10] Many of the presidents in the early years of the nation were chosen from the outgoing president's cabinet (especially the sitting secretary of state) and other high level presidential appointees, but the cabinet is no longer a common source of presidential candidates, and the same is true for the nation's many mayors.[11] About one in seven candidates run for president without ever holding any elective office. That percentage was a little higher in 2016 as one in four of the

**Table 1-2 Current or Most Recent Office Held by Declared Candidates for President: Two Major Parties, 1972–2016**

| Office Held | Percentage of All Candidates Who Held That Office | Number, 1972–2016 | Number, 2016 |
|---|---|---|---|
| President | 6 | 8 | 0 |
| Vice President | 3 | 4 | 0 |
| U.S. Senator | 36 | 53 | 5 |
| U.S. Representative | 12 | 18 | 0 |
| Governor | 24 | 35 | 6 |
| U.S. Cabinet | 3 | 5 | 1 |
| Other | 6 | 9 | 0 |
| None | 10 | 14 | 3 |
| Total | 99 | 146 | 15 |

*Sources:* 1972–1992: *Congressional Quarterly's Guide to U.S. Elections*, 4th ed. (Washington, D.C.: CQ Press, 2001), 522–525, 562. 1996: Paul R. Abramson, John H. Aldrich, and David W. Rohde, *Change and Continuity in the 1996 and 1998 Elections* (Washington, D.C.: CQ Press, 1999), 13. 2000: *CQ Weekly*, January 1, 2000, 22. 2004: *CQ Weekly*, Fall 2003 Supplement, vol. 61, issue 48. The 2008–2016 results were compiled by the authors.

Republican candidates in 2016 (and no Democrats) had not held office previously. The big change, then, was not in the numbers but that one of those relatively politically untested contenders actually won the nomination in 2016, whereas few had left any visible mark at all on the contests in earlier years.

A fourth regularity, also consistent with ambition theory, is that of the many who run in nomination contests without incumbents, only a few put their current office at risk to do so. In 2016 only two senators, Paul and Rubio, were up for reelection. Paul withdrew on February 3, after the first contest of the campaign (the Iowa caucuses). Rubio said he would not run for reelection as a senator, but perhaps because the Florida senatorial primary was so late (August 30), he reentered the senatorial contest after withdrawing from the presidential race and won renomination and then reelection to the Senate.[12]

## THE RULES OF THE NOMINATION SYSTEM

The method that the two major parties use for nominating presidential candidates is unique and includes an amazingly complicated set of rules. To add to the complication, the various formal rules, laws, and procedures in use are changed, sometimes in large ways and invariably in numerous small ways, every four years. As variable as the rules are, however, the nomination system of 1972 has one pair of overriding characteristics that define it as a system The first is that whereas delegates actually choose their party's nominee, it is the general public, at least those who vote in the primaries and attend the caucuses, that chooses the delegates and often instructs them as to how to vote. The second characteristic is that the candidates, as a consequence, campaign in public and to the public for their support, mostly by heavy use of traditional media, such as television and newspapers, and, increasingly, social media, such as Facebook and Twitter. The dynamics of the technology of the media make campaigning in the media dynamic as well. Obama pioneered fund-raising and campaign contacting on social media in 2008 and 2012. Trump adroitly used the "free media" of television and newspaper coverage in lieu of buying campaign ads on them, and he pioneered the use of Twitter, especially, in 2016.

The complexity of the nomination contests is a consequence of four major factors. The first of these, federalism, defines the state as the unit of selection for national nominees and has been central to party nominations for nearly two centuries now. The second factor is the specific sets of rules governing primaries and caucus/convention procedures—established at the level of the national party in terms of general guidelines and then more specifically by state parties and/or state laws—these rules are at the heart of the nomination system of 1972. These rules govern delegate selection (and sometimes dictate instructions for delegates' presidential voting at the convention). The third factor is the set of rules about financing the campaign, which are also the oft-revised products of the reform period itself, starting in 1972. The fourth factor is the way in which candidates react to these rules and to their opponents, strategies that grow out of the keen competition for a highly valued goal. These factors are described in more detail in the sections that follow.

## Federalism or State-Based Delegate Selection

National conventions to select presidential nominees were first held for the 1832 election, and for every nomination since then, the votes of delegates attending the conventions have determined the nominees. Delegates have always been allocated at the state level; whatever other particulars may apply, each state selects its parties' delegates through procedures adopted by state party organizations whether they choose to use caucuses and conventions, by state law, or the party organization wants to use a primary election, or both. Votes at the convention are cast by a state's delegation, and in general the state is the basic unit of the nomination process. Thus there are really fifty separate delegate selection contests in each party.[13] There is no national primary, nor is there serious contemplation of one.

The fact that there are more than fifty separate contests in each party creates numerous layers of complexity, two of which are especially consequential. First, each state is free to choose delegates using any method consistent with the general rules of the national party. Many states choose to select delegates for the parties' conventions via a primary election. States not holding primaries use a combination of caucuses and conventions, which are designed and run by each political party and not by the state government. Caucuses are simply local meetings of party members. Those attending the caucuses report their preferences for the presidential nomination and choose delegates from their midst to attend higher-level conventions such as at the county, congressional district, state, and eventually national levels.

The second major consequence of federalism is that the states are free (within the bounds described as follows) to choose when to hold their primaries or caucuses. These events are thus spread out over time, although both parties now set a time period—the delegate selection "window"—during which primaries and caucuses can be held. Both parties began delegate selection on February 1, 2016, with the Iowa caucuses (a month later than in 2012), Republicans closed their delegate selection process with five states (CA, MT, NJ, NM, and SD) holding primaries on June 7, whereas Democrats in DC held a primary on June 14. The Republicans, concerned about how long the Romney nomination in 2012 took to unfold to victory, not only favored this shortening of the length of the primary season but also tried to regulate front-loading even further. In particular they required that states holding their primaries before March 15 had to use some kind of proportional allocation method so that the delegates awarded to candidates were to some degree proportionate to the votes those candidates received in the primary or caucus. It was not until March 15 that states could use the winner-take-all (WTA) rule, such that the candidate with the most votes wins all that state's delegates.[14] WTA rules are often favored by GOP states, due to the larger impact that state's delegation might have on the race, concentrating their vote on a single candidate.[15]

## The Nomination System of 1972: Delegate Selection

Through 1968 presidential nominations were won by appeals to the party leadership. To be sure public support and even primary election victories could be important in a candidate's campaign, but their importance stemmed from the credibility they would give to the candidacy in the eyes of party leaders. The 1968 Democratic nomination, like so many events that year, was especially tumultuous.[16] The result was that the Democratic Party created a committee, known as the McGovern-Fraser Commission, which proposed a series of reforms that were proposed to the Democratic National Committee between 1969 and early 1972 and then finally adopted by the party convention in 1972. The reforms were sufficiently radical in changing delegate selection procedures that they, in effect, created a new nomination system. Although it was much less aggressive in reforming its delegate selection procedures, the Republican Party did so to a certain degree. However, the most consequential results of the Democratic reforms for our purposes—the proliferation of presidential primaries and the media's treatment of some (notably the Iowa) caucuses as essentially primary-like—spilled over to the Republican side as well.

In 1968 Democratic senators Eugene J. McCarthy of Minnesota and Robert F. Kennedy of New York ran very public, highly visible, primary-oriented campaigns in opposition to the policies of President Lyndon B. Johnson, especially with respect to the conduct of the Vietnam War. Before the second primary, held in Wisconsin, Johnson surprisingly announced, "I shall not seek and I will not accept the nomination of my party for another term as your President."[17] Vice President Hubert H. Humphrey took Johnson's place in representing the presidential administration and the policies of the Democratic Party generally. Humphrey, however, waged no public campaign; he won the nomination without entering a single primary, thereby splitting an already deeply divided party.[18] Would Humphrey have won the nomination had Robert Kennedy not been assassinated the night he defeated McCarthy in California, effectively eliminating McCarthy as a serious contender? No one will ever know. Democrats including Humphrey himself did know, however, that the chaos and violence that accompanied Humphrey's nomination clearly indicated that the nomination process should be opened to more diverse candidacies and that public participation should be more open and more effective in determining the outcome. He thus offered a proposal to create the McGovern-Fraser Commission, as it was popularly called, which was accepted by the Democratic National Committee.

The two most significant consequences of the reforms were the public's great influence on each state's delegate selection proceedings and the proliferation of presidential primaries. Caucus/convention procedures, however, also became timelier, were better publicized, and in short, were more primary-like. Today the media treat Iowa's caucuses as critical events, and the coverage of them is similar to the coverage of primaries—how many "votes" were "cast" for each candidate, for example. Indeed the party organizations formally recognized this fact. The Iowa Republican Party, for example, held a secret balloting among caucus attenders that determined how the delegates to subsequent levels of conventions were to be allocated among supporters of the candidates.[19] Iowa Democrats, in their turn, conducted a standing "vote" of attenders to the same effect.

Whereas the McGovern-Fraser Commission actually recommended greater use of caucuses, many of the state party officials concluded that the easiest way to conform to the new Democratic rules in 1972 was to hold a primary election. Thus the number of states (including the District of Columbia) holding Democratic primaries increased from fifteen in 1968 to twenty-one in 1972 to twenty-seven in 1976, and the number of Republican primaries increased comparably. The numbers peaked in 2000, when forty-three states conducted Republican primaries, and Democratic primaries were held in forty states. In 2016 there were thirty-nine primaries on each side. Thus it is fair to say that the parties' new nomination systems have become largely based on primaries or in more primary-like conventions.

The only major exception to this conclusion is that about 15 percent of delegates to the Democratic National Convention were chosen because they were elected officeholders or Democratic Party officials. Supporters of this reform of party rules (first used in 1984) wanted to ensure that the Democratic leadership would have a formal role to play at the conventions of the party. These "superdelegates" may have played a decisive role in the 1984 nomination of Walter F. Mondale, in the nomination of Obama over Clinton in 2008, and again for Clinton's nomination in 2016, when she, like Mondale and Obama, at one point had a majority of the non-superdelegates but not a majority of all delegates.[20] Each candidate needed only a relatively small number of additional superdelegates to commit to vote for them to win the nomination. All three received those commitments soon after the regular delegate selection process ended, and with that, they were assured the nomination.[21]

The delegate selection process has, as noted, become considerably more front-loaded.[22] The rationale for front-loading was clear enough: the last time California's (actual or near) end-of-season primary had an effect on the nomination process was in the 1964 Republican and the 1972 Democratic nomination contests. Once candidates, the media, and other actors realized, and reacted to, the implications of the reformed nomination system, the action shifted to the earliest events of the season, and nomination contests, especially those involving multiple candidates, were effectively completed well before the end of the primary season. More and more state parties and legislatures (including, for a while, California's) realized the advantages of front-loading, bringing more attention from the media, more expenditures of time and money by the candidates, and more influence to their states if they held primaries sooner rather than later.

Soon, however, other factors started to affect state decisions. First, the rewards for early primaries were concentrated in a relatively small number of the very earliest primaries. And as we have noted, the national parties regulated which ones could go when and threatened to penalize states that violated the national party decisions. Indeed Michigan and Florida were actually penalized in 2008 and 2012 for holding their contests too early in the season. In addition the very early presidential primaries forced states to make an increasingly difficult choice. If they held their presidential primaries early in the year, they had to decide whether to hold the primary elections for all other offices at the same time, which was proving quite a bit earlier than made sense for candidates for local, state, and even national congressional posts, or to pay the costs of running two primaries, one for the president and one much later for all other offices.[23] Some states like California, for example, which were not able to reap the major benefits of being among the very earliest of events, chose to return to late in the season.

If the rationale for front-loading was clear by 1996, when it first became controversial, the consequences were not. Some argued that long-shot candidates could be propelled to the front of the pack by gathering momentum in Iowa and

New Hampshire and could, before the well-known candidates had a chance to react, lock up the nomination early. The alternative argument was that increasing front-loading helps those who begin the campaign with the advantages associated with being a front-runner, such as name recognition, support from state and local party or related organizations, and most of all, money. The dynamic of this adjustment, described in the following paragraphs, can be seen clearly in Figure 1-1, which reports the week in which the winning candidate was assured nomination in contested nomination campaigns since 1976.

Indeed as the primary season has become more front-loaded, the well-known, well-established, and well-financed candidates have increasingly dominated the primaries. Senator George S. McGovern of South Dakota and Carter won the Democratic nominations in 1972 and 1976, even though they began as little-known and ill-financed contenders. George H. W. Bush, successful in the 1980 Iowa Republican caucuses, climbed from being, in his words, "an asterisk in the polls" (where the asterisk is commonly used to indicate less than 1 percent support) to become Reagan's major contender and eventual vice presidential choice and his successor to the presidency. And Colorado senator Gary Hart nearly defeated former Vice President Mondale in 1984. In 1988 the two strongest candidates at the start of the Republican race, George H. W. Bush and Bob Dole, contested vigorously, with Bush winning, while

**Figure 1-1 Length of Multicandidate Campaigns: Two Major Parties, 1976–2016**

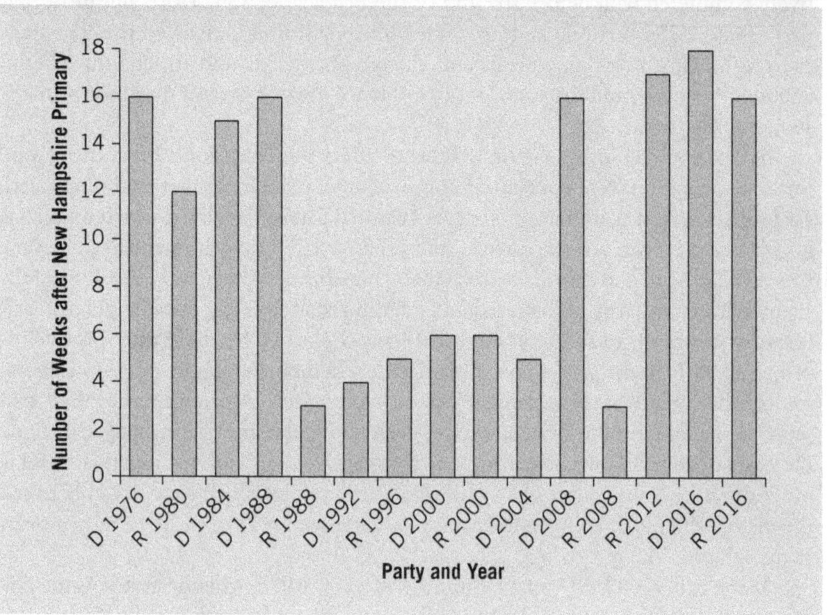


*Source:* Compiled by authors.

their presence basically locked other lesser-known contenders out. Gov. Michael S. Dukakis of Massachusetts, the best-financed and best-organized (albeit little known) Democrat, won the nomination surprisingly easily. Bill Clinton's victory in 1992 appeared, then, to be the culmination of the trend toward an insuperable advantage for the strongest and best-financed candidates. Clinton was able to withstand scandal and defeat in the early going and eventually cruise to victory.

The campaign of former Democratic senator Paul Tsongas of Massachusetts in 1992 illustrates one important reason for Clinton's victory. Tsongas defeated the field in New Hampshire, and as usual, the victory and the media attention it drew opened doors to fund-raising possibilities unavailable to him even days earlier. Yet Tsongas faced the dilemma of whether to take time out of daily campaigning for the public's votes so that he could spend time on fund-raising or to continue campaigning in the upcoming primaries. If he campaigned in those primaries, he would not have the opportunity to raise and direct the funds he needed to be an effective competitor. Front-loading had simply squeezed too much into too short a post-New Hampshire time frame for a candidate to be able to capitalize on early victories as, say, Carter had done in winning the nomination and election in 1976. The events of 1996 supported the alternative argument—that increased front-loading benefits the front-runner—even though it took nearly all of Dole's resources to achieve his early victory that year.[24]

This lesson was not lost on the candidates for 2000, especially George W. Bush. In particular he began his quest in 1999 (or earlier!) as a reasonably well-regarded governor but one not particularly well-known to the public outside of Texas (although, of course, sharing his father's name made him instantly recognizable). He was at that point only one of several plausible contenders, but he worked hard to receive early endorsements from party leaders and raised a great deal of money well ahead of his competition. When others sought to match Bush's early successes in this "invisible primary," they found that he had sewn up a great deal of support. Many, in fact, withdrew before the first vote was cast, suddenly realizing just how Bush's actions had lengthened the odds against them. Bush was therefore able to win the nomination at the very opening of the primary season. Incumbent Vice President Al Gore, on the other side, also benefited from the same dynamics of the invisible primary made manifest by front-loading, although in the more classical role of one who began the nomination season as the odds-on favorite and therefore the one most able to shut the door on his opposition well before it was time for most voters to cast their ballots.[25]

In 2004 there was no strong leader of the contest before the Democratic campaign began. Howard Dean burst on the scene and rather surprisingly into a lead before dropping nearly as suddenly.[26] As a result there was a period of uncertainty in the shape of the contest, followed by solidifying support around long-time senator John Kerry, who thereby benefitted more from lack of anyone able to compete strongly against him than any rule.

The pre-primary period on the Republican side in 2008 was quite variable, with first McCain, then Giuliani, then Romney surging to the front. McCain's campaign was considered all but dead in the water by that point, but it regathered strength before 2007 ended. There was, then, no strong front-runner in the GOP; the campaign was wide open. In fact some pundits imagined former Arkansas Governor Mike Huckabee had become a favorite to win, and so McCain's victory in the Iowa caucuses was a genuine surprise (at least from the perspective of, say, October 2007). On the Democratic side, Hillary Clinton was a clear front-runner. In retrospect it was also clear that Obama had developed an impressive organization both by mobilizing support across the nation and by fund-raising, especially through adroit use of the Internet. Thus once his organizational strength became publicly visible, it was no surprise that he and Clinton easily defeated their rivals. Having boiled down to a two-candidate contest, each had carved out their own bases of support, and neither could decisively defeat the other. Obama did have a slight lead throughout much of the primary season, but because of the superdelegates, it was too slight a lead to be able to secure an outright majority of delegates until after the primary season ended. As heretofore unbound superdelegates determined their choices, they soon favored Obama sufficiently to put him over the top.

The 2012 Republican contest had some similarities to 2008, with Romney moving from his also-ran slot to replace McCain as the candidate who early on seemed strong, lost steam, and then resurged back to victory. One effect of the modest reversal in front-loading was that Romney, even though ahead, was not able to completely shut the door on his opposition until much later in the season. Simply too few delegates were selected as early in 2012 as in, say, 1980. This extended length of time had several effects. The most important appears to have been that the slowing of the delegate selection process, although still relatively highly front-loaded, permitted Romney's opponents to run negative campaigns against him, quite possibly hurting his ability to shape his own image and providing fodder for attacks in the general election campaign before the campaign had selected enough delegates for him to claim what proved to be a rather straightforward nomination victory.

Much the same appeared to happen again in 2016 on the Republican side. The unusual nature of someone like Trump emerging as the leading contender (even after losing the Iowa caucuses but righting his campaign and its dynamic growth in New Hampshire) led to calls for the remaining candidates (fairly soon into the season, the race reduced effectively to Trump versus Cruz, Kasich, and Rubio) and the "Republican establishment" to figure out a way to stop Trump. When that failed to happen, the divided opposition allowed Trump to build his delegate lead to victory.[27] On May 3, the night of the Indiana primary, his last major opponent, Ted Cruz, withdrew his candidacy, although Trump was still short of having a majority of delegates on his side. But from that night onward, he was unchallenged and thus the "presumptive nominee." Thus continued active opposition until May did yield a longer period in which Republicans were criticizing the eventual nomination, sometimes quite strenuously, in spite of a relatively straightforward and convincing win by Trump.

The slowed rate of delegate selection also affected the Clinton-Sanders contest on the Democratic side. Clinton, as she had in 2008, began her quest for nomination as a very strong front-runner, especially after those who appeared likely to be among her strongest opponents, Senator Elizabeth Warren (MA) and Vice President Biden, decided not to run. Of the remaining actual candidates, Sanders effectively had the liberal wing of the party on his own, and the race narrowed almost immediately to a two-person contest. In such races it is typically the case, as here, that both candidates have their own constituency in their party's base and are thus difficult to defeat. That is to say that these races—in 2016 like 2008 and others before them—take a long time to resolve. Even when Clinton had secured an outright majority of delegates (which was at the end of the season anyway), Sanders failed to concede and thus continued to be able to criticize Clinton and to remain a holding place for liberal Democrats who were disenchanted with her.

These effects can be seen in Figure 1-2, which reports the cumulative selection of delegates. As can be seen there, 1976 (the first primary season defined by the rules adopted at the 1972 Democratic convention) shows a slow, gradual increase in the number of delegates selected. It is not until week thirteen, just over a month before the season ends, that 50% of the delegates were selected, and even later that a sufficiently large proportion of the delegates had been selected to make a majority likely to be held by the leading candidate, if he or she faced any opposition at all. The 2000 season was dramatically different, with the 50% mark being reached in week six (indeed reaching nearly two-thirds of the delegates selected by that week). Finally the slight retreat from such heavy front-loading in 2016 is visually apparent, but it is also apparent that it is rather slight, looking far more like the 2000 apogee than the 1976 perigee.

The final consequence—and possibly the most important for differentiating the nomination system of 1972 from its predecessors—is "momentum," the building of success over time during the extended campaign period, such that every nomination has, so far, always been decided before the convention balloting and always going to the candidate who won the greatest support from the party's electorate.

The most significant feature of the nomination process, from the candidates' perspectives, is its dynamic character. This system was designed to empower the general

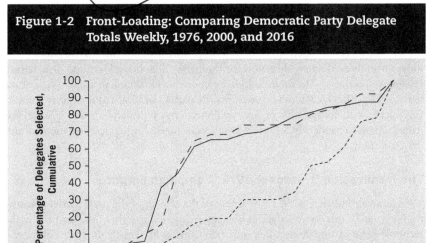

**Figure 1-2 Front-Loading: Comparing Democratic Party Delegate Totals Weekly, 1976, 2000, and 2016**

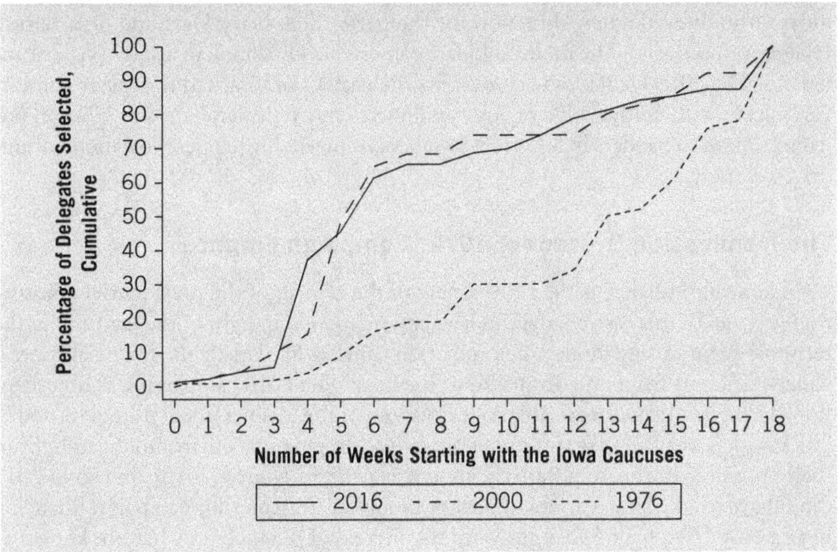

*Source:* Compiled by authors.

public, giving it opportunities to participate more fully in the selection of delegates to the national party conventions. The early state delegate selection contests in Iowa and New Hampshire allowed largely unknown candidates to work a small state or two using the "retail" politics of door-to-door campaigning to achieve a surprising success that would attract media attention and then money, volunteers, and greater popular support. In practice this was exactly the route Jimmy Carter followed in 1976.

John H. Aldrich developed this account of "momentum" in campaigns, using the 1976 campaigns to illustrate its effect. He first showed that there is no stable balance to this process.[28] In practical terms he predicted that one candidate will increasingly absorb all the money, media attention, and public support and thereby defeat all opponents before the convention. He further showed that the tendency for this process to focus rapidly on a single winner increases the *more* candidates there are. This finding was just the opposite of the original speculation and, indeed, what at the time seemed obvious: the greater the number of candidates, the longer it would take to reach victory. But commonsense was not a helpful guide in this case. Like other contests with large numbers of contenders, the Republican race of 2016 illustrates the power of momentum. Trump did not start off the campaign with a large lead in popular support, but he built that over the course of the campaign, eventually all but crushing even his strongest opponents and forcing their mostly early exits.

There is one exception to this pure "momentum" result: the possibility of an unstable but sustainable balance with two candidates locked in a nearly precise tie. Early campaigns offered two illustrations compatible with two candidates in (unstable) equipoise, the 1976 Republican and 1980 Democratic contests. In both the 1984 Democratic and 2008 Democratic contests, the campaigns began with a large number of candidates. Each featured a strong, well-financed, well-known, well-organized candidate (former Vice President Mondale and Hillary Clinton, respectively) who, it turned out, was challenged strongly by a heretofore little-known (to the public) candidate who offered a new direction for the party (Sen. Gary Hart and Sen. Barack Obama, respectively). The multicandidate contest quickly shrank to just two viable candidates. The 2016 Democratic contest fits the pattern of balanced two-party contests very nicely, with neither bloc of voters willing to move from Sanders to Clinton nor from Clinton to Sanders in any great numbers, as inevitably happens in a momentum-driven contest.

## The Nomination System of 1972: Campaign Finance

Campaign finance is the third aspect of the reform of the presidential nomination process. In this case changes in law (and regulation in light of the law) and in the technology for raising money in nomination contests have made the financial context widely different from one campaign to the next. The 2016 campaign was no exception. These candidates were able to learn some of the lessons from strategies tried in 2012, which was the first run under a new (de-)regulatory environment in light of the Supreme Court case popularly known as *Citizens United* (2010), and so in 2012 candidates tried a large variety of new or modified strategies for campaign financing in response. Two major changes were the increased reliance on what are known as independent expenditures by a number of candidates, and Trump's strategy, which focused less on raising money but instead in getting the media to cover his campaign much more highly than those of other candidates. This was a strategy he believed to be a more effective use of "free" media than what impact higher expenditures for purchasing time on the paid media would offer.

Our story begins, however, with the Federal Election Campaign Act of 1971 and especially amendments to that act in 1974 and 1976. The Watergate scandal during the Nixon administration included revelations of substantial abuse in raising and spending money in the 1972 presidential election (facts discovered in part in implementing the 1971 act). The resulting regulations limited contributions by individuals and groups, virtually ending the power of individual "fat cats" and requiring presidential candidates to raise money in a broad-based campaign. The federal government would match small donations for the nomination, and candidates who accepted matching funds would be bound by limits on what they could spend.

These provisions, created by the Federal Election Commission to monitor campaign financing and regulate campaign practices, altered the way nomination campaigns were funded. Still, just as candidates learned over time how to contest most effectively under the new delegate selection process, they also learned how to campaign under the new financial regulations. Perhaps most important, presidential candidates learned—although it is not as true for them as for congressional candidates—that "early money is like yeast, because it helps to raise the dough."[29] They also correctly believed that a great deal of money was necessary to compete effectively.

The costs of running presidential nomination campaigns, indeed campaigns for all major offices, have escalated dramatically since 1972. But a special chain of strategic reactions has spurred the cost of campaigning for the presidential nomination. The *Citizens United* case accelerated the chain reaction by creating a much more fully deregulated environment.

When many states complied with the McGovern-Fraser Commission reforms by adopting primaries, media coverage grew, enhancing the effects of momentum, increasing the value of early victories, and raising the costs of early defeat. By 2008 very few candidates were accepting federal matching funds because doing so would bind them to spending limits in individual states and over the campaign as a whole, and these limits were no longer realistic in light of campaign realities. By 2012, only one candidate, former Louisiana Governor Buddy Roemer, applied for federal funding, and his candidacy was considered sufficiently hopeless that many debates did not even bother to include him among the contestants. No major candidates accepted matching funds in 2016.

Much money was being raised, however. Through May 2008, for example, the fund-raising totals for the three major contenders were $296 million for Obama, $238 million for Clinton, and $122 million for McCain.[30] By the same point in 2012, Romney reported raising $121 million, with Paul having raised $40 million, Gingrich $24 million, and Santorum $22 million. See Table 1-1 for reports on campaign expenditures in 2016. Note that, for example, Clinton and Sanders spent much more than Romney raised in 2012.

The 2008 campaign also marked a dramatic expansion in the use of the Internet to raise money, following on the efforts of Democrat Howard Dean, the former governor of Vermont, in 2004 (and, to an extent, McCain in 2000). Ron Paul, for example, raised more than $6 million on a single day, December 6, 2007, through the Internet. But Obama's success in 2008 served as the model for future campaigns, such as the $55 million he raised in February at a critical moment for the campaign.[31]

The *Citizens United* decision in 2010 changed the landscape dramatically. In the narrow it overturned the 2002 Bipartisan Campaign Reform Act and held that corporations and unions could spend unlimited money in support of political objectives and could enjoy First Amendment free speech rights, just as individuals could. These organizations, however, continued to be banned from direct contribution to candidates and parties. The case, and especially a subsequent one decided by the U.S. Court of Appeals in light of this case, spurred the development of what are known as "super PACs," which are political action committees that can now accept unlimited contributions from individuals, corporations, and unions and spend as much as they like so long as it is not in explicit support of a candidate or party's election campaign or coordinated with their campaign organization.[32]

According to data from the Center for Responsive Politics, expenditures on behalf of the three major nomination contenders were quite large. In 2012 about $14 million was spent on behalf of Romney, $19 million for Gingrich, and $21 million for Santorum. Data from Open Secrets are reported in Table 1-1 for the 2016 campaign. Note that the expenditures on behalf of many candidates, especially Republicans, had as much, or even more, spent on behalf of their campaigns than they spent themselves.[33] These organizations altered the terms of the campaign in that their expenditures had to be independent of the candidates and their (and their party's) organizations. It is therefore not necessarily the case that the candidate and, in the fall, the party will retain total control over the campaign and its messages.

Another consequence of these changes is that what were previously dubbed "fat cats" are once again permitted. The 2012 exemplar was Sheldon Adelson, a casino magnate and a strong supporter of Israel. He contributed $10 million to the Winning Our Future super PAC in support of Newt Gingrich, contributing about half that total before the South Carolina primary and the other half before the next primary in Florida. His public support is rare, however. Most of the super PACs are funded and led by small numbers of individuals, and we often do not know their names.

Note that in 2016, although Trump did raise and spend a good deal of money, much of his expenditures came later in the game, and he made a very public case for not spending a dime of his own money until late into the campaign. Certainly he spent much less than either of the two major Democrats, both of whom raised sums comparable to the Obama-Clinton race in 2008. But he did spend much more than his opponents, with only Rubio being at all close behind. And, of course, he eventually received a lot of support from super PACs, even though Bush also had a great deal spent on his behalf (even if ineffectually). The lessons are that money is very helpful, that early money still must be better than that raised late, that candidates are still trying to figure out the best configuration in this largely deregulated campaign finance regime, and that, as Trump's approach shows, it is not money that is important, but what it will buy. We will discuss his campaign strategy in a little while, but this also raises the final lesson for the future, that if candidates come to rely on super PACs, they risk control over their campaign, or they simply agree to adopt the stances of their party or its backers as their own. This concession to the party and its "image" is greatly strengthened due to the dramatic increase in partisan polarization that began around 1980 and continues to increase today.

## STRATEGY AND THE CANDIDATES' CAMPAIGNS IN 2016: THE ELECTORAL SETTING AND HOW THE CANDIDATES WON THEIR NOMINATIONS

*The Strategic Context:* One of the most dramatic changes of the last half century has been the increase in partisan polarization, which generally means an increasing similarity of attitudes and preferences within each party and a substantial increase in divergence of opinion between the two parties. The leading indicators of this increase in partisan polarization have been among the party elites and especially their elected officeholders.[34] What is less clear is whether the electorate has followed polarization among elites (or, even less obviously, led elite polarization), and if so, how much the electorate has followed (or led). Some argue that there has been little change for decades, especially on such key measures as issue and ideological preferences. In this view polarization in the electorate is relatively small, with the result that the electorate continues to be basically moderate in its views.[35] Others point to at least some increased polarization in preferences between partisan identifiers, particularly among the more attentive and engaged in politics, such as those among the most likely to participate in primaries and caucuses.[36]

The clearest evidence of partisan polarization in the electorate lies in divergences between the two parties in other ways than their attitudes toward issues and even their ideological views. For example, Marc Hetherington and Jason Husser showed that there has been a dramatic decline in trust across party lines, whereas Shanto Iyengar and colleagues have shown that emotional responses have become much more polarized along party lines in the electorate.[37] Finally Gary Jacobson demonstrated that the so-called approval ratings of presidents (something we analyze in Chapter 7 in detail) went from having only a modest amount of partisan differences to becoming deeply divided by party.[38]

Here we illustrate that the context for the 2016 presidential nomination campaign has become much more deeply polarized along party lines than it was in 1980 in terms of overall affective evaluations of the candidates running for the presidential nomination. The ANES ran nation-wide surveys in January 1980 and in January 2016.[39] These years turn out to be especially appropriate ones for this look at partisan polarization of candidate evaluations for two reasons. The 1980 presidential election, as it happens, was the year in which elite partisan polarization turned and began its sharp increase, and thus we have data from the beginning and (current) end points of elite polarization. In addition both parties' nominations were strongly competitive. In both years the Democrats witnessed a strong two-person contest that lasted throughout the primary season. In both years the Republicans chose over a larger number of candidates that more quickly ended with Reagan and Trump's victories, respectively, but were nonetheless hotly contested in January. Especially on the Republican side, contenders argued for their candidacy in part by claiming to be supported by Democrats.

The survey data reported in Figures 1-3 and 1-4 show an increase in partisan polarization in the electorate in two ways. The figures report data using the so-called candidate thermometers, which ask how "warmly" or "coolly" the respondent feels toward the candidate, where 100 is the warmest possible feeling, 50 is neutral (neither warm nor cool), and 0 is the coldest possible feelings toward that candidate.[40] Figure 1-3 reports the difference between how the average Democrat and average Republican evaluated that candidate.[41] This is probably the most direct measure of partisan polarization of candidate evaluations. Those who are concerned about partisan polarization often point to the decline in the ability to work across party lines—the decline in bipartisanship—which is compounded by an apparent growth in emotional hostility to those on the other side of party lines. In Figure 1-4, therefore, we report the percentage of partisans who rate the relevant candidate of the opposite party positively (i.e., warmly or above 50 degrees). Even if there are large gaps in evaluations, as in Figure 1-3, the ability to see the opposition candidate positively bodes more favorably for bipartisanship.

The two figures have strong and reinforcing findings. In 1980, although each party felt more positively toward its own candidates than did those identifying with the other party, the difference between the two parties was fairly muted, with

**Figure 1-3 Difference in Average Thermometer Rating: Selected Candidates, January 1980 and 2016**

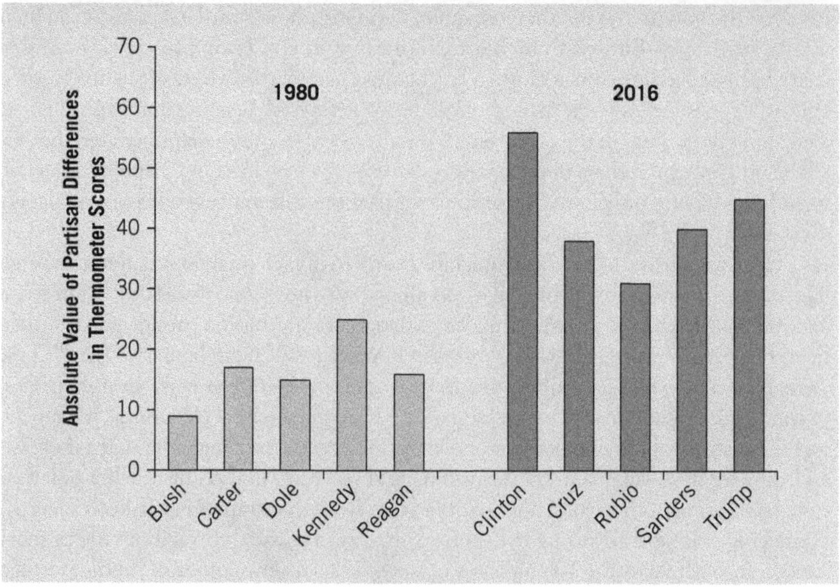

Source: Authors' analysis of "feeling thermometers" is from the respective ANES surveys.

Note: Data are weighted.

**Figure 1-4 Warm Feelings from Opposite Partisans: Selected Candidates, January 1980 and 2016**

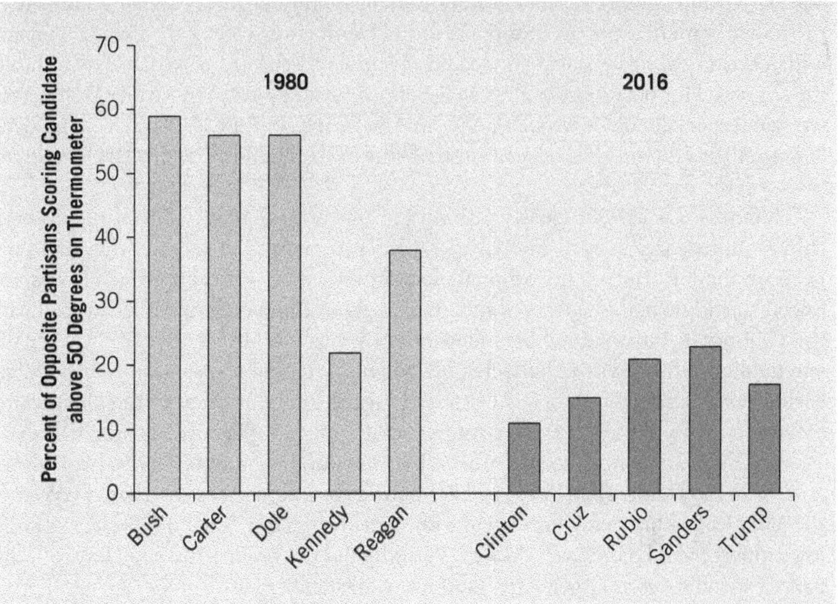


*Source:* Authors' analysis of "feeling thermometers" is from the respective ANES surveys.

*Note:* Data are weighted.

differences typically under 20 degrees on the 100-point scale. Only evaluations of Kennedy were higher, at 27 points. None of these were as large as the smallest partisan gap in 2016, and the partisan polarization between the two eventual nominees was great—more than 40 points for Trump and more than 50 for Clinton. Perhaps even more dramatic, in 1980 *majorities* of the opposition felt warmly toward Carter and toward eventual vice presidential nominee Bush, with Reagan evaluated positively by many Democrats. Conversely, in 2016, none of the candidates were evaluated positively by a quarter of the opposition, and fewer than one in five partisans felt warmly toward the candidate who eventually won the other party's nomination. There was very little chance that either party could nominate a candidate with any appreciable support among the opposition in 2016, quite unlike Reagan's success in winning over "Reagan Democrats" in his campaigns and presidency.[42] Even at the start of the campaign, that is, the contenders were in a strategic context that rewarded focus on one's own party with no incentive to build toward a cross-party coalition, either in open primary states or for the general election—or thereafter when in office. The public has become deeply divided emotionally over our electoral contests even before they have barely begun in a way that simply was not true a generation ago.

Whereas, therefore, it is always true that nomination politics leads candidates to focus on their party to win, this was truer in 2016 than ever before. How, then, did the candidates win? We begin with Democrats. Hillary Clinton started both the 2008 and 2016 campaigns in the enviable position of an unusually well-known candidate in the public, with many areas of support in the Democratic electorate already won and with a great deal of support from leading Democrats and those with access to funding sources. Her position was thus well-defined with appeal to moderate Democrats, women (especially older women), African Americans, and those who have long been "Clintonians." As such if she had a vulnerability in the Democratic primary electorate, it was on the party's left.

Sanders was able to clearly fashion his appeal to that very constituency, even though not nearly as well-known to Democratic voters in January. He had long been on the left. Indeed his original election as mayor of Burlington, VT, was as a Socialist, and he had long served in Congress as an Independent who caucused with the Democrats but retained his independent status. Only recently had he formally and publicly affiliated as a Democrat, making his potential nomination viable. Unlike earlier nomination contests, few contested for the liberal portion of the Democratic electorate, with the apparently strongest contenders, especially Senator Elizabeth Warren (MA), declining to run. Given his late and, in some measures, begrudging entry into the Democratic Party, he lacked the close interactions and shared service to the party leadership that Clinton had with so many of them. And both his lack of seeking support from Democratic donors (Vermont did not require the same level of campaign expenditures as larger states) and his vocal stance against super PACs and other organizations that serve as sources of campaign resources, he also faced obstacles to expanding upon his electoral base. And, indeed, that is how the campaign worked out.

Perhaps the biggest surprise of the Democratic campaign was how Sanders was able to make a strong appeal, especially to younger voters on the left, and to turn college students, among others, into active supporters. As a further result, Clinton, even as she emphasized the more liberal parts of her agenda and adopted more left-wing positions on key issues, was unable to expand her base on the left, as Sanders was demonstrably a liberal (even socialist) candidate, and she was forced to publicly change her stances to try to reach Sanders's supporters. Conversely Sanders had too little standing among Democratic leaders (such as superdelegates) or more moderate Democrats in the public, nor even among the large constituency of African Americans. Thus he too was unable to cut into Clinton's strengths and expand his base of support.

Clinton won the Iowa caucuses (a real victory, given her loss there in 2008) and held Sanders to a relatively small victory in New Hampshire, sitting next door to Sanders's home (see Table 1-3 for delegates won by these two candidates over the nomination campaign). Of course that meant that Sanders did reasonably well in Iowa and won New Hampshire, cementing him as a credible candidate, able to be considered by voters over the long haul. Still, his inability to shake much of her support meant that in the March 1 "Super Tuesday" primaries, most of which were in the South and thus featured two sources of Clinton strength, moderate white Democrats and African Americans, followed by her largely similar victories in the large, industrial states of the "Rust Belt," meant that Sanders fell behind in the count of delegates won, even as he very slowly approached her standing in the public opinion polls. Because the Democratic rules require some form of proportional selection of delegates (i.e., roughly in proportion to the percentage of votes received), Clinton's delegate lead became simply insurmountable.

As noted earlier, however, it took Clinton until June for her to win an absolute majority of the delegates and thus achieve victory, a victory strengthened by heavy support of superdelegates, those party leaders with whom she had so long worked. In short two candidates with clear and distinct appeals were able to hold their own support, but both were unable to expand into that of the opponent. As a result the early lead Clinton had in public opinion polls (8 points in the February CBS/*New York Times* [NYT] poll) held steady throughout the season (the same poll in May had her with a 7-point lead), and that relatively small lead in the national polls became a small but winning majority in the delegate count as state after state selected its delegates.

The Republican side was, of course, rather different in many ways. Still, Trump held a 17-point lead over Cruz, his closest competitor in the January (and February) CBS/NYT poll that in April, just before Cruz withdrew, stood at 13 points. Once delegate selection started, that is, all the sound and fury of Republican candidates attacking each other on increasingly personal grounds had at best minor effects on Trump's public standing and lead in the delegate count. To be sure, in 2016 or 2017, many different Republicans got their day in the sun, but none were able to close the Trump lead.

Perhaps surprisingly Trump lost to Cruz in Iowa (and nearly fell to third place there) but righted his ship in New Hampshire, South Carolina, and virtually everywhere thereafter, consistently winning most of the states with pluralities (only occasionally with actual majorities) but picking up the bulk of the delegates in state after state. Trump did lose two large states, Ohio and Texas, and with those losses in votes, he also lost even larger percentages of their delegates, but these were divided between Kasich and Cruz, respectively (each winning their home states). Even so, Trump was able to carry many other larger states (perhaps most significantly, Rubio's home state of Florida). While opponents considered ways to unite their forces to maximize leverage against Trump, no plan was able to be worked out. Further, after the earliest states had chosen, the Republican Party rules permit states to use WTA rules so that the candidate who wins more of the larger states wins a far higher percentage of the delegates needed to win nomination. Thus Trump was able to move consistently and smoothly toward victory, as can be seen in Table 1-4, which reports the results of each Republican contest.

This relatively placid and straightforward account of how Clinton and Trump won nomination belies the media frenzy that accompanied both campaigns—and especially these two candidates in particular. These circumstances are those that most remember, even though their consistent and largely unchecked (and apparently uncheckable) drives to victory are the real story of how to win nominations in the post-1972 nomination system.

Still, both were tagged with problems (quite reasonably understood as of their own doing) that would dog their campaigns throughout the spring, summer, fall, and in Trump's case, into the White House itself as we discuss in subsequent chapters. Clinton was tarnished with three charges that yielded appearances of corruption—the financing of the Clinton Foundation, the events that led to the deaths of four

**Table 1-3 Democratic Nomination Results, 2016: Bound Delegates Won in State Primaries and Caucuses—Clinton and Sanders**

| Date | State | Clinton | Sanders |
|---|---|---|---|
| 1-Feb | Iowa | 23 | 21 |
| 9-Feb | N.H. | 9 | 15 |
| 20-Feb | Nev. | 20 | 15 |
| 27-Feb | S.C. | 39 | 14 |
| 1-Mar | Ala. | 44 | 9 |
| | Ark. | 22 | 10 |
| | Colo. | 25 | 41 |
| | Ga. | 73 | 29 |
| | Mass. | 46 | 45 |
| | Minn. | 31 | 46 |
| | Okla. | 17 | 21 |
| | Tenn. | 44 | 23 |
| | Texas | 147 | 75 |
| | Vt. | 0 | 16 |
| | Va. | 62 | 33 |
| 5-Mar | Kan. | 10 | 23 |
| | La. | 37 | 14 |
| | Neb. | 10 | 15 |
| 6-Mar | Maine | 8 | 17 |
| 8-Mar | Mich. | 63 | 67 |
| | Miss. | 31 | 5 |
| 15-Mar | Fla. | 141 | 73 |
| | Ill. | 79 | 77 |
| | Mo. | 36 | 35 |
| | N.C. | 60 | 47 |
| | Ohio | 81 | 62 |
| 22-Mar | Ariz. | 42 | 33 |
| | Idaho | 5 | 18 |
| | Utah | 6 | 27 |

| Date | State | Clinton | Sanders |
|---|---|---|---|
| 26-Mar | Alaska | 3 | 13 |
| | Hawaii | 8 | 17 |
| | Wash. | 27 | 74 |
| 5-Apr | Wis. | 38 | 48 |
| 9-Apr | Wyo. | 7 | 7 |
| 19-Apr | N.Y. | 139 | 108 |
| 26-Apr | Conn. | 28 | 27 |
| | Del. | 12 | 9 |
| | Md. | 60 | 35 |
| | Pa. | 106 | 83 |
| | R.I. | 11 | 13 |
| 3-May | Ind. | 39 | 44 |
| 10-May | W.Va. | 11 | 18 |
| 17-May | Ky. | 28 | 27 |
| | Ore. | 25 | 36 |
| 5-Jun | P.R. | 37 | 23 |
| 7-Jun | Calif. | 254 | 221 |
| | Mont. | 10 | 11 |
| | N.J. | 79 | 47 |
| | N.M. | 18 | 16 |
| | N.D. | 5 | 13 |
| | S.D. | 10 | 10 |
| 14-Jun | D.C. | 16 | 4 |
| Listed numbers are for bound delegates. | | | |

*Source:* Kevin Schaul and Samuel Granados, "The Race to the Democratic Nomination," *Washington Post*, October 10, 2017, https://www.washingtonpost.com/graphics/politics/2016-election/primaries/delegate-tracker/democratic/, accessed June 1, 2017.

Americans in Benghazi, Libya, and her use of a private e-mail account while she was secretary of state (and possible misuse of classified material). The latter, of course, continued right up to election day itself. In the spring, as well as in the fall, Trump regularly referred to her as "Crooked Hillary," and his audiences chanted "Lock her up! Lock her up!" Trump made a series of what we would ordinarily have imagined to be candidacy-ending gaffes, but (just as Clinton's poll numbers stayed fixed at a high level in the nomination campaign) no matter how vindictive (calling Cruz's wife "ugly"), mean-spirited ("Little Marco"), lascivious,[43] factually inaccurate, or seemingly outrageously racist his words, Trump simply marched toward victory in the spring. Or, as he put it himself, "I could stand in the middle of 5th Avenue and shoot somebody, and I wouldn't lose voters," Trump said in Sioux City, Iowa, January 24, 2016.[44] Yet these unique features of these two candidates seemed to have had little effect on their nomination campaigns.

*National Party Conventions:* As we noted earlier the purpose of the state primary or caucus convention procedures is to select who will be the delegates from that state to attend their national party convention and/or to instruct those delegates on how to vote for presidential nomination. The delegates are those entrusted with voting on all the convention's major pieces of business. These include resolving any remaining problems that arose in selecting one state's or another's delegations, adopting rules that will govern the party for the next four years, voting on the proposed party platform, and choosing the presidential and vice presidential nominees. Thus the delegates are entrusted with essentially all of the party's major decisions. But, as we have already seen with respect to the presidential nomination, they may cast the formal ballots—and it could well be some day that they will in fact play active roles—but their decision making is so tightly constrained that they almost invariably have no real choices to make. Their choice for presidential nominee is constrained by the vote of the public in their state.[45] The presidential nominee selects a candidate she or he would like to see serve as a running mate, and it has been a very long time since there was any real opposition to that choice.[46]

Party platforms once were regularly contended, as this was the one time when the party leadership could interact and work out just what the party stood for. Although this has not been true in recent years, both parties have had protests over the platform committee's proposals on one issue or another (e.g., the change in the 1980 Republican platform from its long-held stance of endorsing an Equal Rights Amendment to the Constitution for women to opposing it), whereas the last truly contended (nearly violently contended) battle over a platform plank was the debate over the Vietnam War in the 1968 Democratic Convention.

Instead of the traditional role of party conventions serving as the one time the party gathers from around the nation to debate and decide party business, the conventions have changed in recent decades to serve as major public presentations of the party to the nation. This leads the party and its leadership to seek to downplay internal divisions (although when they are really there, they are typically not able to be completely hidden) and present a united front to the public. Their other central role is to serve as the end of the intra-party competition of nominations and the transition to the general election campaign. The acceptance speeches of the nominees (and certainly of the presidential nominee) are generally used to showcase the major themes of the candidates for the general election campaign.

In 2012 the conventions were held late in August, which put the Republicans, especially, at a disadvantage as their nominee was restricted in spending in opposition

**Table 1-4 Republican Nomination Results, 2016: Bound Delegates Won in State Primaries and Caucuses—Trump, Cruz, Rubio, and Kasich**

| | | Trump | Cruz | Rubio | Kasich |
|---|---|---|---|---|---|
| 1-Feb | Iowa | 7 | 8 | 7 | 1 |
| 9-Feb | N.H. | 11 | 3 | 1 | 4 |
| 20-Feb | S.C. | 50 | 0 | 0 | 0 |
| 23-Feb | Nev. | 14 | 6 | 7 | 1 |
| 1-Mar | Ala. | 36 | 13 | 1 | 0 |
| | Alaska | 11 | 12 | 5 | 0 |
| | Ark. | 16 | 15 | 9 | 0 |
| | Ga. | 42 | 18 | 16 | 0 |
| | Mass. | 22 | 4 | 8 | 8 |
| | Minn. | 8 | 13 | 17 | 0 |
| | Okla. | 13 | 15 | 12 | 0 |
| | Tenn. | 33 | 16 | 9 | 0 |
| | Texas | 48 | 104 | 3 | 0 |
| | Vt. | 8 | 0 | 0 | 8 |
| | Va. | 17 | 8 | 16 | 5 |
| 5-Mar | Kan. | 9 | 24 | 6 | 1 |
| | Ky. | 17 | 15 | 7 | 7 |
| | La. | 25 | 18 | 0 | 0 |
| | Maine | 9 | 12 | 0 | 2 |
| 6-Mar | P.R. | 0 | 0 | 23 | 0 |
| 8-Mar | Hawaii | 11 | 7 | 1 | 0 |
| | Idaho | 12 | 20 | 0 | 0 |
| | Mich. | 25 | 17 | 0 | 17 |
| | Miss. | 25 | 15 | 0 | 0 |
| 10-Mar | V.I. | 1 | 0 | 0 | 0 |
| 12-Mar | D.C. | 0 | 0 | 10 | 9 |
| | Wyo. | 1 | 23 | 1 | 0 |

*(Continued)*

**Table 1-4** (Continued)

| | | Trump | Cruz | Rubio | Kasich |
|---|---|---|---|---|---|
| 15-Mar | Fla. | 99 | 0 | 0 | 0 |
| | Ill. | 54 | 9 | 0 | 6 |
| | Mo. | 37 | 15 | 0 | 0 |
| | N.C. | 29 | 27 | 6 | 9 |
| | M.P. | 9 | 0 | 0 | 0 |
| | Ohio | 0 | 0 | 0 | 66 |
| 22-Mar | Ariz. | 58 | 0 | 0 | 0 |
| | Utah | 0 | 40 | 0 | 0 |
| 5-Apr | Wis. | 6 | 36 | 0 | 0 |
| 9-Apr | Colo. | 0 | 30 | 0 | 0 |
| 19-Apr | N.Y. | 89 | 0 | 0 | 6 |
| 26-Apr | Conn. | 28 | 0 | 0 | 0 |
| | Del. | 16 | 0 | 0 | 0 |
| | Md. | 38 | 0 | 0 | 0 |
| | Pa. | 17 | 0 | 0 | 0 |
| | R.I. | 12 | 2 | 0 | 5 |
| 3-May | Ind. | 57 | 0 | 0 | 0 |
| 10-May | Neb. | 36 | 0 | 0 | 0 |
| | W.Va. | 30 | 0 | 0 | 1 |
| 17-May | Ore. | 18 | 5 | 0 | 5 |
| 24-May | Wash. | 41 | 0 | 0 | 0 |
| 7-Jun | Calif. | 172 | 0 | 0 | 0 |
| | Mont. | 27 | 0 | 0 | 0 |
| | N.J. | 51 | 0 | 0 | 0 |
| | N.M. | 24 | 0 | 0 | 0 |
| | S.D. | 29 | 0 | 0 | 0 |

Listed numbers are for bound delegates.

*Source:* Kevin Schaul and Samuel Granados, "The Race to the Democratic Nomination," *Washington Post*, October 10, 2017, https://www.washingtonpost.com/graphics/politics/2016-election/primaries/delegate-tracker/republican/, accessed June 1, 2017.

to President Obama by the rules of the nomination season. Thus they were especially keen to hold their convention earlier in 2016. They choose to hold it in Cleveland July 18–21, whereas the Democrats held theirs in Philadelphia July 25–28.[47]

Trump selected the governor of Indiana, Michael Pence, to be his running mate on July 15. Pence is as understated as Trump is flamboyant and has had considerable experience in politics to balance Trump's outsider status. He has particularly deep religious beliefs, which guide many of his policy positions and, of course, appeals strongly to the large and important religious right in the party. That he hails from a combined Rust Belt, agricultural Midwestern state balanced the ticket, as is a common tradition, counterbalancing a New York City, high-rolling businessman with little formal connections to religion. Whereas the Trump and Pence nominations (and adoption of the party platform) went smoothly enough, there were moments of contention. Perhaps the most obvious was Cruz's unwillingness (often described as "defiance") to endorse Trump's nomination on prime-time television, which resulted in loud booing and heckling. Trump, for his part, stuck pretty closely to the script of his acceptance speech, which outlined a dark vision of contemporary America, leading those who agreed to the conclusion (he hoped) that one needed to vote for him to reverse course.

Clinton, for her part, selected Senator Tim Kaine, Virginia, as her running mate. This choice had less ticket balancing as compared to selecting a candidate from the liberal wing of the party, such as Sanders or Senator Elizabeth Warren (both of whom had featured speeches—Warren gave the keynote address). Although perhaps not quite as similar as Senator Al Gore was to Bill Clinton, Kaine was less about uniting the party (although he certainly did not divide it) than about trying to win the general election. Any worries about major disruption from the left wing were unfounded, and thus the convention presented a united image to the public and allowed Clinton to use her acceptance speech to complete the uniting and begin the general election campaign.

| Election | Winning Candidate | Party of Winning Candidate | Success of Incumbent Political Party |
|---|---|---|---|
| 1932 | Franklin D. Roosevelt | Democrat | Lost |
| 1936 | Franklin D. Roosevelt | Democrat | Won |
| 1940 | Franklin D. Roosevelt | Democrat | Won |
| 1944 | Franklin D. Roosevelt | Democrat | Won |
| 1948 | Harry S. Truman | Democrat | Won |
| 1952 | Dwight D. Eisenhower | Republican | Lost |
| 1956 | Dwight D. Eisenhower | Republican | Won |
| 1960 | John F. Kennedy | Democrat | Lost |
| 1964 | Lyndon B. Johnson | Democrat | Won |
| 1968 | Richard M. Nixon | Republican | Lost |
| 1972 | Richard M. Nixon | Republican | Won |
| 1976 | Jimmy Carter | Democrat | Lost |
| 1980 | Ronald Reagan | Republican | Lost |
| 1984 | Ronald Reagan | Republican | Won |
| 1988 | George H. W. Bush | Republican | Won |
| 1992 | Bill Clinton | Democrat | Lost |
| 1996 | Bill Clinton | Democrat | Won |
| 2000 | George W. Bush | Republican | Lost |
| 2004 | George W. Bush | Republican | Won |
| 2008 | Barack Obama | Democrat | Lost |
| 2012 | Barack Obama | Democrat | Won |
| 2016 | Donald J. Trump | Republican | Lost |

*Source: Presidential Elections, 1789–2008* (Washington, D.C.: CQ Press, 2009); 2012–2016, compiled by authors.

[a]Whigs are classified as the incumbent party because they won the 1840 election. In fact their presidential candidate, William Henry Harrison, died a month after taking office and his vice president, John Tyler, was expelled from the party in 1841.

[b]Republicans are classified as the incumbent party because they won the 1864 election. (Technically Lincoln had been elected on a Union ticket.) In fact after Lincoln's assassination in 1865, Andrew Johnson, a war Democrat, became president.

became Republicans, the Republican Party was not just the Whig Party renamed. The Republicans had transformed the political agenda by capitalizing on opposition to slavery in the territories.[47]

The 1896 contest, the last of four incumbent party losses, is usually considered a critical election because it solidified Republican dominance.[48] Although the Republicans had won five of the seven elections since the end of the Civil War, after Ulysses S. Grant's reelection in 1872, all their victories had been by narrow margins. In 1896 the Republicans emerged as the clearly dominant party, gaining a solid hold in Connecticut, Indiana, New Jersey, and New York, states that they had frequently lost between 1876 and 1892. After William McKinley's defeat of William Jennings Bryan in 1896, the Republicans established a firmer base in the Midwest, New England, and the Mid-Atlantic states. They lost the presidency only in 1912, when the GOP was split, and in 1916, when the incumbent, Woodrow Wilson, ran for reelection.[49] The Republicans would win again in 1920, 1924, and 1928.

The Great Depression ended Republican dominance. The emergence of the Democrats as the majority party was not preceded by a series of incumbent losses. Instead the Democratic coalition forged in the 1930s relied heavily on the emerging working class and the mobilization of new groups into the electorate.

As the emergence of the New Deal coalition demonstrates, a period of electoral volatility is not a necessary condition for a partisan realignment. Nor perhaps is it a sufficient condition. In 1985 Ronald Reagan himself proclaimed that his reelection was indicative of a realignment. Political scientists were skeptical about that claim mainly because the Democrats continued to dominate the U.S. House of Representatives. George H. W. Bush's election in 1988 suggested that Republican dominance indeed might have arrived. But Clinton's 1992 victory called this thesis into question, and his 1996 victory cast further doubts on the idea that a realignment had occurred. After the 2000 election, the Republicans held control of the House, the Senate, and the presidency for the first time since 1953, although they temporarily lost control of the Senate between June 2001 and January 2003.[50] But the closeness of the election called into question any claim of Republican dominance. The Democrats regained the presidency—by a comfortable margin—with Obama's victory in 2008, and they also won relatively large majorities in both houses of Congress, only to lose control of the House and a sizable portion of their advantage in the Senate in the 2010 midterm elections. The election of 2012 gave Obama and the Democrats another four years in the White House, but Congress remained under divided party control. Following the 2016 election the Republicans control the White House and both houses of Congress. Yet, just as unified political control of government following the 2008 election did not launch a period of Democratic dominance, it is unlikely that unified government under the Republicans signals the dawn of GOP ascendancy. No party currently dominates American politics. Volatility persists.

One clear pattern that does emerge when one examines presidential elections across history is that incumbent candidates appear to have an advantage. Between 1792 and 2016, in-office parties retained the White House about two-thirds of the time when they ran the incumbent president but only won half the time—a coin flip—when they did not run an incumbent.[51] Obama's victory in 2012 made him the third straight incumbent president to win reelection. In fact eight of ten postwar incumbent presidents seeking reelection have won, with Ford losing in 1976 and Carter in 1980. The 1976 and 1980 elections were the only successive elections in the twentieth century in which two incumbent presidents in a row lost. The only other elections in which incumbent presidents were defeated in two straight elections were in 1888, when Benjamin Harrison defeated Grover Cleveland, and in 1892, when Cleveland defeated Harrison. With no incumbent on the ballot in 2016, the presidential election was seemingly either party's to win. In Chapter 7, we examine voters' evaluations of presidential performance and how it relates to voting.

## STATE-BY-STATE RESULTS

The modern electoral map is a conglomeration of Republican "red states" and Democratic "blue states." Yet this color pairing has no real historical meaning and, in fact, has only become convention in recent years.[52] In 1976, for instance, election-night news coverage on NBC classified Republican (Ford) wins in blue and Democratic (Carter) victories in red. ABC News featured an electoral map that colored Democratic states in blue and Republican states in yellow.

Whereas the colors on the electoral map may be meaningless, the political geography of presidential elections most certainly is not. Because states deliver the electoral votes necessary to win the presidency, the presidential election is effectively fifty-one separate contests, one for each state and one for the District of Columbia. With the exception of Maine and Nebraska, the candidate who wins the most votes in a state wins all of the state's electors. Regardless of how a state decides to allocate its electors, the number of electors is the sum of its senators (two), plus the number of its representatives in the U.S. House.[53] Since 1964 there have been 538 electors and a majority, 270, is required to win. In 2016 the distribution of electoral votes ranged from a low of three in Alaska, Delaware, Montana, North Dakota, South Dakota, Vermont, Wyoming, and the District of Columbia to a high of fifty-five in California.

Because each state, regardless of population, has two electoral votes for its senators, the smaller states are overrepresented in the Electoral College and the larger states are underrepresented. The twenty least-populated states and the District of Columbia were home to roughly 10.5 percent of the U.S. population according to the 2010 Census, but these states had 16.5 percent of the electoral votes. The nine most-populated states, which had 52.2 percent of the population, had only 44.8 percent of the electoral vote.

Even though smaller states are overrepresented in the Electoral College, presidential campaigns tend to focus their resources on larger states unless pre-election polls suggest that a state is unwinnable. Consider the two most populous states, California and Texas. California's fifty-five electoral votes represent one-fifth of the votes needed to win the Electoral College. Texas has thirty-eight electoral votes, one-seventh of the votes necessary to win. Clearly both are vital for building an Electoral College victory. Yet pre-election polls suggested landslide wins for Clinton in California and Trump in Texas, and neither campaign spent significant time or money in either state. During the general election campaign (from the end of their respective conventions to election day), neither presidential candidate made a public appearance in California, and

Trump visited Texas only twice.[54] Florida, North Carolina, Ohio, and Pennsylvania, on the other hand, were competitive, large states with a total of eighty-two electoral votes at stake, and both candidates visited the four states more than any other. Clinton made twenty-one public appearances in Florida, for instance. Trump, who spent more time on the campaign stump overall, made twenty public appearances each in Florida, North Carolina, and Pennsylvania.[55] Trump won all four states.[56]

States are the building blocks of winning presidential coalitions, but state-by-state results can be overemphasized and may sometimes be misleading for three reasons. First, although much attention is given to battleground states, the nature of broadcast and social media coverage means that candidates must run national campaigns. Candidates can make appeals to specific states and regions, but those messages are likely to be reported across geographic boundaries. Thus, whereas battleground contests and regional bases of support may color a campaign's message and strategy, most campaigns seek to form a broad-based coalition throughout the nation. Indeed, given that forty-four of the forty-eight elections between 1828 and 2016 have resulted in the candidate with the largest number of popular votes also winning a majority of the electoral votes, it would appear that successful campaigns have always been national rather than regional in scope.

Second, comparing state-level election results over time can be misleading and may even conceal change. To illustrate this point we compare the results of two close Democratic victories—John Kennedy's defeat of Richard Nixon in 1960 and Jimmy Carter's defeat of Gerald Ford in 1976—that have many similarities. In both 1960 and 1976, the Republicans did very well in the West, and both Kennedy and Carter needed southern support to win. Kennedy carried six of the eleven southern states—Arkansas, Georgia, Louisiana, North Carolina, South Carolina, and Texas—and gained five of Alabama's eleven electoral votes, for a total of eighty-one electoral votes. Carter carried ten of the eleven southern states (all but Virginia) for a total of 118 electoral votes. Yet the demographic basis of Carter's support was quite different from Kennedy's. In 1960 only twenty-nine percent of African Americans in the South were registered to vote compared with sixty-one percent of whites. According to our analysis of the American National Election Studies, only about one in fifteen of the Kennedy voters in the South was black. In 1976, 63 percent of African Americans in the South were registered to vote compared with 68 percent of whites.[57] We estimate that about one in three southerners who voted for Carter was black. A simple state-by-state comparison would conceal this massive change in the social composition of the Democratic presidential coalition.

Third, state-by-state comparisons do not tell us why a presidential candidate received support. Of course such comparisons can lead to interesting speculation, especially when the dominant issues are related to regional differences. Following the 2016 election, for example, some observers speculated that Trump's victory, particularly in states such as Michigan, North Carolina, Ohio, and Pennsylvania, could be attributed to manufacturing job losses in those states.[58] Yet exit polls from these states show that voters who reported that the economy was the "most important issue facing the economy" were actually more likely to vote for Clinton than Trump.[59] Inference based solely on who won the state may be fallacious and lead to mischaracterizations of the electorate. Indeed similarly constructed inferences often lead to hyperbolic comparisons of "red states" versus "blue states," creating an illusion of a deeply divided electorate.[60] State-level election results should not be used to infer voters' preferences; for this we must examine individual-level survey responses—as we do in later chapters.

With these qualifications in mind, we now turn to the state-by-state results. Figure 3-2 shows Trump's margin of victory over Clinton in all states. As noted earlier both of the parties maintain regional bases of strong support, whereas relatively few states are competitive and truly in play. A continuing base of strength for the Democrats was the Northeast, sweeping eight of the nine states in the region (by an average popular vote margin of 15.3 points).[61] The Democrats have dominated the Northeast in presidential elections since Bill Clinton's election in 1992.[62] But Hillary Clinton was unable to hold the region's second-largest electoral prize, Pennsylvania, which Trump won by a slim 0.72 points. Despite the party's electoral strength in the Northeast, the region is proving to be a precarious base of electoral support for the Democrats. Whereas comparison of vote shares across the last seven elections suggests that the region has not waned in its support of the Democratic Party, the region

**Figure 3-2 Trump's Margin of Victory over Clinton, 2016**

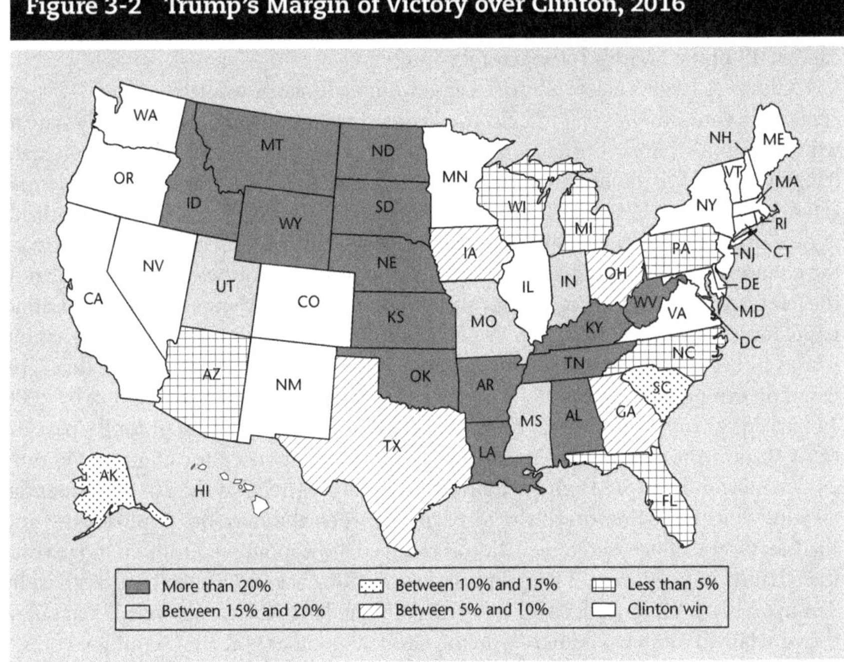


*Source:* Federal Election Commission, "Official 2016 Presidential General Election Results," January 30, 2017, https://transition.fec.gov/pubrec/fe2016/2016presgeresults.pdf. Based on reports of the secretaries of state of the fifty states and the District of Columbia.

*Note:* We classify Maine as being carried by Clinton in 2016. Clinton actually won the statewide race and one of Maine's two congressional districts, thus winning three of the state's four Electoral College votes.

is declining in population and thus carries less weight in the Electoral College. In 1992 the region offered 106 electoral votes. In 2016 that number was only ninety-six, and by one estimate—based on U.S. Census population projections—by the 2024 election, the Northeast's share of electoral votes will decline further to ninety-one.[63] Whether the region continues to vote consistently for the Democratic Party remains to be seen.

Clinton's coalition was not restricted to one region. Outside of the Northeast she carried seven other states, as well as the District of Columbia, by ten percentage points or more, including the electorally rich states of California and Illinois. Clinton's sizable victories in Oregon and Washington continue the Democrat's dominance in those states, which have voted Democratic in each of the last eight presidential elections. Clinton also won pluralities in Nevada and Colorado, although her victories in each did not approach the comfortable majorities secured there by Obama in both 2008 and 2012. Yet Clinton's ability to keep these states in the Democratic column is notable because Nevada had voted Democrat only twice (for Bill Clinton in 1992 and 1996) between 1964 and 2008, and Colorado voted Democrat only once (1992) during that time frame. Clinton was also able to maintain Virginia for the Democrats. Until Obama's victory there in 2008 and 2012, Virginia had not voted Democratic since Lyndon Johnson's 1964 landslide, although the state had been inching toward the Democratic column because of the suburban growth from D.C. But the rest of the South remained unfertile ground for the Democrats in 2016. Clinton was only able to capture 13 of the South's 160 electoral votes.

Clinton's largest electoral prize came from California, where she won 61.7 percent of the vote and the state's 55 electoral votes. In fact California was the only state in which Clinton's margin of victory was bigger than Obama's in 2012. The Golden State has now voted for the Democratic candidates in each of the last seven presidential elections. Between 1952 and 1988, the state voted for the GOP presidential candidate in nine of the ten elections. But in those elections, California did not differ much from the country as a whole: its average level of Republican support was the same as that of the nation as a whole. One reason for this political change is the state's growing Latino population, which increased from 19 percent in 1980 to 39 percent in 2016, overtaking whites to become California's largest ethnic group.[64] According to Mark Baldassare, based on exit polls in 1990, only 4 percent of California voters were Latino; by 2000 14 percent were.[65] In 2016 exit polls indicate that Latinos accounted for 31 percent of the California electorate. Of those voters 71 percent voted for Clinton and only 24 percent for Trump.[66] Perhaps California's greatest effect on the 2016 presidential election is its contribution to the disparity between the national popular vote and the Electoral College outcome. Clinton received a whopping 4.3 million more votes than Trump in California. That surplus of votes alone is greater than that received by Trump in his seven most decisive victories combined.[67] If California were taken out of the vote tally, Trump would have won the national popular vote by 1.4 million votes.[68] Thus California's place in the 2016 election helps demonstrate the logic inherent in the Electoral College, an institution designed by the founders to prevent regional candidates from dominating a national election.[69]

As noted previously Trump's narrow victories in Michigan, Pennsylvania, and Wisconsin—all by less than one percentage point—brought three reliably Democratic states back into the Republican's win column. All three of these states supported Reagan in both 1980 and 1984, and Michigan and Pennsylvania sided with George H. W. Bush in 1988. In the six elections that followed, all three states voted for the Democratic nominee, although not always by comfortable margins. These states represented a substantial haul for Trump, totaling 46 electoral votes (17 percent of the 270 needed for victory). Other states that Trump was able to win, such as Florida and Ohio, are far more variable electorally. Since 1992, for instance, neither state has voted for a presidential candidate of the same party more than twice in a row. Unsurprisingly, these states are typically defined as among the most competitive from election to election. And Ohio continues to be a bellwether for the nation; the Buckeye State has voted for the presidential (Electoral College) winner in every election since 1960, when it voted for Richard Nixon over John F. Kennedy.

The remaining states captured by Trump in 2016 are the core of the Republican electoral coalition. These twenty-two states, which Trump won by an amazing average margin of 23.6 percentage points, all voted Republican in each of the last five presidential elections.[70] Thirteen of these states (Alabama, Arkansas, Idaho, Kansas, Mississippi, Nebraska, North Dakota, Oklahoma, South Carolina, South Dakota, Utah, and Wyoming) have voted Republican in every election dating back to 1980. The problem for Republicans, generally, is that the twenty-two solidly Republican states tend to be smaller in population and result in 180 electoral votes. Texas, with its thirty-eight electoral votes, is the largest state in this coalition, followed by Georgia with sixteen electoral votes, but five of these states have only three electoral votes each. To make the point clearer, consider the subset of thirteen states that have voted Republican since 1980. These thirteen states cumulatively represent sixty-seven electoral votes. This is not much of an advantage when we recall that Democratic-leaning California alone has fifty-five votes.

The region that offered Trump his greatest electoral reward was the South. One hundred forty-seven of Trump's electoral votes were from the South, nearly half of his total (48.4 percent). In the last half century, the South has been transformed into the base of the Republican Party, and this transformation is the most dramatic change in postwar American politics. Clinton's only victory in the South was in Virginia. In 2008 and 2012 Obama cut into the Republican's southern base by winning both Florida and Virginia, and in 2008, he also carried North Carolina. In each of those elections, however, Obama would have won the Electoral College without winning a single southern state. The same is true of Bill Clinton's victories in 1992 and 1996. Yet it is infeasible for the Republicans to win the presidency without southern electoral votes.

Republican strength in the South and Democratic advantage in the Northeast does not mean that sectionalism has beset the country. Indeed regional differences in presidential voting have declined in the postwar period and are currently low by historical standards. This can be demonstrated by statistical analysis. Joseph A. Schlesinger has analyzed state-by-state variation in presidential elections from 1832 through 1988, and we have updated his analyses through 2016.[71] Schlesinger measures the extent to which party competition in presidential elections is divided along geographic lines by calculating the standard deviation in the percentage of the Democratic vote among the states.[72] The state-by-state variation was 10.35 in 2016, slightly higher than the 10.29 deviation in 2012 and the 9.54 deviation in 2008. This suggests that states were slightly more divided in their support for Trump in 2016 than in recent elections.[73]

Schlesinger's analysis clearly reveals the relatively low level of state-by-state variation in the postwar elections.[74] According to his analysis (as updated), all fifteen of the presidential elections from 1888 to 1944 displayed more state-by-state variation than any of the seventeen postwar elections. To a large extent, the decline in state-by-state variation has been a result of the transformation of the South and the demise of local party machines, which has allowed partisan cleavages to become more consistent across states and allowed party competition to increase across the country.[75]

## ELECTORAL CHANGE IN THE POSTWAR SOUTH

The South is a growing region that has undergone dramatic political change. Even though five of the eleven southern states have lost congressional representation since World War II, Florida and Texas have made spectacular gains. In the 1944 and 1948 elections, Florida had only eight electoral votes, but in the 2016 election, it had twenty-nine. In 1944 and 1948, Texas had twenty-three electoral votes; in 2016 it had thirty-eight. Since the end of World War II, the South's electoral vote total has grown from 127 to 160. The South gained seven electoral votes following the 2010 Census and projections suggest that it may gain an extra four by 2024.[76]

The political transformation of the South was a complex process, but the major reason for the change was simple. As V. O. Key, Jr., brilliantly demonstrated in *Southern Politics in State and Nation* in 1949, the main factor in southern politics is race. "In its grand outlines the politics of the South revolves around the position of the Negro. . . . Whatever phase of the southern political process one seeks to understand, sooner or later the trail of inquiry leads to the Negro."[77] And it was the national Democratic Party's sponsorship of African American civil rights that shattered the party's dominance in the South.[78]

Between the end of Reconstruction in 1877 and the end of World War II, the South was functionally a one-party system. Unified in its support of racial segregation and in its opposition to Republican social and economic policies, the South was a Democratic stronghold—the "Solid South." Indeed in fifteen of the seventeen elections from 1880 to 1944, all eleven southern states voted Democratic. Between 1896 (the first election after many southern states adopted the "white primary") and 1944, the average Democratic Party vote share in presidential elections was 71.6 percent.[79] The only major defections were in 1928, when the Democrats ran Alfred E. Smith, a Roman Catholic. As a result the Republican candidate, Herbert Hoover, won five southern states. Even then six of the most solid southern states voted for Smith, even though all but Louisiana were overwhelmingly Protestant.

After Reconstruction ended in 1877, many southern blacks were prevented from voting, and in the late nineteenth and early twentieth centuries, several southern states changed their voting laws to further disenfranchise blacks. The Republicans effectively ceded those states to the Democrats. Although the Republicans garnered black support in the North, they did not attempt to enforce the Fifteenth Amendment, which bans restrictions on voting on the basis of "race, color, or previous condition of servitude."

In 1932 a majority of African Americans in the North remained loyal to the Republicans; although by 1936 Franklin D. Roosevelt had won the support of northern blacks. But Roosevelt made no effort to win the support of southern blacks, most of whom remained disenfranchised. Even as late as 1940, about 70 percent of the nation's blacks lived in the states of the old Confederacy. Roosevelt carried all eleven of these states in each of his four victories. His 1944 reelection, however, was the last contest in which Democrats carried all eleven southern states.

World War I led to massive migration of African Americans from the agrarian South and into the industrial North, where—given the absence of laws restricting their suffrage—many would enjoy the franchise for the first time. The influx of African Americans alarmed some Democratic politicians in the North, who would likely see their electoral prospects decline unless they were able to siphon a share of African American voters who were loyal to the party of Lincoln. In 1932 African American voters in most major cities in the North voted for Herbert Hoover by a roughly two-to-one margin.[80] To appeal to African American voters, many northern Democrats encouraged their party to adopt a supportive position toward civil rights. By 1948 President Harry Truman was making explicit appeals to blacks through his Fair Employment Practices Commission, and in July 1948 he issued an executive order ending segregation in the armed services.[81] These policies led to defections from the "Dixiecrats" and cost Truman four southern states in the 1948 election; he still won the seven remaining southern states by an average margin of 26.2 points. In 1952 and 1956 the Democratic candidate, Adlai E. Stevenson, de-emphasized appeals to blacks, although his opponent, Dwight Eisenhower, still made inroads in the South. In 1960 Kennedy also played down appeals to African Americans, and southern electoral votes were crucial to his win over Nixon.[82] Kennedy also strengthened his campaign in the South by choosing a Texan, Lyndon Johnson, as his running mate. Clearly Johnson helped Kennedy win Texas, which he carried by only two percentage points.

If Johnson as running mate aided the Democrats in the South, Johnson as president played a different role. His explicit appeals to African Americans, including leading the Civil Rights Act into law in 1964, helped end Democratic dominance in the South. Barry Goldwater, the Republican candidate, had voted against the Civil Rights Act as a member of the Senate, creating a sharp difference between the two candidates. Goldwater carried all five states in the Deep South.[83] The only other state he won was his native Arizona. In 1968 Hubert Humphrey, who had long championed black equality, carried only one southern state, Texas, which he won with only 41 percent of the vote. He was probably aided by George Wallace's third-party candidacy because Wallace, a segregationist, won 19 percent of the Texas vote. Wallace carried Alabama, Arkansas, Georgia, Louisiana, and Mississippi, while Nixon carried the remaining five southern states. Nixon won every southern state in 1972, and his margin of victory was greater in the South than in the rest of the nation. Although Carter won ten of the eleven southern states in 1976 (all but Virginia), he carried a minority of the vote among white southerners.

In 1980 Reagan won every southern state except Georgia, Carter's home state. In his 1984 reelection victory, Reagan carried all the southern states, and his margin of victory in the South was greater than his margin outside it. In 1988 George H. W. Bush was victorious in all eleven southern states, and the South was his strongest region. Four years later, in 1992, Clinton, a native of Arkansas, made some inroads in the South and somewhat greater inroads in 1996. All the same the South was the only predominantly Republican region in 1992, and in 1996 Bob Dole won a majority of the electoral vote only in the South and mountain states. In 2000 the South was the only region in which Bush carried every state, and more than half of his electoral votes came from that region. Bush again carried every southern state in 2004, along with all of the states in the Mountain West. As was the case four years earlier, more than half of his electoral votes came from the states of the old Confederacy. Despite slippage in 2008 and 2012, Republicans have won every southern state in five of the twelve elections (1972, 1984, 1988, 2000, and 2004) between 1972 and 2016.

Although the transformation of the South is clearly the most dramatic change in postwar American politics, the 2016 election underscores that the Republicans do not hold the same level of dominance in the region that the Democrats once enjoyed. The average Republican vote share in the South between 1972 and 2016 was 54.1 points—much smaller than the 71.6 vote share that we reported earlier for the Democrats from 1896 to 1944. Florida is highly competitive. Bill Clinton won the Sunshine State in 1996, and in 2000 George W. Bush carried the disputed contest by a negligible margin. Obama narrowly won Florida in both 2008 and 2012, and Trump won the state by 1.2 percentage points. Trump won North Carolina by 3.7 points, but it too remains competitive. The state narrowly voted for Obama—by a 0.3 percentage-point margin—in 2008 and for Romney—by a slim two-point margin—in 2012. Although Virginia did not vote Democratic between 1968 and 2004, the growing number of suburbanites in northern Virginia has made the state more competitive, and the Democrats have now captured the state in three straight elections. Even in Georgia Democrats see Atlanta and its close-in suburbs as fertile ground to make the state competitive.[84] Clinton carried Georgia in 1992, and McCain won by only 5.2 percentage points in 2008. Republicans have an advantage in the South, to be sure, but Democrats are competitive in few a southern states, thus allowing the South to keep its place of prominence in modern presidential politics.

Some scholars predict that the South will play a part in the next major transformation in American politics, one they argue could make the Electoral College less competitive. John Judis and Ruy Teixeira contend that shifting demographics, specifically a growing professional class and an increase in America's nonwhite population, are setting the stage for an "emerging Democratic majority."[85] Central to this argument is that in the next two decades, the proportion of Latinos in the electorate is likely to double.[86] Latino growth in the South, where African Americans already compose a large share of the electorate, could greatly benefit the Democrats. Three southern states—Arkansas, North Carolina, and South Carolina—were among the top five states in Hispanic population growth between 2000 and 2010 according to the U.S. Census.[87] And Texas (19 percent) and Florida (8 percent) already have the second- and third-largest Hispanic populations, respectively. It is assumed by Judis and Teixeira that further growth in the Latino population could make Texas a Democratic-leaning state and Florida a safe Democratic state by the 2024 election cycle, giving Democrats, who already hold advantages in the electorally rich states of California and New York, an easier path to victory in the Electoral College.[88]

We have heard predictions of impending electoral realignment before, and as in the past, we encourage caution when evaluating these claims.[89] As noted earlier, after his reelection in 1984, Ronald Reagan proclaimed that his victory represented a Republican realignment. Indeed some scholars went so far as to argue that the Republicans held an electoral vote "lock."[90] But the Democrats won two consecutive elections in the 1990s. The scenario outlined by Judis and Teixeira offers reason for optimism for the Democrats and pessimism for the Republicans. Yet there are two major assumptions undergirding this scenario that complicate things for the Democrats. First, it should not be assumed that Latino voting participation will increase proportionately with Latino population growth; it has not thus far. As noted in a Pew Research Center report, the "[n]umber of Latino eligible voters is increasing faster than the number of Latin voters in presidential election years."[91] Hispanics were 24 percent of Florida's population but only 18 percent of voters on election day. In Texas Hispanics were 39 percent of the population but only 24 percent of the electorate.[92] For Democrats to make real substantial gains in the near future, voter participation among Latinos—particularly those in Texas—must grow at a faster rate to become commensurate with the group's share of the population. Second, it should not be assumed that Latinos will continue to support Democrats at the same levels. The Latino vote is not monolithic and has changed somewhat over time (we will have more to say about Latino political preferences in Chapter 8). For instance, Cuban Americans in Florida, many of whom fled their homeland to escape Fidel Castro's dictatorship, have long been a reliable voting bloc for Republicans. "In Florida, Cubans were about twice as likely as non-Cuban Latinos to vote for Donald Trump" in 2016.[93] But recent evidence shows that second- and third-generation Cuban Americans are more liberal and more likely to vote Democratic than the elder generation.[94] This is good news for Democrats, of course, but it also serves to remind both parties that old loyalties are not easily maintained and that voters respond to changing issues and interests, not simply on the basis of ethnicity. However, this battle for Latino votes plays out, it appears the South will be the focus of both parties' attention for many elections to come.

## THE ELECTORAL VOTE BALANCE

Elections often conclude with the winning party making hyperbolic claims of electoral mandates and partisan realignments. However, as we have seen, comparing presidential elections results over time suggest that party competition for the presidency is high in the postwar period. Today's presidential elections are national in scope, and the Electoral College provides no significant barrier to either political party. Moreover, Andrew Gelman, Jonathan N. Katz, and Gary King present compelling evidence that since the 1950s partisan biases created by the Electoral College are negligible.[95]

Despite Trump's victory in 2016, short-term factors suggest that Democrats are currently advantaged. Since 1988 the Democrats have won the presidency in four of seven elections and the popular vote in six out of the seven. But the recent past is not always a guide to the future. Consider the fact that in the six elections between 1968 and 1988, the Republicans held the advantage, winning five of the six and several by significant margins.[96] Republican strength in the 1980s was soon replaced by Democratic victories in the 1990s. Yet because competition for the presidency has always rested upon some assessment of a candidate's relative strength in each of the states, recent election results often guide how parties develop future electoral strategies.[97] In Figure 3-3, we illustrate how the states have voted in each of the last five elections.

Figure 3-3 creates an illusion of Republican dominance. Twenty-two states have voted Republican in each of the past five elections—an impressive number, to be sure. But the geographic expanse of these Republican states belies their electoral power. These solidly Republican states only tally 180 electoral votes (33 percent of all available electoral votes). Texas with thirty-eight electoral votes is the only large state among the twenty-two, and five of these states have the minimum of three votes. Two other states, Indiana and North Carolina, have voted Republican in four of the five elections, accounting for twenty-six electoral votes. Both states voted for Obama in 2008. The Republicans have won Florida and Ohio (forty-seven electoral votes combined) in three of the last five elections, but both voted for Obama in 2008 and 2012. In total these twenty-six "Republican states" represent 253 electoral votes, seventeen votes shy of the 270 needed to win the Electoral College.

**Figure 3-3 Results of the 2000, 2004, 2008, 2012, and 2016 Presidential Elections**

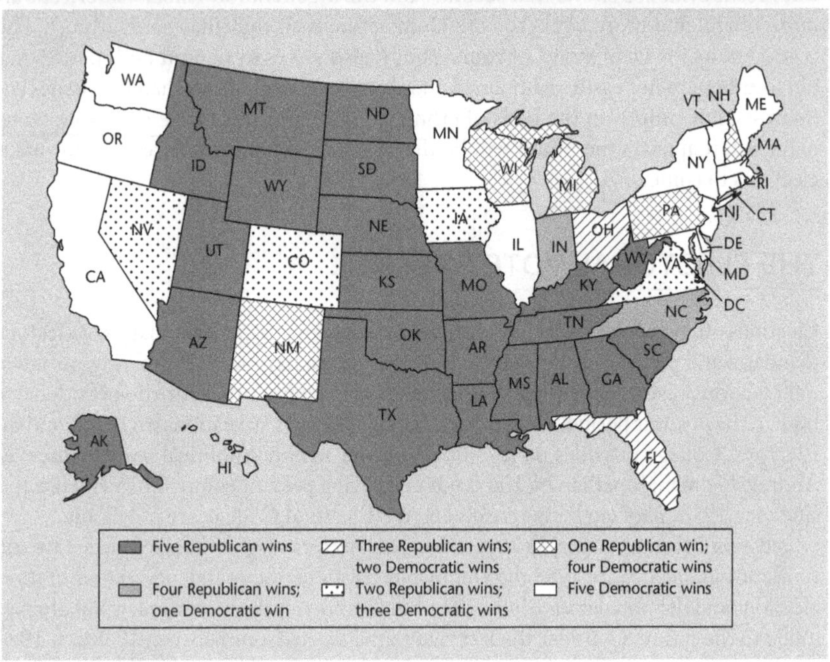


*Source:* Compiled by authors.

This leaves Democrats with twenty-four states and the District of Columbia, which total 285 electoral votes, exceeding the majority needed. Of these, fifteen states and the District of Columbia have voted Democratic in five straight elections. Although seemingly less impressive than the twenty-two states held comfortably by the Republicans, the solidly Democratic group represents 285 electoral votes (53 percent of all the available electoral votes). Five states—Michigan, New Hampshire, New Mexico, Pennsylvania, and Wisconsin (55 electoral votes collectively)—have voted Democratic in four of the five elections. And four states—Colorado, Iowa, Nevada, and Virginia (34 votes in sum)—have voted Democratic on three of the last five occasions.

If we were solely to use these five elections as the basis for determining battleground states for 2020, it would be a narrow field of play. Only six states fall into the "three-out-of-five" categories: Colorado, Florida, Iowa, Nevada, Ohio, and Virginia (three voted for Clinton; three voted for Trump in 2016). In this hypothetical, the Democratic candidate in 2020 would only have to win Florida to win the Electoral College. Indeed with 251 electoral votes on the safer side of their ledger, the Democrats could reach 270 electoral votes with a wider variety of coalitions than the Republicans. The Republicans, on the other hand, start with only 206 electoral votes in the safe column and cannot create a winning electoral coalition without Florida. Even with Florida in the win column, the Republicans would need a minimum of three additional states in their coalition to reach 270. Of course the odds of a Republican victory were just as long in 2016.

Undoubtedly the current electoral map presents a challenge for the GOP. But this is not the first time in recent history that the Electoral College map has appeared so uninviting for one of the parties and generally uncompetitive. Figure 3-4 illustrates over-time changes in the electoral balance of the Electoral College. Similar to Figure 3-3, we calculated how each of the states voted in the prior five elections but did so for each election from 1988 to 2016.[98] We then categorized states that voted for the same party in three of the five previous elections as "highly competitive." States that voted for the same party in four of the five elections were labeled "sometimes competitive," and those that voted for the same party in each of the five were labeled "uncompetitive."[99]

The figure shows that the number of uncompetitive states has more than doubled since the 2000 election. Thirty-eight of the fifty states currently appear to be uncompetitive, having voted for one of the two parties consistently over each of the last five elections. This rise coincides with a decline in the number of highly competitive states, which as noted earlier is now down to six (in 1996 the number of highly competitive states was twenty-six!). This alone would suggest a lack of electoral competition. But perhaps the clearest message conveyed by the figure is that the current electoral vote balance is likely subject to change . . . indeed, perhaps rapid change. The competitive balance in 1988 was similar to what we see today. Following that election, only eight states were considered highly competitive, and twenty-six were uncompetitive. Yet the challenge confronting Democrats following the 1988 elections was arguably more daunting than that confronting Republicans today. Whereas there are thirty-eight uncompetitive states following the 2016 elections, sixteen are Democratic and twenty-two are Republican states. In 1988, however, twenty-five of the twenty-six

**Figure 3-4 Competitive Balance in the Electoral College, 1988–2016**

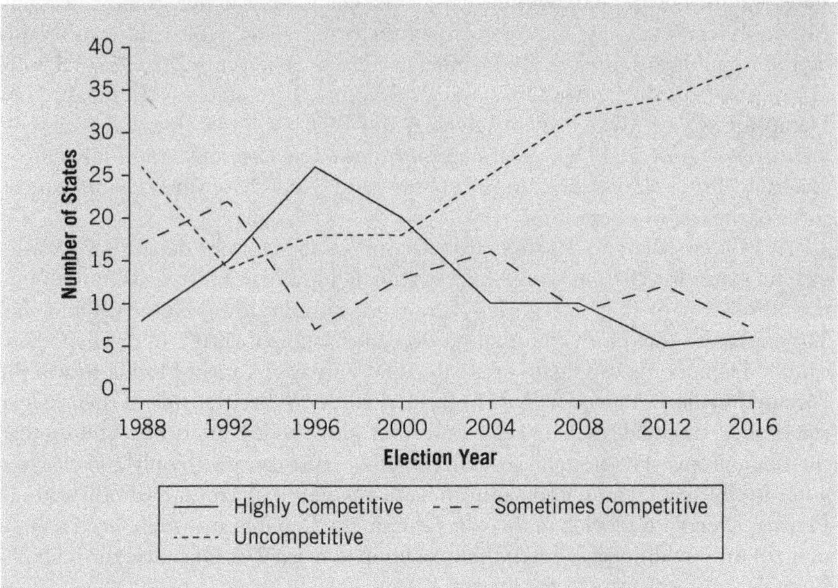


*Source:* Calculated by the authors.

uncompetitive states were Republican states. Based on the electoral vote balance alone, no one could have reasonably predicted Democratic victories in 1992 and 1996.

To assess the future prospects of the major parties, we must go beyond analyzing official election statistics. Although these statistics are useful for understanding competitive outcomes and future party strategies, they tell us little about why Americans vote the way they do or whether they vote at all. To understand how social coalitions have changed over time, as well as the issue preferences of the electorate, we must turn to surveys. They reveal how Trump was able to win election despite the public's relatively positive assessment of the Obama presidency. Furthermore, to determine the extent to which Americans really are polarized along party lines, we must study surveys to examine the way in which the basic party loyalties of the American electorate have changed during the postwar period. Thus, in the next five chapters, our study turns to survey data to examine the prospects for continuity and change in American electoral politics.

PART TWO

# VOTING BEHAVIOR IN THE 2016 PRESIDENTIAL ELECTION

# CHAPTER FOUR

# WHO VOTED?

More than 136 million Americans cast ballots in the 2016 presidential election—more than any prior election in U.S. history. Yet this number is less impressive when one considers that some 93 million Americans who were eligible to vote did not.[1] Overall the turnout rate in 2016 was 54.7 percent of the population (59.3 percent if we count only those eligible to vote), a one percentage point increase from the 2012 election but roughly 2.2 points lower than 2008, the last presidential election without an incumbent on the ballot.

Voter turnout in the United States is lower than in any other Western industrialized democracy. In Table 4-1, we present average turnout rates during the postwar period for twenty-five democracies, including the United States.[2] Clearly there is much variation in turnout among these democracies. And although it is not our goal to provide a full accounting of these differences, several points are worth noting.[3] Australia and Belgium, which have the highest turnout rates shown in Table 4-1, are among several democracies with laws that enforce some form of compulsory voting. Although the penalties for not voting are relatively mild, compulsory voting obviously increases turnout.[4] A country's electoral system has also been shown to affect voter turnout rates. In democracies that use some form of proportional representation (PR) system, political parties have an incentive to mobilize the electorate broadly because every vote contributes to a party's proportional share. In plurality rule, winner-take-all systems, such as the United States and Britain, many electoral units are not competitive, and get-out-the-vote efforts are likely to be of little value.[5] Differences among party systems may also encourage the lower social classes to vote in some societies and do little to encourage them to vote in others.

No matter whether one is examining turnout in legislative or presidential elections, the United States clearly lags behind other industrialized democracies in voter participation. To be fair, U.S. congressional elections, especially midterm elections, are not wholly comparable to parliamentary elections in these other democracies. In the United States, the head of government is elected separately from the legislature. The president, for instance, remains in office regardless of the outcomes of the congressional midterms. In parliamentary systems, the head of government, typically a prime minister, is dependent upon the performance of his/her legislative party in

**Table 4-1 Voter Turnout in National Elections, 1945–2017 (Percent)**

| Country | National Parliamentary | Presidential |
|---|---|---|
| Australia (28) | 94.8 | |
| Belgium (22) | 92.1 | |
| Luxembourg (15) | 90.0 | |
| Malta (18) | 89.4 | |
| Austria (21) | 89.0 | (13) 85.2 |
| Italy (18) | 88.1 | |
| Iceland (21) | 88.0 | (8) 92.2 |
| New Zealand (24) | 87.4 | |
| Denmark (26) | 86.1 | |
| Sweden (21) | 85.5 | |
| Netherlands (22) | 85.0 | |
| Germany (18) | 83.1 | |
| Norway (18) | 79.9 | |
| Greece (20) | 77.1 | |
| Israel (21) | 76.4 | |
| Finland (20) | 74.1 | (11) 73.5 |
| Spain (13) | 73.2 | |
| United Kingdom (19) | 73.0 | |
| Ireland (19) | 71.7 | (7) 56.9 |
| Canada (23) | 71.4 | |
| Portugal (15) | 71.4 | (9) 63.6 |

| Country | National Parliamentary | Presidential |
|---|---|---|
| France (19) | 71.3 | (10) 81.1 |
| Japan (27) | 68.1 | |
| Switzerland (18) | 54.6 | |
| United States (36) | 44.6 | (18) 55.4 |

*Source:* All countries except United States: mean level of turnout computed from results in International Voter Turnout Database, http://www.idea.int/data-tools/data/voter-turnout. U.S. turnout results: 1946–2010: U.S. Census Bureau, *Statistical Abstract of the United States, 2012* (Washington, D.C.: Government Printing Office, 2012), Table 397, 244, https://www.census.gov/prod/2011pubs/12statab/election.pdf. U.S. results for 2012, 2014, and 2016 were calculated by authors; total votes cast in U.S. House elections obtained from Clerk of the House of Representatives, "Statistics of the Presidential and Congressional Election," http://history.house.gov/Institution/Election-Statistics/Election-Statistics/; voting-age population estimates obtained from Michael P. McDonald, United States Elections Project, http://www.electproject.org/home/voter-turnout/voter-turnout-data.

*Note:* For all countries except the United States, turnout is computed by dividing the number of votes cast by the number of people registered to vote. For the United States, turnout is computed by dividing the number of votes cast for the U.S. House of Representatives (or for president) by the voting-age population. Numbers in parentheses are the number of parliamentary or presidential elections. For all countries with bicameral legislatures, we report turnout for the lower house.

parliamentary elections. Even in a semipresidential system such as France, the president may be forced to replace his prime minister and cabinet as a result of a National Assembly election. Yet, even when the president is on the ballot, turnout for U.S. House elections during the eighteen presidential elections since World War II was only 51.4 percent, which is substantially lower than that of any democracy except for Switzerland. Indeed turnout for U.S. presidential elections ranks well below voting rates in Austria, Finland, France, Iceland, and Portugal. Voter participation in U.S. presidential elections is roughly equivalent to presidential turnout in Ireland, where the presidency is essentially a ceremonial position.

Although not evident in Table 4-1, it is important to note that voter turnout in most democracies has declined significantly over the postwar period. Indeed, by our analysis, seventeen of the twenty-five democracies have experienced a statistically significant decline in voter participation, by an average of roughly 2.4 percentage points per decade.[6] Great Britain, for instance, has seen turnout declines as large as twelve percentage points in recent elections. In our sample of democracies, average parliamentary turnout during the 1990s was 78.3 percent ($N = 67$); average turnout since then has dropped roughly five percentage points to 73.8 percent ($N = 114$). This average remains substantially higher than turnout in U.S. national elections.

In comparative perspective the low turnout rate of the United States can be explained in part by institutional differences. But this does little to explain the tremendous amount of individual-level variation in voter turnout that occurs within the United States. If roughly 55 percent of Americans participate in presidential elections, that means 45 percent *do not*. Thus, before discovering how people voted in the 2016 election, we must answer a more basic question: who voted? The answer to this question is partly institutional because federal and state laws in the United States—both historically and still today—often serve to inhibit (and sometimes facilitate) individuals' ability to vote. Political parties also play a role in affecting individuals' turnout decisions because parties' electoral strategies help define which voters are mobilized. And, of course, personal characteristics, such as an individual's socioeconomic status, political predispositions, and feelings of efficacy, contribute to someone's decision to go to the polls. Using survey data from the 2016 American National Election Study, we will consider how each of these factors affected who voted in the most recent presidential election. Before doing so, however, it is important to place the study of voter turnout in the United States in a broader historical context.[7]

## VOTER TURNOUT, 1789–1916

As noted by the historian Alexander Keyssar, "At its birth, the United States was not a democratic nation—far from it. The very word democracy had pejorative overtones, summoning up images of disorder, government by the unfit, even mob rule."[8] Between 1789 and 1828 popular elections were not the norm in the United States. The Constitution did not require the Electoral College to be selected by popular vote, so many state legislatures simply appointed their presidential electors. Indeed, as late as the election of 1824, six of the twenty-four states appointed their slate of electors. Because U.S. senators were also appointed by state legislatures, voting in national elections was essentially limited to casting ballots for members of the House of Representatives.[9] Even then voter participation was strictly limited. Race exclusions and property requirements, combined with the lack of female suffrage, effectively narrowed the eligible electorate during this period to white male landowners.[10] As a result of this limited electoral competition and restricted suffrage, voter turnout rates during this period are the lowest in American history.

The presidential election of 1828 is the first election in which the vast majority of states chose their presidential electors by popular vote, thus making it the first for which meaningful measures of voter turnout can be calculated.[11] Historical records can be used to determine how many people voted in presidential elections, but constructing a measure of the turnout rate requires us to choose an appropriate denominator. Turnout in presidential elections is typically determined by dividing the total number of votes cast for president by the voting-age population.[12] But, given limited voting rights, should the turnout denominator be all people who are old enough to vote? Or should it include only those who were eligible to vote? The answer will greatly affect our estimates of turnout in presidential elections through 1916 because voting rights differed significantly among the states during this time. Women, for instance, were eligible to vote in a handful of states before the ratification of the Nineteenth

Amendment in 1920.[13] Clearly women should be included in the turnout denominator in states where they had the right to vote, but including them in the states where they could not vote would grossly deflate our estimates of turnout.

In Figure 4-1 we present two sets of estimates of turnout in presidential elections from 1828 through 1916. The alternative estimates reflect the difference in the choice of denominator used to measure the turnout rate. The first set was compiled by Charles E. Johnson, Jr., who calculated turnout by dividing the number of votes cast for president by the voting-age population. The second set is based on calculations by Walter Dean Burnham, who measures turnout by dividing the total number of votes cast for president by the number of Americans eligible to vote (the voting-eligible population). Burnham excludes African Americans before the Civil War, and from 1870 on, he excludes aliens where they were not allowed to vote, basing his estimates on what he calls the "politically eligible" population. But the main difference between Burnham's estimates and Johnson's estimates is that Burnham excludes women from the turnout denominator in states where they could not vote.

**Figure 4-1 Voter Turnout in Presidential Elections, 1828–1916**

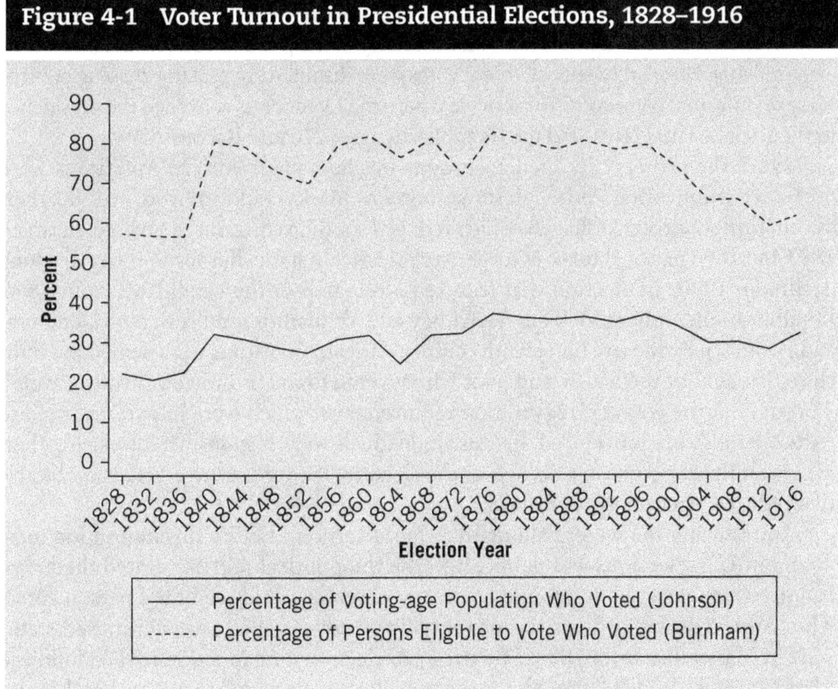


*Sources:* Estimates of turnout among the voting-age population based on Charles E. Johnson, Jr., *Nonvoting Americans,* series P-23, no. 2, U.S. Department of the Census (Washington, D.C.: Government Printing Office, 1980), 2; estimates of turnout among the population eligible to vote based on calculations by Walter Dean Burnham, "The Turnout Problem," in *Elections American Style,* ed. A. James Reichley (Washington, D.C.: Brookings, 1987), 113–114.

*Note:* Johnson's estimate for 1864 is based on the entire U.S. adult population. Burnham's estimate for that year excludes the eleven Confederate states that did not take part in the election.

Most political scientists would consider Burnham's calculations more meaningful than Johnson's. But whichever set of estimates one employs, the pattern of change is very similar. One clearly sees the effect of the advent of mass political parties and reemergence of two-party competition on voter participation. There is a large increase in turnout after 1836, when both the Democrats and Whigs began to employ popular appeals to mobilize the electorate. Turnout jumped markedly in 1840, during the "Log Cabin and Hard Cider" campaign in which William Henry Harrison, the hero of the Battle of Tippecanoe (1811), defeated the incumbent Democrat, Martin van Buren. Turnout waned somewhat after 1840, only to increase by roughly ten percentage points in 1856 after the Republican Party, founded in 1854, polarized the nation by taking a clear stand against slavery in the territories. In Abraham Lincoln's election in 1860, four out of five eligible white men went to the polls.

Turnout vacillated during the Civil War and Reconstruction era. The presidential election of 1864, held just weeks after General Sherman's Union troops seized Atlanta, saw a decline in turnout. Voter participation increased in 1868, but the turnout rate declined sharply in the 1872 election, the first to take place after African Americans were granted suffrage by the ratification of the Fifteenth Amendment.[14] Voter participation peaked in the 1876 contest between Republican Rutherford B. Hayes and Democrat Samuel J. Tilden. Although Tilden won a plurality of the popular vote, he did not win an electoral majority, and twenty electoral votes were disputed. To end the ensuing controversy, an informal compromise was made where the Democrats conceded the presidency to the Republican, Hayes, and the Republicans agreed to end Reconstruction.

Once the protection of federal troops was lost, many African Americans were prevented from voting. Although some southern blacks could still vote in 1880, their overall turnout dropped sharply, which reduced southern turnout as a whole. Between 1880 and 1896 national turnout levels were relatively static, but turnout began a long decline in 1900, an election that featured a rematch of the candidates from 1896, Republican incumbent William McKinley and William Jennings Bryan (Democrat and Populist). By the late nineteenth century, African Americans were denied the franchise throughout the South, and poor whites often found it difficult to vote as well.[15] Throughout the country, registration requirements, which were in part designed to reduce fraud, were introduced. Because individuals were responsible for placing their names on the registration rolls before the election, the procedure created an obstacle that reduced electoral participation.[16]

Introducing the secret ballot also reduced turnout. Before this innovation most voting in U.S. elections was public. Because the political parties printed their own ballots, which differed in size and color, any observer could see how a person voted. The "Australian ballot"—as the secret ballot is often called—was first used statewide in Massachusetts in 1888.[17] By the 1896 election nine in ten states had followed Massachusetts's lead.[18] Although the secret ballot was designed to reduce fraud, it also reduced turnout.[19] When voting was public, men could sell their votes, but candidates were less willing to pay for a vote if they could not see it delivered. Ballot stuffing was also more difficult when the state printed and distributed the ballots. Moreover, the Australian ballot also proved to be an obstacle to participation for many illiterate voters, although this was remedied in some states by expressly permitting illiterate voters to seek assistance.[20]

As Figure 4-1 shows, turnout trailed off rapidly in the early twentieth century. By the time the three-way contest was held in 1912 among Democrat Woodrow Wilson, Republican William Howard Taft, and Theodore Roosevelt, a Progressive, only three in five politically eligible Americans were going to the polls. In 1916 turnout rose slightly, but just over three-fifths of eligible Americans voted, and only one-third of the total adult population went to the polls.

## VOTER TURNOUT, 1920–2016

With the extension of suffrage to all women by constitutional amendment in 1920, the rules that governed eligibility for voting became much more uniform across the states. This makes it easier to calculate turnout from 1920 onward, and we provide estimates based on both the voting-age and voting-eligible populations. As suffrage becomes more universal, these two populations grow in similarity (and the large gap between the measures that is evident in Figure 4-1 dissipates). Indeed these alternative measures of voter turnout produce fairly similar estimates, although differences have increased since 1972. In the modern period we prefer focusing on turnout among the voting-age population for two reasons. First, it is difficult to estimate the size of the eligible population. Walter Dean Burnham and coauthors Michael P. McDonald and Samuel L. Popkin have made excellent efforts to provide these estimates.[21] Even so Burnham's estimates of turnout differ from McDonald and Popkin's, with the latter reporting somewhat higher levels of turnout in all five elections between 1984 and 2000. One difficulty in determining the eligible population is estimating the number of ineligible felons.[22] Incarceration rates, which have grown markedly during the last four decades, are frequently revised, and the number of permanently disenfranchised is nearly impossible to measure satisfactorily.[23] According to McDonald, in 2016 more than 1.4 million prisoners were ineligible to vote, as were 2.2 million on probation and more than 508,000 on parole.[24]

Second, excluding noneligible adults from the turnout denominator may yield misleading estimates, especially when U.S. turnout is compared with turnout levels in other democracies. For example, about one in ten voting-age Americans cannot vote, whereas in Britain only about one in fifty is disenfranchised. In the United States about one in seven black males cannot vote because of a felony conviction. As Thomas E. Patterson writes in a critique of McDonald and Popkin, "To ignore such differences, some analysts say, is to ignore official attempts to control the size and composition of the electorate." [25]

In Table 4-2, we show the percentage of the voting-age population who voted for the Democratic, Republican, and minor-party and independent candidates ("other candidates") between 1920 and 2016. The table also shows the percentage that did not vote as well as the overall size of the voting-age population.

Hillary Clinton won 48.2 percent of the popular vote in 2016, a plurality, but this number does mean that her supporters composed a comparable portion of the voting age population. As Table 4-2 shows, it is more likely for a majority of American adults to stay away from the polls on election day than support any one candidate. In all the elections between 1920 and 2016, except 1964, the percentage that did not vote

**Table 4-2 Percentage of Adults Who Voted for Each of the Major-Party Candidates, 1920–2016**

| Election Year | Democratic Candidate | | Republican Candidate | | Other Candidates | Did Not Vote | Total | Voting-Age Population |
|---|---|---|---|---|---|---|---|---|
| 1920 | 14.8 | James M. Cox | 26.2 | *Warren G. Harding* | 2.4 | 56.6 | 100 | 61,639,000 |
| 1924 | 12.7 | John W. Davis | 23.7 | *Calvin Coolidge* | 7.5 | 56.1 | 100 | 66,229,000 |
| 1928 | 21.1 | Alfred E. Smith | 30.1 | *Herbert C. Hoover* | 0.6 | 48.2 | 100 | 71,100,000 |
| 1932 | 30.1 | *Franklin D. Roosevelt* | 20.8 | Herbert C. Hoover | 1.5 | 47.5 | 100 | 75,768,000 |
| 1936 | 34.6 | *Franklin D. Roosevelt* | 20.8 | Alfred M. Landon | 1.5 | 43.1 | 100 | 80,174,000 |
| 1940 | 32.2 | *Franklin D. Roosevelt* | 26.4 | Wendell Willkie | 0.3 | 41.1 | 100 | 84,728,000 |
| 1944 | 29.9 | *Franklin D. Roosevelt* | 25.7 | Thomas E. Dewey | 0.4 | 44.0 | 100 | 85,654,000 |
| 1948 | 25.3 | *Harry S. Truman* | 23.0 | Thomas E. Dewey | 2.7 | 48.9 | 100 | 95,573,000 |
| 1952 | 27.3 | Adlai E. Stevenson | 34.0 | *Dwight D. Eisenhower* | 0.3 | 38.4 | 100 | 99,929,000 |
| 1956 | 24.9 | Adlai E. Stevenson | 34.1 | *Dwight D. Eisenhower* | 0.4 | 40.7 | 100 | 104,515,000 |
| 1960 | 31.2 | *John F. Kennedy* | 31.1 | Richard M. Nixon | 0.5 | 37.2 | 100 | 109,672,000 |
| 1964 | 37.8 | *Lyndon B. Johnson* | 23.8 | Barry M. Goldwater | 0.3 | 38.1 | 100 | 114,090,000 |
| 1968 | 26.0 | Hubert H. Humphrey | 26.4 | *Richard M. Nixon* | 8.4 | 39.1 | 100 | 120,285,000 |
| 1972 | 20.7 | George S. McGovern | 33.5 | *Richard M. Nixon* | 1.0 | 44.8 | 100 | 140,777,000 |

| Election Year | Democratic Candidate | | Republican Candidate | | Other Candidates | Did Not Vote | Total | Voting-Age Population |
|---|---|---|---|---|---|---|---|---|
| 1976 | 26.8 | *Jimmy Carter* | 25.7 | Gerald R. Ford | 1.0 | 46.5 | 100 | 152,308,000 |
| 1980 | 21.6 | Jimmy Carter | 26.8 | *Ronald Reagan* | 4.3 | 47.2 | 100 | 163,945,000 |
| 1984 | 21.6 | Walter F. Mondale | 31.3 | *Ronald Reagan* | 0.4 | 46.7 | 100 | 173,995,000 |
| 1988 | 23.0 | Michael S. Dukakis | 26.9 | *George H. W. Bush* | 0.5 | 49.7 | 100 | 181,956,000 |
| 1992 | 23.7 | *Bill Clinton* | 20.6 | George H. W. Bush | 10.8 | 44.9 | 100 | 189,493,000 |
| 1996 | 24.1 | *Bill Clinton* | 19.9 | Bob Dole | 4.9 | 51.1 | 100 | 196,789,000 |
| 2000 | 24.8 | Al Gore | 24.5 | *George W. Bush* | 1.9 | 48.8 | 100 | 205,813,000 |
| 2004 | 26.7 | John F. Kerry | 28.1 | *George W. Bush* | 0.6 | 44.6 | 100 | 220,804,000 |
| 2008 | 30.0 | *Barack Obama* | 26.0 | John McCain | 0.8 | 43.2 | 100 | 230,917,000 |
| 2012 | 27.4 | *Barack Obama* | 25.2 | Mitt Romney | 0.9 | 46.5 | 100 | 240,926,957 |
| 2016 | 26.3 | Hillary Clinton | 25.2 | *Donald J. Trump* | 3.1 | 45.4 | 100 | 250,055,734 |

*Sources:* Voting-age population, 1920–1928: U.S. Census Bureau, *Statistical Abstract of the United States*, 1972, 92nd ed. (Washington, D.C.: Government Printing Office, 1972), Table 597, 373. Voting-age population, 1932–2000: U.S. Census Bureau, *Statistical Abstract of the United States, 2004–2005*, 124th ed. (Washington, D.C.: Government Printing Office, 2004), Table 409, 257. Voting-age population, 2004–2016: Michael P. McDonald, United States Election Project, http://www.electproject.org/home/voter-turnout/voter-turnout-data. Number of votes cast for each presidential candidate and the total number of votes cast for president: Federal Election Commission, "Official 2016 Presidential General Election Results," January 30, 2017, https://transition.fec.gov/pubrec/fe2016/2016presgeresults.pdf.

*Note:* The names of the winning candidates are italicized.

easily exceeded the share cast for the winning candidates. In 2016 only 26.3 percent of American adults could be counted as a Clinton voter (25.2 percent of the adult population cast ballots for Trump). In both absolute and proportional terms, fewer Americans voted for either Clinton or Trump than voted for Obama in 2012 or 2008. Of course, it was Trump who won the Electoral College and the presidency. Yet the proportion of Americans who supported Trump in 2016 was well below the average for all winning presidential candidates before 2008 (29.1 percent).

Figure 4-2 illustrates the percentage of the voting-age population that voted for president in each of these twenty-five elections as well as the percentage of the politically eligible population between 1920 and 1944 and the voting-eligible population between 1948 and 2016.[26] The extent to which these trend lines diverge depends on the percentage of the voting-age population that is eligible to vote. In eras when few people were ineligible, such as between 1940 and 1980, it makes very little difference which turnout denominator one employs. Today, however, there is a much larger noncitizen population, and incarceration rates are nearly 2.5 times higher than they were in 1980. Back in 1960, when turnout peaked, only 2.2 percent of voting-age Americans were not citizens; in 2016 8.4 percent were not. In 1960 only 0.4 percent of Americans were ineligible to vote because of their felony status; in 2016, 1.3 percent was ineligible. Thus as Figure 4-2 shows, in 1960 there was very little difference between turnout among the voting-age population and turnout among the voting-eligible population. In the 2016 election 136,669,237 votes were cast for president. Because the voting-age population was 250,055,734, turnout among this population was 54.7 percent. But, according to McDonald, the population eligible to vote was only 230,585,915. Using this total as our denominator, turnout was 59.3 percent. If we use McDonald's measure to calculate turnout in all eighteen postwar presidential elections, turnout would rise from 55.4 percent to 58.2 percent. However, U.S. presidential turnout would still be lower than turnout in parliamentary elections in any country except Switzerland and lower than in presidential elections in any country except Ireland.

Turnout among the voting-age population generally rose between 1920 and 1960. Two exceptions were the elections of 1944 and 1948, when turnout decreased markedly due to social dislocations during and after World War II. Campaign-specific conditions sometimes account for increases in turnout in certain elections. In 1928, for instance, it is plausible to attribute the jump in voter turnout to the candidacy of Alfred Smith, the first Catholic candidate to receive a major-party nomination. The increase in 1936 partly reflects Franklin Roosevelt's efforts to mobilize the lower social classes, especially the industrial working class. The extremely close contest between Republican Vice President Richard Nixon and the second Catholic candidate, Democrat John F. Kennedy, may account, in part, for the high turnout in 1960, when it rose to 62.8 percent of the voting-age population and was slightly higher among the politically eligible population.[27] The presidential election of 1960 produced the highest level of turnout among voting-age adults in American history. Yet the turnout percentage for the politically eligible population in 1960 was far below the typical levels found between 1840 and 1900. Moreover, the U.S. turnout in 1960 was still well below the average level of turnout in most advanced democracies (see Table 4-1).

**Figure 4-2 Percentage of Voting-Age Population and of the Politically Eligible and Voting-Eligible Population Voting for President, 1920–2016**

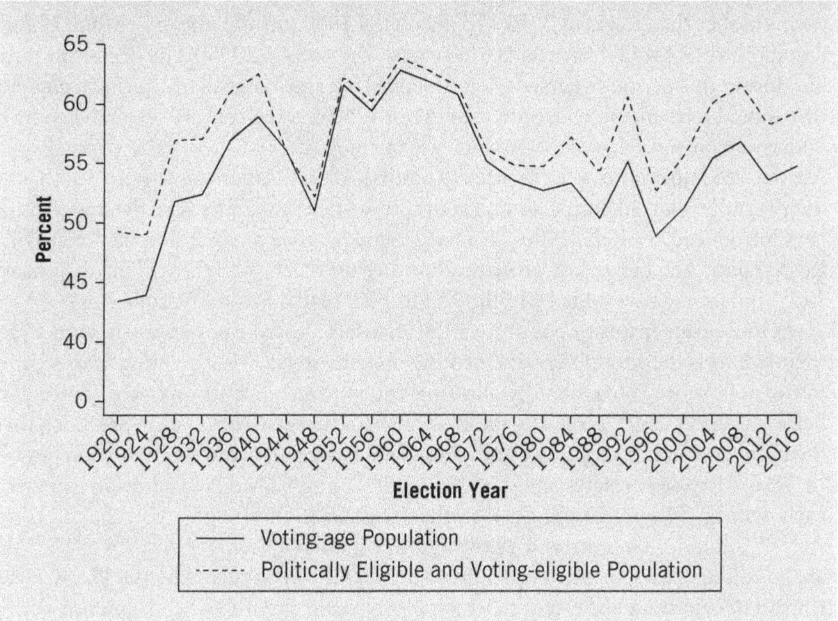


*Sources:* Voting-age population, see Table 4-3 in this volume. Politically eligible population, 1920–1944: Walter Dean Burnham, "The Turnout Problem," in *Elections American Style*, ed. A. James Reichley (Washington, D.C.: Brookings, 1987), 113–114. Voting-eligible population, 1948–2000: Michael P. McDonald and Samuel L. Popkin, "The Myth of the Vanishing Voter," *American Political Science Review* 95 (December 2001): 966. Voting-eligible population, 2000–2016: Michael P. McDonald, United States Election Project, http://www.electproject.org/home/voter-turnout/voter-turnout-data.

Although short-term forces drove turnout upward in specific elections, long-term forces also contributed to the increase in turnout during this period. Three examples—not an exhaustive list certainly—help illustrate how long-term forces affect turnout. First, women who came of age before the Nineteenth Amendment, perhaps out of habit or long-held social expectations, often failed to exercise their right to vote once suffrage was granted. But women who came of age after 1920 were more likely to turn out, and as this younger generation of women gradually replaced older women in the electorate, turnout levels rose.[28] Second, because all states restrict voting to citizens, immigrants enlarge the voting-age population but do not increase the number of voters until they become citizens. After 1921, however, as a result of restrictive immigration laws, the percentage of the population that was foreign-born declined. Over time this led to an increase in turnout as a percentage of the voting-age population. Finally, levels of education rose markedly throughout the twentieth century, a change that acts as an upward force on turnout. Americans who have attained higher levels of education are much more likely to vote than those with lower levels of education.

From 1960 to 1980 voter turnout in the United States declined with each election, followed by a variable pattern through 2016. Turnout among the voting-age population in 1960—the highest in the modern period—was roughly eight percentage points higher than it was in 2016. (To match the 1960 turnout rate, more than 20 million more voters would have had to have gone the polls in 2016!) The decline in turnout during this period occurred even though there were several institutional changes that should have increased turnout. Between 1960 and the century's end, the country underwent changes that tended to increase turnout. After passage of the Voting Rights Act of 1965, turnout rose dramatically among African Americans in the South, and their turnout spurred voting among southern whites too. Less restrictive registration laws introduced since the 1990s also have made it easier to vote. The National Voter Registration Act, better known as the "motor voter" law, went into effect in January 1995, and it may have added 9 million additional registrants to the rolls.[29]

One recent institutional innovation that has altered the way many voters cast their ballots is the adoption of early voting in many states.[30] Early voting makes going to the polls more convenient by allowing voters to cast ballots on one or more days before election day.[31] Texas was the first state to use early voting in 1988. Since then the number of states adopting early voting laws has increased in every election period. In 2016 thirty-seven states and the District of Columbia had laws allowing in-person early voting. The remaining states offer some form of absentee voting, and three states, Colorado, Oregon, and Washington, conducted voting strictly by mail.[32] We analyzed the 2016 Current Population Survey (CPS) conducted by the U.S. Census Bureau to determine the extent to which voters made use of these convenience-voting mechanisms in 2016.[33] Figure 4-3 shows that early voting varies greatly among the states. Nationally, 38.6 percent of Americans reported voting early. The three states with vote-by-mail reported rates of early voting greater than 80 percent, while at the lower end, eleven states (all of which have absentee voting only) reported rates of less than 10 percent.[34]

And yet despite all of the institutional changes related to voting since the 1960s, turnout has not increased. Except for a small increase in turnout in 1984, turnout among the voting-age population clearly declined in each election between 1960 and 1988, falling most between 1968 and 1972.[35] Turnout then rose almost five points in 1992, perhaps as a result of Ross Perot's third-party candidacy.[36] But in 1996 turnout fell some six percentage points, reaching only 48.9 percent. In 2000, 2004, and 2008, turnout rose. Both George W. Bush elections were expected to be close going into election day, and this may have stimulated voter participation. In 2008 Barack Obama's historic campaign as the nation's first African American nominee from a major party excited many minority and young voters. Although few people expected that election to be close, the Obama campaign ran an inventive ground game, incorporating many Internet-based technological advances in their attempt to get out the vote. Although some observers expected a large increase in turnout in 2008, it rose only 1.4 percentage points. But it rose nevertheless. Unfortunately, the increased levels of voter turnout between 1996 and 2008 were not extended or sustained in 2012, when turnout declined by roughly three percentage points, whereas 2016 only made up a third of that decline.

**Figure 4-3 Percentage of Voters Who Voted Early, by State, 2016**

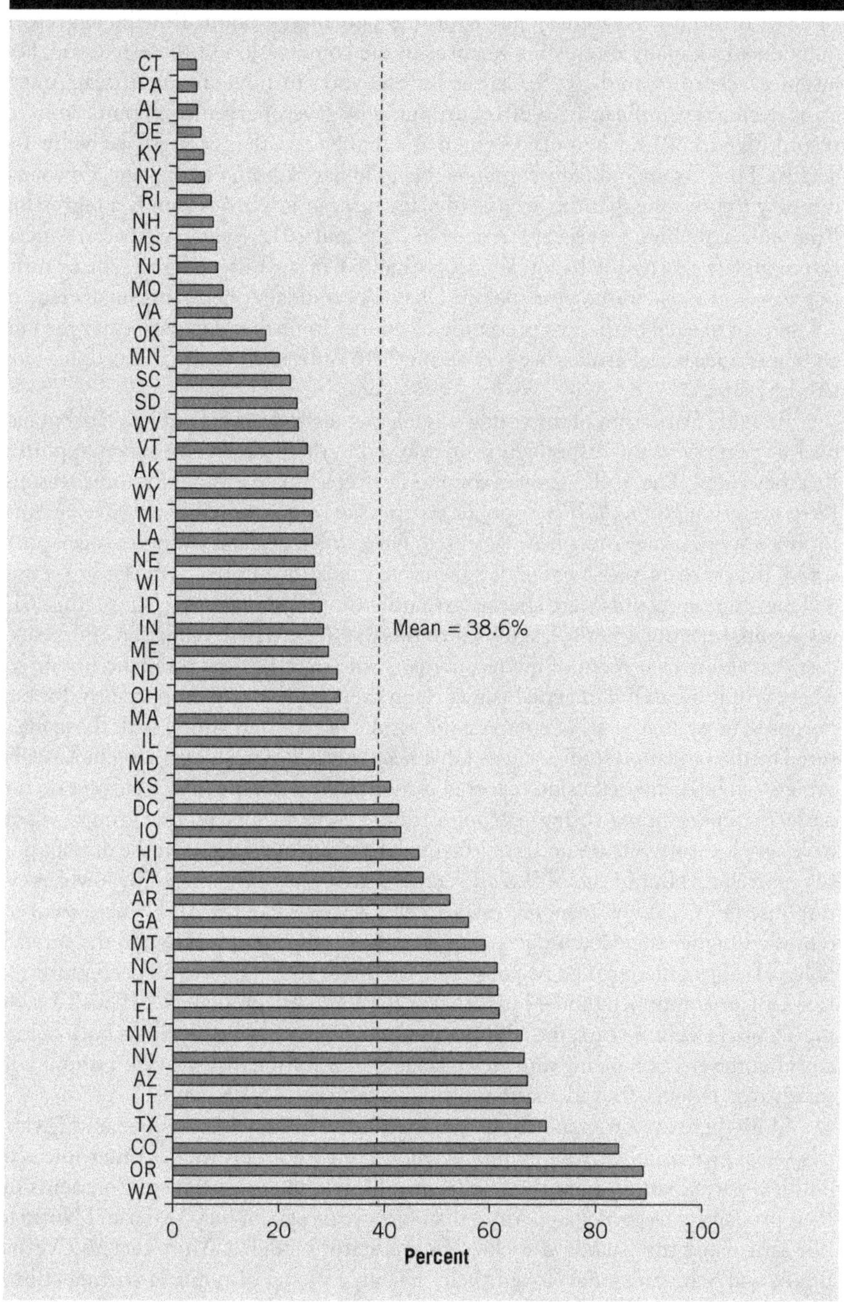


*Source:* U.S. Census Bureau, 2016 Current Population Study, November Supplement.

*Note:* Data are weighted.

## VOTER TURNOUT AMONG SOCIAL GROUPS

In 2016 turnout increased by just over one percentage point. But the aggregate numbers mask many interesting nuances in the composition of the electorate. For instance, according to the U.S. Census Bureau, voter turnout among African Americans declined significantly in 2016, dropping by seven percentage points from its record high in 2012, when blacks voted at a higher rate than whites (see below for details). This was undoubtedly consequential to Hillary Clinton's campaign. Of course it is easy to presume that the decline in black turnout in 2016 is simply a regression from unusually high levels experienced in 2008 and 2012, when an African American candidate was on the ballot. Yet, according to Census Bureau figures, black turnout was on the rise in the years before Obama's candidacy, increasing an average of 3.3 percent in each of the two preceding elections. To further compare voter turnout among various social groups, we rely on the 2016 American National Election Study (ANES) survey.[37]

Roughly 59 percent of the voting-eligible population turned out in 2016, but just over 85 percent of the respondents interviewed in the postelection survey reported that they voted. The ANES surveys commonly overestimate turnout for three reasons. First, even though the ANES respondents are asked a question that provides reasons for not voting, some voters falsely claim to have voted, perhaps owing to social pressure.[38] In past years ANES has undertaken vote validation efforts in which state voting and registration records were checked to authenticate respondents' claims—the 2012 presidential election was the last for which this was done. These validation efforts suggest that about 15 percent of the respondents who say that they voted did not do so, whereas only a handful of actual voters claim they did not vote. Importantly, for our purposes, most analyses that compare the results of reported voting with those measured by the validation studies suggest that *relative* levels of turnout among most social groups can be compared using reported turnout.[39] Second, the ANES surveys do not perfectly represent the voting-age population. Lower socioeconomic groups, which have very low turnout, are underrepresented. Discrepancies between the distribution of reported turnout in the ANES and actual turnout are exacerbated by low survey-response rates.[40] When response rates are low, surveys like the ANES tend to overrepresent higher socioeconomic groups and those who are interested in the survey's political subject matter. The response rate for the 2016 ANES was 50 percent for the face-to-face component and 44 percent for the Internet component.[41] Third, during presidential election years, the ANES attempts to interview respondents both before and after the election. Being interviewed before the election may provide a stimulus to survey respondents, thus increasing turnout among the ANES sample.

With these caveats in mind, we examine differences in voter turnout among various social groups. Nearly all empirical studies of turnout (as well as other forms of political participation) note the importance of individuals' social environments on their propensity to participate. More than forty years ago, Sidney Verba and Norman Nie articulated the "standard socioeconomic status model."[42] More recently, Verba, Brady, and Schlozman developed their "resource model of political participation," by which they argue that individuals' resources, particularly time, money, and civic skills, facilitate political participation.[43] Individuals high in socioeconomic status are also more likely to be located in social networks that encourage participatory norms. In the following sections we examine patterns of voter participation among various social groups.

## Race, Gender, Region, and Age

Table 4-3 compares reported turnout among social groups using the 2016 ANES survey. To many observers the 2016 election reflected growing levels of resentment among white Americans toward a political system that in their view, seemed to cater to minorities and immigrants and an economic system that valued global trade and devalued the domestic manufacturing jobs usually held by working-class whites.[44] Trump's populist message seemed tailored to these voters. But did white voters flock to the polls in disproportionate numbers in 2016? What about turnout among other social groups; what can we say about their levels of voter participation? Was voter turnout in 2016 significantly different than in years past?

Our analysis begins by comparing African Americans and whites.[45] In both the 2008 and 2012 election studies, whites and blacks reported voting at equal rates. In 2016, however, white respondents reported voting at a higher rate than that of blacks, a difference of four percentage points. Data from the CPS also suggest that whites were more likely to vote in 2016 than blacks, 65.3 percent to 59.6 percent. This gap, it is important to note, is more attributable to a decrease in black turnout than an upswing in white turnout. Whether one is using the ANES or the CPS, white turnout between 2012 and 2016 increased only minimally—by one percentage point. Black turnout, on the other hand, declined precipitously. According to the ANES, reported turnout among blacks decreased from 87 percent in 2012 to 84 percent in 2016. Both figures are likely inflated due to overreporting among ANES survey participants. Estimated turnout rates from CPS are lower generally and suggest a steeper decline: in 2012, CPS estimated black turnout to be 66.6 percent, dropping to 59.6 percent in 2016.

Of course, voter turnout levels among black voters were not always close to those of whites, and this marks a significant change in voting behavior (and American politics generally) over the last half century. In 1964, the year prior to the passage of the Voting Rights Act, the CPS reported whites were 12.2 percentage points more likely to vote than blacks. By 2004 this difference was reduced to 5.4 percent.[46] As noted earlier, in 2012, for the first time, black turnout was estimated to be higher than white turnout, although the gap was not large. The reversion of black voter turnout to roughly 2004 levels is a statistic worth watching because black voters are a sizable component of the Democratic Party's electoral coalition.

Roughly 11 percent of the 2016 ANES sample (face-to-face and Internet) is composed of self-identified African American respondents, making it possible to make within-group comparisons. As with earlier ANES surveys, blacks with higher levels of education are more likely to vote than those with lower levels of education. Blacks with college degrees were ten percentage points more likely to vote than those with only a high school diploma, and turnout among younger blacks continues to lag behind older generations. In 2016 the ANES shows a slightly higher turnout for black women than men, a difference of 2.7 percentage points; exit polls indicate that black women were 7 percent of the electorate, whereas black men were 5 percent. Perhaps the most influential variable for predicting voter turnout among blacks is income. By our estimate, using the ANES, blacks in the upper quartile (top 25 percent) of income are roughly 20 percentage points more likely to vote than those in the bottom quartile (lowest 25 percent).[47]

Table 4-3 reveals that turnout among Latinos was lower than turnout among whites and African Americans. This is consistent with the historical record. Low levels of Latino turnout have typically been attributed to lower levels of education, income, and English language skills, and some have demonstrated differences between native- and foreign-born Latinos—although evidence varies on this issue—as well as ethnic group.[48] ANES data reveal the importance of education as a predictor of Latino participation; college graduates were 10.5 percentage points more likely to vote than Latinos with only a high school degree. Yet, unfortunately, while the 2016 ANES sample includes roughly 12 percent Latinos, data regarding their ethnicity (e.g., Mexican-American, Puerto Rican, etc.) were not publicly available at the time of this study. To examine differences among Latinos, we turn to the CPS. The Census Bureau data show that Latinos (47.6 percent) were significantly less likely to vote than blacks (59.6 percent) and non-Latino whites (65.3 percent) and, for the first time since 1996, were slightly less likely to vote than Asian Americans (49.3 percent). The data also show that foreign-born, naturalized Latinos were eight percentage points more likely to vote than native-born Latinos. And ethnicity seems to matter as well, but these differences may be confounded by political geography. Turnout among Mexican Americans (the lowest among Latino groups) was roughly 9.5 percentage points lower than that of Cuban Americans. This difference is likely attributable to Mexican Americans, many of whom live in California and Texas, residing in uncompetitive states, whereas many Cuban Americans live in the battleground state of Florida. Overall, though, Latino turnout in 2016 was roughly equal to that experienced in 2012 (a difference of 0.2 percent).

The 2016 presidential election was the first to feature a woman as one of the major party nominees, and gender differences in voter turnout might be expected. To be sure women have voted at higher rates than men for some time now. The 1980 election was the last year in which the ANES surveys show white males to have a clear tendency to report voting more often than white females. Early ANES surveys show a clear decline in the turnout differential that advantaged men. In 1952, 1956, and 1960, the average male advantage was just over ten points, whereas in the 1964, 1968, 1972, and 1976 elections, the gap narrowed to an average of just over five points. This pattern of a long period of male advantage in turnout followed by a long period of female advantage has also been evident in midterm elections. In the 2008 election white women were seven points more likely than white men to report voting, the largest female advantage in any of the presidential elections we studied prior to that year.[49] But the gender gap in voting may have declined some in 2012. The 2012 ANES shows that white women were only four points more likely to vote than white men, a gap that is comparable to that found in that year's CPS.

The data for 2016 presents a somewhat mixed view of the gender gap in turnout. The ANES suggests that among whites, gender differences in turnout might have declined even further than that shown in 2012: 88 percent of the study's white female respondents reported voting compared to 87 percent of white men. The gender differences found in the 2016 CPS, however, are a bit larger. Among non-Hispanic whites,

**Table 4-3 Percentage of Electorate Who Reported Voting for President, by Social Group, 2016**

| Social Group | Did Vote | Did Not Vote | Total | ($N$)[a] |
|---|---|---|---|---|
| Total electorate | 85 | 15 | 100 | (3,254) |
| **Electorate, by race** | | | | |
| African American | 84 | 16 | 100 | (366) |
| White | 88 | 12 | 100 | (2,273) |
| Other | 77 | 23 | 100 | (598) |
| Latinos (of any race) | 73 | 27 | 100 | (381) |
| **Whites, by gender** | | | | |
| Female | 88 | 12 | 100 | (1,187) |
| Male | 87 | 13 | 100 | (1,069) |
| **Whites, by region** | | | | |
| New England and Mid-Atlantic | 89 | 11 | 100 | (440) |
| North Central | 87 | 13 | 100 | (547) |
| South | 86 | 14 | 100 | (604) |
| Border | 87 | 13 | 100 | (196) |
| Mountain and Pacific | 90 | 10 | 100 | (485) |
| **Whites, by birth cohort** | | | | |
| Before 1946 | 95 | 5 | 100 | (316) |
| 1947–1956 | 93 | 7 | 100 | (392) |
| 1957–1966 | 89 | 11 | 100 | (515) |
| 1967–1976 | 84 | 16 | 100 | (328) |
| 1977–1986 | 85 | 15 | 100 | (325) |
| 1987–1994 | 77 | 23 | 100 | (245) |
| 1995–1998 | 81 | 19 | 100 | (110) |
| **Whites, by level of education** | | | | |
| Not high school graduate | 67 | 33 | 100 | (132) |
| High school graduate | 85 | 15 | 100 | (578) |
| Some college | 87 | 13 | 100 | (689) |
| College graduate | 93 | 7 | 100 | (510) |
| Advanced degree | 94 | 6 | 100 | (350) |

*(Continued)*

**Table 4-3** (Continued)

| Social Group | Did Vote | Did Not Vote | Total | (*N*)[a] |
|---|---|---|---|---|
| **Whites, by annual family income** | | | | |
| Less than $15,000 | 77 | 23 | 100 | (193) |
| $15,000–34,999 | 82 | 18 | 100 | (333) |
| $35,000–49,999 | 86 | 14 | 100 | (248) |
| $50,000–74,999 | 87 | 13 | 100 | (406) |
| $75,000–89,999 | 92 | 8 | 100 | (221) |
| $90,000–124,999 | 90 | 10 | 100 | (355) |
| $125,000–174,999 | 94 | 6 | 100 | (230) |
| $175,000 and over | 91 | 9 | 100 | (208) |
| **Whites, by union membership**[b] | | | | |
| Member | 90 | 10 | 100 | (361) |
| Nonmember | 87 | 13 | 100 | (1,906) |
| **Whites, by religion** | | | | |
| Jewish | 99 | 1 | 100 | (57) |
| Catholic | 90 | 10 | 100 | (477) |
| Protestant | 91 | 9 | 100 | (763) |
| None | 81 | 19 | 100 | (483) |
| **White Protestants, by whether born again** | | | | |
| Not born again | 92 | 8 | 100 | (333) |
| Born again | 91 | 9 | 100 | (426) |
| **White Protestants, by religious commitment** | | | | |
| Medium or low | 92 | 8 | 100 | (321) |
| High | 90 | 10 | 100 | (303) |
| Very high | 96 | 4 | 100 | (127) |
| **White Protestants, by religious tradition** | | | | |
| Mainline | 96 | 4 | 100 | (328) |
| Evangelical | 90 | 10 | 100 | (216) |

*Source:* Authors' analysis of the 2016 ANES survey.

[a]Sample includes both face-to-face and Internet respondents. Numbers are weighted.

[b]Respondent or family member in union.

the CPS estimates a 3.8 percentage-point gap in turnout, with women (60.1 percent) voting at a higher rate than men (56.3 percent). Exit polls also found a similar gender difference in turnout, estimating that white women composed 37 percent of the electorate and white men accounted for 34 percent.

Surveys are not needed to study turnout in the various regions of the country. Because we have estimates of both the voting-age population and the voting-eligible population for each state, we can measure turnout once we know the number of votes cast for president. According to McDonald's estimates, turnout among the voting-age population ranged from a low of 38.3 percent in Hawaii (42.2 percent of the voting-eligible population) to a high of 69.4 percent in Minnesota (74.2 percent of the voting-eligible population). But regional differences as a whole were small. According to our calculations, among the voting-age population in the South, 52.9 percent voted; outside the South, 55 percent did. Among the voting-eligible population, 59.2 percent of southerners voted; outside the South, 60 percent did. There are small regional differences among whites. As the data in Table 4-3 show, 86 percent of southern whites said they voted; this estimate is lower but not significantly different from the estimates for whites outside the South. We used CPS state-level estimates to calculate white non-Latino turnout in the eleven southern states. The CPS estimates turnout in the South to be 55.5 percent and 59.4 percent turnout outside the South. This relatively small difference (3.9 percent) reflects a fundamental change in postwar voting patterns since the Voting Rights Act of 1965. The one-party South was destroyed, electoral competition increased, and with blacks enfranchised for the first time since the turn of the twentieth century, turnout increased among whites as well. Outside the South, turnout has declined.

Young Americans are more likely to have higher levels of formal education than their elders, and one might thus expect them to have higher levels of turnout. But they do not. Voter participation tends to increase with age, and this is supported by the ANES data presented in Table 4-3. This relationship is often attributed to changes in the life cycle; as people get older, settle down, and develop more community ties, they develop a greater appreciation for the role of government and politics in their lives, and they participate more.[50] Others argue that the effect of "life-changing" events may be overstated and that the greater likelihood of voter turnout with age is a product of greater political learning as people grow older.[51] Whatever the cause the relationship between age and voter turnout is evident in each of the studies we examined.

In both 2008 and 2012 the Obama campaign expended great effort trying to mobilize young voters. But this effort had limited success at best. Exit polls report that in 2008, eighteen- to twenty-nine-year-olds composed 18 percent of the electorate; in 2012 that number was 19 percent. These numbers represent a modest increase from the 2004 election, where the youngest cohort of voters represented 17 percent of the electorate. In the 2016 primary campaign, the youth vote was most energized by the candidacy of the seventy-four-year-old, Bernie Sanders, than by Trump or Clinton.[52] With Sanders out of the race and without the concerted efforts to mobilize young voters as during the Obama campaigns, some may have wondered if the so-called Millennials would turn out to the polls in the general election.[53] Exit polls suggest that young voters once again composed 19 percent of the electorate, as they did in 2012. However, it is important to remember that exit polls are not nationally representative but instead tend to focus on competitive states. Thus to examine voting participation among young people more broadly, we examined Census Bureau estimates. The CPS reports turnout by age group, with eighteen- to twenty-four-year-olds being the youngest cohort for which estimates are provided. The 2016 CPS estimates turnout for this cohort to have been 39.4 percent, a small increase (although within the margin of error) of the 38 percent estimated in 2012. In the thirteen battleground states we identified in Chapter 2, the CPS reports that turnout among Millennials was approximately 43.7 percent; in non-battleground states, it was only 35.6 percent (a difference of 8.1 percentage points). However, it is important to put these numbers into perspective. Young voters, even those in battleground states, are far less likely to vote than their elders. According to CPS estimates, nationally, adults who were forty-five years old or older participated in the election at a rate of 64.1 percent, roughly 1.6 times more likely than the youngest cohort. Thus age continues to be an important predictor of voter turnout rates in the United States.

## Income and Union Membership

Jan Leighley and Jonathan Nagler argue that there is no better measure of an individual's social class than income, and income is strongly linked to voter participation.[54] The 2016 ANES shows that respondents' family income is related to reported turnout. White respondents with family incomes less than $15,000 were over thirteen percentage points less likely to vote than those with incomes over $90,000. We found strong relationships between income and validated turnout in 1980, 1984, and 1988 and between income and reported turnout in all the presidential elections between 1982 and 2012. Earlier analyses of ANES data also demonstrate a strong relationship between family income and turnout in all the presidential elections between 1952 and 1976 and all the midterm elections between 1958 and 1978.[55] Previous CPS surveys have also shown a strong relationship between income and turnout, and the data for 2016 are no different. The CPS data show that turnout among all respondents with incomes less than $15,000 was 36.9 percent, whereas turnout among those with incomes greater than $100,000 was 74.5 percent.

Surveys over the years have found a weak and inconsistent relationship between union membership and turnout. Being in a household with a union member may create organizational ties that encourage voting. And unions have also been an important mobilizing agent for the Democratic Party, which for a significant portion of the postwar period relied on white working-class support as part of its electoral coalition. Yet Leighley and Nagler argue that the small and sporadic empirical association between union membership and turnout may result from union mobilization efforts increasing turnout among members and nonmembers alike. To support their claim they provide evidence that the decline in union membership since 1964 has resulted in a decrease in voter turnout among low and middle-class income groups regardless of membership. Exit polls show that voters from union households made up eighteen percent of the electorate. The 2016 ANES shows the effect of union membership to be small, with members reporting turnout at a slightly higher rate (3 percent more) than nonmembers. In both 2008 and 2012, we found no difference in turnout between union members and nonmembers.

## Religion

Religion continues to play a powerful role in American public life.[56] A 2014 survey by the Pew Research Center shows that 82 percent of Americans say that religion is an important part of their lives, and over half say they attend religious services on at least a monthly basis.[57] Religious individuals tend to have strong social networks, which facilitate the transmittal of political information and ease the costs of voting.[58] Churches also serve as direct and indirect vehicles for voter mobilization.[59]

In the earlier postwar years, Catholics were more likely to vote than Protestants, but these differences have declined.[60] The low turnout of Protestants, clearly documented by ANES surveys conducted between 1952 and 1978, resulted largely from two factors.[61] First, Protestants were more likely to live in the South, which was once a low turnout region. And, second, Protestants were more likely to be black, a group that had much lower turnout than whites. We have always compared turnout or reported turnout by comparing white Catholics with white Protestants. Except for the 1980 election, when there were no differences between Catholics and Protestants, Catholics were more likely to vote when vote validation measures were used (1984 and 1988). Catholics were also more likely to report voting in the five elections between 1992 and 2004, but in 2008 and 2012 Protestants and Catholics were equally likely to turn out. The 2016 ANES inquired about respondents' religious affiliations and practices, and as seen in Table 4-3, Protestants and Catholics once again reported turning out in roughly equal rates. Exit polls estimate that Protestants composed 27 percent of the electorate, whereas Catholics were 23 percent.[62] Fifteen percent of the electorate did not profess a religion.

Between 1952 and 1996 Jews had higher reported turnout than either Protestants or Catholics in six of the seven presidential elections as well as in five of the six midterm elections between 1958 and 1978. We found Jews to have higher levels of turnout or reported turnout in all seven elections between 1980 and 2012. In 2016, although exit polls estimated that Jewish voters represented only 3 percent of the electorate, the ANES suggests that Jews were nearly ten percentage points more likely to vote than Protestants or Catholics—the highest turnout level among any religious group.

For nearly three decades, fundamentalist Protestants have been a pivotal player in American politics. As we will see in Chapter 5, fundamentalist Protestants are conservative on social issues, such as abortion and same-sex marriage, and tend to throw their support overwhelmingly toward Republican presidential candidates. Indeed Christian conservative churches and organizations expend considerable resources mobilizing voters through get-out-the-vote efforts and attempt to galvanize supporters through the circulation of voter information guides.[63] In examining turnout among white fundamentalist Protestants since the 1992 election, we have found that the success of these groups in mobilizing their supporters has varied from election to election. In 2016 we found no statistically significant difference in reported turnout between Protestants who say they are born-again Christians and those who say they are not.[64]

Lyman A. Kellstedt argues that religious commitment is an important factor contributing to voting behavior.[65] Using multiple indicators we were able to construct a measure of religious commitment using the ANES.[66] To score "very high" on this measure, respondents had to report attending church at least once a week. In addition they had to say that religion provided "a great deal" of guidance in their lives and to believe that the Bible is literally true or the "word of God." In 1992, 1996, 2000, and 2004, respondents who scored very high on this measure were the most likely to report voting, but in 2008 there was only a weak relationship between religious commitment and whether white Protestants said they voted. We lacked the data necessary to measure religious commitment in 2012. The 2016 ANES shows that white Protestants with very high religious commitment are about four to six percentage points more likely to vote than those with lower levels of commitment. The 2016 exit polls show that 33 percent of voters said they attended church weekly or more; 16 percent of the electorate reported attending monthly; 29 percent declared they attend religious services only a few times a year; and 22 percent identified as never attending religious services.

Most white Protestants can be classified into two categories, mainline and evangelical, which according to Pew Research Center's Religious Landscape Survey, make up more than two-fifths of the total U.S. adult population.[67] As R. Stephen Warner has pointed out, "The root of the [mainline] liberal position is the interpretation of Christ as a moral teacher who told his disciples that they could best honor him by helping those in need." By contrast, says Warner, "the evangelical interpretation sees Jesus (as they prefer to call him) as one who offers salvation to anyone who confesses in his name." Liberal or mainline Protestants stress the importance of sharing their abundance with the needy, whereas evangelicals see the Bible as a source of revelation about Jesus.[68]

In classifying Protestants as mainline or evangelical, we rely on their denomination. For example, Episcopalians, Congregationalists, and most Methodists are classified as mainline, whereas Baptists, Pentecostals, and many small denominations are classified as evangelicals.[69] In 1992, 1996, 2000, 2008, and 2012, white mainline Protestants were more likely than white evangelicals to report voting. And we find similar evidence in 2016 with mainline Protestants being six percentage points more likely to report voting than evangelicals. These results are scarcely surprising because mainline Protestants have higher levels of formal education than evangelicals. Only in 2004, when fundamentalist churches launched a massive get-out-the-vote effort, were white evangelicals as likely to report voting as white mainline Protestants.

## Education

Surveys consistently reveal a strong relationship between formal education and electoral participation. The tendency for better-educated citizens to be more likely to vote is one of the most extensively documented facts in the study of politics. Indeed in their classic study, *Who Votes?*, Raymond E. Wolfinger and Steven J. Rosenstone note the "transcendent power of education" as a predictor of voter turnout.[70] Better-educated Americans have higher levels of political knowledge and political awareness; they also are more likely to possess the resources—money, time, and civic skills—that reduce the information costs of voting.[71]

The 2016 ANES reveals a strong relationship between formal education and voter turnout. Whites who did not graduate from high school were nearly twenty-six percentage points less likely to report voting than those who graduated college. The 2016 CPS also found a strong relationship between education and reported voter turnout. Among all citizens (i.e., regardless of race) with less than a high school education, only 34.3 percent reported voting, and among those with only a high school diploma, 51.5 percent said they cast a ballot. Among those citizens with some college-level education, 63.3 percent reported voting, and among college graduates, turnout was 76.3 percent.

Earlier we noted that education was also strongly associated with voter turnout for African Americans and Latinos. According to the 2016 ANES, blacks with less than a high school education turned out at a reported rate of 86.2 percent (a number likely inflated by few observations fitting into this category), whereas those with a high school diploma reported turning out at a 79.8 percent rate. Turnout among African Americans with some college education was 88.7 percent, and among those with a college degree, it was 91.2 percent. Turnout differences among Latinos at varying levels of education were quite sharp. Latinos with less than a high school education turned out a reported rate of 72.4 percent; the rate was 71.2 percent among Latinos who are high school graduates. Turnout among Latinos with some college education was 65.6 percent, and for those with a college degree, turnout was 88.3 percent.

## CHANGES IN TURNOUT AFTER 1960

The postwar turnout rate peaked in 1960. According to the U.S. Census Bureau, in that year, only 43.2 percent of whites and 20.1 percent of blacks twenty-five years and older were high school graduates. By 2010, 87.6 percent of whites and 84.2 percent of blacks were high school graduates. In 1960 only 8.1 percent of whites and 3.1 percent of blacks were college graduates. By 2010, 30.3 percent of whites and 19.8 percent of blacks had obtained college degrees. The growth in educational attainment is a remarkable change in American society, and this social transformation plays a central role in one of the longest-standing empirical puzzles in the study of political behavior, a puzzle Richard A. Brody labels the "puzzle of political participation."[72] Given that education is a strong predictor of voter turnout at the individual level, why did national turnout levels decline between 1960 and 1980, and why did they stabilize, roughly speaking, thereafter, during a time when education levels rose dramatically?

Political scientists have studied the postwar changes in voter turnout extensively over the past several decades. Given the influence of education on turnout, one would expect increasing levels of education would lead to a substantial increase in turnout over this time, and certainly not a decline in voter participation of any degree, as happened between 1960 and 1980. This suggests that any stimulating effect of education on voter turnout was likely offset by other factors that depressed it. Some scholars argue that the decline in turnout was a function of social forces, such as the changing age distribution of the electorate and a decline in social institutions generally. Others point to institutional changes, such as the expansion of suffrage to eighteen-year-olds or to the ways in which the political parties conduct their campaigns as sources for the decline in voter turnout. Still others argue that the decline in voter turnout reflected changes in political attitudes that are fundamental for encouraging political participation.

The research by McDonald and Popkin provides one important part of the explanation for why turnout among the voting-age population has declined during the past half century. The percentage of noncitizens among the voting-age population in the United States has increased markedly from less than 2 percent in 1960 to 8.5 percent in 2010.[73] Moreover, in 1960, fewer than half a million people were incarcerated or were convicted felons, whereas in 2012 about five million were. This has resulted in an expansion in the number of ineligible voters in the United States. These changes would tend to reduce turnout among the voting-age population. Of course neither the growth in noncitizens nor the increased number of disenfranchised felons is so large (large though these changes are) as to be sufficient for explaining the entire decline in turnout from 1960 onward. Moreover, these factors have increased at a higher rate in recent decades, but turnout no longer appears to be in decline.

In a comprehensive study of the decline in turnout between 1960 and 1988, Ruy Teixeira identifies three of the social forces that contributed to declining levels of voter participation.[74] After 1960 the electorate became significantly younger as the post-World War II baby boomer generation (those born between 1946 and 1964) came of age. Thus the largest cohort in the electorate consisted of baby boomers, who were of an age when participation is lowest. Of course, boomers are considerably older today and now reside in the age cohort that is most likely to turnout, so they should be fueling an increase in participation. Teixeira also cites the decline in the percentage of Americans who were married, and married people are more likely to vote than those who are unmarried. He also points to declining church attendance as contributing to the decline in voter turnout.[75] Teixeira argues that the decline in church attendance, which reduces Americans' ties to their communities, was the most important of these three factors in reducing turnout and suggests that voter participation would have declined even further had education not been a countervailing force.[76]

Steven J. Rosenstone and John Mark Hansen also develop a comprehensive explanation for the decline in turnout. Using data from the ANES, they examine the effect of expanded suffrage (estimating that the inclusion of eighteen-, nineteen-, and twenty-year-olds in the 1972 elections likely caused about a one percentage point decline in turnout) and reduced voter registration requirements on voting. They found that reported turnout declined eleven percentage points from the 1960s to the 1980s. Yet their analysis also demonstrates that the increase in formal education was the most important factor preventing an even greater decline in voter participation. They estimate that turnout would have declined sixteen percentage points if it had not been for the combined effect of rising education levels and liberalized election laws.[77] Next we discuss another institutional change that they argue contributed substantively to the decline in turnout—a change in the way political parties conduct electoral campaigns.

Most analysts agree that attitudinal changes contributed to the decline in electoral participation. Indeed our own analysis has focused on the effects of attitudinal changes, particularly the influence of changes in party loyalties and the role of what George I. Balch and others have called feelings of "external political efficacy"—that is, the belief that political authorities will respond to attempts to influence them.[78] These are the same two fundamental attitudes analyzed by Teixeira in his first major study of turnout, and they are among the attitudes examined by Rosenstone and Hansen.[79] We found these attitudes contributed to the decline in turnout from 1960 through 1980, and they have remained influential in every presidential election we have studied from 1980 to 2016.[80]

To measure party identification, we use a standard set of questions to gauge individuals' psychological attachment to a partisan reference group.[81] In Chapter 8, we examine how party identification contributes to the way people vote. But party loyalties also contribute to *whether* people vote. Strong feelings of party identification contribute to one's psychological involvement in politics.[82] Moreover, party loyalties also reduce the time and effort needed to decide how to vote and thus reduce the costs of voting.[83] In every presidential election since 1952, the ANES studies have shown that strong partisans are more likely to vote than weaker partisans and independents who lean toward one of the parties. And in every election since 1960, independents with no partisan leanings have been the least likely to vote.

Partisanship is an important contributor to voters' decisions to turn out, but the strength of party loyalties in the United States has varied over time. Between 1952 and 1964 the percentage of self-identified "strong partisans" among the white electorate never fell below 25 percent. It then fell to 27 percent in 1966 and continued to fall, reaching its lowest level in 1978, when only 21 percent of voters identified strongly with one of the two major parties. In more recent years party identification has risen; indeed, by 2004, it had returned to 1952–1964 levels. After a temporary decline in 2008 due to a decrease in Republican loyalties, the percentage of whites who were strong party identifiers rose to just over 30 percent in 2012 and reached 37.4 percent in 2016.[84]

Feelings of political efficacy also contribute to voter participation. Citizens may expect to derive benefits from voting if they believe that government is responsive to their demands. Conversely, those who believe that political leaders will not or cannot respond to popular demands may see little reason to engage in political participation.[85] In fourteen of the sixteen elections between 1952 and 2012, Americans with high levels of political efficacy were more likely to vote than those at lower levels of efficacy.[86]

From 1960 to 1980 feelings of political efficacy dropped precipitously, and they remain low and in decline today. In 1956 and 1960, 64 percent of whites reported high levels of political efficacy, with only 15 percent scoring low. In 2016 few Americans felt that that government responded to their needs. Indeed efficacy was at an all-time low. Only 21.6 percent of whites scored "high" on our measure of political efficacy, and 52.3 percent scored "low." Incredibly the portion of respondents with low levels of political efficacy increased roughly seven percentage points since 2012.

The steepest declines in partisan attachment and political efficacy occurred between 1960 and 1980, contemporaneous with the sharpest decline in voter participation. Our analysis of voter turnout during this two-decade period suggests that the combined impact of the decline in party identification and the decline in beliefs about government responsiveness accounts for roughly 70 percent of the decline of electoral participation. The ANES reports a decline in validated turnout among white voters of 10.3 percentage points between 1960 and 1980. By our estimates, if there had been no decline in either partisan attachments or external political efficacy, the decline in turnout would have been only 2.9 percentage points.[87] In previous volumes we have noted the persistent role these attitudes play in predicting voter turnout in subsequent election years. Whereas party loyalties have rebounded to 1952–1964 levels, Americans' feelings of efficacy remain anemic, thus preventing a substantial increase in turnout levels. Using a rather simple algebraic procedure, we can estimate the percentage of whites in 2016 who would have reported voting for president had strength of partisanship, and external political efficacy remained at 1960 levels.[88] Our estimate suggests that reported turnout among whites in 2016 would be 1.5 percentage points higher if not for these attitudinal changes.

In Table 4.4 we present the joint relationship between strength of party identification, feelings of efficacy, and reported electoral participation in the 2016 presidential election. As we have found in the past, strength of party identification and feelings of political efficacy are weakly related, but both contribute to turnout. Reading across each row reveals that strength of party identification is positively related to reported electoral participation, but the strength of this relationship has been weaker in the past two elections relative to years we have studied. The difference in reported voting among whites with strong partisanship and those describing themselves as independents who lean toward a party is six percentage points for those high in efficacy and eight points for those low in efficacy. These differences were much smaller in 2012, but in 2008, we reported differences of fifteen percentage points for those high in efficacy and thirty-four points for those low in efficacy. Reading down each column, we see a consistent relationship between feelings of political efficacy and reported voting within each partisan group—on the magnitude of six to nine percentage point differences. This suggests that the record-low level of political efficacy in 2016—52.3 percent report "low" levels of efficacy—was distributed among strong, weak, and nonpartisans alike and that efficacy had a strong relationship with decisions to turn out. This finding is similar to what we found in 2012, when political efficacy was at a then record low (50 percent scored "low"). In 2008, by comparison, we found a strong relationship between feelings of efficacy and reported turnout in only one partisan group: independents who lean toward a political party. In that year 43.7 percent of respondents reported low feelings of political efficacy.

A comprehensive analysis of the role of attitudinal factors would have taken into account other factors that might have eroded turnout. For instance, as has been well documented, there has been a substantial decline in trust during the past four decades, a decline that appears to be occurring in a large number of democracies.[89] In 1964, when political trust among whites was highest, 77 percent of whites trusted the government to do what was right just about always or most of the time, and 74 percent of blacks endorsed this view.[90] Political trust reached a very low level in 1980, when only 25 percent of whites and 26 percent of blacks trusted the government. Trust rebounded during the Reagan years, but it fell after that, and by 1992 trust was almost as low as it was in 1980. After that, trust rose in most elections, and by 2004, 50 percent of whites and 34 percent of blacks trusted the government. But trust dropped markedly among whites during the next four years, and it dropped somewhat among blacks. In 2008, 30 percent of whites and 28 percent of blacks trusted the government.[91] In 2012, after the first term of the first black president, 19 percent of whites—a sharp decline—and 40 percent of blacks—a sharp increase—trusted the government in Washington to do what is right. Among Latinos, trust declined by six points over the course of Obama's first term from 36 to 30 percent. In 2016 trust in government

**Table 4-4 Percentage of Whites Who Reported Voting for President, by Strength of Party Identification and Sense of External Political Efficacy, 2016**

| Score on External Political Efficacy Index | Strength of Party Identification | | | | | | | |
|---|---|---|---|---|---|---|---|---|
| | Strong Partisan | | Weak Partisan | | Independent Who Leans toward a Party | | Independent with No Partisan Leaning | |
| | % | (N) | % | (N) | % | (N) | % | (N) |
| High | 97 | (236) | 91 | (140) | 91 | (118) | 66 | (34) |
| Medium | 88 | (201) | 89 | (134) | 91 | (129) | 66 | (50) |
| Low | 93 | (454) | 82 | (314) | 85 | (300) | 75 | (150) |

*Source:* Authors' analysis of the 2016 ANES survey.

*Note:* The numbers in parentheses are the totals on which the percentages are based. Sample includes both face-to-face and Internet respondents. Numbers are weighted.

was in marked decline among all groups. Only 8.6 percent of whites profess trust in government, whereas 20.8 percent of blacks and 17.8 of Latinos did.

Although the decline in trust in government would seem to be an obvious explanation for the decline in turnout since the 1960s, scholarship shows little evidence supporting this. In most years Americans who distrusted the government were as likely to vote as those who were politically trusting. In the past two elections, the evidence has been mixed. In 2012 we found some evidence for a relationship between trust in government and turnout. Respondents who trusted the government in Washington to do what is right were nine percentage points more likely to vote than those who expressed no trust in government. This relationship was not dependent upon the race of the voter. In 2016 trust in government—or, better put, the lack thereof—seemed to motivate white voters but not blacks or Latinos. For blacks and Latinos we see no statistically significant relationship between trust in government and voter turnout. However, among whites, those who claimed to "never" trust the government were roughly seven percentage points more likely to vote than those who trusted the government "most of the time" or "always." Whether these disaffected voters turned out to vote for Donald Trump, a candidate who pledged to "drain the swamp," that is Washington, warrants investigation in Chapter 7.

## ELECTION-SPECIFIC FACTORS

Focusing on long-term stable factors related to voting, such as social demographics and partisan attachments, might give one the impression that election-specific factors may not matter. Yet in any election there will be political and nonpolitical circumstances that affect voting. Among the nonpolitical factors shown to affect voter turnout is election day weather. Bad weather is likely to increase the physical costs of voting and make it more difficult for potential voters to get to the polls. A study by Brad T. Gomez, Thomas G. Hansford, and George A. Krause, which examined county-level voter turnout in every presidential election from 1944 to 2000, showed that for every inch of rain a county received above its thirty-year average rainfall, turnout declined by nearly one percentage point.[92] In close elections a nonpolitical factor like weather could have real political consequences by keeping voters in some localities away from the polls and potentially changing electoral outcomes.[93]

Politics matters, too, of course. Not all elections are competitive, and one factor that stimulates voter turnout is the expected closeness of the outcome.[94] According to the rational choice theory of voting developed by Anthony Downs and refined by William H. Riker and Peter C. Ordeshook, a person's expected benefit from voting increases in close elections because the probability that one's vote will directly affect the outcome is higher.[95] Close elections also make it easier for potential voters to become politically informed as heightened media coverage, television advertising, and interpersonal discussion of politics help create an information-rich environment. And parties and candidates are more likely to engage in get-out-the-vote efforts when election outcomes hang in the balance.

In Chapter 2 we identified the thirteen battleground states in the 2016 election.[96] Early predictions suggested these states might have close elections. According to the 2016 CPS, average voter turnout (voting-age population) in these thirteen states was 60.0 percent, whereas the average in non-battleground states was 54.6 percent.

At the individual level, perceptions of the closeness of the presidential election may vary from person to person. These perceptions may be informed by the actual competitiveness of the election in the individual's state, or they may reflect the expected outcome of the Electoral College. But people sometimes espouse a distorted view of the competitive nature of the election. As Rosenstone and Hansen note, "[t]his may reflect ignorance, excitability, wishful thinking, accurate assessments of the leanings of friends and localities, or sober recollections of the inconstancy of public opinion polls."[97] Our analysis of the ANES shows that the percentage who thinks the election will be close varies greatly from election to election. For example, in 1996, only 52 percent of whites thought the election between Bill Clinton and Bob Dole would be close, but in 2000, 88 percent thought the contest between Gore and Bush would be close. In 2008 there were clear racial differences in individuals' perceptions of the competitiveness of the election. Among whites 82 percent thought the election would be close; among blacks only 69 percent did. These racial differences were remarkably persistent in 2012. In 2016, 72.6 percent of ANES respondents thought the election would be close. Racial differences in perception were once again evident; 75 percent of whites thought the election would be close, whereas 62.2 percent of blacks and 64.8 percent of Latinos thought so. These racial and ethnic differences may be a function of differences in partisan attachment. Republicans (78.7 percent) were significantly more likely than Democrats (63.8 percent) to think the election was going to be close. To the extent that perceptions of closeness are related to decisions to turn out, these partisan differences suggest that Democrats may have been overconfident in their party's chances to win and, perhaps, less motivated to go to the polls.

The most direct way that campaigns attempt to influence turnout is through get-out-the-vote efforts. Modern campaigns expend exorbitant amounts of money and effort trying to bring their voters to the polls. Campaigns employ local phone banks and door-to-door canvassing; they use direct mail and social networking technology and even old-fashioned political rallies all in an effort to stimulate voter interests. But to what effect? Over a decade ago political scientists Donald Green and Alan Gerber began a research agenda aimed at answering this question. Green and Gerber use field experiments to gauge the effectiveness of voter mobilization tactics.[98] The field experiments typically use voter registration rolls to randomly assign a subset of voters into "treatment" and "control" conditions. Those assigned to the treatment group are exposed to the specific get-out-the-vote tactic being tested, whereas those in the control group are not.[99] After the election the voter rolls are reexamined to determine whether voter turnout was higher among those in the treatment group than those in control group, thus providing evidence that the mobilization tactic *caused* an increase in turnout. Green and Gerber's work, as well as that undertaken subsequently by others, suggests, among other things, that voters tend to respond best to personalized methods and messages, such as door-to-door canvassing, than impersonal techniques, such as "robocalls."[100] Pressure from one's social network is also important in mobilizing voters to the polls. In one of their most well-known experiments to date, Gerber and Green, joined by Christopher Larimer, find that voters are more likely to turn out—by an increased probability of 8.1 percentage points—when they are told prior to election day that their decision to vote will be publicized to their neighbors. This experiment not only demonstrates the effectiveness of social pressure in mobilizing voters; it provides supporting evidence for the argument that the historic decline in turnout could have been caused in part by the concomitant decline in Americans' willingness to join associational groups, such as fraternal organizations and churches.

Unlike these experimental designs, it is difficult to estimate the *causal* effect of mobilization on turnout using surveys. Consider the fact that campaigns often contact voters based on how likely they are to vote. Can we really say that mobilization causes turnout, or does the potential for turnout cause mobilization? Because the survey environment typically measures whether the individual was contacted by a political party and the individual's reported turnout contemporaneously, it is hard to establish for certain which variable came first. Thus an analysis of the relationship between whether an individual was contacted by a political party and their reported turnout using the 2016 ANES is likely to only establish correlation, not causation.[101]

The longitudinal nature of the ANES does offer interesting insights into changes in the mobilization of the electorate, however. Most notably the percentage of Americans who say they have been contacted by a political party increased after the 1960 election. In 1960, 22 percent of the electorate said a political party had contacted them.[102] By 1980, 32 percent said they had been contacted. The upward trend abated in 1992, when only 20 percent said they had been contacted by a political party. The percentage that said they had been contacted by a political party grew in 1996 and in 2000, and it increased slightly between 2000 and 2004. It grew again somewhat in 2008, when 43 percent said they had been contacted, with whites somewhat more likely to claim they were contacted (45 percent) than blacks (38 percent). In 2012, 39 percent of the electorate said a political party had contacted them, a decrease from four years earlier. This number dropped precipitously in 2016, when only 31.8 of respondents reported contact by one of the parties. That party contact went down in 2016 may not be a surprise to close observers of the campaigns. Much was made during the general election season about the limited resources dedicated by the Trump campaign to the mobilization "ground game."[103] Indeed our estimates show that Republicans were more than three percentage points less likely to be contacted by a party than Democrats, 32.9 to 36.2, respectively. The study of party contact rates over time may shed further light on changes in turnout. Similar to education, increased levels of party contact over time may have prevented the decline from being even greater.

## DOES LOW VOTER TURNOUT MATTER?

Many bemoan the low levels of turnout in U.S. elections. Some claim that low rates of voter participation undermine the legitimacy of elected political leaders. Seymour Martin Lipset, for instance, argues that the existence of a large bloc of nonparticipants in the electorate may be potentially dangerous because it means that many Americans have weak ties to the established parties and political leaders.[104] This may increase the prospects of electoral instability or perhaps political instability generally. Others argue that the low levels of turnout, at minimum, increase the probability that American elections produce "biased" outcomes, reflecting the preferences of an active political class while ignoring those who may be alienated or disenfranchised.

Turnout rates may also increase the electoral fortunes of one party over the other. Conventional wisdom holds that because nonvoters are more likely to come from low socioeconomic-status groups and ethnic minorities—groups that tend to vote Democratic—higher turnout benefits the Democrats. James DeNardo, using aggregate election data from 1932 to 1976, and Thomas Hansford and Brad Gomez, using aggregate data from 1948 to 2000, provide evidence that increases in turnout enlarge the vote share of Democratic candidates, although the nature of the relationship is more complex and weaker than one might assume.[105]

Elected officials appear convinced that their reelection fates depend on the level of turnout.[106] Over the past several decades, at both the national and state level, legislators have debated a number of laws aimed at making it easier (or sometimes harder) for citizens to vote. Bills that make it easier to register to vote, such as the 1993 motor voter law, and bills that promote convenience voting mechanisms, such as early voting or vote by mail, have typically divided legislators along strict party lines with Democrats supporting efforts to expand the electorate and Republicans opposing them.

More recently Republicans have led in the push to require voter identification at the polls, typically by requiring the presentation of a government-issued identification card, such as a driver's license. At the time of the 2016 election, these bills had passed in thirty-four states.[107] After the 2012 election, North Carolina, which had a Republican legislature and governor, passed a strict voter identification requirement. In addition to requiring people to show photo identification, the North Carolina law condensed the number of early voting days, abolished same-day registration, and eliminated out-of-precinct voting. Supporters of the North Carolina bill argued that the bill attempted to increase the integrity of elections; opponents of the bill argued that the aim of the bill was voter suppression, particularly minority voters.[108] In July 2016 the Fourth Circuit Court of Appeals struck down the North Carolina law, stating that the state legislature had acted with "discriminatory intent" and that the law targeted the state's black voters with "almost surgical precision" to reduce their voter participation.[109] In May 2017 the U.S. Supreme Court rejected the state's appeal of the case.[110]

In our analyses of the 1980, 1984, and 1988 presidential elections, we argued that among most reasonable scenarios, increased turnout would not have led to Democratic victories.[111] In 1992 increased turnout coincided with the Democratic victory but not a higher share of the Democratic vote. Our analyses suggest that Bill Clinton benefited from increased turnout but that he benefited more by converting voters who had supported George H. W. Bush four years earlier.[112] Despite the six percentage point decline in turnout between 1992 and 1996, Clinton was easily reelected. Even so there is some evidence that the decline in turnout cost Clinton votes.[113]

In view of the closeness of the 2000 contest, it seems plausible that a successful get-out-the-vote effort by the Democrats could have swung the election to Al Gore. In 2004 turnout rose by over four percentage points, regardless of how it is measured. But Bush won with a majority of the popular vote, even though his margin over Kerry was small. Our analyses suggest that the Republicans were more successful in mobilizing their supporters than the Democrats. Some argue that the GOP gained because in eleven states proposals to ban same-sex marriages were on the ballot. But, as we have shown, turnout was only one point higher in the states that had these propositions on the ballot than in the states that did not.[114] Bush won nine of the eleven states with such a proposition, but of those nine states only Ohio was closely contested, and turnout increased by nine percentage points there.

In 2008 many argued that Obama's victory was aided by the mobilization of new voters, particularly blacks, Latinos, and eighteen- to twenty-five-year-olds. But we found little evidence of turnout effects in the 2008. The ANES data suggest that Republican identifiers were more likely to vote than Democrats in 2008, and Obama would have enjoyed an increase in support had Democrats and Republicans voted at the same rate. However, we found no additional evidence that higher turnout would have benefited Obama.[115]

As was the case in 2008, Obama was able to win the 2012 election in spite of Republican identifiers turning out at a higher rate than Democrats. Our analyses showed that if we assume that each of the Democratic identifiers had turnout as high as Republican identifiers and assume that the additional Democrats drawn to the polls would have vote the same way as the Democrats who did not, Obama would have gained about 1.5 percentage points.

As argued originally by the authors of *The American Voter*, if nonvoters and occasional voters hold preferences that differ from those of regular (or core) voters, then variation in turnout is likely to have meaningful electoral implications.[116] Thus, in Table 4-5, we examine whether respondents reported voting for president in 2016, according to their party identification, their positions on the issues (the "balance-of-issues" measure), and their evaluations of the performance of the incumbent president

(Obama), which party is best able to handle the important problems facing the country, and their beliefs about whether the country is going in the right direction (the summary measure of "retrospective" evaluations).

Although Hillary Clinton won the popular vote, her party did not win the turnout battle. Table 4-5 shows that strong Republicans were more likely to vote than strong Democrats by four percentage points, and independents who felt close to the Republican Party were more likely to vote than those who leaned toward the Democrats by three percentage points. Among weak identifiers, the Democrats had the advantage but only by two percentage points. If we assume that each of the low-turnout groups had turnouts as high as each of the comparable high-turnout groups, and assume that the additional voters drawn to the polls voted the same way as actual voters, we estimate that Hillary Clinton would have gained about 1.5 percentage points to her popular vote total—whether this would have affected Clinton's Electoral College fortunes is difficult to determine.

In Chapter 6, we examine the issue preferences of the electorate. For every presidential election between 1980 and 2008, we built a measure of overall issue preferences based on the seven-point scales used by the ANES surveys to measure the issue preferences of the electorate.[117] But we have found little or no evidence of issue differences between those who vote and those who do not.

In 2016 our overall measure of issues preferences is based on scales measuring the respondent's position on six issues: (1) reducing or increasing government services, (2) decreasing or increasing defense spending, (3) government health insurance, (4) government job guarantees, (5) government helping blacks, and (6) protecting the environment.[118] As Table 4-5 shows partisan differences on the balance-of-issues scale do not contribute significantly to differences in voter turnout. Respondents who are strongly Republican on the issues were one percentage point more likely to report voting than those who are strongly Democratic. Respondents who were moderately Democratic were four points more likely to vote than those who were moderately Republican on the issues. Those who were slightly Republican on the issues were equally likely to vote as those who lean toward the Democrats on the issues. Based on our simulation, if the differences in turnout based on issue preference were leveled out, Clinton would have gained about 1.3 percentage points to her popular vote total.

In Chapter 7 we discuss the retrospective evaluations of the electorate. Voters, some analysts argue, make their decisions based not just on their evaluation of policy promises but also on their evaluation of how well the party in power is doing. In past studies we used a summary measure based on presidential approval, an evaluation of the job the government was doing dealing with the most important problem facing the country, and an assessment of which party would do a better job dealing with this problem. Across each of the elections that we have studied, the relationship between retrospective evaluations and turnout has been weak, at best, and often nonexistent.

In 2016 we employed a summary measure based on the respondent's approval of the president, the respondent's evaluation of how good a job the government had been doing over the last four years, and the respondent's belief about whether things in the country are going in the right direction or are on the wrong track. Although 53 percent of voters approved of President Obama, they overwhelmingly

**Table 4-5 Percentage of Electorate Who Reported Voting for President, by Party Identification, Issue Preferences, and Retrospective Evaluations, 2016**

| | Voted | Did Not Vote | Total | (N) |
|---|---|---|---|---|
| Strong Democrat | 90 | 10 | 100 | (747) |
| Weak Democrat | 84 | 16 | 100 | (453) |
| Independent, leans Democratic | 84 | 16 | 100 | (351) |
| Independent, no partisan leaning | 67 | 33 | 100 | (358) |
| Independent, leans Republican | 87 | 13 | 100 | (376) |
| Weak Republican | 82 | 18 | 100 | (392) |
| Strong Republican | 94 | 6 | 100 | (563) |
| **Electorate, by scores on balance-of-issues measure** | | | | |
| Strongly Democratic | 92 | 8 | 100 | (323) |
| Moderately Democratic | 88 | 12 | 100 | (327) |
| Slightly Democratic | 81 | 19 | 100 | (495) |
| Neutral | 81 | 19 | 100 | (465) |
| Slightly Republican | 81 | 19 | 100 | (609) |
| Moderately Republican | 84 | 16 | 100 | (555) |
| Strongly Republican | 93 | 7 | 100 | (478) |
| **Electorate, by scores on summary measure of retrospective evaluations of incumbent party** | | | | |
| Strongly opposed | 91 | 9 | 100 | (999) |
| Moderately opposed | 77 | 23 | 100 | (396) |
| Slightly opposed | 80 | 20 | 100 | (189) |
| Neutral | 76 | 24 | 100 | (392) |
| Slightly supportive | 86 | 14 | 100 | (449) |
| Moderately supportive | 89 | 11 | 100 | (248) |
| Strongly supportive | 90 | 10 | 100 | (525) |

*Source:* Authors' analysis of the 2016 ANES survey.

*Note:* Sample includes both face-to-face and Internet respondents. Numbers are weighted. Chapter 6 describes how the balance-of-issues measure was constructed, and Chapter 7 describes how the summary measure of retrospective evaluations was constructed. Both measures differ slightly from those presented in previous volumes of *Change and Continuity*, so care should be given when comparing to earlier election studies.

(72.5 percent) believed that the nation was headed on the "wrong track." On our summary scale roughly half of the respondents, 48.8 percent, had negative views of recent governmental performance; 37.2 percent had a positive view. Yet, interestingly, those who were supportive were more likely to vote on balance. Whereas those with the strongest views turned out in roughly equal proportions, those who were slightly or moderately supportive of the incumbent party were nine percentage points more likely to vote than those who opposed the incumbent party slightly or moderately. Thus, in our simulation, evening out turnout differences based on retrospective evaluations brings more voters with negative views of the recent past into the equation. Nevertheless, adding more voters to the tally, even those with a pessimistic view of things, would have aided the Democratic candidate, Clinton. If turnout differences between retrospective subgroups are eliminated, Clinton would have gained 1.1 percentage points.

In most elections higher turnout is unlikely to affect the outcome. But in close elections, like that held in 2016, variation in voter turnout is most likely to have an effect on who wins or loses. In our analyses the largest and most consistent turnout effects that we see are associated with differences in voter participation among party identifiers. Consistent with other scholarship we found that higher turnout benefits the Democrats but only to a small degree.[119] Moreover, we have found limited evidence in our analyses to support the argument that low voter turnout biases election outcomes on the basis of issue preferences or retrospective evaluations. Because in most presidential contests increased turnout would not have affected the outcome, some analysts might argue that low turnout does not matter.[120]

Despite this evidence we do not accept the conclusion that low turnout is unimportant. We are especially concerned that turnout is low among the disadvantaged. Some observers believe this is so because political leaders structure political alternatives in a way that provides disadvantaged Americans with relatively little political choice. Frances Fox Piven and Richard A. Cloward, for example, acknowledge that the policy preferences of voters and nonvoters are similar, but they argue that this similarity exists because of the way that elites have structured policy choices:

> "Political attitudes would inevitably change over time," they maintain, "if the allegiance of voters from the bottom became the object of partisan competition, for then politicians would be prodded to identify and articulate the grievances of and aspirations of the lower-income voters in order to win their support, thus helping to give form and voice to a distinctive political class."[121]

We cannot accept this argument, either, mainly because it is highly speculative and there is little evidence to support it. The difficulty in supporting this view may in part stem from the nature of survey research itself because questions about public policy are usually framed along lines of controversy as defined by mainstream political leaders. Occasionally, however, surveys pose radical policy alternatives, and they often ask open-ended questions that allow respondents to state their own preferences. We find no concrete evidence that low turnout leads American political leaders to ignore the policy preferences of the electorate.

Nevertheless, low turnout can scarcely be healthy for a democracy. As we have shown much of the initial decline in U.S. voter turnout following the 1960s could be attributed to decreases in partisan attachment and external political efficacy. Partisan identification has largely returned to 1960s levels, but turnout has not increased proportionally. Feelings of political efficacy have continued to decline and, as we reported, were at an all-time low in 2016. If turnout remains low because an ever-growing segment of the American public believe that "public officials don't care much what people like me think" and "people like me don't have any say about what the government does," then concern seems warranted.

CHAPTER FIVE

# SOCIAL FORCES AND THE VOTE

Although voting is an individual act, group characteristics influence voting choices because individuals with similar social characteristics may share similar political interests. Group similarities in voting behavior may also reflect past political conditions. The partisan loyalties of African Americans, for example, were shaped by the Civil War. Black loyalties to the Republican Party, the party of Lincoln, lasted through the 1932 election, and the steady Democratic voting of southern whites, the product of those same historical conditions, lasted even longer, at least through 1960.

It is easy to see why group-based loyalties persist over time. Studies of pre-adult political learning suggest that partisan loyalties are often passed on from generation to generation.[1] And because religion, ethnicity, and to a lesser extent, social class are often transmitted across generations as well, social divisions have considerable staying power. The interactions of social group members also reinforce similarities in political attitudes and behaviors.

Politicians often make group appeals. They recognize that to win an election, they need to mobilize the social groups that supported them in the past while attempting to cut into their opponents' bases of support. These group-based electoral coalitions often become identified at election time with the particular candidate being supported and the nature of the particular campaign, creating what we might think of as "Trump voters" or "Clinton voters," for example. Yet group-based electoral coalitions tend to be relatively stable from one election to the next, so it is perhaps best to think of these social-group loyalties as the basis for partisan coalitions, for example, "Republican voters" or "Democratic voters." Indeed political scientists often identify periods of significant electoral change, "realignments," by virtue of observing dramatic and lasting shifts in group-based support from one party to another. Thus examining the social forces that influence voting behavior is a crucial aspect for understanding change and continuity within an electoral system.

To place the 2016 presidential election within the context of recent electoral history, we examine the evolution of the Democratic Party's broad and diverse electoral coalition from its zenith in the years following the New Deal to its eventual unraveling and how the subsequent shifting of white political loyalties structures the major parties' bases and electoral competition today. It is sometimes said that Democrats tend to think in group terms more than Republicans, but it is most certainly the case that both of the major parties count on the support of core groups as part of the electoral bases. Yet the historical alteration of the Democratic Party's group-based coalition provides an important examination of how partisan allegiances change over time and how this has changed both parties' electoral fortunes. Beginning with the election of Franklin D. Roosevelt in 1932, the Democrat Party brought together sometimes disparate groups, a "coalition of minorities" that included both union and nonunion working-class households, both African Americans and native white southerners, and both Jews and Catholics. Yet by the late twentieth century, the coalition was in decline. African Americans maintained, even strengthened, their loyalty to the Democrats, but southern white conservatives have drifted to their more natural ideological home on the right and are now more likely to identify with the Republican Party. Working-class voters are a cross-pressured group who sometimes side with the Democrats on economic issues but sometimes agree with Republicans on social issues.[2] Union membership in the United States has declined greatly, making it difficult for the party to mobilize working-class voters. Jewish voters remain loyal to the Democrats, but non-white Catholic voters now support the two major parties at the roughly the same rate, and churchgoing Catholics now lean toward the Republican Party. And a growing Latino population appears to be joining the Democratic coalition.

The 1992 and 1996 presidential elections provide an example of the fragile nature of the Democratic coalition. Bill Clinton earned high levels of support from only two of the groups that made up the New Deal coalition formed by Roosevelt—African Americans and Jews. Most of the other New Deal coalition groups gave fewer than half of their votes to Clinton. Fortunately for him, in a three-way contest (it included independent candidate Ross Perot), only 43 percent of the vote was needed to win. Despite a second candidacy by Perot, the 1996 election was much more of a two-candidate fight, and Clinton won 49 percent of the popular vote. He gained ground among the vast majority of groups analyzed in this chapter, making especially large gains among union members (a traditional component of the New Deal coalition) and Latinos. In many respects the Democratic losses after 1964 can be attributed to the party's failure to hold the loyalties of the New Deal coalition groups.

In 2008 Barack Obama's victory returned a Democrat to the White House. His victory marked the first time since 1976 that a Democrat won the presidency with a majority of the popular vote. But Obama did not restore the New Deal coalition. Obama gained nearly a fourth of his total vote from black voters. This was possible because black turnout equaled white turnout and because blacks voted overwhelmingly Democratic. Yet, among the groups that we examined, only blacks and Jews (a small segment of the electorate, to be sure) gave a clear majority of their vote to Obama. Obama had only a slight edge among white union members, and he split the white Catholic vote with the Republican nominee, John McCain. Among white southerners, a mainstay of the New Deal coalition, Obama won only a third of the vote.[3]

In 2012 the coalitional divisions of 2008 were accentuated slightly. As noted in Chapter 4, 2012 marked the first time in the nation's history that turnout among African Americans exceeded that of whites. Combined with the group's extraordinarily high level of support for Obama, we estimated that blacks were between 23.7 and 24.4 percent of Obama's reelection electorate. No other Democratic presidential winner has received as large a share of his vote from the black electorate than Obama.

Conversely, Obama lost support from southern whites and non-Latino Catholics, core groups that were once part of his party's electoral coalition.

## HOW SOCIAL GROUPS VOTED IN 2016

Table 5-1 presents the results of our analysis of how social groups voted in the 2016 presidential election.[4] Among the 2,564 respondents who said they voted for president, 48.8 percent said they voted for Hillary Clinton, 44.0 percent for Donald Trump, and 7.2 percent for other candidates—results that are within roughly two percentage points of the actual results (see Table 3-1). The American National Election Studies (ANES) are the best source of data for analyzing change over time, but the total number of self-reported voters is sometimes small. This can make group-based analysis tenuous if the number of sample respondents within a group is exceedingly small. Therefore, we will often supplement (sometimes by necessity) our analysis with the exit polls (pool polls) conducted by Edison Research for a consortium of news organizations.[5] For the 2016 exit polls, 24,558 voters were interviewed. Most were randomly chosen as they left 350 polling places from across the United States on election day. Respondents who voted absentee or voted early were contacted via telephone, totaling 4,398 telephone interviews in all.[6] For comparison we will sometimes reference the 2012 exit polls, for which 26,565 voters were interviewed.

### Race, Gender, Region, and Age

Political differences between African Americans and whites are far sharper than any other social cleavage.[7] According to the 2016 ANES, 90 percent of black voters supported Clinton (see Table 5-1), similar to the pool poll, which indicates that 89 percent did. Clinton's level of support among black voters in 2016 was smaller than Obama's level of support (98 percent) as reported in the 2012 ANES, although the differences are negligible according to the exit polls. Based on the ANES survey, we estimate that 20.1 percent of Clinton's vote came from blacks; our analysis of the pool poll suggests that 22.2 percent did. These estimates are smaller than those associated with Barack Obama's 2012 electorate, which as we noted earlier, composed roughly 24 percent of his electoral coalition. This reduction in the proportional share of African Americans in the Democratic candidate's coalition appears to be driven primarily by the decline in voter turnout among blacks from 2012 to 2016 (see Chapter 4). Nevertheless, this is a sizable, and relatively high, contribution to the Democratic electorate and suggests that the party is heavily reliant on black voters for their electoral fortunes. Clinton's electorate is estimated to have been between 54.5 (exit poll) and 59.2 (ANES) percent white.

In comparison, African Americans comprised a very small portion of the Trump coalition. Based on the ANES estimates only 6.4 percent of blacks voted for Trump, 8 percent according to the exit polls. These estimates suggest that between 1.5 to 2.1 percent of all Trump voters were black, approximately 1 to 1.3 million of Trump's 63 million voters. Four years earlier, the Republican nominee, Mitt Romney, constructed an electorate that was estimated to be 1.9 percent black, thus roughly comparable to

## Table 5-1 How Social Groups Voted for President, 2016 (Percent)

| Social Group | Clinton | Trump | Other | Total | (*N*)[a] |
|---|---|---|---|---|---|
| Total electorate | 49 | 44 | 7 | 100 | (2,564) |
| **Electorate, by race** | | | | | |
| African American | 90 | 6 | 4 | 100 | (275) |
| White | 39 | 54 | 7 | 100 | (1,854) |
| Other | 64 | 26 | 9 | 99 | (422) |
| Latino (of any race) | 69 | 23 | 8 | 100 | (255) |
| **Whites, by gender** | | | | | |
| Female | 41 | 53 | 7 | 101 | (967) |
| Male | 37 | 55 | 8 | 100 | (872) |
| **Whites, by region** | | | | | |
| New England and Mid-Atlantic | 53 | 43 | 4 | 100 | (377) |
| North Central | 38 | 56 | 7 | 101 | (442) |
| South | 24 | 69 | 7 | 100 | (473) |
| Border | 40 | 51 | 9 | 100 | (168) |
| Mountain and Pacific | 46 | 45 | 10 | 101 | (393) |
| **Whites, by birth cohort** | | | | | |
| Before 1946 | 32 | 66 | 3 | 101 | (286) |
| 1947–1956 | 44 | 53 | 4 | 101 | (329) |
| 1957–1966 | 36 | 57 | 8 | 101 | (423) |
| 1967–1976 | 36 | 56 | 9 | 101 | (259) |
| 1977–1986 | 47 | 43 | 10 | 100 | (267) |
| 1987–1994 | 35 | 50 | 15 | 100 | (176) |
| 1995–1998 | 60 | 35 | 6 | 101 | (83) |
| **Whites, by level of education** | | | | | |
| Not high school graduate | 35 | 58 | 7 | 100 | (77) |
| High school graduate | 33 | 62 | 6 | 101 | (463) |
| Some college | 30 | 63 | 8 | 101 | (564) |
| College graduate | 42 | 48 | 10 | 100 | (437) |
| Advanced degree | 64 | 31 | 5 | 100 | (306) |

| Social Group | Clinton | Trump | Other | Total | (*N*)[a] |
|---|---|---|---|---|---|
| **Whites, by annual family income** | | | | | |
| Less than $15,000 | 30 | 63 | 7 | 100 | (140) |
| $15,000–34,999 | 39 | 51 | 10 | 100 | (259) |
| $35,000–49,999 | 37 | 57 | 6 | 100 | (201) |
| $50,000–74,999 | 38 | 58 | 5 | 101 | (335) |
| $75,000–89,999 | 36 | 58 | 6 | 100 | (186) |
| $90,000–124,999 | 39 | 51 | 10 | 100 | (292) |
| $125,000–174,999 | 45 | 48 | 6 | 99 | (205) |
| $175,000 and over | 53 | 39 | 8 | 100 | (169) |
| **Whites, by union membership[b]** | | | | | |
| Member | 49 | 47 | 4 | 100 | (311) |
| Nonmember | 37 | 55 | 8 | 100 | (1,542) |
| **Whites, by religion** | | | | | |
| Jewish | 79 | 20 | 2 | 101 | (54) |
| Catholic | 37 | 56 | 7 | 100 | (405) |
| Protestant | 31 | 63 | 6 | 100 | (645) |
| None | 61 | 28 | 11 | 100 | (363) |
| **White Protestants, by whether born again** | | | | | |
| Not born again | 46 | 48 | 6 | 100 | (285) |
| Born again | 18 | 75 | 6 | 99 | (358) |
| **White Protestants, by religious commitment** | | | | | |
| Medium or low | 45 | 50 | 5 | 100 | (272) |
| High | 27 | 64 | 9 | 100 | (256) |
| Very high | 7 | 90 | 3 | 100 | (112) |
| **White Protestants, by religious tradition** | | | | | |
| Mainline | 44 | 52 | 5 | 101 | (294) |
| Evangelical | 19 | 76 | 5 | 100 | (175) |

*Source:* Authors' analysis of the 2016 ANES survey.

[a]Sample includes both face-to-face and Internet respondents. Numbers are weighted.

[b]Respondent or family member in union.

Trump's.[8] Based on the ANES we estimate that Trump's electoral coalition was 84.5 percent white; the exit poll estimate is 87.8 percent white. But this figure is not atypical for Republican presidential nominees. In 2012, for example, it is estimated that 90 to 93 percent of Romney voters were white, larger than the Trump electorate. Clearly, while the Democratic Party is increasingly reliant on black voters as a part of their coalition, the Republican Party is almost wholly dependent upon white voters.

The Democrats continue to hold a decided edge among Latino voters, but Clinton's level of support among Latinos was less than that received by Obama in 2008 and 2012. In his initial election, Obama garnered 75 percent of the Latino vote, and he did equally well in his reelection. As seen in Table 5-1, the ANES reports that Clinton received 69 percent of the Latino vote, a figure in line with the level of Latino support received in 2004 by Democratic nominee John Kerry, who won support from 67 percent from the group. The exit polls suggest that Clinton won 66 percent of the Latino vote. Latinos, of course, are not a homogeneous group.[9] Cuban Americans in South Florida, for example, have traditionally voted Republican, although younger generations now lean Democrat. Unfortunately, we cannot examine differences among Latino groups using the ANES. The pool poll, however, shows that Cuban American voters in Florida split 54 percent to 41 percent in Trump's favor; four years ago, the poll reported that the group voted 50–47 percent in Romney's favor. The data do not allow us to examine the voting behavior of other Latino groups.

Based on data from the ANES and the pool polls, we estimate that Latinos (of all ethnicities) composed roughly 14.2 to 15.1 percent of Clinton's 2016 electorate, depending on the data source, and between 5.2 to 6.7 percent of the Trump electorate. The exit poll estimate for Trump's Latino electorate size (6.7 percent) actually marks a small, one percentage point increase of Romney's Latino electorate (5.7 percent) in 2012. Trump's level of support among Latinos is likely surprising to many given that during the campaign, candidate Trump threatened to build a wall on the Mexican border, deport undocumented immigrants, and described Mexican immigrants as "bringing drugs; they're bringing crime; they're rapists."[10] The battle over the Latino vote is a potentially important one. The U.S. Census predicts that the size of the Latino electorate could grow by as much as 40 percent in the next twelve years. If Latinos' current rate of support for the Democrats were to continue, we estimate that nearly one in five Democratic votes will be cast by Latinos by 2028. This puts tremendous pressure on Republicans. The GOP already lags well behind Democrats in support among Latinos and African Americans; about 34 to 37 percent of Clinton's voters came from these two groups, whereas somewhere between 6.7 to 8.8 percent of Trump's voters did. If Republicans cannot make inroads with these two minority groups, they will be forced to increase their support—through increased turnout and vote share—from white voters.

Gender differences in voting behavior have been pronounced in some European societies, but they have been relatively weak in the United States.[11] Gender differences, whereby men disproportionately support the Republican Party and women the Democratic Party, emerged in the 1980 election and have been found in every election since. According to the exit polls, the "gender gap" was eight percentage points in 1980, six points in 1984, seven points in 1988, four points in 1992, eleven points in 1996, twelve points in 2000, seven points in 2004, seven points in 2008, and ten points in 2012. According to the 2016 exit polls, 54 percent of women and 41 percent of men voted for Clinton, a gap of thirteen points. Among whites Trump received a majority of votes from both men and women, although men were significantly more likely to support him. Trump received 52 percent of the white female vote and 62 percent of the white male vote, for a gap of ten points.

As the gender gap began to emerge, some feminists hoped that women would play a major role in defeating the Republicans.[12] But as we pointed out more than three decades ago, a gender gap does not necessarily help the Democrats.[13] For example, in 1988, George H. W. Bush and Michael Dukakis each won half of the female vote, but Bush won a clear majority of the male vote. Thus Bush benefited from the gender gap in 1988. However, two decades later the role of gender was reversed. In 2008 Obama and McCain split the male vote, whereas Obama won a clear majority among women. By the same logic, then, Obama benefited from the gender gap in 2008. During the intervening elections, Clinton benefited from the gender gap in both 1992 and 1996, and George W. Bush benefited in 2000 and 2004.

Unlike the pool polls, the 2016 ANES (see Table 5-1) finds evidence of a much smaller gender gap in voting. We find a small, two percentage point difference between white women and men in their support for Trump. Like the exit polls, the ANES shows that a majority of white men and women voted for Trump. Hillary Clinton, despite being the first female major party nominee for president, received only 41 percent of the vote from white females, who gave Trump 53 percent of their vote. Among all women voters, Clinton received 55.4 percent of the vote. Thus a significant portion of her support among females is driven by minority women.

As for marital status, in all of our analyses of ANES surveys between 1984 and 2012, we found clear differences between married women and single women.[14] Among all women voters who were married, 42.7 percent voted for Clinton; among those who were never married, 70.2 percent did—a 27.5 point difference. This difference remains large, 16.1 points, if we limit our analysis to white women. Interestingly the 2016 election is one of the few where we see a large marriage gap among men. Among all men, married voters were nineteen points less likely to vote for Clinton than men who had never been married. Indeed the majority of married men (52.3 percent) voted for Trump, whereas the majority of single men (54.3 percent) supported Clinton. This overall difference cannot be attributed wholly to racial differences. Among white men, married voters were 14.6 percentage points less likely to vote for Clinton than those who have never married.

Since the 2000 election, exit polls have shown that sexual orientation is related to the way people vote. In 2000, 70 percent of the respondents who said they were gay, lesbian, or bisexual voted for Gore; in 2004, 77 percent voted for Kerry; in 2008, 70 percent voted for Obama; and in 2012, 76 percent voted for Obama. Although it is difficult to confirm, Obama's ability to increase his support among the LGBT community may have resulted from his actions as president. Obama signed legislation repealing the "don't ask, don't tell" law, which allowed gays to serve in the military so long as they were not open about their sexual orientation, and in May 2012, he unexpectedly declared his support for the legalization of same-sex marriage.[15] In the 2016 exit polls, 5 percent of respondents said that they were gay, lesbian, bisexual, or transgender. Of these voters, 77 percent said they voted for Clinton, thus matching the level of support received by Kerry in 2004 and Obama in 2012. In the five ANES surveys that have inquired about sexual orientation, self-acknowledged homosexuals made up approximately 4 percent of the electorate.[16] In 2016, 5.3 percent of the ANES respondents said they were gay, lesbian, or bisexual.[17] Among homosexual or bisexual voters (*N* = 149), 76 percent voted for Clinton. This is down from the 83 percent of the vote that Obama earned from this group.

As described in Chapter 3, in the 2016 election the political variation among states was higher than in 2012 (and greater than in any election since 1964), suggesting that states were slightly more divided in their support for Trump in 2016 than in recent elections. And there were clear regional differences among white voters. As Table 5.1 shows, Trump garnered electoral majorities from white voters in three of the five regions. Trump, like all recent Republican nominees, fared best in the South, where he won 69 percent of the white vote (consistent with Romney's share in the region four years earlier). Clinton won only 24 percent of the vote among white southerners. The exit poll shows that she fared only marginally better among whites in the one southern state she carried, Virginia, where she captured 35 percent of the white vote. Obama won 38 percent of the vote in Virginia in 2012, a state he too won outright; thus it does not appear that Clinton improved her position among white Virginians despite the presence of the commonwealth's former governor and current U.S. senator on the ballot as her running mate. Trump also won majorities in the border region on the South and in the north central states, but Clinton won a plurality in the Mountain and Pacific region and a majority in the New England and mid-Atlantic region. Exit polls were taken in thirteen of the twenty-two states that define these two regions, and our analysis of these state-level results shows that Clinton outpolled Trump among whites in only four of these states—California, Maine, Oregon, and Washington.

Between Ronald Reagan's election in 1980 and Bill Clinton's reelection in 1996, young voters were more likely to vote Republican than their elders, and the Democrats did best among Americans who came of age before World War II (born before 1924). This was not the case in the 2000, 2004, 2008, and 2012 elections. In these elections the ANES surveys show that Republicans did well among white voters who entered the electorate in the 1980s and who may have been influenced by the pro-Republican tide during the Reagan years. Yet among white voters, those who entered the electorate in the mid-1990s or later, Democrats outgained Republicans. If Democrats were optimistic about their future because of these trends among young voters, they were no doubt ecstatic about Obama's exceptional performance among young adults in 2008. According to the 2008 ANES surveys, Obama won 57 percent of the vote among whites born between 1979 and 2000 (those who were between the ages of eighteen and twenty-nine at the time of the election). The ANES shows Obama lost ground among young white voters in 2012. But Obama remained quite strong among younger nonwhite voters. Indeed, among all voters, Obama won clear majorities with voters thirty-nine years old and younger.

The ANES shows that Trump won majorities from each of the four oldest cohorts (forty and over). Except for eighteen- to twenty-one-year-olds, who were decidedly pro-Clinton, the younger cohorts, overall, were competitive. Among white voters thirty-nine years old or younger, Clinton won a plurality of the vote, 45.3 to

Trump's 43.7 percent. Interestingly the younger cohorts were significantly more likely than older cohorts to cast a ballot for third-party candidates. In 2016, 11 percent of whites under the age of thirty-nine voted for someone other than Clinton or Trump. The pool poll also shows a relationship between age and voting behavior, but unlike the ANES, these polls suggest that whites of all ages supported Trump more than Clinton (although it should be noted that the cohorts are defined differently by the survey organizations). The pool poll shows that Trump fared best among older whites (forty-five and older), earning roughly 60 percent of the vote; he won a plurality of whites (47 percent) between eighteen to twenty-nine years old.

## Social Class, Education, Income, and Union Membership

Traditionally the Democratic Party has fared well among the relatively disadvantaged. It has done better among the working class, voters with lower levels of formal education, and the poor. Moreover, since the 1930s most union leaders have supported the Democratic Party, and union members have been a mainstay of the Democratic presidential coalition. We have been unable to measure social class differences using the 2012 and 2016 ANES surveys because the occupational codes we use to classify respondents as working class (manually employed) and middle class (non-manually employed) are restricted access for privacy concerns and unavailable at the time of this writing. But we do have substantial evidence that class differences as defined by occupation have been declining—a trend found in other advanced democracies.[18] Differences between the more educated and the less educated were relatively strong in 2016, as were income effects.

In 1992 and 1996 Bill Clinton fared best among whites who had not graduated from high school, whereas both George H. W. Bush and Bob Dole fared best among whites who were college graduates (but without advanced degrees). In 1992 Clinton won more than half of the major-party vote among whites with advanced degrees, and in 1996 he won almost half the major-party vote among this group. In 2000 there was a weaker relationship between education and voting preferences, and in 2004 Kerry did best among whites in the highest and lowest educational categories. The 2008 ANES survey found only a weak relationship between level of education and the vote among whites. Moreover, the only educational group among which Obama won a majority of the vote was the small number who had not graduated from high school. In 2012 the ANES showed no discernible relationship between educational attainment and vote choice among whites. Romney won majorities among whites from all levels of education, but he did slightly better among those with a high school degree and those with some college.

In Table 5-1, we see the relationship between education and vote choice in the 2016 ANES. The evidence shows that Trump won clear majorities among whites who had not completed high school, high school graduates, and those with some college. Clinton did much better among whites with a college degree and won a majority of the vote from whites with postgraduate degrees. Indeed, if we collapse these two top categories, we find that Clinton won a majority (51.1 percent) from all whites with college degrees. Thus here we see partial evidence in support of the recent claim that support for Democratic candidates among whites tends to be limited to those who are educated and living in urban areas.[19] Unfortunately we cannot fully test this claim because data identifying whether respondents live in rural or urban areas is not publicly provided by the ANES. The 2016 exit polls—which, again we remind readers, are not nationally representative—also show a strong relationship between education and vote choice among whites. Trump won 18 percentage points more support from those whites without college degrees than he did from those with college degrees.

Scholars such as Jeffrey M. Stonecash and Larry M. Bartels argue that voting differences according to income have been growing in the United States.[20] We find little evidence to support this claim, however. Instead we find evidence that the relationship between income and voting has varied considerably in recent decades and in no discernible pattern. In his victories in 1992 and 1996, for example, Clinton clearly fared much better among the poor than among the affluent. The relationship between income and voting preferences was weaker in both 2000 and 2004, although whites with an annual family income of $50,000 and above were more likely to vote for Bush. In 2008 the ANES data revealed a strong relationship between the respondent's family income and voting choice. Like Clinton's victories, Obama did better among those with lower incomes than those who were wealthier. Among whites with annual family incomes below $50,000, a majority voted for Obama. In all income groups above that level, a majority voted for McCain. Moreover, among whites with family incomes of $150,000 and above, over three in four voted Republican. The 2012 ANES showed a weak negative relationship between annual family income and voting for Obama. In fact, across all income categories except for those making between $125,000 and $174,999, Romney won a majority of the white vote. Obama's majority among this high-income group is perhaps a bit surprising given the expectation many have that wealth is positively related to support for the Republican Party.

The 2016 ANES shows a relationship between income and vote choice similar to that seen in 2012. Once again, the Republican nominee, Trump, did best among whites in the six lowest income categories, winning majorities from all income groups under $125,000. Clinton won a majority among the top earners in our sample, and among top two income categories combined, she won a 48.7 to 44.3 plurality. If we include voters of all races and ethnicities in the analysis, the relationship between income and the vote appears to flip, with low-income voters being more likely than the more affluent to support Clinton. The exit polls, which do not report a breakdown of income and vote share based on race, support this general finding. Thus, as was the case in 2012, it appears that much of the relationship between social class—in this case, measured by income and education—and the vote is conditioned by race and ethnicity.

According to the ANES surveys, Bill Clinton made major gains among white union households between 1992 and 1996. But the 2000 ANES survey shows that Gore slipped twelve percentage points from Clinton's 1996 total, whereas George W. Bush gained sixteen points over Dole's. The 2004 ANES survey shows that Bush made no gains among union households but gained six points among nonunion households. In 2008 the ANES survey shows a five-point loss for the Democrats among white union households but a seven-point gain among nonunion households. Four years later Obama's vote share among white voters in nonunion households declined markedly, a five percentage point drop. This allowed Romney to dominate Obama among nonunion households: 61 to 38 percent.

Our estimates show that despite his appeals to working-class whites and union members, particularly, Trump did no better among union members than Romney did four years earlier, capturing 47 percent of the vote.[21] And Trump's level of support among nonunion whites was lower (55 percent) than Romney's (61). Yet, among union workers, Clinton performed approximately 4 points lower than Obama in 2012, winning a 49 percent plurality. Among nonunion whites, Clinton's 37 percent share was roughly equal to Obama's. Four percent of union workers voted for a third-party candidate in 2016. The exit polls also suggest that Clinton won union voters (51 percent), whereas Trump won nonmember households (48 percent).

## Religion

Religious differences have long played a major role in American politics.[22] In the postwar period, Catholics tended to support the Democrats, whereas white Protestants, especially those outside the South, tended to favor the Republicans. Jews consistently voted more Democratic than any other major religious group. Yet the religious cleavages of old, partly reflecting ethnic differences between Protestants and Catholics, do not necessarily hold today. As noted by David E. Campbell, "the last thirty years have seen a re-sorting of the parties' electoral coalitions along religious lines."[23] As ethnic differences have faded through assimilation and as social and moral issues have become more politically salient, religious denomination plays a smaller role in defining partisan loyalties. Indeed the role of religion in modern politics is not so much about denomination as it is about what Campbell calls "religious devotional style" or religiosity. Today Christian voters who classify themselves as devout in their beliefs and practices—regardless of denomination—tend to support the Republican Party.[24] This has allowed the Republicans to benefit electorally from a "coalition of the religious," which brings together groups that are sometimes theologically and politically disparate (if not antagonistic), evangelical Christians, traditionalist Catholics, and Mormons.[25]

In the 2016 election Hillary Clinton won a plurality of the Catholic vote (47.6 to 45.3 percent), much smaller than Barack Obama's majority (55.1 to 44.9 percent) with the group four years earlier against Mitt Romney. But Clinton's plurality support among *all* Catholics belies her relationship with *many* Catholic voters, as well as the Church hierarchy, and says much about ethnic changes among American Catholics.[26] Roughly three in ten voters in 2016 was a self-identified Catholic, but the "Catholic vote" is hardly a monolith. White Catholics voted in favor of Donald Trump, awarding him 55.9 percent of the vote to Clinton's 30.8 percent. Obama did markedly better among white Catholic voters four years earlier, when the 2012 ANES showed that he garnered 47.2 percent of the white Catholic vote to Romney's 52.8 percent. Obviously Clinton's primary source of support among American Catholics was from Latinos, who represent about a third of all Catholics in the United States (and also a third of Catholic voters in the 2016 ANES).[27]

Although the Republican Party has been successful among white Protestants, it has been more successful among some than others. The Republican emphasis on traditional values may have special appeal to Protestants who share them. George W. Bush's policies such as limiting funding for embryonic stem cell research, calling for an amendment to the U.S. Constitution to ban same-sex marriage, and appointing conservatives to the federal courts may have appealed to Christian conservatives. But Romney's Mormon faith and previous support for abortion rights—although he has consistently opposed same-sex nuptials and stem cell research—may have given some socially conservative evangelical Protestants cause for concern. In 2016 the question was whether white Christian conservatives would lend their support to Donald Trump, a nominal mainline Protestant who has been married three times and was secretly recorded making lewd comments about his own treatment of women

We focus here on differences among white Protestants. For example, for the 1992, 1996, 2000, 2008, and 2012 ANES surveys, we examined differences between white Protestants who said they were "born again" and those who had not had this religious experience.[28] In all five surveys, white born-again Protestants were more likely to vote Republican than those who were not. In 2016, 47.6 percent of the white Protestants who said they had not had this religious experience voted for Trump; among those who said they were born again, 75.3 percent voted for Trump. Among born-again Protestants, Clinton only received 18.4 percent of the vote. The 2016 pool poll also asked Protestants if they considered themselves born again or not. According to this survey, among born-again Christians—roughly one-fourth of all Protestants—Trump outpolled Clinton 80 percent to 16 percent. Finally white Protestants affiliated with evangelical denominations were 24 percentage points more likely to vote for Trump than those who were affiliated with mainline congregations.

As we noted earlier Campbell argues that the role of religion in modern politics is not so much about denomination as it is about "religious devotional style" or religiosity. The point is similarly made by Lyman A. Kellstedt, who argues that religious commitment has an important effect on voting behavior.[29] According to the 2012 ANES, religious commitment was strongly associated with voting for the Republican nominee, Mitt Romney. Figure 5-1 presents the results from the ANES for all Protestants and Catholics voters, and religious commitment appears to have mattered in 2016.[30] Trump won nearly 90 percent of the vote from those voters who held a "very high" religious commitment; among whites who had low levels of religious commitment, Clinton won 49.8 to 42.3. This division is particularly pronounced among Protestants. White Protestants with very high religious commitment were approximately 40 percentage points more likely to vote for Trump than those with low religious commitment. White Catholics with "high" levels of commitment were 18 percentage points more likely to vote for Trump than white Catholics with low commitment.[31]

## HOW SOCIAL GROUPS VOTED DURING THE POSTWAR YEARS

Although we found sharp racial/ethnic and religious differences in voting, most other social differences in voting behavior were relatively modest in 2016. How does this election compare with other presidential elections? Do the relationships between social variables and the vote found in 2016 result from long-term trends that have changed the importance of social factors? To answer these questions, we will examine the voting behavior of social groups that were an important part of the Democrat's New Deal coalition during the postwar years. Understanding the nature of this broad coalition and its subsequent collapse helps place current American politics into a broader historical perspective—and, in our view, this helps us understand better that the politics that brought Donald Trump to office in 2016 are not very different from (indeed are a product of) the politics of the recent past. Our analysis, which will begin with the 1944 election between Roosevelt and Thomas Dewey, uses a simple measure to assess the effect of social forces over time.

In his lucid discussion of the logic of party coalitions, Robert Axelrod analyzed six basic groups that made up the Democrat's New Deal coalition: the poor, southerners, blacks (and other nonwhites), union members (and members of their families), Catholics and other non-Protestants such as Jews, and residents of the twelve largest metropolitan areas.[32] John R. Petrocik's more comprehensive study of the Democratic coalition identified fifteen groups and classified seven of them as predominantly Democratic: blacks, lower-status native southerners, middle- and upper-status southerners, Jews, Polish and Irish Catholics, union members, and lower-status, border-state whites.[33] A more recent analysis by Harold W. Stanley, William T. Bianco, and Richard G. Niemi analyzes seven pro-Democratic groups: blacks, Catholics, Jews, women, native white southerners, members of union households, and the working class.[34] Our own analysis focuses on race, region, union membership, social class, and religion.

The contribution that a social group can make to a party's coalition depends on three factors: the relative size of the group in the total electorate, its level of turnout compared with that of the total electorate, and its relative loyalty to the political party.[35] The larger a social group, the greater its contribution can be. For example, African Americans make up 11.3 percent of the electorate; the white working class makes up about 30 percent. Thus the potential contribution of blacks is smaller than that of the white working class. Historically the electoral power of blacks was limited by their relatively low turnout. But black turnout has increased substantially in recent elections and has been comparable to white turnout. Moreover, because blacks vote overwhelmingly Democratic, their contribution to the Democratic Party can be greater than their group size would indicate. And the relative size of their contribution grows as whites desert the Democratic Party.

## Race

We begin by examining racial differences, which we can trace back to 1944 by using the National Opinion Research Center (NORC) study for that year.[36] Figure 5-1 shows the percentages of white and black major-party voters who voted Democratic for president from 1944 to 2016. (All six figures in this chapter are based on major-party voters only.) After emancipation and the passage of the Fifteenth Amendment, most blacks voters—when not deprived of their voting right under Jim Crow—tended to vote for the Republican Party, the "Party of Lincoln." By 1932, however, those old allegiances had begun to change, and the GOP could no longer count of the solid support of black voters. Although most African Americans voted Democratic from 1944 to 1960, a substantial minority voted Republican. Yet the political mobilization of blacks, spurred by the civil rights movement and by the Republican candidacy of Barry Goldwater in 1964, evaporated black support for the Republican Party, and the residual Republican loyalties of older blacks were discarded between 1962 and 1964.[37]

**Figure 5-1 Major-Party Voters Who Voted Democratic for President, by Race, 1944–2016 (Percent)**

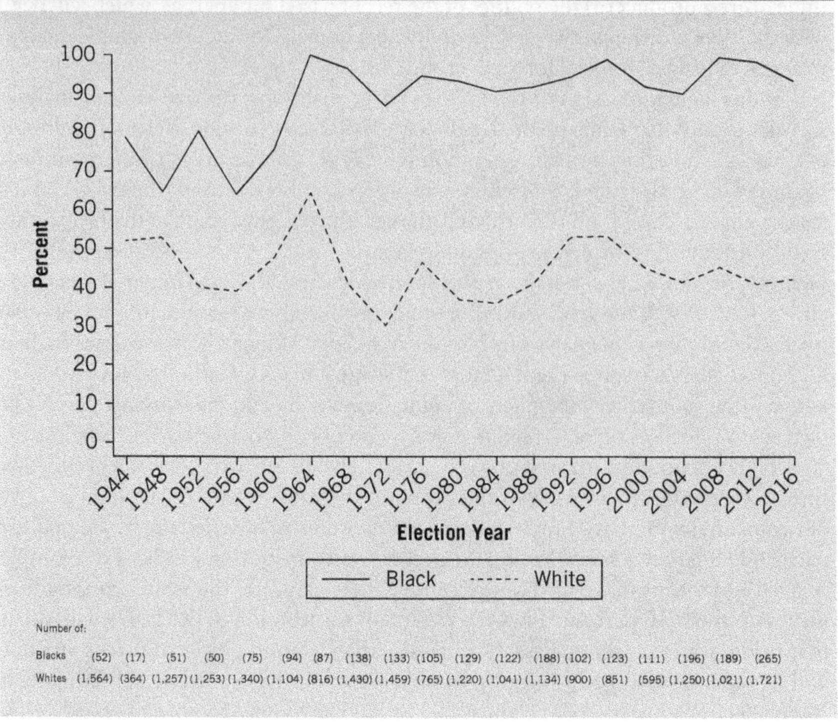


*Source:* Authors' analysis of the ANES surveys.

*Note:* Numbers are weighted.

Although the Democrats made substantial gains among blacks, they lost ground among whites. From 1944 to 1964 the Democrats gained a majority of the white vote in three of six elections. Since 1964 the Democrats have never again won a majority of the white vote. However, in a two-candidate contest, a Democrat can win with just under half the white vote, as the 1960, 1976, 2008, and 2012 elections demonstrate. (Of course, in 2016, Hillary Clinton won the popular vote while only capturing 39.2 percent of the white vote. But her relatively low levels of support among white voters also hurt her in several states, such as Pennsylvania and Wisconsin, which cost her in the Electoral College.) In the three-candidate contests of 1992 and 1996, Bill Clinton was able to win with only about two-fifths of the white vote.[38]

The gap between the two trend lines in Figure 5-1 illustrates the overall difference in the Democratic vote between whites and blacks. Table 5-2 shows the overall level of "racial voting" in the six elections from 1944 to 2016 as well as four other measures of social cleavage.

**Table 5-2 Relationship of Social Characteristics to Presidential Voting, 1944–2016**

| | Election Year (Percentage-Point Difference) | | | | | | | | | | | | | | | | | | |
|---|---|---|---|---|---|---|---|---|---|---|---|---|---|---|---|---|---|---|---|
| | 1944 | 1948 | 1952 | 1956 | 1960 | 1964 | 1968 | 1972 | 1976 | 1980 | 1984 | 1988 | 1992 | 1996 | 2000 | 2004 | 2008 | 2012 | 2016 |
| Racial voting[a] | 27 | 12 | 40 | 25 | 23 | 36 | 56 | 57 | 48 | 56 | 54 | 51 | 41 | 47 | 47 | 49 | 54 | 57 | 51 |
| **Regional voting[b]** | | | | | | | | | | | | | | | | | | | |
| Among whites | — | — | 12 | 17 | 6 | −11 | −4 | −13 | 1 | 1 | −9 | −5 | −10 | −8 | −20 | −10 | −14 | −16 | −22 |
| Among entire electorate (ANES surveys) | — | — | 9 | 15 | 4 | −5 | 6 | −3 | 7 | 3 | 3 | 2 | 0 | 0 | −10 | 1 | −11 | −2 | −11 |
| Among entire electorate (official election results) | 23 | 14 | 8 | 8 | 3 | −13 | −3 | −11 | 5 | 2 | −5 | −7 | −6 | −7 | −8 | −8 | −10 | −9 | −6 |
| **Union voting[c]** | | | | | | | | | | | | | | | | | | | |
| Among whites | 20 | 37 | 18 | 15 | 21 | 23 | 13 | 11 | 18 | 15 | 20 | 16 | 12 | 23 | 12 | 21 | 8 | 15 | 11 |
| Among entire electorate | 20 | 37 | 20 | 17 | 19 | 22 | 13 | 10 | 17 | 16 | 19 | 15 | 11 | 23 | 11 | 18 | 6 | 10 | 9 |

*(Continued)*

**Table 5-2** (Continued)

| | Election Year (Percentage-Point Difference) | | | | | | | | | | | | | | | | | | |
|---|---|---|---|---|---|---|---|---|---|---|---|---|---|---|---|---|---|---|---|
| | 1944 | 1948 | 1952 | 1956 | 1960 | 1964 | 1968 | 1972 | 1976 | 1980 | 1984 | 1988 | 1992 | 1996 | 2000 | 2004 | 2008 | 2012 | 2016 |
| **Class voting**[d] | | | | | | | | | | | | | | | | | | | |
| Among whites | 19 | 44 | 20 | 8 | 12 | 19 | 10 | 2 | 17 | 9 | 8 | 5 | 4 | 6 | –6 | 3 | 3 | — | — |
| Among entire electorate | 20 | 44 | 22 | 11 | 13 | 20 | 15 | 4 | 21 | 15 | 12 | 8 | 8 | 9 | 2 | 4 | 4 | — | — |
| **Religious voting**[e] | | | | | | | | | | | | | | | | | | | |
| Among whites | 25 | 21 | 18 | 10 | 48 | 21 | 30 | 13 | 15 | 10 | 16 | 18 | 20 | 14 | 8 | 19 | 15 | 16 | 7 |
| Among entire electorate | 24 | 19 | 15 | 10 | 46 | 16 | 21 | 8 | 11 | 3 | 9 | 11 | 10 | 7 | 2 | 5 | 9 | 7 | 13 |

*Sources:* Authors' analysis of a 1944 NORC survey, official election results, and ANES surveys.

*Notes:* All calculations are based upon major-party voters. — indicates not available.

[a]Percentage of blacks who voted Democratic minus percentage of whites who voted Democratic.

[b]Percentage of southerners who voted Democratic minus percentage of voters outside the South who voted Democratic. Comparable data for region were not available for the surveys conducted in 1944 and 1948.

[c]Percentage of members of union households who voted Democratic minus percentage of members of households with no union members who voted Democratic.

[d]Percentage of working class that voted Democratic minus percentage of middle class that voted Democratic. The data for occupation needed to classify respondents according to their social class for 2012 and 2016 are restricted for privacy concerns.

[e]Percentage of Catholics who voted Democratic minus the percentage of Protestants who voted Democratic.

From 1944 to 1964 racial differences in voting ranged from a low of twelve percentage points to a high of forty points. These differences then rose to fifty-six percentage points in 1968 (sixty-one points if Wallace voters are included with Nixon voters) and did not fall to the forty percentage point level until 1992.[39] Racial voting was higher in the 1996, 2000, and 2004 contests but increased markedly in the elections of Barack Obama. In 2008 there was a forty-four percentage point gap between blacks and whites, and in 2012 that gap increased to fifty-seven points, matching the record high level of racial voting found in 1972. Obama's elections exhibit the highest levels of racial voting in any elections in which the Democratic candidate has won. In 2016 racial differences in voting contracted only slightly, by six points, to a fifty-one percentage point gap. Thus America has not experienced a racial gap in voting of less than forty percentage points since 1964, more than a half century ago.

Not only did African American loyalty to the Democratic Party increase sharply after 1960, but black turnout rose considerably from 1960 to 1968 because southern blacks were enfranchised. And while black turnout rose, white turnout outside the South declined. Between 1960, when overall turnout was highest, and 1996, when postwar turnout was lowest, turnout fell by about fifteen percentage points among the voting-age population.[40] Between 1996 and 2008, turnout in the United States rose by roughly eight percentage points. In the 2000 and 2004 election, turnout among whites and blacks increased at approximately the same rate. Yet in the 2008 and 2012 election, the groups moved in opposite directions, with black turnout continuing to rise and white turnout declining to the point where black turnout exceeded white turnout in 2012. Yet the trend lines reversed course between 2012 and 2016. As noted in Chapter 4, black voter turnout declined by seven percentage points, whereas white turnout increased 1.2 percentage points.

From 1948 to 1960 African Americans never accounted for more than one Democratic vote in twelve. In 1964, however, Johnson received about one in seven of his votes from blacks, and blacks contributed a fifth of the Democratic totals in both 1968 and 1972. In the 1976 election, which saw Democratic gains among whites, Jimmy Carter won only about one in seven of his votes from blacks, and in 1980, one in four. In the next three elections, about one in five Democratic votes were from blacks. In 1996 about one in six of Clinton's votes came from black voters, and in 2000 about one in five of Gore's votes did. In 2004 between a fifth and a fourth of Kerry's total vote was provided by black voters. Both Gore and Kerry came very close to winning, even with this heavy reliance on African American voters. In both 2008 and 2012, black voters accounted for about one-fourth of Obama's total vote. No Democratic presidential winner had ever drawn this large a share of his total vote from these voters. Hillary Clinton received about one in five of all of her votes from blacks, lower than the share received by Obama but comparable to that received by the Democratic nominees in 1984, 1988, 1992, 2000, and 2004. Thus it is fair to say that Obama's elections aside, the size of the Democratic Party black electoral base has been relatively consistent over the past three decades.

## Region

White southerners' desertion of the Democratic Party is arguably the most dramatic change in postwar American politics . . . and the most consequential for the electoral fortunes of the Republican Party. As we saw in Chapter 3, regional differences can be analyzed using official election statistics, but these statistics are of limited use in examining race-related differences in regional voting because election results are not tabulated by race. Consequently we rely on survey data to document the dramatic shift in voting behavior among white southerners.

As Figure 5-2 reveals, white southerners were somewhat more Democratic than whites outside the South in the 1952 and 1956 contests between Dwight Eisenhower and Adlai Stevenson and in the 1960 contest between John Kennedy and Richard Nixon.[41] But in the next three elections, regional differences were reversed, with white southerners voting more Republican than whites outside the South. In 1976 and 1980, when the Democrats fielded Jimmy Carter of Georgia as their standard-bearer, white southerners and whites outside the South voted very much alike. But since 1980 southern whites have been less likely than nonsouthern whites to vote Democratic, by an average difference of 12.6 percentage points. In 1984 and 1988 white southerners were less likely to vote Democratic than whites from any other region. In 1992 and 1996 Bill Clinton and his running mate, Al Gore, were both from the South. Even so, George H. W. Bush in 1992 and Bob Dole in 1996 did better among white southerners than among whites from any other region.[42] In 2000 the Democrats ran the southerner Gore, with Joseph Lieberman of Connecticut as his running mate. The Republican candidate, George W. Bush, the governor of Texas, was also a southerner, and his running mate, Dick Cheney, who had become a resident of Texas, moved back to Wyoming to reestablish his residence.[43] In 2004 the Democrats ran John Kerry, the junior senator from Massachusetts, although John Edwards, his running mate, was from North Carolina. But in both these contests, the Democratic vote in the South was low, and the Democrats did substantially better outside the South. In both 2008 and 2012, neither party ran a southerner on its ticket. In Obama's 2008 election, the Democrats made gains among both white southerners and among whites outside the South. But, as Figure 5-2 shows, the Democrats' support among whites in both regions receded in 2012. In 2016 both Hillary Clinton and Donald Trump were residents of New York. Although Clinton could claim a connection to the South, having been the First Lady of the State of Arkansas for eleven years, this was of little help to the Democratic nominee. Regional differences among whites set a record high for the modern period in 2016, with white southerners being twenty-two percentage points less likely to vote Democratic than white nonsoutherners.

Regional differences among whites from 1952 to 2016 are summarized in Table 5-2. The negative signs for 1964, 1968, 1972, and 1984–2016 reveal that the Democratic candidate fared better outside the South than in the South. As we saw in Chapter 3, in 1968 Wallace had a strong regional base in the South. If we include Wallace voters with Nixon voters, regional differences change markedly, moving from –4 to –12.

Table 5-2 also presents regional differences for the entire electorate. Here, however, we present two sets of estimates: (1) the ANES results from 1952 to 2016 and (2) the results we computed using official election statistics. Both sets of statistics indicate that regional differences have been reversed, but these results are often different and in many cases would lead to substantially different conclusions. The 2004 election provides a clear example. According to the 2004 ANES survey, voters in the South

**Figure 5-2 White Major-Party Voters Who Voted Democratic for President, by Region, 1952–2016 (Percent)**

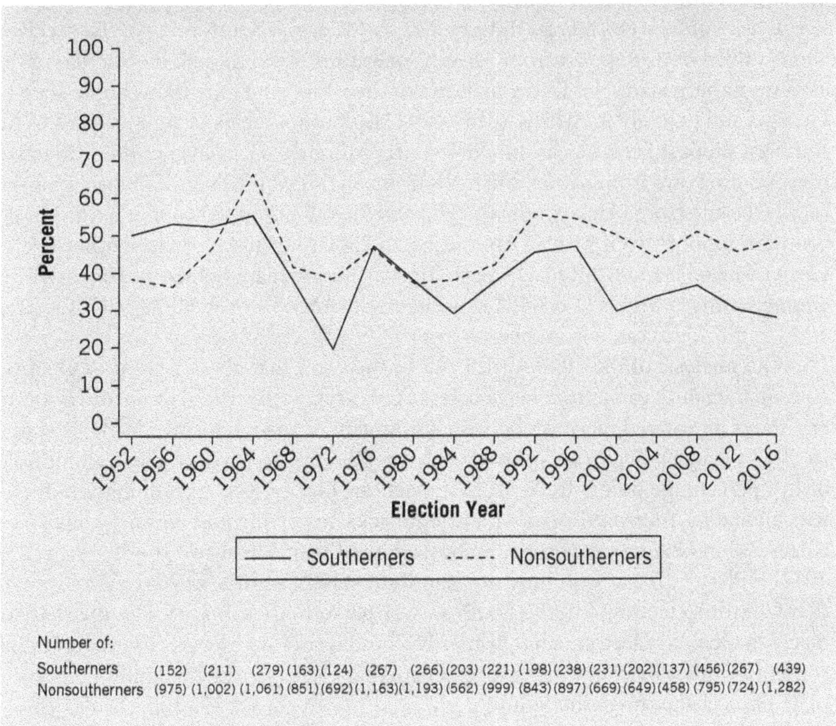


*Source:* Authors' analysis of ANES surveys.

*Note:* Numbers are weighted.

were as likely to vote Democratic as voters outside the South. But we know that this result is wrong. After all Bush won all the southern states, whereas Kerry won nineteen states outside the South as well as the District of Columbia. In fact the official statistics show that southerners were eight points more likely to vote Republican than voters outside the South. In this case, the ANES results, which are based on a sample of eight hundred voters, overestimated the number of Democratic voters in the South. This should remind us of a basic caution in studying elections: always turn to the actual election results before turning to the survey data.

Surveys are useful in demonstrating the way in which the mobilization of southern blacks and the defection of southern whites from the Democratic Party dramatically transformed the Democratic coalition in the South.[44] According to our analysis of ANES surveys, between 1952 and 1960 Democratic presidential candidates never received more than one in fifteen of their votes in the South from blacks. In 1964 three in ten of Johnson's southern votes came from black voters, and in 1968 Hubert Humphrey received as many votes from southern blacks as from southern whites. In 1972, according to these data, George McGovern received more votes from southern blacks than from southern whites.

Black voters were crucial to Carter's success in the South in 1976; he received about a third of his support from African Americans. Even though he won ten of the eleven southern states, he won a majority of the white vote only in his home state of Georgia and possibly in Arkansas. In 1980 Carter again received about a third of his southern support from blacks. In 1984 Walter Mondale received about four in ten of his southern votes from blacks, and in 1988 one in three of the votes Michael Dukakis received came from black voters. In 1992 and 1996 Clinton won about a third of his southern support from African Americans. In 2000 four in ten of the southern votes Gore received came from blacks. A southern running mate helped Kerry very little among southern whites in 2004. According to the ANES survey, about half of Kerry's votes in the South came from blacks.

Our analysis of the 2008 ANES survey indicates that about a third of Obama's votes in the South came from black voters. And blacks were crucial to the three southern states he carried, because he won a minority of the white vote in those states. In 2012 Obama's electorate in the South was roughly 38 percent black, an increase of five percentage points from his first election. This reflects a combination of factors, including increased turnout among blacks, lower turnout among whites, and a decrease in Obama's vote share among whites. Obama won two southern states in 2012. Hillary Clinton won only one southern state, Virginia, in 2016. We estimate that Clinton's electorate in the South was 41 percent black, larger than the share of blacks in Obama's electorate but primarily a product of lower levels of support among southern whites. By comparison we estimate that blacks represented only 1.3 percent of Trump's electorate in the South.

## Union Membership

Figure 5-3 shows the percentage of white union members and nonmembers who voted Democratic for president from 1944 to 2016. Over the course of the postwar period, Democrats have enjoyed a higher level of support from union members than nonmembers, but this has not always resulted in a majority of union votes. In all six elections between 1944 and 1964, the majority of white union members (and members of their households) voted Democratic. In 1968 Humphrey won a slight majority of the union vote, although his total would be cut to 43 percent if Wallace voters were included. The Democrats won about three-fifths of the union vote in 1976, when Jimmy Carter defeated Gerald Ford. In 1988 Dukakis appears to have won a slight majority of the white union vote, although he fell well short of Carter's 1976 tally. In 1992 Bill Clinton won three-fifths of the major-party union vote and won nearly half the total union vote. In 1996 the ANES data show him making major gains and winning 70 percent of the major-party vote among union members. In 2000 Gore won a majority of the union vote, but he was well below Clinton's 1996 tally. In 2004 Kerry did slightly better than Gore among white union voters, but Bush did somewhat better among nonmembers. Because there are more nonmembers than members, this shift worked to Bush's advantage. In 2008 the Democrats' support among white union members declined from 2004 levels, but Obama nonetheless won a small majority of white union voters. Obama made significant gains among nonmembers in 2008, obviously a net benefit for the Democrats. Obama maintained his majority support among white union members in 2012, again winning about 53 percent of the white union vote. But Obama's support from whites from nonmember households dropped precipitously, by roughly six points.

Hillary Clinton's support among union members was slightly less than that received by Obama in his two elections. Nevertheless, Clinton won a majority of white union voters, 51.4 percent, while receiving 40.4 percent support from nonunion whites. Clearly unions continue to be an important vehicle for mobilizing white voters' support for the Democratic Party, but the gap in support from union versus nonunion voters has contracted some since the heyday of the New Deal coalition.

Differences in presidential voting between union members and nonmembers are presented in Table 5-2. Because in 1968 Wallace did better among union members

**Figure 5-3 White Major-Party Voters Who Voted Democratic for President, by Union Membership, 1944–2016 (Percent)**

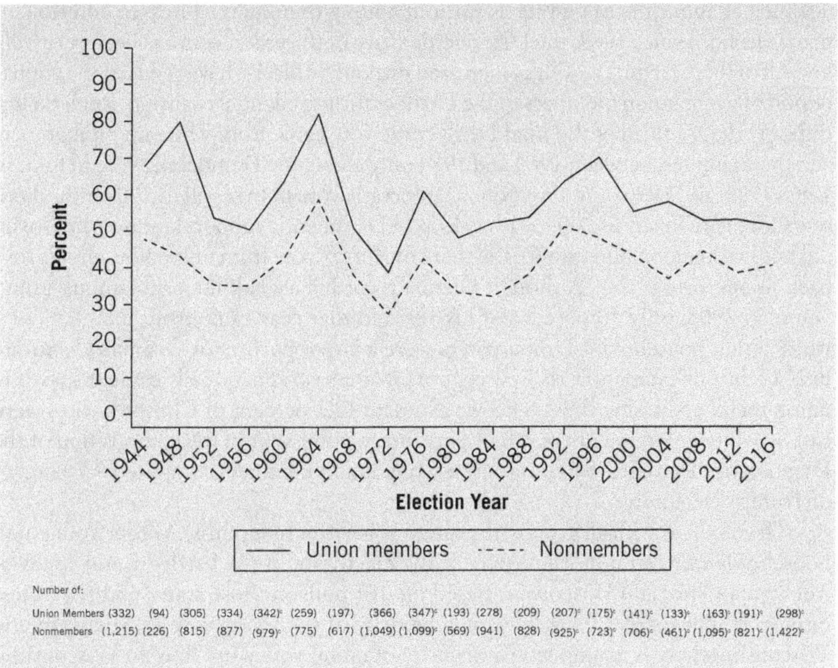

Percent

100 90 80 70 60 50 40 30 20 10 0

1944 1948 1952 1956 1960 1964 1968 1972 1976 1980 1984 1988 1992 1996 2000 2004 2008 2012 2016

Election Year

Union members ----- Nonmembers

Number of:

Union Members (332) (94) (305) (334) (342)[c] (259) (197) (366) (347)[c] (193) (278) (209) (207)[c] (175)[c] (141)[c] (133)[c] (163)[c] (191)[c] (298)[c]

Nonmembers (1,215) (226) (815) (877) (979)[c] (775) (617) (1,049) (1,099)[c] (569) (941) (828) (925)[c] (723)[c] (706)[c] (461)[c] (1,095)[c] (821)[c] (1,422)[c]

*Source:* Authors' analysis of ANES surveys.

*Note:* "Union members" indicates that the respondent is a union member or lives in a union household. "Nonmembers" indicates that the respondent is not a union member nor lives in a union household. Data are weighted.

than nonmembers, including Wallace voters, with Nixon voters reducing union voting from thirteen percentage points to ten. Union voting was highest in 1948, a year when Truman's opposition to the Taft-Hartley Act gained him strong union support.[45] Union voting was low in 1992 and 2000, when white union members were only slightly more likely to vote Democratic than nonmembers. Because Bush did better among nonmembers in 2004, the differences between members and nonmembers rose to twenty-one points. Differences between members and nonmembers were sharply reduced in 2008, reaching the lowest level in any of the preceding seventeen elections, although the differences were expanded—due to a loss in vote share among white nonunion households—during his reelection bid in 2012. In 2016 the gap in member/nonmember voting differential decreased by four percentage points with symmetrical forces seemingly at play; union members lowered their support for the Democratic nominee by two points, whereas nonmembers increased their support by two points. Table 5-2 also shows the results for the entire electorate, but because blacks are about as likely to live in union households as whites, including blacks has little effect in most years.

The percentage of the total electorate composed of white union members and their families has declined during the postwar years. White union members and their families made up 25 percent of the electorate in 1952; in 2016, according to the ANES survey, they made up only 16 percent.[46] Turnout among white union members has declined at about the same rate as turnout among nonunion whites. In addition, in many elections since 1964, the Democratic share of the union vote has been relatively low. All of these factors, as well as increased turnout by blacks, have reduced the contribution of white union members to the Democratic presidential coalition. Remarkably, through 1960, a third of the total Democratic vote came from white union members and their families; between 1964 and 1984 only about one Democratic vote in four; in 1988, 1992, and 1996 only about one Democratic vote in five; and in 2000 only about one Gore vote in six. In 2004, with a drop in Democratic support among whites who did not live in union households, the share of Kerry's vote from union households rose back to one vote in five. Although Obama recorded a small majority among union voters in 2008, only 10 percent of his votes in that year came from members of a white union household.[47] Union voters were a larger portion of Obama's electorate in 2012; by our estimation 16.1 percent of Obama's votes nationally came from white union members. Using the ANES we estimate 12.3 percent of Clinton's votes were cast by white union members, a four percentage point shift in the composition of the Democratic electorate. By comparison white union members composed 9.7 percent of Trump's electorate.

Of course, as with all groups, the union vote is not monolithic. Voters from union households were an important part of the electorate in the battleground states of Michigan, Ohio, and Wisconsin. Based on exit polls in those states and regardless of race, it appears that Clinton won a majority of the union vote in Michigan and Wisconsin, whereas Trump won a majority of union voters in Ohio. In Wisconsin it is estimated that 21 percent of all voters were union members; of these Clinton won 53 to 43 percent. By our estimate, 24 percent of Clinton's voters in Wisconsin were from union households (19.1 percent of Trump voters). Clinton also did well garnering union support in Michigan, where roughly 28 percent of the electorate belong to unions. Of these voters Clinton won 53 to 40 percent. In Michigan 31.4 percent of Clinton voters were union members (23.6 percent of Trump voters). Despite this support, of course, Clinton lost both states. She also lost Ohio, but in the Buckeye State, union voters were decidedly pro-Trump. The billionaire Republican won 54 percent of union voters to Clinton's 41 percent. Approximately one quarter of all Trump voters in Ohio were union members; one-fifth of Clinton's voters were.

## Social Class

The broad social cleavage between manually employed workers (and their dependents) and non-manually employed workers (and their dependents) is especially valuable for studying comparative behavior.[48] For this reason we present the results of our analysis in Figure 5-4, even though we are not yet able to analyze the ANES results for 2012 and 2016 due to a lack of available data. The figure shows the percentage of white major-party voters who voted Democratic among the working class and the middle class in all the presidential elections between 1944 and 2008.

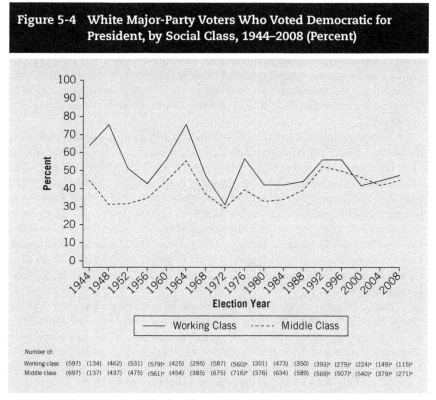

**Figure 5-4 White Major-Party Voters Who Voted Democratic for President, by Social Class, 1944–2008 (Percent)**

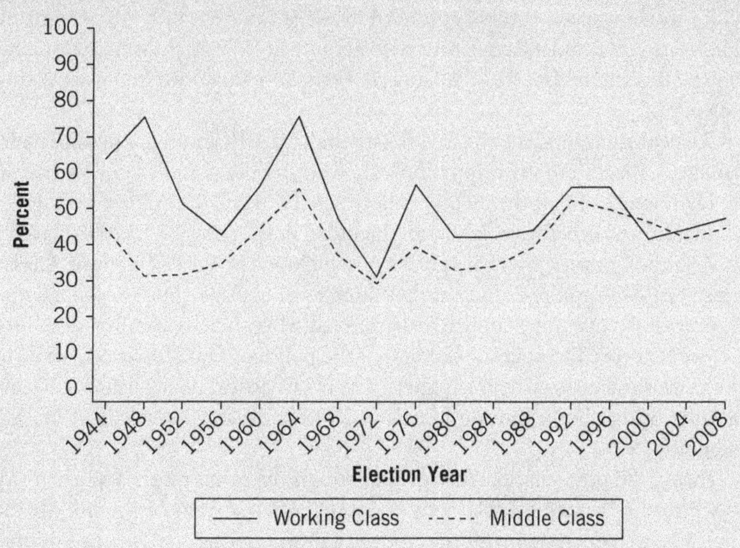

Percent

Election Year

Working Class ----- Middle Class

Number of:

| | | | | | | | | | | | | | | | | | |
|---|---|---|---|---|---|---|---|---|---|---|---|---|---|---|---|---|---|
| Working class | (597) | (134) | (462) | (531) | (579)[a] | (425) | (295) | (587) | (560)[a] | (301) | (473) | (350) | (393)[a] | (279)[a] | (224)[a] | (149)[a] | (115)[a] |
| Middle class | (697) | (137) | (437) | (475) | (561)[a] | (454) | (385) | (675) | (716)[a] | (376) | (634) | (589) | (569)[a] | (507)[a] | (540)[a] | (379)[a] | (271)[a] |

*Source:* Authors' analysis of a 1944 NORC survey and ANES surveys.

*Note:* Numbers are weighted.

In all fourteen presidential elections between 1944 and 1996, the white working class voted more Democratic than the white middle class. But as Figure 5-4 shows, the percentage of white working-class voters who voted Democratic has varied considerably from election to election. It reached its lowest level in 1972, during the Nixon-McGovern contest. Carter regained a majority of the white working-class vote class in 1976, but he lost it four years later. Bill Clinton won only two-fifths of the vote among working-class whites in the three-candidate race of 1992, although he did win a clear majority of the major-party vote among working-class whites. The 1996 election again featured a strong third-party candidate, but Clinton won half of the working-class vote and a clear majority of the major-party vote among this group. In 2000 Gore won only two-fifths of the vote among working-class whites, and 2000 is the only election during these years in which the Democratic presidential candidate did better among middle-class whites than among working-class whites. Support for the Democrats among the white working class increased slightly in 2004, but their vote share among the middle class declined, and John Kerry failed to win a majority among either group. The 2008 ANES is the last survey for which we have data on working-class and middle-class voting. Figure 5-4 shows that Obama improved his party's standing among working-class and middle-class voters in 2008, gaining around three percentage points among each group, but he failed to win a majority from either.

Although levels of class voting have varied over the last six decades, they have clearly followed a downward trend, as Table 5-2 reveals.[49] Class voting was even lower in 1968, if Wallace voters are included with Nixon voters, because 15 percent of white working-class voters supported Wallace, whereas only 10 percent of white middle-class voters did. Class voting was very low in 1972, mainly because many white working-class voters deserted McGovern. Only in 2000 do we find class voting to be negative.[50]

Class voting trends are affected substantially if African Americans are included in the analysis. Blacks are disproportionately working class, and they vote overwhelmingly Democratic. In all the elections between 1976 and 1996, class voting is higher when blacks (and other nonwhites) are included in the analysis. In 2000 class voting is positive (although very low) when blacks are included in our calculations. Class voting increased in 2004 and remained at that same level in 2008. The overall trend toward declining class voting is somewhat dampened when blacks are included. However, black workers vote Democratic because of the politics of race, not necessarily because they are working class. Obviously there was no statistical relationship between social class and voting choice among blacks in 2008 because 99 percent of blacks voted Democratic.[51]

During the postwar years the proportion of the electorate made up of working-class whites has remained relatively constant, whereas that of the middle class has grown. The percentage of whites in the agricultural sector has declined dramatically. Turnout fell among both the middle and working classes after 1960, but it fell more among the working class. Declining turnout and defections from the Democratic Party by working-class whites, along with increased turnout by blacks, have reduced the total white working-class contribution to the Democratic presidential coalition.

In 1948 and 1952 about half the Democratic vote came from working-class whites, and from 1956 through 1964, this social group supplied more than four in ten

Democratic votes. Its contribution fell to just over a third in 1968 and then to under a third in 1972. In 1976, with the rise in class voting, the white working class provided nearly two-fifths of Carter's total, but it provided just over a third four years later in Carter's reelection bid. In 1984 more than a third of Mondale's total support came from this group, and in 1988 Dukakis received more than two in five of his votes from this group. In both 1992 and 1996, working-class whites provided three in ten votes of Clinton's total, but in 2000 this group accounted for only about a fifth of Gore's votes. In 2004, with a drop in middle-class support for the Democratic candidate, Kerry received just under a fourth of his vote from working-class whites. Obama obtained only 15 percent of his votes from white working-class voters, a significant departure from 2004 and far below the group's contribution to the Democratic coalition in the early postwar years.

The white middle-class contribution to the Democratic presidential coalition amounted to fewer than three in ten votes in 1948 and 1952, and just under one-third in 1956, stabilizing at just over one-third in the next five elections. In 1984 Mondale received fewer than two in five of his votes from middle-class whites, and in 1988 Dukakis received more than two in five. In 1992 more than two in five of Clinton's total votes came from this group, rising to a half in 1996. In 2000 Gore received two-fifths of his total vote from middle-class whites, and in 2004 Kerry received just over two-fifths. In 2008 Obama received around 37 percent of his votes from middle-class whites. In all of the elections between 1984 and 2008, the Democrats received a larger share of their vote from middle-class whites than from working-class whites. The increasing middle-class contribution stems from two factors: (1) although objectively the middle class is shrinking, the percentage of individuals who classify themselves as "middle class" has increased, and (2) class differences are eroding.[52] The decline in class differences is a widespread phenomenon in advanced industrialized societies.[53]

Of course our argument that class-based voting is declining depends on the way in which we have defined social class. Different definitions may yield different results. For example, in a major study depending on a far more complex definition that divides the electorate into seven social categories, Jeff Manza and Clem Brooks, using ANES data from 1952 to 1996, conclude that class differences are still important.[54] But their findings actually support our conclusion that the New Deal coalition has eroded. For example, they found that professionals were the most Republican class in the 1950s, but that by the 1996 election they had become the most Democratic.

## Religion

Voting differences among major religious groups have also declined during the postwar years. Even so, as Figure 5-5 reveals, in every election since 1944, Jews have been more likely to vote Democratic than Catholics, and Catholics have been more likely to vote Democratic than Protestants.[55]

As Figure 5-5 shows a large majority of Jews voted Democratic in every election from 1944 to 1968, and although the percentage declined in Nixon's landslide over McGovern in 1972, even McGovern won a majority of the Jewish vote. In 1980 many Jews (like many Gentiles) were dissatisfied with Carter's performance as president, and some resented the pressure he had exerted on Israel to accept the Camp David

## Figure 5-5 White Major-Party Voters Who Voted Democratic for President, by Religion, 1944–2016 (Percent)

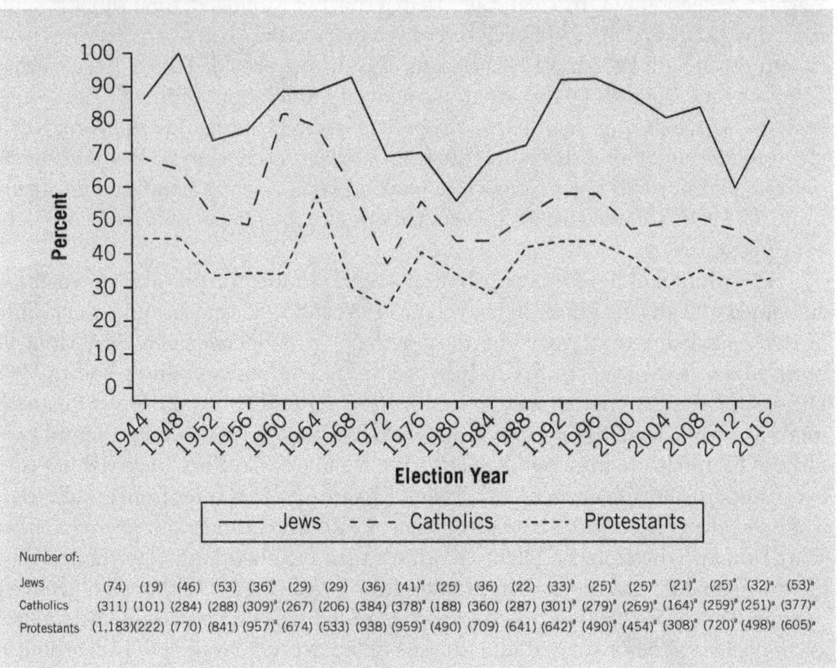


*Source:* Authors' analysis of a 1944 NORC survey and ANES surveys.

*Note:* Numbers are weighted.

Accords, which returned the Sinai Peninsula—captured by Israel in 1967 during the Six Day War—to Egypt. A substantial minority of Jews supported third-party candidate John Anderson that year, but Carter still outpolled Reagan. Both Mondale in 1984 and Dukakis (whose wife is Jewish) in 1988 won a clear majority of the Jewish vote. The Jewish Democratic vote surged in 1992, with Clinton winning nine in ten major-party voters. With Lieberman, an observant Jew, as his running mate, Gore, too, won overwhelming Jewish support in 2000. Bush was strongly pro-Israel in his foreign policy, but Kerry won solid support among Jewish voters, although there may have been some Republican gains. In 2008 some Jews may have had reservations about Obama's commitment to Israel's security, but even so he may have made slight gains among Jewish voters. The data show that Obama's support among white Jewish voters dropped significantly in 2012 to 59.8 percent. Obama had a rocky relationship with the Israeli prime minister, Benjamin Netanyahu, during his first term, and the decline in his support among Jewish voters between 2008 and 2012 may reflect these tensions. Hillary Clinton was able to regain high levels of Jewish support in 2016. According to the ANES Clinton won 80.1 percent of the Jewish two-party vote. Obviously, on the whole, Jewish voters' loyalty to the Democratic Party remains very strong.

A majority of white Catholics voted Democratic in six of the seven elections from 1944 to 1968. The percentage of Catholics voting Democratic surged in 1960, when the Democrats fielded a Catholic candidate, John Kennedy, but Catholic support was still very high in Johnson's landslide four years later.[56] In 1968 a majority of white Catholics voted Democratic, although Humphrey's total is reduced from 60 percent to 55 percent if Wallace voters are included. In 1976 Carter won a majority among white Catholics, but the Democrats did not win a majority of the major-party vote among white Catholics again until 1992. In his 1996 reelection Clinton again won over half of the major-party vote among white Catholics. Four years later, George W. Bush outpolled Al Gore among white Catholics. Even in 2004, when the Democrats ran a Catholic presidential candidate, Bush outscored Kerry among white Catholic voters. Based on 2008 ANES data, Obama won half the vote among white Catholics. He won slightly less than half in the 2008 pool poll. Obama's two-party vote share among white Catholics declined, however, in 2012, falling to 47.2 percentage points. Hillary Clinton's white Catholic support in 2016 declined even further to 40 percent of the two-party vote share. Catholics had once been firmly footed in the Democrats' New Deal coalition, but the party's support for abortion rights—first formally espoused in the 1976 party platform—places it odds with the Catholic Church and many of the faithful.[57] As we noted earlier, much of the Democrats' support from white Catholics comes from those who are less devout in their religious practices as well as the Latino Catholic population. Nevertheless, on average, Democrats continue to do better among white Catholics than among white Protestants.

Our measure of religious voting shows considerable change from election to election, although there was a downward trend from 1968 to 2000, when religious differences reached their lowest level. Religious differences were somewhat higher in both 2004 and 2008 (see Table 5-2). Even though white Protestants were more likely than white Catholics to vote for Wallace in 1968, including Wallace voters in our total has little effect on religious voting (it falls from thirty points to twenty-nine points). Religious differences were small in the 1980 Reagan-Carter contest, but since then they have varied. Because the Latino Catholic electorate is projected to grow, religious voting may rise in future elections.

Including African Americans in our calculations reduces religious voting. Blacks are much more likely to be Protestant than Catholic, and including blacks in our calculations adds a substantial number of Protestant Democrats. In 2016, for example, religious voting is reduced from seven points to five points when blacks are included. However, when we look at the electorate as a whole, we see that religious voting increases significantly to thirteen points; this is driven primarily by the inclusion of Latinos.[58]

The Jewish contribution to the Democratic Party has declined in part because Jews did not vote overwhelmingly Democratic in 1972, 1980, 1984, 1988, 2004, and 2012 and in part because Jews make up a small and declining share of the electorate. During the 1950s, Jews were about a twentieth of the electorate. But the most recent estimates suggest that only about one American in fifty is Jewish.[59]

Although Jews make up only about 2 percent of the population, three-fourths of the nation's Jews live in seven large states—New York, California, Florida, New Jersey, Pennsylvania, Massachusetts, and Illinois—which together had 178 electoral votes in 2016.[60] More important, two of these states are battleground states: Florida, where Jews make up 3.3 percent of the population, and Pennsylvania, where they make up 2.3 percent. In recent elections Florida has witnessed very close presidential elections, and in 2016, Trump won Pennsylvania by slightly more than 44,000 votes. In these close elections, even a relatively small group, like Jewish voters, can be influential in presidential politics. Overall, however, the electoral significance of Jews is lessened because five of these large states are not battleground states. For example, Jews make up 8.4 percent of the population in New York, far more than any other state. Although Jewish voters could influence New York's twenty-nine electoral votes, a Democratic candidate who does not win by a comfortable margin in New York is very likely to lose the election.[61]

According to our estimates based on ANES surveys, in 1948 Truman received about a third of his total vote from white Catholics. In 1952 Stevenson won three-tenths of his vote from white Catholics but only one-fourth in 1956. In 1960, Kennedy, the first Catholic president, received 37 percent of his vote from Catholics, but the Catholic contribution fell—owing to an ebb in Catholic turnout—to just under three in ten votes when Johnson defeated Goldwater in 1964. In 1968 three-tenths of Humphrey's total vote came from white Catholics but only a fourth of McGovern's vote in 1972. White Catholics provided just over a fourth of Carter's vote in his 1976 victory, but in his 1980 loss to Reagan, just over a fifth came from this source. Mondale received just under three in ten of his votes from white Catholics, and Dukakis received a fifth of his vote from this group. According to our analysis based on ANES surveys, just over a fifth of Bill Clinton's vote came from white Catholics in 1992 and just over a fourth in 1996. The ANES surveys suggest that both Kerry and Bush received about a fifth of their votes from white Catholics. In 2008, less than a fifth of Obama's vote came from white Catholics, and in 2012, 17.4 percent of the votes cast for Obama were from white Catholics. White Catholics composed 16.6 percent of Hillary Clinton's electoral coalition, roughly half the size of the group's contribution to the New Deal coalition. (Twenty-six percent of Trump's voters were white Catholics.)

The contrast between the 1960 and 2004 elections is the most striking comparison across the eight decades in our investigation. In both elections the Democrats fielded a Catholic presidential candidate. But Kennedy received over twice as large a share of the Catholic vote as Kerry. Religious differences were massive in 1960 and relatively modest in 2004. Well over a third of Kennedy's votes came from white Catholics, but only about one-fifth of Kerry's did. Obviously the social characteristics of the Catholic community changed over the span of the forty-four years between these elections. Of course there were also social issues that may have led many Catholics to vote Republican in 2004 that were simply not on the political agenda four decades earlier.[62]

As the data reveal, in all of the elections between 1944 and 1996, the effects of class and religion were cumulative (see Figure 5-6). In every one of these fourteen elections, working-class Catholics were more likely to vote Democratic than any other group. And in all these elections, middle-class Protestants were the most likely to vote Republican. In 2000 middle-class Catholics were the most likely to vote Democratic and middle-class Republicans the most likely to vote Republican. In 2004 and 2008, as in the vast majority of past elections, working-class Catholics were the most Democratic group. Middle-class Protestants were somewhat more likely to vote Republican than middle-class Catholics. All the same, middle-class Protestants are the most consistent group, supporting the Republicans in all seventeen elections. We lack data on the effect of class and religion in the 2012 and 2016 elections.

The relative importance of social class and religion can be assessed by comparing the voting behavior of middle-class Catholics with that of working-class Protestants. Religion was more important than social class in predicting the vote in all elections between 1944 and 2008, except those in which social class was more important than

**Figure 5-6 White Major-Party Voters Who Voted Democratic for President, by Social Class and Religion, 1944–2008 (Percent)**

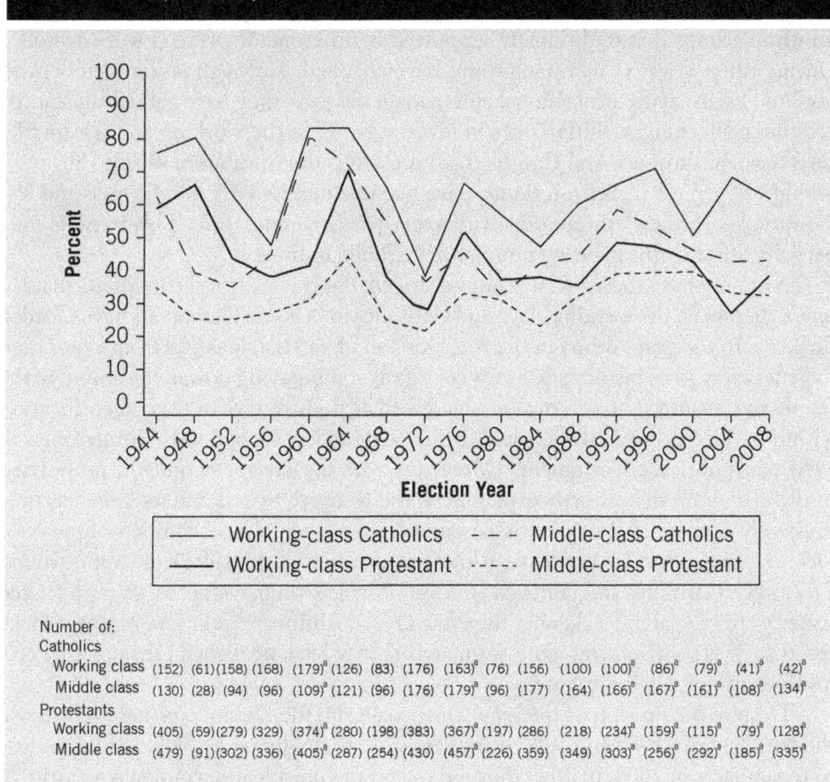


| Number of: | 1944 | 1948 | 1952 | 1956 | 1960 | 1964 | 1968 | 1972 | 1976 | 1980 | 1984 | 1988 | 1992 | 1996 | 2000 | 2004 | 2008 |
|---|---|---|---|---|---|---|---|---|---|---|---|---|---|---|---|---|---|
| Catholics | | | | | | | | | | | | | | | | | |
| Working class | (152) | (61) | (158) | (168) | (179)[a] | (126) | (83) | (176) | (163)[a] | (76) | (156) | (100) | (100)[a] | (86)[a] | (79)[a] | (41)[a] | (42)[a] |
| Middle class | (130) | (28) | (94) | (96) | (109)[a] | (121) | (96) | (176) | (179)[a] | (96) | (177) | (164) | (166)[a] | (167)[a] | (161)[a] | (108)[a] | (134)[a] |
| Protestants | | | | | | | | | | | | | | | | | |
| Working class | (405) | (59) | (279) | (329) | (374)[a] | (280) | (198) | (383) | (367)[a] | (197) | (286) | (218) | (234)[a] | (159)[a] | (115)[a] | (79)[a] | (128)[a] |
| Middle class | (479) | (91) | (302) | (336) | (405)[a] | (287) | (254) | (430) | (457)[a] | (226) | (359) | (349) | (303)[a] | (256)[a] | (292)[a] | (185)[a] | (335)[a] |

*Source:* Authors' analysis of a 1944 NORC survey and ANES surveys. The data for occupation needed to classify respondents according to their social class for 2012 and 2016 are restricted for privacy concerns.

*Note:* Numbers are weighted.

religion—1948 (by a considerable margin), 1976, and 1980—and the one, 1964, in which class and religion were equally important. However, all of these trend lines have been converging, suggesting that traditional sources of cleavage are declining in importance.

## WHY THE NEW DEAL COALITION BROKE DOWN

The importance of race increased substantially after 1960, but all of the other factors we have examined have declined in importance. The effects of region on voting behavior have been reversed, with the Republicans now enjoying an advantage in the South, especially when we compare southern whites with whites outside the South. As the national Democratic Party strengthened its appeals to African Americans during the 1960s, party leaders endorsed policies that southern whites opposed, and many of them deserted the Democratic Party. The migration of northern whites to the South also may have reduced regional characteristics.

Although the Democratic Party's appeals to blacks may have weakened its hold on white groups that traditionally supported it, other factors were at work as well.[63] During the postwar years these groups have changed. Although union members do not hold high-paying professional and managerial jobs, they have gained substantial economic advantages. Differences in income between the working and the middle class have diminished. And Catholics, who often came from more recent European immigrant groups than Protestants, have become increasingly middle class and less identified with their ethnic roots with every passing generation. This trend is only partially offset by the growing number of Catholic Latinos.

Not only have these social groups changed, but the historical conditions that led union members, the working class, and Catholics to become Democrats have receded further into the past. Although the transmission of partisan loyalties from generation to generation gives historically based coalitions some staying power, the ability of the family to transmit partisan loyalties decreased as the strength of party identification within the electorate weakened during the 1960s and 1970s and were formed anew in a changed political environment.[64] Moreover, with the passage of time the proportion of the electorate that directly experienced the Roosevelt years and its wake has progressively declined. New policy issues, unrelated to the political conflicts of the New Deal era, have tended to erode party loyalties among traditionally Democratic groups. Edward G. Carmines and James A. Stimson provide strong evidence that race-related issues were crucial in weakening the New Deal coalition.[65] And more recently social issues such as abortion and same-sex marriage may have weakened Democratic Party loyalties among Catholic voters.

Despite the erosion of the New Deal coalition, the Democrats managed to win the presidency in 1992 and 1996, came very close to holding it in 2000, and came close to regaining it in 2004. In 2008 they did regain the presidency, winning a majority of the popular vote for the first time since 1976. And they won a popular-vote majority again in 2012. In his 1992 victory Bill Clinton boosted his share of the major-party vote among union members, the white working class, and even among white southerners. He focused on appeals to middle America, and in both 1992 and 1996, he paid as low a price as possible to gain the black vote. Clinton was the first Democrat to win in an election in which blacks made up more than 15 percent of the Democratic vote. In 1996 Clinton once again won with more than 15 percent of his votes provided by blacks. But the 1992 and 1996 elections were three-candidate contests. Our calculations suggest that under typical levels of turnout among its various coalition groups, it would be exceedingly difficult for a Democrat to win a two-candidate contest in which blacks made up a fifth or more of his or her total coalition—difficult but not impossible.

With the 2008 and 2012 elections, we see the ingredients (and challenges) of building a modern Democratic coalition. Obama gained about a fourth of his total tally from black voters. This was possible because black turnout equaled or exceeded white turnout and because blacks voted overwhelmingly Democratic. The Democrats also enjoyed strong support from Latino voters, and population growth makes this group an increasingly larger share of the Democratic coalition. The Democrat's New Deal coalition was often described as a "coalition of minorities"—increasingly the minorities at the heart of the new Democratic electoral coalition are blacks and Latinos.

The 2016 election brought many of the electoral challenges confronting both parties to the fore. For the Democrats, while they were able to capture the national popular vote, the party's losses in nearly every battleground state were brought about, in large measure, by the same symptoms. To win, the modern Democratic coalition must not only maintain their recent levels of support from blacks and Latinos, but they must turn these voters out to the polls. African American turnout declined by seven percentage points in 2016, and Latino turnout remains lower than that of any other racial/ethnic group. At the same time the Democratic Party's increasing reliance on its minority constituents may exacerbate its losses among a growing number of disaffected, white working-class voters, who feel the party has lost touch with their interests. Indeed, as we have seen in our analysis, over the last forty years, the Democratic Party has lost ground with every segment of the white electorate, save the most educated (and, possibly, urban dwellers).

With the end to racial segregation in the formerly "solid" Democratic South in the 1960, the Republican Party moved quickly (and successfully) to capture the partisan loyalties of white southerners. With the exception of the elections of its native sons, Jimmy Carter in 1976 and Bill Clinton in 1992 and 1994, the South has been solidly Republican since 1964. In the South political change was quick. But the broadening of the Republican Party's electoral coalition to include large segments of the bygone Democratic New Deal coalition, including white Catholic voters and the white working class, occurred at a much slower rate of change, indeed, decades in the making. Much has been made of Donald Trump's resonance with disaffected white voters, tired of immigration, tired of seeing jobs moving overseas, tired of a government that, in their view, seems to care little about them and cannot be trusted. Yet careful examination of the electoral record shows that these "Trump voters" have been "Republican voters" for quite some time now, although the GOP's share of these voters has grown with each passing decade. On balance the evidence shows that the American electorate in 2016 is remarkably similar to electorates of the last few decades.

CHAPTER SIX

# CANDIDATES, ISSUES, AND THE VOTE

In this chapter and the two that follow, we examine some of the concerns that underlie voters' choices for president. Even though scholars and politicians disagree about what factors voters employ and how they employ them, there is general consensus on several points. First, voters' attitudes or preferences determine their choices. There may be disagreement over exactly which attitudes shape behavior, but most scholars agree that voters deliberately choose to support the candidate they believe will make the best president. For decades there had also been general agreement that, as Campbell et al., in *The American Voter*, originally argued, it is the tripartite attitudes toward the candidates, the issues, and the parties that is the most important set of attitudes in shaping the vote.[1] In these three chapters, we start with voters' considerations just before casting their ballots and then turn to their earlier ones, ending with the most important long-term attitudinal force shaping the vote, party identification.

Subsequent work has raised other sets of attitudes to greater prominence, beyond attitudes towards the candidates, the issues, and the parties. One flows from what Campbell et al. rather dismissively referred to as the "nature of the times."[2] Anthony Downs and V. O. Key developed two different accounts of "retrospective voting."[3] Morris Fiorina extended Downs's perspective and provided a wealth of empirical tests of that account, which became the disciplinary norm and which will be used to examine the 2016 election in Chapter 7.[4]

More recently Christopher Achen and Larry Bartels claimed that all kinds of matters, including those for which no reasonable person would hold the government accountable, are treated as "retrospective" by voters.[5] They argued for an enhanced role for partisan loyalties, above and beyond that which Campbell et al. argued for originally. They saw that, similar to Donald Green et al., partisanship can serve as the basis of a voter's political identity, that is, how one thinks and feels about politics.[6] It is true that group loyalties, such as the very high levels of racial voting patterns already discussed, are powerful forces in the vote, and perhaps partisan loyalties have become as intense. In Chapter 8 we will take up party identification in detail in these terms, among others. Whereas Campbell et al. placed party identification at the center of their understanding of voting and elections, the increased partisan polarization appears to have strengthened this particular type of group loyalty even further, often in emotional rather than or in addition to cognitive terms. Whether all of these forces, retrospective and group-based loyalties, among others, can be summarized simply as attitudes, beliefs, or preferences is a newly reopened question. For here we take it that these all can be fit sufficiently comfortably into the consensus view that attitudes shape behavior, and the debate is over which of these matter, when, and with what consequences.

In this chapter we look first at the relationships among several measures of candidate evaluations and the vote, beginning with the "feeling thermometers" used by the ANES to measure affect toward the candidates. After this brief analysis we examine aspects of the major components of these evaluations: voters' perceptions of the candidates' personal qualities and of the candidates' professional qualifications, and competence to serve as president.[7] As we will see there is a very powerful relationship between thermometer evaluations of candidates and the vote and an only somewhat less strong one between evaluations of candidate traits and the vote. It might seem obvious that voters support the candidate they like best, but in 1968, 1980, 1992, 1996, and 2000, the presence of a significant third candidate complicated decision-making for many voters.[8]

We conceive of attitudes toward the candidates as the most direct influence on the vote itself, especially the summary evaluations encapsulated in the "feeling thermometers," as we used in Chapter 1. But attitudes toward the issues and the parties help shape attitudes toward the candidates and thus the vote.[9] With that in mind we turn to the first part of our investigation of the role of issues. After analyzing the problems that most concerned the voters in 2016, we discuss the two basic forms of issue voting: that based on prospective issues and that based on retrospective issues. In this chapter we investigate the impact of prospective issues. In doing so we consider one of the enduring questions about issue voting—how much information the public has on the issues and candidates' positions on them—and is this sufficient for casting an issues-based vote? Our analyses provide an indication of the significance of prospective issues in 2016 and compare their impact as shown in earlier election surveys. Chapter 7 examines retrospective issues and the vote, and Chapter 8 examines partisan identification and assesses the significance of both parties and issues for voting in 2016 and in earlier elections.

## ATTITUDES TOWARD THE CANDIDATES

Although the United States has a two-party system, there are still ways in which other candidates can appear on the ballot or run a write-in candidacy. The 2016 presidential election was a two-person race for all intents and purposes, but many other candidates were running as well.[10] Two other political parties qualified for inclusion on nearly all state ballots. The Libertarian Party nominated Gary Johnson for president (as they had in 2012), winning about 4.5 million votes (about 3.3 percent; by comparison Clinton won about 65.8 million or 48.3 percent, whereas Trump won 63 million votes, or 46.2 percent). Jill Stein was the Green Party's presidential nominee (also as in 2012), winning about close to 1.5 million votes (or 1.1 percent). Both Johnson, who appeared on all ballots, and Stein, who appeared on forty-two state ballots and that of DC, greatly increased their vote from 2012 but obviously fell far short of being competitive for a single Electoral College vote.

As a result we consider 2016 to be a nearly pure, two-person contest, and thus we limit our attention to Hillary Clinton and Donald Trump. We want to know why people preferred one candidate over the other, and therefore how they voted, and by extension, why Clinton won the popular vote (which is what the ANES survey, as most surveys, is designed to measure), whereas Trump won the election by virtue of his Electoral College majority.

If attitudes determine choices, then the obvious starting point in a two-person race is to imagine that people voted for the candidate they preferred. This may sound obvious, but as we have noted, in races with three or more candidates, people do not necessarily vote for the candidate they most prefer.[11] Respondents who rank a major-party candidate highest among three candidates vote overwhelmingly for the major-party candidate. On the other hand respondents who rank a third-party or independent candidate highest often desert that candidate to vote for one of the major-party candidates, which we believe may result from voters using strategic considerations to avoid "wasting" their vote on a candidate who has little chance of winning.

Happily for understanding the 2012 presidential election, in a strictly two-person race, people overwhelmingly vote for the candidate they prefer. This close relationship can be demonstrated by analyzing the "feeling thermometer." This measure is a scale that runs from 0 to 100 degrees, with 0 indicating "very cold" or negative feelings, 50 indicating neutral feelings, and 100 indicating a "very warm" or positive evaluation.[12]

The data for 2016 are reported in Table 6-1. As the data in Part A of the table illustrate, there was a close balance in the electorate between those ranking Clinton higher than Trump (48 percent of respondents) and those ranking Trump higher (46 percent).[13] The closeness of these overall ratings of the candidates to the actual vote choice is clear in Part B of the table. In particular it depicts the powerful relationship between these assessments and the vote, in which almost everyone supported the candidate they rated higher—all but 1 percent of those who rated the Democrat higher and 2 percent of those who rated the Republican higher voted for that party's nominee. The relatively small percentage who tied the two candidates voted much closer to the mental coin flip that would imply—55 percent for Clinton.

Perhaps due to the relatively high levels of unpopularity of the two major-party candidates, 15 percent of the respondents rated Johnson highest on the thermometer, and 20 percent so rated Stein. But very few of those respondents voted for their third-party favorite. Johnson received only 17 percent of the vote from those who rated him highest (with 45 percent voting for Clinton, 34 percent for Trump, and the rest scattered). Those who claimed to feel most warmly toward Stein did not stick with her at all; she received only 4 percent of that vote (with 48 percent voting for Clinton and 38 for Trump). Clearly, in this case, affective evaluations did not lead to behavior. Rather strategic calculations about wasting votes and chances of winning weighed heavily.

Overall, then, these summary evaluations are quite proximate to the vote in a two-candidate race. This finding is particularly strong in 2016, but the general pattern of more than nine in ten supporting their preferred candidates is commonplace, and so it is worth noting that the small percentages voting for highly regarded third-party candidates in 2016 is found also in earlier elections. These preferences about the major-party candidates are, therefore, but a first, very close, step back from the vote to the discovery of underlying reasons that explain how people came to the choices they did.

**Table 6-1 Relative Ranking of Presidential Candidates on the Feeling Thermometer: Response Distribution and Vote Choice, 2016**

| | Rated Clinton Higher Than Trump on Thermometer | Rated Clinton Equal to Trump on Thermometer | Rated Trump Higher Than Clinton on Thermometer | Total | (*N*) |
|---|---|---|---|---|---|
| **A. Distribution of responses** | | | | | |
| Percent | 48 | 6 | 46 | 100 | (3612) |
| **B. Major-party voters who voted for Clinton** | | | | | |
| Percent | 99 | 55 | 2 | 53 | (2366) |
| (*N*) | (1199) | (52) | (1115) | | |

*Source:* Authors' analysis of the 2016 ANES survey.

*Note:* The numbers in parentheses in Part B of the table are the totals on which the percentages are based. Only respondents who rated both candidates on the scale are included.

That is to say that we are led to the next obvious question: Why did more people rate Clinton or Trump more warmly? The ANES asked a series of questions about how people view the candidates as people and as potential presidents, six of which are reported in Table 6-2A. These cover different aspects of attributes we might like a president to possess: speaking his or her mind, providing strong leadership, caring about people, and being knowledgeable, even-tempered, and honest.[14] The 2016 campaign presented quite a different mixture compared to the 2008 or 2012 contests in that both candidates in 2016 were perceived negatively on most of these traits. In 2008, for example, Obama and McCain were both perceived quite positively on most (but not all) of these traits, whereas 2012 illustrated a case in which the electorate had mixed views about both nominees. As for 2016 Clinton was perceived net positively in terms of being knowledgeable. The electorate was about evenly divided in considering her to be even-tempered and speaking her mind. Providing strong leadership was net negative for her, but only modestly so, whereas caring about people like you [the respondent] was more clearly negative, and honesty was very decidedly negative, perhaps reflecting Trump's repeated campaign nickname of "Crooked Hillary." For his part Trump was very clearly seen as speaking his own mind (which may or may not have been perceived positively by respondents, as we will see). However, all else was net negative in evaluation, with providing strong leadership fairly solidly so and the other traits very negative overall. The public saw Trump as only very slightly more honest than Clinton, and in the other four traits, Clinton was clearly more positively evaluated.[15]

**Table 6-2A Distribution of Responses on Presidential Candidate Trait Evaluations, 2016 (Percent)**

| | Extremely Well | Very Well | Moderately Well | Slightly Well | Not Well at All | Total | (*N*) |
|---|---|---|---|---|---|---|---|
| **Clinton** | | | | | | | |
| Speaks mind | 12 | 23 | 28 | 17 | 20 | 100 | (4251) |
| Provides strong leadership | 14 | 20 | 22 | 15 | 29 | 100 | (4255) |
| Really cares about people like you | 11 | 16 | 20 | 16 | 37 | 100 | (4251) |
| Knowledgeable | 25 | 27 | 24 | 13 | 11 | 100 | (4249) |
| Even-tempered | 13 | 22 | 29 | 17 | 19 | 100 | (4244) |
| Honest | 5 | 10 | 21 | 15 | 49 | 100 | (4250) |
| **Trump** | | | | | | | |
| Speaks mind | 56 | 25 | 8 | 4 | 7 | 100 | (4250) |
| Provides strong leadership | 12 | 18 | 18 | 14 | 38 | 100 | (4246) |
| Really cares about people like you | 7 | 12 | 18 | 12 | 51 | 100 | (4245) |
| Knowledgeable | 7 | 15 | 22 | 17 | 39 | 100 | (4241) |
| Even-tempered | 3 | 5 | 19 | 18 | 55 | 100 | (4250) |
| Honest | 7 | 15 | 20 | 14 | 44 | 100 | (4246) |

*Source:* Authors' analysis of the 2016 ANES.

*Note:* Numbers are weighted.

In Table 6-2B we report the percentage of major-party voters with differing assessments of these traits who voted for Clinton and Trump, respectively. These trait evaluations were quite differently related to the vote for the two candidates. For Clinton the relationship is quite like what one might expect. She won the support of nearly everyone (with the only partial exception of the "speaks her mind" trait) who thought the trait described her extremely well and quite high majorities among those who responded "very well" and even "moderately well." Those who responded "slightly well" or "not at all well" did not support her highly at all.[16] For evaluations of traits describing Trump, much the same is true for four of the six traits (strong leadership, really cares, knowledgeable, and honest). The pattern for "speaks mind" is still decreasing with decreasing fit of the trait for Trump, but the variable is quite a bit more weakly related to the vote, largely due to the large percentage picking the "extremely well" response. Whereas relatively few picked the top two categories for "even-tempered" for describing Trump, the pattern is clearly different. Those who said "moderately well" were the most likely to vote for Trump, followed by the "very well" and "slightly well" categories, with the two extremes quite a bit lower.[17] As a general rule, then, we find trait evaluations provide context and underpinning for understanding why some felt warmly toward one candidate or the other, and indeed, they show the public responded to the observations of the campaign in an at least somewhat bipartisan way. However, these remain only one more step removed from the vote than the candidate thermometer questions.

What might lie even further from the vote? Candidates and their supporters campaign on the assessments of the two candidates (decidedly not bipartisan with much negative campaigning!), but they also spend a great deal of time discussing a variety of issues. These are both prospective—what I or my opponent will do if elected—and retrospective—how Obama or the Democrats succeeded or failed in handling public policy in the last four or even eight years. These, we might expect, stand farther removed from the vote and thus help shape how these global or more specific assessments of the candidates came about. The rest of this chapter examines issues as they are discussed prospectively, leaving retrospective assessments for Chapter 7 and differences in this partisan-polarized world for Chapter 8.

## PROSPECTIVE EVALUATIONS

Public policy concerns enter into the voting decision in two very different ways. In any election two questions become important: How has the incumbent president and party done on policy? And how likely is it that his opponent (or opponents) would do any better? Voting based on this form of policy appraisal is called retrospective voting and will be analyzed in Chapter 7.

The second form of policy-based voting involves examining the candidates' policy platforms and assessing which candidate's policy promises conform most closely to what the voter believes the government should be doing. Policy voting, therefore, involves comparing sets of promises and voting for the set that is most like the voter's own preferences. Voting based on these kinds of decisions is called prospective voting because it involves examining the promises of the candidates about future actions. In

**Table 6-2B Major-Party Vote for Clinton and Trump by Presidential Candidate Trait Evaluations, 2016 (Percent)**

| | Extremely Well | Very Well | Moderately Well | Slightly Well | Not Well at All |
|---|---|---|---|---|---|
| **Clinton** | | | | | |
| Speaks mind | 82 | 70 | 63 | 38 | 13 |
| (*N*) | (280) | (583) | (647) | (377) | (486) |
| Provides strong leadership | 96 | 91 | 66 | 23 | 4 |
| (*N*) | (396) | (500) | (480) | (288) | (710) |
| Really cares about people like you | 95 | 95 | 80 | 42 | 8 |
| (*N*) | (299) | (418) | (445) | (336) | (874) |
| Knowledgeable | 90 | 65 | 28 | 13 | 5 |
| (*N*) | (730) | (625) | (494) | (275) | (248) |
| Even-tempered | 95 | 84 | 52 | 22 | 6 |
| (*N*) | (386) | (549) | (604) | (364) | (469) |
| Honest | 95 | 98 | 93 | 75 | 13 |
| (*N*) | (118) | (273) | (502) | (340) | (1139) |
| **Trump** | | | | | |
| Speaks mind | 55 | 48 | 32 | 15 | 4 |
| (*N*) | (1425) | (553) | (169) | (68) | (155) |
| Provides strong leadership | 97 | 90 | 66 | 29 | 4 |
| (*N*) | (343) | (447) | (394) | (307) | (879) |
| Really cares about people like you | 96 | 97 | 89 | 58 | 9 |
| (*N*) | (189) | (326) | (413) | (254) | (1188) |
| Knowledgeable | 92 | 93 | 79 | 41 | 7 |
| (*N*) | (162) | (356) | (534) | (388) | (929) |
| Even-tempered | 55 | 84 | 90 | 77 | 20 |
| (*N*) | (61) | (115) | (458) | (411) | (1327) |
| Honest | 89 | 91 | 84 | 48 | 7 |
| (*N*) | (183) | (385) | (460) | (323) | (1021) |

*Source:* Authors' analysis of the 2016 ANES.

*Note:* The numbers in parentheses are the totals on which the percentages are based. The numbers are weighted.

this chapter we examine prospective evaluations of the two major-party candidates in 2016 and how these evaluations relate to voter choice.

The last twelve elections show some remarkable similarities in prospective evaluations and voting. Perhaps the most important similarity is the perception of where the Democratic and Republican candidates stood on issues. In these elections the public saw clear differences between the major-party nominees. In all cases the public saw the Republican candidates as conservative on most issues, and most citizens scored the GOP candidates as more conservative than the voters themselves. And in all elections the public saw the Democratic candidates as liberal on most issues, and most citizens viewed the Democratic candidates as more liberal than the voters themselves. As a result many voters perceived a clear choice based on their understanding of the candidates' policy positions. The candidates presented the voters with, as the 1964 Goldwater campaign slogan put it, "a choice, not an echo." The *average* citizen, however, faced a difficult choice. For many, Democratic nominees were considered to be as far to the left as the Republican nominees were to the right. In general the net effect of prospective issues over recent elections has been to give neither party a decided, potentially long-term, advantage on policy.

One of the most important differences among these elections, however, was the mixture of issues that concerned the public. Each election presented its own mixture of policy concerns. Moreover, the general strategies of the candidates on issues differed in each election. In 1980 Jimmy Carter's incumbency was marked by a general perception that he was unable to solve pressing problems. Ronald Reagan attacked that weakness both directly (e.g., by the question he posed to the public during his debate with Carter, "Are you better off today than you were four years ago?") and indirectly. The indirect attack was more future oriented. Reagan set forth a clear set of proposals designed to convince the public that he would be more likely to solve the nation's problems because he had his own proposals to end soaring inflation, to strengthen the United States militarily, and to regain respect and influence for the United States abroad.

In 1984 the public perceived Reagan as a far more successful president than Carter had been. Reagan chose to run his reelection campaign by focusing primarily on the theme that things were much better by 1984 (as illustrated by his advertising slogan "It's morning in America"). Walter Mondale attacked that claim by arguing that Reagan's policies were unfair and by pointing to the rapidly growing budget deficit. But Reagan countered that Mondale was another "tax and spend" Democrat, and the "Great Communicator," as some called him, captured a second term.

The 1988 campaign was more similar to the 1984 than to the 1980 campaign. George H. W. Bush continued to run on the successes of the Reagan-Bush administration and promised no new taxes. ("Read my lips," he said. "No new taxes!") Michael S. Dukakis initially attempted to portray the election as one about "competence" rather than "ideology," arguing that he had demonstrated his competence as governor of Massachusetts and that Bush, by implication, was less competent. Bush countered that it really was an election about ideology, and that Dukakis was just another liberal Democrat from Massachusetts.

The 1992 election presented yet another type of campaign. Bush used the success of the 1991 Persian Gulf War to augment his claim that he was a successful world leader, but Bill Clinton attacked the Bush administration on domestic issues, barely discussing foreign affairs at all. He sought to keep the electorate focused on the current economic woes and argued for substantial reforms of the health care system, hoping to appeal to Democrats and to spur action should he be the first Democrat in the White House in twelve years. At the same time, he sought to portray himself not as another "tax and spend" liberal Democrat but as a moderate "New Democrat."

In 1996 Clinton ran a campaign typical of a popular incumbent; he focused on what led people to approve of his handling of the presidency and avoided mentioning many specific new programs. His policy proposals were a lengthy series of relatively inexpensive, limited programs. Bob Dole, having difficulties deciding whether to emphasize Clinton's personal failings in the first term or to call for different programs for the future, decided to put a significant tax cut proposal at the center of his candidacy under either of those campaign strategies.

In 2000 the candidates debated a broad array of domestic issues—education, health care, social security, and taxes the most prominent among them—often couched in terms of a newfound "problem," federal government budget surpluses. Typically these issues (except for taxes) have favored Democratic contenders, and Republicans often avoided detailed discussions of all except taxes on the grounds that doing so would make the issues more salient to voters and would highlight the Democratic advantages. George W. Bush, however, spoke out on education, in particular, as well as health care and Social Security to a lesser extent, believing he could undercut the traditional Democratic advantage. For his part Al Gore had the advantage of his belief (backed by public opinion polls) that the public was less in favor of tax cuts than usual and more in favor of allocating budget surpluses to buttress popular domestic programs.

In 2004, by contrast, Bush and Kerry had less choice about what issues to consider. With wars under way in Iraq, in Afghanistan, and against terrorism, neither candidate could avoid foreign policy considerations. Bush preferred to emphasize that Iraq was part of the war on terrorism, whereas Kerry argued that it was not and indeed that it was a costly distraction from it. Similarly 2004 opened with the economy slumping. The Democrats, including Kerry, attacked the Bush administration policies, while Bush countered by saying that the economy was actually improving—in large part because of his successful policies. As the year wore on, the economy did in fact improve, although not so much as to remove all criticism.

The 2008 campaign began as one in which the Democrats tried to emphasize their opposition to the Bush policies in Iraq and their concern about the war in Afghanistan. On the domestic front Obama emphasized health care reform, improved environmental policies, and other aspects of his agenda that called for "change." McCain, conversely, began with a spirited defense of the war in Iraq, and especially the "surge" in the war effort there. By fall, however, the economy had swept aside virtually every other issue but war from consideration and replaced war as topic number one. Indeed so worrisome were the economic events of the fall that candidates could ill afford to do anything but relate any domestic issue to their plans for fighting the economic downturn.

In 2012 both the Obama and Romney camps anticipated a close contest. Romney's side wanted to make the campaign be about Obama and his successes or failures in office—retrospective voting concerns—on the grounds that the economy had not recovered sufficiently to justify returning Obama to office. This was made problematic first by Romney's statement that Obama's supporters were 47 percent of the electorate whom he characterized as people "who live off government handouts" and do not "care for their lives," and then by Hurricane Sandy and the appearance of successful performance by Obama, reinforced by a leading Republican figure, Gov. Chris Christie (NJ), saying that Obama was doing his job very well. Obama, for his part, approached issues rather more like Clinton did in 1996, offering a series of popular but relatively small domestic initiatives ("small ball" as it was called at times) and his emphasis on how the economy was not where everyone hoped but it was improving and would do so quicker with Democrats in office.

In 2016 Clinton's nomination campaign had many positions that reflected Obama and her service to his administration. In that sense many were retrospective or at least made attacking her through attacking Obama and his policies fair game. Sanders's lengthy challenge to her nomination led her to break with Obama on several key issues, such as the Trans Pacific Partnership (TPP), which Obama had developed and championed (and she had once supported), which was a proposed international agreement among nations that bordered the Pacific, as part of Obama's "pivot" toward China. Conversely she did not change her support for the Paris Agreement (*Accord de Paris*), an international agreement to work to reduce the level of carbon effluent and thus reduce the risk of climate change, or the North American Free Trade Agreement that Bill Clinton (and George H. W. Bush) had developed and seen through to enactment. On the domestic side, although she had her own ideas about how to improve by building on the Affordable Care Act, "Obamacare" was the base of her position. Essentially the same was true on many aspects of domestic policy. But, like the TPP, her advocacy of free access to community and junior colleges marked new directions from the past. Thus, it is fair to say that her platform was a mixture of retrospective and prospective issues. Trump relentlessly attacked Obama and Clinton's support of Obama's policies in the sense of retrospective evaluations. And, of course, he also had signature issues that would represent prospective policies, "repeal and replace" Obamacare, build a wall to keep new immigrants from crossing the Mexican border, deporting all illegal (undocumented) immigrants, and baring entry for all Muslims. Of course he also often advocated different policies in the campaign and even more often provided insufficient detail to be confident on just what he sought to do. Nonetheless, he was clearly providing very strong retrospective critiquing while advocating for prospective policies.

## Most Important Issues in the Public

What did the public care about most? From 1972 to 2004, we were able to use ANES surveys to assess this question. In 2012 we examined exit polls, conducted as voters were leaving the voting booth, and the various interested parties (news media, etc.) formed a pool to conduct that poll.[18] We did so again for 2016.

In the four elections from 1984 through 2000, the great majority of responses revolved around domestic issues rather than foreign policy, perhaps because of the end of the Cold War.[19] In those elections, and even the four before them (when foreign affairs were more important) prior to 2004, two major categories of domestic issues dominated. From 1976 to 1992, in good times and bad, by far the more commonly cited issue was the economy. Yet, in 1972, 1996, 2000, and then in 2004 as well, the most frequently cited problems were in the social issues category, such as either social welfare issues or concerns about public order. In 2004, for example, nearly half (49 percent) cited social issues, whereas 29 percent (the highest since 1984, i.e., since the Cold War) cited foreign and defense issues. Mostly that was the war in Iraq in particular (18 percent). In 2008 (shifting to the pooled exit poll) 63 percent of voters said the economy was most important, with the war in Iraq selected by 10 percent and the war on terror by 9 percent. That high a percentage selecting the economy should come as no surprise as we were in the midst of the initial decline into the "Great Recession," the most severe since the Great Depression.

Table 6-3A reports the results of the exit poll for the 2012 and 2016 elections. Foreign policy in 2012 continued to drop in concern as U.S. involvement in Iraq was over (at least temporarily) and the war in Afghanistan was diminishing (at least temporarily). Only 5 percent selected foreign policy as most important. It was the economy that remained dominant, as 59 percent selected it as their chief concern, whereas 15 percent more said it was the deficit. The latter had been a key part of the Tea Party and Republican leadership concerns through 2010 and into 2012 (it is of course an issue that touches on the economy and on the role of the government and so is not purely about the economy nor about the government). Another large portion, 18 percent, said that health care was the most important problem, whereas selection of other options was rare.

In 2016 the economy remained the most important concern, dropping only slightly to 52 percent of voters, even though the economy had improved noticeably over the intervening four years. Foreign policy increased to 13 percent as both wars rekindled and as Trump critiqued our involvement in foreign trade and international relations generally. The two issues that, in effect, replaced health care and the budget deficit as concerns (those two dropping to low percentages in 2016) were terrorism (18 percent of the voting public) and immigration (13 percent); both appear to us to be made into popular concerns as much by Trump's campaigning as for any other reason. These issues are sometimes referred to as "intermestic," that is, as having both international and domestic dimensions. Indeed one part of the partisan debate over these issues is precisely whether the international or domestic aspects of these issues are predominant.

Table 6-3B illustrates that people's concerns played a role in their voting. Those concerned about two of Trump's most regularly discussed issues in 2016, terrorism and immigration, were indeed considerably more likely to support him than to vote for Clinton. Conversely Clinton had a clear advantage on foreign policy generally. The vote was closer among those who were concerned about the economy, something both candidates raised often and emphasized greatly in their campaigns. Given the interpretation often heard about the concerns of white working-class voters, it was Clinton who held an eleven-point lead among those who stated that the economy was their most important concern.

**Table 6-3 Most Important Problem as Seen by the Electorate, 2012 and 2016, and Reported Vote for Clinton and Trump in 2016 (Percent)**

**Table 6-3A**

| Problem | 2012 | 2016 |
|---|---|---|
| The economy | 59 | 52 |
| Foreign policy | 5 | 13 |
| Terrorism | — | 18 |
| Immigration | — | 13 |
| Health care | 18 | — |
| Federal budget deficit | 15 | — |

**Table 6-3B Percent reporting voted for**

| | Obama | Romney | Clinton | Trump |
|---|---|---|---|---|
| The economy | 47% | 51% | 52% | 41% |
| Foreign policy | 56% | 33% | 60% | 33% |
| Terrorism | — | — | 40% | 57% |
| Immigration | | 33% | 64% | |
| Health care | 75% | 24% | — | — |
| Federal budget deficit | 32% | 66% | — | — |

*Sources:* 2012 and 2016 National Election Exit Polls. Question in 2012 asked 10,798 respondents about which of the four issues were the most important issue facing the country and 24,558 respondents in 2016. The two percentages do not sum to 100%, with the rest reporting that they voted for some other candidate or did not answer the question. For 2016: http://www.cnn.com/election/results/exit-polls, accessed 6/15/2017. For 2012: https://ropercenter.cornell.edu/polls/us-elections/how-groups-voted/how-groups-voted-2012/. Accessed June 17, 2017.

## ISSUE POSITIONS AND PERCEPTIONS

Since 1972 the ANES surveys have included issue scales designed to measure the preferences of the electorate and voters' perceptions of the positions the candidates took on the issues.[20] The questions are therefore especially appropriate for examining prospective issue evaluations. We hasten to add, however, that voters' perceptions of where the incumbent party's nominee stands may well be based in part on what the president has done in office as well as on the campaign promises he or she made as the party's nominee. This is especially likely when the incumbent vice president is nominated, such as Vice President Gore in 2000, or when someone who played a prominent role in the presidential administration, such as former secretary of state Clinton in 2016, is nominated. The policy promises of the opposition party candidate may also be judged in part by what that candidate's party did when it last held the White House. Nevertheless, the issue scales generally focus on prospective evaluations and are very different from those used to make the retrospective judgments examined in Chapter 7.

The issue scales will be used to examine several questions: What alternatives did the voters believe the candidates were offering? To what extent did the voters have issue preferences of their own and relatively clear perceptions of candidates' positions? Finally how strongly were voters' preferences and perceptions related to their choice of candidates?

Figure 6-1 shows the seven-point issue scales used in the 2016 ANES survey. The figure presents the average (median) position of the respondents (labeled "S" for self) and the average (median) perceptions of the positions of Clinton and Trump (labeled "C" and "T"). The issues raised in 2016 probe the respondents' own preferences and perceptions of the major-party nominees on whether government should spend more or less on social services; whether defense spending should be increased or decreased; whether health insurance should be provided by the government or by private insurance; whether the government should see to it that everyone has a job and a good standard of living or let citizens get ahead on their own; whether the government should provide aid to blacks or whether they should help themselves; and whether the government should protect the environment at the cost of jobs and a good standard of living. These issues were selected for inclusion in the ANES survey because they are controversial and generally measure long-standing partisan divisions. As a result the average citizen comes out looking reasonably moderate on these issues. In every case the average citizen falls between the positions corresponding to the average placements of the two candidates. On many issues asked in 2012, the typical citizen is near the center of the scale, generally falling between one-half point to the left and one-half point to the right of the midpoint of four. Only on the environment scale was the average citizen more than a full point—in this case a bit more than a point and a half to the left—of the center. The basic message is that on average, the public in 2012 was mostly moderate on these long-standing issues.

Note that, on five of six of the scales, on all but the defense spending measure the average citizen is at least very slightly to the liberal end of the scale. Because we use the median as our measure of "average," that means that more than half of the respondents were at least slightly liberal and may have been very liberal on those five issues. That is actually a change from 2012 (in which all six of these issue scales were also included).[21] In that year the average citizen also was to the left on five of six of these issue scales. The exception was aid to blacks, where the average citizen

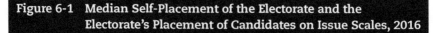

Figure 6-1 Median Self-Placement of the Electorate and the Electorate's Placement of Candidates on Issue Scales, 2016

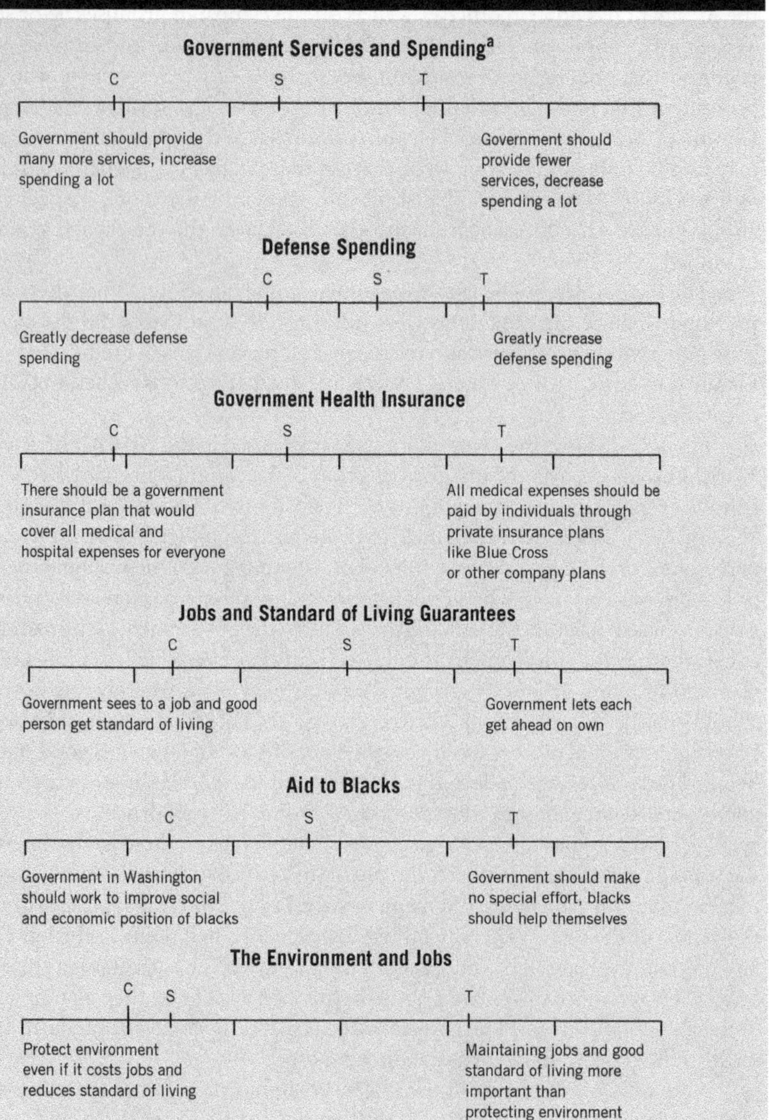


*Source:* Author's analysis of the 2016 ANES.

*Note:* S = median self-placement of the respondents; T = median placement of Trump; C = median placement of Romney.

[a]Reversed from actual scoring to make a "liberal" response closer to point 1 and a "conservative" response closer to point 7.

was at 4.4. On health care the average citizen was somewhat more liberal in 2016 than 2012, so whereas the Republican concerns about "Obamacare" may indeed have had an effect on public opinion, it did not generate greater opposition but, if anything, greater support for the program. Perhaps more likely, the public had, on balance, become adjusted to having "Obamacare" and apparently found it to their liking so that effect did not change opinion that greatly. One might also imagine that the Republican and Tea Party and Freedom Caucus appeals to reduce the size of the federal government might have made a difference. If so they had effects very similar to health care. In fact respondents were at least slightly more liberal on average on every issue but defense spending in 2016 compared to 2012. This was particularly clear with respect to the aid to blacks scale, in which the average respondent was more than a half point further to the left in 2016 than in 2012. Still, in most cases, the average citizen was only slightly left of center and better seen as moderate than even moderately liberal. The exception was the jobs and environment issue, on which the average citizen was clearly to the left of center, as they have been on this issue in most elections.

Generally, on issue scales used between 1980 and 2016, the public has viewed the Democratic candidate as more liberal and the Republican candidate as more conservative than the average member of the public.[22] Indeed these differences are often quite large, and as it happens, this is especially so in 2016. Except for defense spending, they exceed three points (with a maximum difference of six points) on every issue scale.[23] This set of differences is perhaps the greatest we have yet measured.

That effect appears to be due more to perceptions on the Republican side. Perceptions of Clinton generally were very similar to those of Obama four years earlier, although mostly just a bit more centrist. The rather ironic exception is aid to blacks, where respondents saw her just slightly to the left of where they had placed Obama. Trump, for his part, was generally seen as more conservative than Romney had been seen in 2012, although often this difference was small (and on government services and spending, he was seen as very slightly more moderate). The largest difference was his more conservative stances on defense spending, the environment, and aid to blacks. Overall the public saw quite large differences between the offerings of the two candidates. No matter how much or how little the public may have been polarized in 2012, it saw that alleged polarization dividing the two candidates, even more so than in preceding elections.

Although voters saw clear differences between the candidates, the average voter faced a difficult choice. Clinton was seen to the left of the average respondent, and Trump was seen to the right on every issue, and the average voter was rarely much closer to one candidate than the other (the exception being much closer to Clinton on the environment). Of course we cannot at this point go much further on these overall figures. The choice is made not by a mythical average voter choosing over what the respondents as a whole thought the candidates offered, but it is made by individual voters considering what they think about these issues. To consider a voter's choices, then we must look inside these averages to assess the individual behavior that makes up those averages.

## ISSUE VOTING CRITERIA

### The Problem

Because voting is an individual action, we must look at the preferences of individuals to see whether prospective issues influenced their votes. In fact the question of prospective voting is controversial. In their classic study of the American electorate, *The American Voter*, Angus Campbell and his colleagues pointed out that the public is often ill-informed about public policy and may not be able to vote on the basis of issues.[24] They asked themselves what information voters would need before an issue could influence the decision on how to vote, and they answered by posing three conditions. First, the voters must hold an opinion on the issue; second, they must learn what the government is doing on the issue; and third, they must perceive a difference between the policies of the two major parties. According to the authors' analysis, only about one-quarter to one-third of the electorate in 1956 could meet these three conditions, and they therefore concluded that relatively few were likely to vote on the basis of issues.

Although it is impossible to replicate the analysis in *The American Voter*, we can adapt the authors' procedures to the 2016 electorate. ANES data, in fact, focus even more directly on the actual choice citizens must make—the choice among the candidates. The first criterion is whether respondents claim to have an opinion on the issue. This is measured by whether they placed themselves on the issue scale as measured by Campbell et al. Second, the respondents should have some perception of the positions taken by the candidates on an issue. This is measured by whether they could place both major-party candidates on that issue. Although some voters might perceive the position of one candidate and vote on that basis, prospective voting involves a comparison between or among alternatives, so the expressed ability to perceive the stands of the contenders seems a minimal requirement of prospective issue voting. Third, the voter must see a difference between the positions of the candidates. Failing to see a difference means that the voter perceived no choice on the issue, perhaps because he or she failed to detect actual distinctions between the candidates. This failure might arise from lack of attention to the issue in the campaign. It also may arise from instances in which the candidates actually did take very similar positions on the issue, and respondents were thus, on average, reflecting that similarity, as we believe was truer of the candidates on most issues in 1976 than in other campaigns. Actual similarity of positions is rare in this era of partisan polarization, although this happens at times on specific issues. Clinton and Trump, for example, both opposed and said they would end any attempt to ratify the TPP.

A voter might be able to satisfy these criteria but misperceive the offerings of the candidates. This leads to a fourth condition, which we are able to measure more systematically than was possible in 1956: Do the respondents accurately perceive the relative positions of the two major-party candidates—that is, do they see Trump as more conservative than Clinton? This criterion does not demand that the voter have an accurate perception of what the candidate proposes, but it does expect the voter to recognize that Clinton, for example, favored spending more on social services than did Trump.

In Table 6-4, we report the percentages of the sample that met the four criteria on the six issue scales used in 2016.[25] We also show the average proportion that met these criteria for all scales and compare those averages to comparable averages for all issue scales used in the eleven preceding elections.[26] Column I of Table 6-4 reveals that most people felt capable of placing themselves on the issue scales, and this capability was common to all election years.[27]

Nearly as many of the public also placed both candidates on the scales. Indeed a higher percentage satisfied these two criteria in 2016 than any other election. The environmental/jobs issue yielded the lowest percentage satisfying these criteria in 2016, but even that scale yielded a higher percentage, at 81, than the average in any other year (which was highest in 1996 with an average of 80 percent). The 83 percent average for 2016 in Column II is the highest of any election for which we have relevant data.

Although there is a decline in the percentage also seeing differences between the two candidates on these issues, the main point is that 2016 is a high watermark in this regard. Indeed considering this third criterion makes 2016 stand out even more clearly. In 2016 over three in four, on average, satisfied the first three criteria: they placed both themselves and both candidates on the issue scale, and they placed the candidates at two different positions on the scale.

Finally, a very high—the highest by far—percentage met all four issue voting criteria, with more than two in three doing so on average. As the reader can see, the average meeting all four criteria in 2016 was higher than the average meeting the first three criteria in any other election year. And compare 2016 with 1976. In the earlier election only one in four met these criteria on average. In that year relatively few could see differences between Gerald Ford and Jimmy Carter on issues and therefore could hardly have also gotten them in the correct order! But now, by 2016, the idea of polarization seems to have fully settled into the presidential electorate. That is to say they saw the candidates as taking consistently and starkly different positions on just about every major issue (or at least every one of these six), and there was very little disagreement about that point in the electorate. They saw the Republican and the Democratic Party nominees as polarized, more so than ever before over the last twelve elections. Although it could be that Clinton and Trump were uniquely ideological candidates, we believe it more likely that the sustained polarization between the two party elites is becoming clearer to the public.

The data in Table 6-4 suggest that the potential for prospective issue voting was high in 2016. Therefore, we might expect these issues to be rather closely related to voter choice. We will examine voter choice on these issues in two ways. First, how often did people vote for the closer candidate on each issue? Second, how strongly related to the vote is the set of all issues taken together?

## APPARENT ISSUE VOTING IN 2016

### Issue Criteria and Voting on Each Issue

The first question is to what extent did people who were closer to a candidate on a given issue actually vote for that candidate—that is, how strong is apparent issue

## Table 6-4 Four Criteria for Issue Voting, 2016, and Comparisons with 1972–2012 Presidential Elections

| Issue Scale | Percentage of Sample Who . . . | | | |
|---|---|---|---|---|
| | I Placed self on scale | II Placed both candidates on scale[a] | III Saw differences between Clinton and Trump | IV Saw Clinton as more "liberal" than Trump |
| Government spending/services | 82 | 81 | 72 | 70 |
| Defense spending | 84 | 82 | 71 | 67 |
| Government health insurance | 86 | 85 | 74 | 73 |
| Jobs and standard of living | 86 | 85 | 75 | 73 |
| Aid to blacks | 86 | 84 | 73 | 78 |
| Jobs and the environment | 81 | 80 | 70 | 67 |
| **Average[b]** | | | | |
| 2016 (6) | 84 | 83 | 73 | 71 |
| 2012 (6) | 86 | 76 | 67 | 60 |
| 2008 (7) | 88 | 78 | 61 | 51 |
| 2004 (7) | 89 | 76 | 62 | 52 |
| 2000 (7) | 87 | 69 | 51 | 41 |
| 1996 (9) | 89 | 80 | 65 | 55 |
| 1992 (3) | 85 | 71 | 66 | 52 |
| 1988 (7) | 86 | 66 | 52 | 43 |
| 1984 (7) | 84 | 73 | 62 | 53 |
| 1980 (9) | 82 | 61 | 51 | 43 |
| 1976 (9) | 84 | 58 | 39 | 26 |
| 1972 (8) | 90 | 65 | 49 | 41 |

*Source:* Authors' analysis of ANES surveys.

*Note:* Columns II, III, and IV compare the Democratic and Republican nominees. Third-party or independent candidates John Anderson (1980), Ross Perot (1992 and 1996), and Ralph Nader (2000 and 2004) were excluded.

[a]Until 1996 respondents who could not place themselves on a scale were not asked to place the candidates on that issue scale. Although they were asked to do so in 1996, 2000, 2004, 2008, 2012, and 2016, we excluded them from further calculations to maintain comparability with prior surveys.

[b]Number in parentheses is the number of issue scales included in the average for each election year survey.

voting?[28] In Table 6-5 we report the proportion of major-party voters who voted for Clinton by where they placed themselves on the issue scales. We divided the seven points into the set of positions that were closer to where the average citizen placed Trump and Clinton (see Figure 6-1).[29] Note that whereas the average perceptions of the two candidates did vary from issue to issue, the net effect of that variation did not make a great deal of difference. In particular, on five of the six issues (all but defense spending), respondents who placed themselves to the left of the midpoint, that is, on points 1, 2, or 3, were closer to where the electorate as a whole thought Clinton stood. Similarly those to the right of the midpoint were always closer to the perception of Trump. On three issues, those who placed themselves at point 4, the midpoint, were closer to where the electorate thought Trump stood, on defense spending "4s" were closer to Clinton's position, and on the jobs and standard of living and the aid to blacks scales, those at 4 were essentially equidistant from both candidates. We see this as support for the idea that the two parties and their candidates and officeholders have achieved a balanced polarization with consistent deviation for the policy center toward their party's extreme (liberal for Democrats, conservative for Republicans), on issue after issue, and that by 2016, the public sees clearly even the presidential candidates being consistent with their party's positions.

Table 6-5 reveals the clear relationship between the voters' issue positions and the candidate they supported on the six scales. Those who adopted positions at the "liberal" end of each scale were very likely to vote for Clinton. If we define liberal as adopting position 1 or 2, Clinton received at least three in four votes and usually more on each scale. Indeed that was even true for those at point 3, the most slightly liberal position, on every issue except the environmental issue. Clinton received fewer than one in four votes on any issue scale from those at the two most conservative positions, whereas Trump carried a clear majority of the vote from those at point 5 on any of the scales. Those at the midpoint of 4 on any issue except the environment gave Clinton a three in five vote majority, and those in this in-between position often were a plurality on that issue. The major exception was the jobs and the environment scale, in which the distribution was shifted much farther to the left than on any of the other issues. Although the midpoint was still a common position, many more were to the left than in the middle. Those at the middle position gave a two to one majority to Trump on this one issue. Otherwise the midpoint marked a clear transition with large majorities voting for Clinton when they were to the left, and large majorities voting for Trump on the right, and the 4 position being clearly in between. Regardless of the details, these are the patterns we would expect if voters voted for the closer candidate on an issue.

The information on issues can be summarized, as it is in Table 6-6, to illustrate what happens when voters met the various conditions for issue voting. In the first column of Table 6-6, we report the percentage of major-party voters who placed themselves closer to the average perception of Trump or Clinton and who voted for the closer candidate. To be more specific the denominator is the total number of major-party voters who placed themselves closer to the electorate's perception of Trump or Clinton. The numerator is the total number of major-party voters who were both closer to Clinton and voted for her plus the total number of major-party voters who were both closer to Trump and voted for him.

**Table 6-5 Major-Party Voters Who Voted for Clinton, by Seven-Point Issue Scales, 2016 (Percent)**

| | Closer to Median Perception of Clinton | | | Closer to Median Perception of Trump | | | | |
|---|---|---|---|---|---|---|---|---|
| **Issue Scale** | **1** | **2** | **3** | **4** | **5** | **6** | **7** | **(*N*)** |
| Government spending/services[a] | 84 | 88 | 82 | 61 | 30 | 16 | 9 | |
| (*N*) | (160) | (208) | (393) | (481) | (315) | (268) | (254) | (2,079) |
| Defense spending | 79 | 81 | 82 | 66 | 42 | 24 | 23 | |
| (*N*) | (103) | (148) | (242) | (549) | (431) | (351) | (283) | (2,107) |
| Government health insurance | 84 | 82 | 74 | 60 | 39 | 21 | 12 | |
| (*N*) | (398) | (221) | (237) | (392) | (260) | (278) | (362) | (2,148) |
| Jobs and standard of living | 79 | 85 | 82 | 64 | 46 | 23 | 14 | |
| (*N*) | (212) | (179) | (302) | (436) | (368) | (339) | (315) | (2,151) |
| Aid to blacks | 88 | 90 | 84 | 65 | 38 | 20 | 17 | |
| (*N*) | (245) | (198) | (230) | (464) | (246) | (325) | (432) | (2,140) |
| Jobs and the environment | 82 | 78 | 61 | 33 | 21 | 16 | 14 | |
| (*N*) | (549) | (337) | (298) | (348) | (215) | (181) | (115) | (2,043) |

*Source:* Authors' analysis of the 2016 ANES.

*Note:* Numbers in parentheses are the totals on which percentages are based. Numbers are weighted.

[a]Reversed from actual scoring to make a "liberal" response closer to 1 and a "conservative" response closer to 7.

If voting were unrelated to issue positions, we would expect 50 percent of voters to vote for the closer candidate on average. In 2016, on average, 75 percent voted for the closer candidate. As can be seen in the comparisons to earlier elections, this is by far the highest level of apparent issue voting since these issue scales were widely used,

**Table 6-6 Apparent Issue Voting, 2016, and Comparisons with 1972–2012 Presidential Elections (Percent)**

| Issue Scale | Percentage of Voters Who Voted for Closer Candidate and . . . | | |
|---|---|---|---|
| | Placed self on issue scale | Met all four issue voting criteria | Placed self but failed to meet all three other criteria |
| Government spending/services | 72 | 77 | 60 |
| Defense spending | 71 | 79 | 64 |
| Government health insurance | 72 | 78 | 67 |
| Jobs and standard of living | 76 | 82 | 72 |
| Aid to blacks | 81 | 85 | 73 |
| Jobs and the environment | 76 | 85 | 58 |
| **Average**[a] | | | |
| 2016 (6) | 75 | 81 | 66 |
| 2012 (6) | 63 | 68 | 58 |
| 2008 (7) | 62 | 71 | 47 |
| 2004 (7) | 67 | 75 | 51 |
| 2000 (7) | 60 | 68 | 40 |
| 1996 (9) | 63 | 74 | 41 |
| 1992 (3) | 62 | 70 | 48 |
| 1988 (7) | 62 | 71 | 45 |
| 1984 (7) | 65 | 73 | 46 |
| 1980 (9) | 63 | 71 | 48 |
| 1976 (9) | 57 | 70 | 50 |
| 1972 (8) | 66 | 76 | 55 |

*Source:* Authors' analysis of ANES surveys.

*Note:* An "apparent issue vote" is a vote for the candidate closer to one's position on an issue scale. The closer candidate is determined by comparing self-placement to the median placements of the two candidates on the scale as a whole. Respondents who did not place themselves or who were equidistant from the two candidates are excluded from the calculations.

In 2008, analyses conducted on the randomly selected half-sample asked questions with the traditional wording, except aid to blacks, which was asked of the full sample with same (traditional) wording.

[a]Number in parentheses is the number of seven-point issue scales included in the average for each election year survey.

that is, from 1972 to date. These figures do not tell the whole story, however, because those who placed themselves on an issue but failed to meet some other criterion were unlikely to have cast a vote based on that issue. In the second column of Table 6-6, we report the percentage of those who voted for the closer candidate on each issue among voters who met all four conditions on that issue. The third column reports the percentage that voted for the closer candidate among voters who placed themselves but failed to meet all three of the remaining conditions

Those respondents who met all four conditions were more likely to vote for the closer candidate on any issue. Indeed until this year there has been relatively little difference, on average, across all elections, with about seven in ten such voters supporting the closer candidate. But this year the percentage jumped to greater than eight in ten, higher even than the erstwhile most ideologically charged election in 1972. By contrast, for those respondents who failed to meet the last three of the conditions on issue voting, voting was essentially random with respect to the issues, although surprisingly high in 2016, at 66 percent.[30]

The strong similarity of all election averages in the second and third columns suggests that issue voting seems more prevalent in some elections than others because elections differ in the number of people who clearly perceive differences between the candidates. In all elections about seven in ten who satisfied all four conditions voted consistently with their issue preferences; in all elections those who did not satisfy all the conditions on perceptions of candidates voted essentially randomly with respect to individual issues. As we saw earlier the degree to which such perceptions vary from election to election depends more on the strategies of the candidates than on the qualities of the voters. Therefore, the relatively low percentage of apparent issue voting in 1976, for example, results from the perception of small differences between the two rather moderate candidates. The larger magnitude of apparent issue voting in 2016 stems primarily from the greater clarity with which most people saw the positions of the two nominees. Surely this is a consequence of the polarization of the two parties among candidates and office holders.

## The Balance-of-Issues Measure

In prospective issue voting voters compare the full set of policy proposals made by the candidates. Because nearly every issue is strongly related to the vote, we might expect the set of all issues to be even more strongly so. To examine this relationship we constructed an overall assessment of the issue scales to arrive at what we call the balance-of-issues measure. We give individuals a score of +1 if their positions on an issue scale were closer to the average perception of Trump, a score of –1 if their positions were closer to the average perception of Clinton, and a score of 0 if they had no preference on an issue or put themselves on point 4 on the two issues in which that was essentially equidistant from the two candidates' positions. The scores for all six issue scales were added together, creating a measure that ranged from –6 to +6. For example, respondents who were closer to the average perception of Clinton's positions on all seven scales received a score of –6. A negative score indicated that the respondent was, on balance, closer to the public's perception of Clinton, whereas a positive score indicated the respondent was, overall, closer to the public's perception of Trump. We collapsed this thirteen-point measure into seven categories, running from strongly Democratic through neutral to strongly Republican. We have used this scale since 1980 (see Abramson et al., 2016, and sources cited therein). The results are reported in Table 6-7.

As can be seen in Table 6-7A, 19 percent of respondents were in the two most strongly Democratic positions, whereas 30 percent were strongly or moderately Republican. Approximately equal proportions were in the three middle categories, totaling together just over half the electorate. Thus the balance-of-issues measure tilted slightly in the Republican direction, but was much more evenly balanced than the more heavily pro-Republican tilt in 2012.

The balance-of-issues measure was quite strongly related to the vote, as the findings for the individual issues would suggest (see Table 6-7B). Clinton won the vast majority of the votes from those in the strongly, moderately, and even the slightly Democratic categories. She won a bit more than six in ten votes from those in the neutral category and almost held her own in the slightly Republican category. Her support dropped off dramatically from that point. Indeed this relationship between the net balance-of-issues measure and the vote is stronger in 2016 than we have ever found before.

## The Abortion Issue

Clearly abortion was not the major issue in the 2016 election that it has been in some earlier ones. Even so it has been in most elections; it did play a significant, even if smaller, role in 2012; and it is likely to remain consequential in future elections. One special role that it played in 2016 was based on the belief that which party would get to fill the open seat on the Supreme Court would have a major role in the position the Court would likely take on this issue in the future. And, of course, policy about abortions plays a large role in partisan polarization. The Republican national platform has taken a strong pro-life stand since 1980, whereas the Democratic Party became increasingly strongly pro-choice. In addition it is one of a complex set of issues that define much of the social issues dimension, one of two major dimensions of domestic policy (economics being the second) into which most domestic policies—and most controversial issues—fall. Abortion has been central to the rise of social conservatism in America, virtually back to its modern emergence in the wake of the Supreme Court decision, *Roe v. Wade* (1973), which made abortion legal throughout the United States.

The second reason for examining this issue is that it is another policy question about which respondents were asked their own views as well as what they thought Trump's and Clinton's positions were—a battery that has been asked for the last several elections.[31] It differs from (and is therefore hard to compare directly with) the seven-point issue scales, however, because respondents were given only four alternatives, but each was a specified policy option:

1. By law, abortion should never be permitted.
2. The law should permit abortion only in case of rape, incest, or when the woman's life is in danger.

**Table 6-7 Distribution of Electorate on Net Balance-of-Issues Measure and Major-Party Vote, 2016 (Percent)**

| | Net Balance of Issues | | | | | | | | |
|---|---|---|---|---|---|---|---|---|---|
| | Strongly Democratic | Moderately Democratic | Slightly Democratic | Neutral | Slightly Republican | Moderately Republican | Strongly Republican | Total | (*N*) |
| | A. Distribution of responses | | | | | | | | |
| | 9 | 10 | 16 | 16 | 19 | 17 | 13 | 100 | (4267) |
| | B. Major-party voters who voted for Clinton | | | | | | | | |
| Percent | 97 | 91 | 82 | 62 | 47 | 21 | 3 | 53 | (2379) |
| (*N*) | (267) | (251) | (348) | (297) | (423) | (411) | (381) | | |

*Source:* Authors' analysis of the 2016 ANES.

*Note:* Numbers are weighted. The numbers in parentheses in Part B of the table are the totals on which the percentages are based.

**Table 6-8 Percentage of Major-Party Voters Who Voted for Clinton, by Opinion about Abortion and What They Believe Trump's and Clinton's Positions Are, 2016**

| | Respondent's Position on Abortion | | | | | | | |
|---|---|---|---|---|---|---|---|---|
| | Abortion should never be permitted | | Abortion should be permitted only in the case of rape, incest, or danger to health of the woman | | Abortion should be permitted for other reasons, but only if a need is established | | Abortion should be a matter of personal choice | |
| | % | (*N*) | % | (*N*) | % | (*N*) | % | (*N*) |
| All major-party voters | 23 | (324) | 29 | (583) | 52 | (324) | 73 | (1123) |
| Major-party voters who placed both candidates, who saw a difference between them, and who saw Clinton as more pro-choice than Trump | 14 | (237) | 26 | (458) | 50 | (246) | 78 | (884) |
| Major-party voters who did not meet all three of these conditions | 48 | (87) | 41 | (125) | 59 | (78) | 57 | (239) |

*Source:* Authors' analysis of the 2016 ANES.

*Note:* Numbers in parentheses are the totals on which the percentages are based. Numbers are weighted.

3. The law should permit abortion for reasons *other than* rape, incest, or danger to the woman's life but only after the need for the abortion has been clearly established.
4. By law, a woman should always be able to obtain an abortion as a matter of personal choice.

Table 6-8 reports percentages voting for Clinton for various groups of respondents. For example, about three in four voters who believe that abortion should be a matter of personal choice voted for her, whereas about one in four who thought it should never be permitted did so. Substantial numbers of voters met all four conditions on this issue and, for them, their position was even more strongly related to the vote, as almost seven in eight who thought abortion should be a matter of personal choice voted for Obama, but only one in seven who thought it should not be permitted did so. For those who did not meet all conditions for casting an issue-based vote, their voting was essentially the random coin flip one would expect. Thus the abortion issue adds to our previous findings.

## CONCLUSION

Our findings suggest that for major-party voters, prospective issues were important in the 2016 election. In fact 2016 stands out as one in which prospective issues played about as strong a role in shaping their vote as any other. Prospective issues are particularly important for understanding how citizens voted. They cannot alone account for Clinton's victory in the popular vote nor Trump's in the electoral vote. Those for whom prospective issues gave a clear choice, however, voted consistently with those issues. But most people were located between the candidates as the electorate saw them. Indeed on most issues the majority of people were relatively moderate, and the candidates were perceived as more conservative and more liberal, respectively. Moreover, when the conditions for issue voting are present, there can be a strong relationship between the position voters hold and their choice between the major-party candidates. And, it appears, that perhaps due to the lengthening period for which the two parties have polarized on most important policies facing the electorate, a remarkably high proportion of the electorate met the conditions for casting an issue-based vote on many of the issues considered here. For these reasons we conclude that voters took prospective issues into account in 2016, but it is also our conclusion that they also considered other factors. In the next chapter we will see that the second form of policy voting, that based on retrospective evaluations, was among those other factors, as it has been in previous presidential elections.

CHAPTER SEVEN

# PRESIDENTIAL PERFORMANCE AND CANDIDATE CHOICE

Just as in most elections, the presidential candidates focused more on the economy than any other issue in 2016. Clinton robustly defended the record of the Obama administration on the economy, pointing to such evidence as eight years of growth from the very low point the American economy had hit in 2008. Trump, in contrast, did not argue that those facts were incorrect (although there was not 100 percent agreement on what the facts were); he argued in part for a different interpretation of the same facts (growth was too slow) and in part for a completely different part of the record (e.g., job losses to other nations), possible because the economy is so complex and multifaceted.[1] Compared to Romney in 2012, he was not free to argue as strongly against the Obama record because it had an eight-year run of steady, if unspectacular, growth, instead of only four. But he was in a far stronger position than McCain in 2008, having to defend the Bush administration during the campaign while the economy imploded.

But this was also hardly the first election in which candidates thought carefully about how they would present themselves with respect to the successes or failures of the incumbent president and his party. To the extent that voters were considering the successes and failures of the incumbent president and his party in these cases, perhaps in comparison to what they thought his opponent and the opponent's party would have done had they been in office, voters were casting a retrospective vote. And certainly the eight-year record of the Democratic administration and the memory of the collapse of the economy in September 2008, which occurred under then president George W. Bush's term, provided the raw materials for a strong retrospective evaluation set of claims by candidates, ones that well might have been absorbed by the public.

Retrospective evaluations are concerns about policy, but they differ significantly from the prospective evaluations considered in the last chapter.[2] Retrospective evaluations are, as the name suggests, concerns about the past. These evaluations focus on outcomes, with what actually happened, rather than on the policy means for achieving those outcomes, which are at the heart of prospective evaluations. For example, after his reelection in 2004, George W. Bush argued that there was a looming problem in

Social Security and proposed private accounts as a solution. Even though other events soon intervened to draw attention away from this policy, some Democrats argued against the president on the grounds that creating private accounts would actually make the problem worse. These Democrats agreed with Bush that there was a problem, but they were focusing on concerns they had about the policy means that Bush proposed to solve that problem, a classic response in terms of prospective evaluations. Other Democrats argued that there really was no serious problem with Social Security in the first place. Such arguments focused on policy outcomes, which are the basis of retrospective judgments. This scenario illustrates the difference between prospective and retrospective judgments but also suggests that the two are often different sides of the same policy coin, which is indeed the basic point of the Downs-Fiorina perspective.

## WHAT IS RETROSPECTIVE VOTING?

A voter who casts a ballot for the incumbent party's candidate because the incumbent was, in the voter's opinion, a successful president or votes for the opposition because, in the voter's opinion, the incumbent was unsuccessful is said to have cast a retrospective vote. In other words retrospective voting decisions are based on evaluations of the course of politics over the last term in office and on evaluations of how much the incumbent should be held responsible for what good or bad outcomes occurred. V. O. Key, Jr., popularized this argument by suggesting that the voter might be "a rational god of vengeance and of reward."[3]

The more closely a candidate can be tied to the actions of the incumbent, the more likely it is that voters will decide retrospectively. The incumbent president cannot escape such evaluations, and the incumbent vice president is usually identified with (and often chooses to identify him- or herself with) the administration's performance. The electorate has frequently played the role of Key's "rational god" because an incumbent president or vice president has stood for election in twenty-five of the thirty-one presidential elections since 1900 (all but 1908, 1920, 1928, 1952, 2008, and 2016). In 2016 Clinton was an only slightly less central part of at least the first term of the Obama administration than Vice President Biden. More importantly she proudly tied herself to the Obama administration throughout her campaign.

Key's thesis has three aspects. First, retrospective voters are oriented toward outcomes rather than the policy means to achieve them. Second, these voters evaluate the performance of the incumbent only, all but ignoring the opposition. Finally they evaluate what has been done, paying little attention to what the candidates promise to do in the future. Does this kind of voting make sense? Some suggest an alternative, as we discuss next, but note that if everyone did, in fact, vote against an incumbent whose performance they thought insufficient, then incumbents would have very strong incentives to provide such sufficiently high levels of performance to avoid the wrath of the electorate.

Anthony Downs was the first to develop in some detail an alternative version of retrospective voting.[4] His account is one about information and its credibility to the voter. He argues that voters look to the past to understand what the incumbent party's candidate will do in the future. According to Downs parties are basically consistent in their goals, methods, and ideologies over time. Therefore, the past performances of both parties and perhaps their nominees may prove relevant for making predictions about their future conduct. Because it takes time and effort to evaluate campaign promises and because promises are just words, voters find it faster, easier, and safer to use past performance to project the administration's actions for the next four years. Downs also emphasizes that retrospective evaluations are used in making comparisons among the alternatives presented to the voter. Key sees a retrospective referendum on the incumbent's party alone. Downs believes that retrospective evaluations are used to compare the candidates as well as to provide a guide to the future. Even incumbents may use such Downsian retrospective claims. In 1996, for example, Clinton attempted to tie his opponent, Senator Bob Dole, to the performance of congressional Republicans because they had assumed the majority in the 1994 election. Clinton pointedly referred to the 104th Congress as the "Dole-Gingrich" Congress. Twenty years later a different Clinton was trying to tie evaluations of her expected performance to those of the Obama administration in which she had served.

Morris P. Fiorina elaborates on and extends Downs's thesis.[5] Here we focus especially on Fiorina's understanding of party identification, which was a completely new addition to the Downsian perspective. Fiorina claimed that party identification plays a central role in this perspective on retrospective voting. It differs from that of Campbell et al., however.[6] He argued that "citizens monitor party promises and performances over time, encapsulate their observations in a summary judgment termed 'party identification,' and rely on this core of previous experience when they assign responsibility for current societal conditions and evaluate ambiguous platforms designed to deal with uncertain futures."[7] We return to Fiorina's views on partisanship in Chapter 8.[8]

Retrospective voting and voting according to issue positions, as analyzed in Chapter 6, differ significantly. The difference lies in how concerned people are with societal outcomes and how concerned they are with the policy means to achieve desired outcomes. For example, everyone prefers economic prosperity. The disagreement among political decision makers lies in how best to achieve it. At the voters' level, however, the central question is whether people care only about achieving prosperity or whether they care about, or even are able to judge, how to achieve this desired goal. Perhaps they looked at high inflation and interest rates in 1980 and said, "We tried Carter's approach, and it failed. Let's try something else—anything else." They may have noted the long run of relative economic prosperity from 1983 to 1988 and said, "Whatever Reagan did, it worked. Let's keep it going by putting his vice president in office." In 1996 they may have agreed with Clinton that he had presided over a successful economy, and so they decided to remain with the incumbent. In 2016 just how these concerns would play was uncertain. Would the public judge the economy as improving sufficiently, or was its improvement too little, too late?

Economic policy, along with foreign and defense policies, are especially likely to be discussed in these terms because they share several characteristics. First, the outcomes are clear, and most voters can judge whether they approve of the results. Inflation and unemployment are high or low; the economy is growing, or it is not. The country is at war or at peace; the world is stable or unstable.[9] Second, there is often near consensus on the desired outcomes; no one disagrees with peace or prosperity, with world stability, or with low unemployment. Third, the means to achieving these ends are often very complex, and information is hard to understand; experts as well as candidates and parties disagree over the specific ways to achieve the desired ends. How should the economy be improved, and how could terrorism possibly be contained or democracy established in a foreign land?

As issues, therefore, peace and prosperity differ sharply from policy areas such as abortion, in which there is vigorous disagreement over ends among experts, leaders, and the public. On still other issues, people value both ends *and* means. The classic cases often revolve around the question of whether it is appropriate for government to take action in a particular area at all. Ronald Reagan was fond of saying, "Government isn't the solution to our problems; government *is* the problem." For example, should the government provide national health insurance? After decades of trying, the Democrats, under the Obama administration, had finally succeeded in passing the Affordable Care Act (ACA), a program labeled "Obamacare" by the Republicans. Republicans continued to try to roll back the law or keep it from being implemented. Few disagree with the end of better health care, but they disagree over the appropriate means to achieve it. The choice of means touches on some of the basic philosophical and ideological differences that have divided Republicans and Democrats for decades.[10] For example, in the 1984 presidential campaign, Walter Mondale agreed with Reagan that the country was in a period of economic prosperity and that prosperity was a good thing, but he also argued that Reagan's policies were unfair to the disadvantaged. In the 1992 campaign, Bill Clinton and Ross Perot claimed that Reagan's and George H. W. Bush's policies, by creating such large deficits, were creating the conditions for future woes. Clearly, then, disagreement was not over the ends but over the means and the consequences that would follow from using different means to achieve them.

Two basic conditions must be met before retrospective evaluations can affect voting choices. First, individuals must connect their concerns with the incumbent and the actions the president and his or her party took in office. This condition would not be present if, for example, a voter blamed earlier administrations with sowing the seeds that become the "Great Recession," blamed an ineffective Congress or Wall Street, or even believed that the problems were beyond anyone's control. Second, individuals, in the Downs-Fiorina view, must compare their evaluations of the incumbent's past performance with what they believe the nominee of the opposition party would do. For example, even if they thought Obama's performance on the economy was weak, voters might have compared that performance with programs supported by Trump in 2016 and concluded that his efforts would not result in any better outcome and might even make things worse.

In this second condition a certain asymmetry exists, one that benefits the incumbent. Even if the incumbent's performance has been weak in a certain area, the challenger still has to convince voters that he or she could do better. It is more difficult, however, for a challenger to convince voters who think the incumbent's performance has been strong that he or she, the challenger, would be even stronger. This asymmetry advantaged Republican candidates in the 1980s but worked to Bob Dole's disadvantage in 1996 and to Bush's in 2000 and his putative successor in 2008. Would this asymmetry apply to 2016? Or perhaps would both sides have the more difficult problem of convincing the electorate they could handle important problems when current performance was judged as neither especially strong nor especially weak?

We examine next some illustrative retrospective evaluations and study their impact on voter choice. In Chapter 6 we looked at issue scales designed to measure the public's evaluations of candidates' promises. For the incumbent party the public can evaluate not only its promises but also its actions. We compare promises with performance in this chapter, but one must remember that the distinctions are not as sharp in practice as they are in principle.[11] The Downs-Fiorina view is that past actions and projections about the future are necessarily intertwined.

## EVALUATIONS OF GOVERNMENT PERFORMANCE ON IMPORTANT PROBLEMS

"Do you feel things in this country are generally going in the right direction, or do you feel things have pretty seriously gotten off on the wrong track?"[12] This question is designed to measure retrospective judgments, and the responses are presented in Table 7-1A. In the appendix to this book, we report responses to the question the ANES had asked in prior surveys, comparing the respondents' evaluations of

**Table 7-1 Evaluation of Government Performance and Major-Party Vote, 2012 and 2016 (Percent)**

| Evaluation | 2012 | 2016 |
|---|---|---|
| **A. Evaluation of government performance during the last four years** | | |
| Right track | 33 | 25 |
| Wrong track | 67 | 75 |
| Total | 100 | 100 |
| (*N*) | (1958) | (4239) |
| **B. Percentage of major-party vote for incumbent's party nominee** | | |
| Right track | 94 | 94 |
| (*N*) | (430) | (663) |
| Wrong track | 30 | 36 |
| (*N*) | (804) | (1700) |

*Source:* Authors' analysis of the 2012 and 2016 ANES surveys.

*Note:* The numbers in parentheses are the totals on which the percentages are based. Numbers are weighted.

government performance on the problem that each respondent identified as the single most important one facing the country.[13] The most striking finding in Table 7-1A is that in 2016, as in 2012, just one in four thought the country was on the right track. These questions are asked by many polling agencies to gauge the feelings of the public, and Real Clear Politics (https://www.realclearpolitics.com/) reports an averaging across these many polling outfits. Using their aggregated data[14] we find that overall, the public has viewed things as being on the wrong track since June 2009, and the election period in 2016 was roughly typical of the perceptions of the country since then.[15]

If the voter is a rational god of vengeance and reward, we can expect to find a strong relationship between the evaluation of government performance and the vote. Such is indeed the case (see Table 7-1B). Nine in ten who thought the country was on the right track voted for Clinton. Only a few more than one in three who thought the country was on the wrong track voted for her.

According to Downs and Fiorina, it is important for voters not only to evaluate how things have been going but also to assess how that evaluation compares with the alternative. In most recent elections, including 2016, respondents have been asked which party would do a better job of solving the problem they named as the most important. Table 7-2 shows the responses to these questions. These questions are clearly oriented toward the future, but they may call for judgments about past performance, consistent with the Downs-Fiorina view. Respondents were not asked to evaluate policy alternatives, and thus responses were most likely based on a retrospective comparison of how the incumbent party handled things with a prediction about how the opposition would fare. We therefore consider these questions to be a measure of comparative retrospective evaluations.

Table 7-2A shows that the public had different views about which party was better at handling their important concerns. In particular there is pretty close to an even three-way split among those thinking that one party or the other was better or that there was no difference between the two parties in this regard. To be sure, there were fewer who said the Democrats were better, but the five-point difference between the two parties is slighter than usual. This is not much different from some earlier elections, including major Republican defeats (such as in 1996), solid victories (such as in 1988), and even landslide victories (such as in 1972). In 2008, by contrast, very few selected the "neither party" option and only one in four selected the Republican Party as better. Thus the Democratic Party held a huge advantage on this measure, one of the rare instances in which a clear majority thought one party would be better. But by 2012 the Democrats had lost their advantage, even though the Republicans had not really gathered a major advantage either. This set of responses persisted into 2016.

Table 7-2B reveals that the relationship between the party seen as better on the most important political problem and the vote is very strong. Clinton won nearly all the votes from those who thought the Democrats would be better. Trump was able to hold nearly all of those who thought the Republican Party better able to handle the most important problem. The candidates essentially split the "no difference" category evenly.

The data presented in Tables 7-1 and 7-2 have an important limitation. The first question, analyzed in Table 7-1, refers to an impression of how the country is going and not the incumbent president nor even the government. The question examined in Table 7-2 refers to which political party would handle the most important problem

**Table 7-2 Evaluation of Party Seen as Better on Most Important Political Problem and Major-Party Vote, 2012 and 2016 (Percent)**

| Better party | 2012 | 2016 |
|---|---|---|
| **A. Distribution of responses on party seen as better on most important political problem** | | |
| Republican | 31 | 35 |
| No difference | 31 | 35 |
| Democratic | 38 | 30 |
| Total | 100 | 100 |
| (*N*) | (1884) | (3578) |
| **B. Major-party voters who voted Democratic for president** | | |
| Republican | 7 | 6 |
| (*N*) | (436) | (923) |
| No difference | 56 | 64 |
| (*N*) | (405) | (933) |
| Democratic | 98 | 99 |
| (*N*) | (429) | (792) |

*Source:* Authors' analysis of the 2012 and 2016 ANES surveys.

*Note:* The numbers in parentheses are the totals on which the percentages are based. Numbers are weighted. Question wording: "Which political party do you think would be the most likely to get the government to do a better job in dealing with this problem?"

better and does not directly refer to the incumbent—and we believe it is the assessment of the incumbent that relates most directly to voters' evaluations of the candidates for president. Thus we will look more closely at the incumbent and at people's comparisons of his and the opposition's performance where the data are available to permit such comparisons.

## ECONOMIC EVALUATIONS AND THE VOTE FOR THE INCUMBENT

More than any other, economic issues have been highlighted as suitable retrospective issues. The impact of economic conditions on congressional and presidential elections has been studied extensively.[16] Popular evaluations of presidential effectiveness, John E. Mueller has pointed out, are strongly influenced by the economy.[17] A major reason for Jimmy Carter's defeat in 1980 was the perception that economic performance had been weak during his administration. Reagan's rhetorical question in the 1980 debate with Carter, "Are you better off than you were four years ago?" indicates that politicians realize the power such arguments have over the electorate. Reagan owed his sweeping reelection victory in 1984 largely to the perception that economic performance by the end of his first term had become, after a deep recession in the middle, much stronger.

If people are concerned about economic outcomes, they might start by looking for an answer to the sort of question Reagan asked. Table 7-3A presents ANES respondents' perceptions of whether they were financially better off than one year earlier, including the 2000–2016 election surveys (the appendix reports these back to 1972).[18] The economy grew steadily and strongly over the Clinton administration. Thus, by 2000 about a third felt better off, whereas far fewer felt worse off in 2000 than in any of the seven preceding elections (see appendix Table A7-3). More than half responded in 2000 that they were about the same as a year ago. In 2004 more than two in five reported feeling better off, the most popular response. The year 2008, however, was a different story, because half the respondents said they were worse off, with only a third saying they were better off and very few feeling their finances were the same. Simply 2008 was a terrible year for the economy, and everyone knew it (even though not everyone suffered). The situation in 2012 presented little to help or harm either side. A few more thought they were better off than worse off, but each view was held by close to two in five. Only one in four in claimed his or her situation was the same as in 2008. The continued slow but steady improvement over eight years, for 2016, as compared with only four for 2012, suggests that the Obama administration should have been somewhat more favorably reviewed by the public in 2016 compared to 2012, which appears to be true, at least in terms of the decline of "worse off" responses. In some ways 2016 was like 2000. Clinton, like Obama, had inherited a troubled economy from a Republican president, and as they left office they could point to more or less eight years of consistent growth. To be sure, the bad economy Clinton inherited was far better than that received by Obama, but the gains under Clinton were more spectacular than Obama's too. Still, the electorate overall felt they had had broadly similar results: around three in ten being better off, with fewer being a bit worse off, but about half said they were about the same.

In Table 7-3B we see how the responses to this question are related to the two-party presidential vote. In 2008 that relationship was not particularly strong. McCain was able to win just over half the votes of those who felt better off, just as he did among those relatively few who felt neither better nor worse off. Obama won support from a clear majority of that half of the electorate who felt worse off, winning more than three in five of their votes. But in 2012 that relationship strengthened. That is, the extent that the family's financial situation shaped the vote was as strong as the Reagan and senior Bush reelection contests, and the Clinton reelection campaign was not far behind. For 2016 the results are even stronger, and almost exactly the same as the landslide reelection of Reagan in 1984. It is quite obvious that personal economic situations are rarely as strongly related to the vote as in 2016 but, more importantly,

**Table 7-3 The Public's Assessment of Their Personal Financial Situation and Major-Party Vote, 2000–2016**

| Response | "Would you say that you (and your family) are better off or worse off financially than you were a year ago?" | | | | |
|---|---|---|---|---|---|
| | 2000[a] | 2004 | 2008 | 2012 | 2016 |
| **A. Distribution of responses** | | | | | |
| Better now | 33 | 43 | 32 | 41 | 28 |
| Same | 53 | 25 | 18 | 24 | 47 |
| Worse now | 14 | 32 | 50 | 36 | 25 |
| Total | 100 | 100 | 100 | 101 | 100 |
| (*N*) | (907) | (1,203) | (2,307) | (1,800) | (4,256) |
| **B. Major-party voters who voted for the incumbent party nominee for president** | | | | | |
| Better now | 56 | 65 | 53 | 65 | 73 |
| (*N*) | (164) | (354) | (491) | (456) | (681) |
| Same | 51 | 50 | 52 | 49 | 50 |
| (*N*) | (291) | (207) | (280) | (274) | (1132) |
| Worse now | 45 | 28 | 38 | 31 | 33 |
| (*N*) | (56) | (219) | (778) | (414) | (560) |

*Source:* Authors' analysis of ANES surveys.

*Note:* The numbers in parentheses are the totals on which the percentages are based. Numbers are weighted.

[a]This question was asked of a randomly selected half-sample in 1972.

sufficiently well-distributed such that even strong relationships to the vote advantage one candidate over the other sufficiently to play a major role in the outcome. In most cases the middle category bulges with lots of people and thus neither helps nor hurts a party or president greatly.

People, that is, may "vote their pocketbooks," but they are at least as likely to vote retrospectively based on their judgments of how the economy as a whole has been faring across the country (see Table 7-4A).[19] And personal and national economic experiences can be quite different. In 1980, for example, about 40 percent of respondents thought their own financial situation was worse than the year before, but responses to the 1980 ANES survey revealed that twice as many (83 percent) thought the national economy was worse off than the year before (see Table A7-4 in the appendix). In 1992 the public gave the nation's economy a far more negative assessment than they gave their own financial situations. That was not the case in 1996 and 2000, when respondents gave broadly similar assessments of their personal fortunes and those of the nation. But then in 2004 the public had much more negative views of the economy as a whole, although (naturally) the public saw the economy in 2008 in the most negative terms ever observed in these surveys. Fully nine in ten respondents believed that the economy was worse off. That changed substantially again in 2012. Here the views leaned slightly negatively, but it was not too far from an even three-way split among better, same, and worse, with better trailing worse by only seven points. In 2016 responses were quite similar to those in 2012, albeit slightly more positive, as the "worse" category was five points lower and the "stayed same" category in the middle, five points larger.

In Table 7-4B, we show the relationship between responses to these items and the major-party vote for president. The relationship between these measures and the vote is always strong. Moreover, a comparison of Table 7-3B and Table 7-4B reveals that in general, the vote is more closely associated with perceptions of the nation's economy than it is with perceptions of one's personal economic well-being. In 2012 the relationship was as strong as any we have been able to assess, with 2016 only slightly less strongly so. The difference in votes cast in 2012 for Obama between the "better" and the "worse" categories was fully sixty percentage points, with the "same" category essentially splitting their votes evenly. This wide difference declined modestly, but remained greater than forty points, in 2016. Thus both personal and national economic circumstances mattered a great deal in the two most recent elections.

To this point we have looked at personal and national economic conditions and the role of the government in shaping them. We have not yet looked at the extent to which such evaluations are attributed to the incumbent. In Table 7-5A, we report responses to the question of whether people approved of the incumbent's handling of the economy from the elections of 2000 through 2016 (and the same data are reported for elections between 1980 and 1996 in the appendix, Table A7-5). Although a majority approved of Reagan's handling of the economy in both 1984 and 1988, fewer than one in five held positive views of the economic performance of the Carter administration. In 1992 evaluations of George H. W. Bush were also perceived very negatively. In 1996 evaluations of Clinton's handling of the economy were stronger than those of incumbents in the previous surveys. By 2000 evaluations of Clinton's handling of the economy were even stronger, with three of every four respondents approving. Evaluations of George W. Bush's handling of the economy in 2004 were more negative than positive, although not nearly as negative of those of Jimmy Carter or of his father. By 2008 evaluations of Bush's handling of the economy were very negative. But in 2012 evaluations of Obama's handling of the economy were quite like those of Bush in 2004. In 2016 evaluations were positive and very similar to those of the Reagan administration in 1988.

The bottom-line question is whether these views are related to voter choice. According to the data in Table 7-5B, the answer is yes. Those who held positive views

**Table 7-4 The Public's View of the State of the National Economy and Major-Party Vote, 2000–2016**

| Response | "Would you say that over the past year the nation's economy has gotten . . .?" | | | | |
|---|---|---|---|---|---|
| | 2000[a] | 2004 | 2008 | 2012 | 2016 |
| **A. Distribution of responses** | | | | | |
| Better | 39 | 24 | 2 | 28 | 28 |
| Stayed same | 44 | 31 | 7 | 36 | 42 |
| Worse | 17 | 45 | 90 | 35 | 30 |
| Total | 100 | 100 | 99 | 99 | 100 |
| (*N*) | (1,787) | (1,196) | (2,313) | (1,806) | (4,261) |
| **B. Major-party voters who voted for the incumbent party nominee for president** | | | | | |
| Better | 69 | 87 | 69 | 86 | 88 |
| (*N*) | (408) | (211) | (34) | (339) | (724) |
| Stayed same | 45 | 88 | 57 | 48 | 50 |
| (*N*) | (487) | (243) | (109) | (425) | (992) |
| Worse | 31 | 20 | 44 | 16 | 18 |
| (*N*) | (154) | (319) | (1,425) | (382) | (658) |

*Source:* Authors' analysis of ANES surveys.

*Note:* The numbers in parentheses are the totals on which percentages are based. Numbers are weighted.

[a]We combine the results using standard and experimental prompts that contained different word orderings in 2000, 2004, and 2008.

of the incumbent's performance on the economy were very likely to vote for that party's candidate, whereas those who did not were just as likely to vote against him or her. Nearly nine in ten of those holding a positive view of Obama's handling of the economy voted for Clinton; only about one in ten who disapproved of his handling of the economy supported her. This relationship is once again as strong as we have yet observed. The economy was a vitally important factor in the 2012 and 2016 elections as all three retrospective evaluations of the economy are clearly and strongly related to the vote.

**Table 7-5 Evaluations of the Incumbent's Handling of the Economy and Major-Party Vote, 2000–2016**

| Response | Approval of incumbent's handling of the economy | | | | |
|---|---|---|---|---|---|
| | 2000 | 2004 | 2008 | 2012 | 2016 |
| **A. Distribution of responses** | | | | | |
| Positive view | 77 | 41 | 18 | 42 | 53 |
| Negative view | 23 | 59 | 82 | 58 | 47 |
| Total | 100 | 100 | 100 | 100 | 100 |
| (*N*) | (1,686) | (1,173) | (2,227) | (1,698) | (4,221) |
| **B. Major-party voters who voted for the incumbent party nominee** | | | | | |
| Positive view | 67 | 91 | 89 | 92 | 89 |
| (*N*) | (768) | (341) | (313) | (476) | (1,253) |
| Negative view | 11 | 17 | 33 | 13 | 11 |
| (*N*) | (233) | (431) | (1,200) | (618) | (1,109) |

*Source:* Authors' analysis of ANES surveys.

*Note:* Numbers are weighted.

## FOREIGN POLICY EVALUATIONS AND THE VOTE FOR THE INCUMBENT

Foreign and economic policies are, as we noted earlier, commonly evaluated by means of retrospective assessments. These policies share the characteristics of consensual goals (peace and prosperity, respectively, plus security in both cases), complex technology, and difficulty in ascertaining relationships between means and ends. Foreign policy differs from economic policy in one practical way, however. As we noted in the last chapter, economic problems are invariably a major concern, but foreign affairs are salient only sporadically. Indeed foreign affairs are of sufficiently sporadic concern that most surveys, including the ANES, only occasionally have many measures to judge their role in elections. Moreover, what part of our foreign policy is under scrutiny changes from election to election, especially when there are wars that are at the center of choice.

In 2016, therefore, we report on a more general evaluation, similar to that of approval of economic performance. In particular, in Table 7-6A are responses to the question of whether the respondent approves or not of Obama's handling of foreign

**Table 7-6 President's Handling of Foreign Relations and Major-Party Vote, 2016 (Percent)**

| Evaluation | |
|---|---|
| **A. "Do you approve or disapprove of the way the president is handling foreign relations?"** | |
| Approve | 50 |
| Disapprove | 50 |
| Total | 100 |
| (*N*) | (4203) |
| **B. Percentage of major-party vote for incumbent's party nominee** | |
| Approve | 89 |
| (*N*) | (1173) |
| Disapprove | 16 |
| (*N*) | (1187) |

*Source:* Authors' analysis of the 2016 ANES survey.

*Note:* The numbers in parentheses in Part B are the totals on which the percentages are based. The numbers in Parts A and B are weighted.

relations. This leaves great latitude in aggregating responses over what might well be very different parts of the world in the voters' minds.

The responses to this question are an exact tie. Half the public approved, half did not, and this made a considerable difference to voters. Consider Table 7-6B. Overall, nine in ten approvers voted for Obama's party successor, whereas only one in six of those who disapproved voted for her.

The key points in all of these data seem to be the following. First, as we saw in Chapter 6, foreign policy was just not seen as especially important in the public. This tempered all of the findings and made 2016 quite different from, say, 2004, when foreign policy and evaluations of the wars were near the top of nearly everyone's list of political concerns. Second, retrospective evaluations of all sorts are often strongly related to the vote, and this was especially so in 2016, when the vote differential was at an all-time high on many measures, including especially those that are often more weakly related to the vote (such as "pocketbook" voting).

## EVALUATIONS OF THE INCUMBENT

Fiorina distinguishes between "simple" and "mediated" retrospective evaluations.[20] By simple, Fiorina means evaluations of the direct effects of social outcomes on the person, such as one's financial status, or direct perceptions of the nation's economic well-being. Mediated retrospective evaluations are evaluations seen through or mediated by the perceptions of political actors and institutions. Approval of Obama's handling of the economy and the assessment of which party would better handle the most important problem are examples.

As we have seen, the more politically mediated the question, the more closely the responses align with voting behavior.[21] Perhaps the ultimate in mediated evaluations is the presidential approval question: "Do you approve or disapprove of the way [the incumbent] is handling his job as president?" From a retrospective voting standpoint, this evaluation is a summary of all aspects of the incumbent's service in office. Table 7-7 reports the distribution of overall evaluations and their relationship to major-party voting in the last five elections.[22]

Table A7-6 reveals that incumbents Richard Nixon (1972), Gerald Ford (1976), Ronald Reagan (1984), and Bill Clinton (1996) enjoyed widespread approval, whereas only two respondents in five approved of Jimmy Carter's and of George H. W. Bush's

**Table 7-7 President's Handling of the Job and Major-Party Vote, 2000–2016**

| | "Do you approve or disapprove of the way [the incumbent] is handling his job as president?" | | | | |
|---|---|---|---|---|---|
| **Response** | **2000** | **2004** | **2008** | **2012** | **2016** |
| **A. Distribution of responses** | | | | | |
| Approve | 67 | 51 | 27 | 50 | 53 |
| Disapprove | 33 | 49 | 73 | 50 | 47 |
| Total | 100 | 100 | 100 | 100 | 100 |
| (*N*) | (1,742) | (1,182) | (2,245) | (1,704) | (4,226) |
| **B. Major-party voters who voted for the incumbent party's nominee** | | | | | |
| Approve | 74 | 91 | 88 | 92 | 91 |
| (*N*) | (662) | (408) | (441) | (537) | (1,263) |
| Disapprove | 13 | 6 | 26 | 6 | 8 |
| (*N*) | (366) | (372) | (1,075) | (568) | (1,102) |

*Source:* Authors' analysis of ANES surveys.

*Note:* The numbers in parentheses in Part B are the totals on which percentages are based. Numbers are weighted.

handling of the job in 1980 and 1992, respectively. This situation presented Carter and the senior Bush with a problem. Conversely, highly approved incumbents, such as Reagan in 1984 and Clinton in 1996—and their vice presidents as beneficiaries in 1988 and 2000, respectively—had a major advantage. Clinton dramatically reversed any negative perceptions held of his incumbency in 1994 so that by 1996 he received the highest level of approval in the fall of an election year since Nixon's landslide reelection in 1972. Between 1996 and 2000 Clinton suffered through several scandals, one of which culminated in his impeachment in 1998. Such events might be expected to lead to substantial declines in his approval ratings, but instead his ratings remained high—higher even than Reagan's at the end of his presidency. The evaluations in 2004 present a more varied picture. For the first time in nine elections, the proportions approving and disapproving of George W. Bush were almost exactly the same. In view of what we have seen so far, it should come as no surprise that evaluations of Bush turned dramatically by 2008 so that he was by far the least approved incumbent during this period, with nearly three in four respondents disapproving of his handling of the office. Obama's approval ratings in 2012 were, again, much like Bush's in 2004, here coming out exactly evenly divided between approval and disapproval.[23] By 2016 his approval increased so that it was positive, six points higher than his disapproval rating. Thus, although there was nearly an even-up balance for Clinton to work with in 2016, it was slightly more positive than the victorious Bush in 2004.

If it is true that the more mediated the evaluation, the more closely it seems to align with behavior, and if presidential approval is the most mediated evaluation of all, then we would expect a powerful relationship with the vote. As Table 7-7B (and Table A7-6 in the appendix) illustrates, that is true over the full set of elections for which we have the relevant data. As we have seen before, the approval ratings in 2004, 2012, and 2016 are about as strongly related to the vote as is possible. More than nine in ten who approved of Obama's performance voted for Clinton; only 8 percent who disapproved voted for her.

## THE IMPACT OF RETROSPECTIVE EVALUATIONS

Our evidence strongly suggests that retrospective voting has been widespread in all recent elections. Moreover, as far as data permit us to judge, the evidence is clearly on the side of the Downs-Fiorina view. Retrospective evaluations appear to be used to make comparative judgments. Presumably, voters find it easier, less time-consuming, and less risky to evaluate the incumbent party based on what its president did in the most recent term or terms in office than on the nominees' promises for the future. But few people base their votes on judgments of past performance alone. Most use past judgments as a starting point for comparing the major contenders with respect to their likely future performances.

In analyzing previous elections, we constructed an overall assessment of retrospective voting and compared that overall assessment across elections. We then compared that net retrospective assessment with our balance-of-issues measure. Our measure is constructed by combining the question asking whether the United States is on the right or on the wrong track, the presidential approval measure, and the assessment of which party would better handle the problem the respondent thinks is the single most important.[24] The combination of responses to these three questions creates a seven-point scale ranging from strongly negative evaluations of recent and current conditions to strongly positive evaluations of performance in these various areas. For example, those who thought the nation was on the right track, approved of Obama's job performance, and thought the Democratic Party would better handle the most important problem are scored as strongly supportive of Obama in their retrospective evaluations in 2016.

In Table 7-8, we present the results of this measure.[25] The data in Table 7-8A indicate that there was a substantial diversity of responses but that the measure was skewed modestly against the incumbent. By this measure more than one in four were strongly opposed to the performance of the Obama administration, with another fifth moderately or slightly opposed. One in nine was neutral, while a bit over one in five were slightly or moderately supportive, and one in seven was strongly supportive of the Obama administration.

Table 7-8B presents a remarkably clear example of a very strong relationship between responses and votes, with greater than 90 percent of those in any of the three supportive categories voting for Clinton and very few of those moderately or strongly opposed voting for her. The slightly opposed split their votes about evenly, whereas Clinton held the votes of eight in ten of those scored neutral on this measure. Thus for five of the seven categories, the valence of evaluations alone tells you everything you need to know about their voting choices. Perhaps because there appears to be some belief that even though the country may not be on the right track and even though the economy (the most common choice of most important problem) is not as strong as many would like, many voters appear to hold Obama less responsible for the problems and more generous in their evaluations of his performance in terms of the responses to these concerns due, perhaps, to remembrances of Bush's highly negatively evaluated handling of the economy in 2008 and attribution of the problems to Bush or even those outside the government.

We cannot really compare 2016 with any other election on this measure, but we can at least make broad generalizations.[26] In earlier years it was reasonable to conclude that the 1980 election was a clear and strong rejection of Carter's incumbency. In 1984 Reagan won in large part because voters perceived that he had performed well and because Mondale was unable to convince the public that he would do better. In 1988 George H. W. Bush won in large part because Reagan appeared to have performed well—and people thought Bush would stay the course. In 1992 Bush lost because of the far more negative evaluations of his administration and of his party than had been recorded in any election since 1980. In 1996 Clinton won reelection in large part for the same reasons that Reagan won in 1984: He was viewed as having performed well on the job, and he was able to convince the public that his opponent would not do any better. In 2000 Gore essentially tied George W. Bush because the slightly pro-incumbent set of evaluations combined with a very slight asymmetry against the incumbent in translating those evaluations into voting choices. In 2004 there was a slight victory for the incumbent because more thought he had performed well than poorly. And 2008 was most like 1980, with a highly skewed distribution

**Table 7-8 Summary Measure of Retrospective Evaluations of the Obama Administration and Major-Party Vote, 2016**

| | Strongly Opposed | Moderately Opposed | Slightly Opposed | Neutral | Slightly Supportive | Moderately Supportive | Strongly Supportive | Total (*N*) |
|---|---|---|---|---|---|---|---|---|
| **A. Distribution of responses** | | | | | | | | |
| Percent | 29 | 14 | 7 | 13 | 14 | 8 | 15 | 100 (3,578) |
| **B. Major-party voters who voted for Clinton** | | | | | | | | |
| Percent | 1 | 22 | 50 | 79 | 97 | 93 | 99 | 53 |
| (*N*) | (817) | (225) | (116) | (221) | (352) | (190) | (430) | (2351) |

*Source:* Authors' analysis of the 2016 ANES survey.

*Note:* Numbers are weighted. The numbers in Part B are the totals on which the percentages are based.

working against the Republicans (likely the most skewed measure of all, subject to wording differences). In 2012 evaluations, once again, paralleled those (with a different measure) from 2004, with an outcome not substantially different—slightly negative evaluations overall but not so negative as to cost the incumbent reelection. In many respects one of the lessons from considering these data is that 2016 looked a great deal like a repeat of 2012 on these measures as well as others. Thus, Bush and Obama won reelection after their first terms with relatively modest pluralities. That Bush's successor lost in 2008 was due to the dramatic economic collapse of the nation during the campaign, which otherwise might have looked like 2016. In 2016 Clinton received the boost of standing with her party's incumbent president, but it was an even more modest boost than retrospective evaluations gave Obama in 2012 (and Bush in 2004), enough for her to win by two percentage points but not enough to ensure her victory in the Electoral College. As we noted in discussing presidential approval scores, like so much else, these have become much more polarized by partisanship in the electorate, with the net result that it is a tightly constrained range of possible evaluations being shaped strongly by party identification, as we will see in the next chapter.

How do retrospective assessments compare with prospective judgments? As described in Chapter 6, prospective issues, especially our balance-of-issues measure, have become more strongly related to the vote over the last few elections, peaking in 2016. There appears, that is, to be a significant extent of partisan polarization in the electorate in terms of their evaluations of the choices and their vote, even if not in terms of their own opinions about issues. Table 7-9 reports the impact of both types of policy evaluation measures on the major-party vote in 2016. Both policy measures were collapsed into three categories: pro-Democratic, neutral, and pro-Republican. Reading down each column we see that controlling for retrospective evaluations, prospective issues are modestly related to the vote in a positive direction. Or, to be more precise, they are modestly related to the vote among those whose retrospective evaluations are nearly or actually neutral, with a small but real effect among those inclined to evaluate the Obama administration negatively. It is thus really only among those whose retrospective evaluations did not even moderately incline them toward either party that prospective evaluations are related to the vote. Note, however, that even in this column, Clinton received the votes of nearly more than four in five who were neutral on retrospective issues.

Reading across each row, we see that retrospective evaluations are very strongly related to the vote. This is true no matter what prospective evaluations respondents held. Thus we can conclude that in 2016, retrospective evaluations shaped voting choices to a great extent. Prospective evaluations were still important but only for those without a moderate or strong partisan direction to their retrospective judgments.

Together the two kinds of policy measures take us a long way toward understanding voting choices. Essentially everyone whose retrospective and prospective evaluations inclined them toward the same party voted for the candidate of that party. This accounting of voting choices is stronger when considering both forms of policy evaluations than when looking at either one individually.[27]

**Table 7-9 Major-Party Voters Who Voted for Clinton, by Balance-of-Issues and Summary Retrospective Measures, 2016**

| | Summary Retrospective | | | | | | | |
|---|---|---|---|---|---|---|---|---|
| | Strongly or Moderately Democratic | | Slightly Supportive or Slightly Opposed or Neutral | | Strongly or Moderately Republican | | Total | |
| Net balance of issues | % | (*N*) | % | (*N*) | % | (*N*) | % | (*N*) |
| Democratic | 99 | (409) | 92 | (376) | 21 | (76) | 89 | (866) |
| Neutral | 96 | (93) | 86 | (94) | 10 | (101) | 62 | (297) |
| Republican | 94 | (118) | 66 | (218) | 4 | (865) | 24 | (1,215) |
| Total | 98 | (620) | 83 | (688) | 6 | (1,042) | 53 | (2,379) |

*Source:* Authors' analysis of the 2016 ANES survey.

*Note:* Numbers are weighted. Numbers in parentheses are the totals on which percentages are based. For the condensed measure of retrospective voting, we combine respondents who are strongly positive (or negative) toward Hillary Clinton and the Democratic Party with respondents who are moderately positive (or negative). We combine respondents who are slightly positive (or negative) with those who are neutral (see Table 7-8). For the condensed balance-of-issues measure, any respondent who is closer to Trump is classified as pro-Republican. The neutral category is the same as the seven-point measure (see Table 6-7).

## CONCLUSION

In this and the previous chapter, we have found that both retrospective and prospective evaluations were strongly related to the vote in 2016. Indeed just as 2012 presents an unusually clear case of retrospective evaluations being a very powerful reason for Obama's victory, the mixed evaluations in 2016 provided both Clinton and Trump with a large base of votes before voters turned to consider the characteristics of the candidates and their promises. Whereas retrospective evaluations are always strong, they genuinely stand out both in 2012 and in 2016. In 1992, for example, dissatisfaction with George H. W. Bush's performance and with his and his party's handling of the most important problem—usually an economic concern in 1992—goes a long way toward explaining his defeat, whereas satisfaction with Clinton's performance and the absence of an advantage for the Republicans in being seen as able to deal with the most important concerns of voters go a long way toward explaining his 1996 victory. In 2000 prospective issues favored neither candidate because essentially the same number of major-party voters was closer to Bush as was closer to Gore. The Democrat had a modest advantage on retrospective evaluations, but Bush won greater support among those with pro-Republican evaluations than did Gore among those with pro-Democratic evaluations. The result was another even balance and, as a result, a tied outcome. Although Kerry was favored on prospective evaluations in 2004, his advantage was counterbalanced by Bush's slight advantage based on retrospective evaluations, leading to a Bush reelection victory with only a slight gain in the popular vote. By 2008 the public had turned quite negative on Bush's performance, and that led to a major advantage for the Democrats. In 2012, there was a return, essentially, to the 2004 patterns, except with a Democrat as incumbent and with retrospective judgments focusing more heavily on the economy and less heavily on international affairs. In a number of respects, 2016 was a continuation of the patterns of 2012, with perhaps a little more strength.

Even so our explanation remains incomplete. For example, why did so many of those in the middle or neutral category on retrospective evolutions support Clinton, even those inclined toward Trump on prospective policies? Even more importantly we have not accounted for *why* people hold the views they expressed on these two measures. We cannot provide a complete account of the origins of people's views, of course, but there is one important source we can examine: party identification. This variable, which we have used in previous chapters, provides a powerful way in which the typical citizen can reach preliminary judgments. As we will see partisanship is strongly related to these judgments, especially to retrospective evaluations.

CHAPTER EIGHT

# PARTY LOYALTIES, POLICY PREFERENCES, AND THE VOTE

In Chapter 5 we discussed the influence of social forces such as race and ethnicity on voting behavior. We noted that, for example, African Americans do not vote Democratic simply because of their race. Instead race and other social forces provide the context for electoral politics and thus influence how voters reach their decisions. In Chapters 6 and 7 we studied the effects of various perceived traits of the candidates and of both prospective and retrospective evaluations on the vote. The question for here is why, for example, did some voters approve of Obama's performance, whereas others did not? Partisanship is an important part of the answer, indeed perhaps the single most important part of the answer, because it is the most important factor connecting voters' backgrounds, social settings, and their more immediate assessments of issues and the candidates. Thus a major part of the explanation of why African Americans vote overwhelmingly Democratic are the various events and actions that made the Democratic Party attractive (and the Republican Party unattractive) to them. The reason why some people approved of Obama's performance, whereas others did not, is largely because some are Republicans and some are Democrats. Party is therefore the third of the triumvirate of "candidates, issues, and parties"—that is, evaluations of the parties are one of three major forces that shape voting behavior. Party identification may be more foundational even than that. Party may, that is, provide additional, indirect effects, explaining, for example, why voters have the evaluations of candidates and of issues they do.

Partisanship is not the only force that helps connect context and evaluation, but it has proven to be by far the most important for understanding elections. Its dual role in directly and indirectly affecting voting makes it unusually critical for understanding why U.S. citizens vote as they do. Most Americans identify with a political party—one reason why it is so central. Their identification then influences their political attitudes and, ultimately, their behavior. In the 1950s and 1960s, Angus Campbell and his coauthors of *The American Voter*, along with other scholars, began to emphasize the role of party loyalties.[1]

Although today few people deny that partisanship is central to political attitudes and behavior, many scholars question the interpretation of the evidence gathered during that period. Two main alternatives have been proposed, and we examine them, along with an attempt to make sense of how party identification may have changed in part because of the rise of partisan polarization over the 1980s into today. Thus we ask two questions: What is party identification? And how does it actually structure other attitudes and behavior? We then examine the role that party identification played in the 2016 presidential election.

## PARTY IDENTIFICATION AS LOYALTY: THE ORIGINAL VIEW

According to Angus Campbell and his colleagues, party identification is "the individual's affective orientation to an important group-object in his environment," in this case a political party.[2] In other words an individual recognizes that two major political parties are playing significant roles in elections (and presumably, observing its role in governing and policy making) and develops an affinity for one of them. Partisanship, therefore, represents an evaluation of the two parties, but its implications extend to a wider variety of political phenomena. Campbell and his colleagues measured partisanship by asking individuals which party they identified with and how strong that identification was.[3] If an individual did not identify with one of the parties, he or she may have either "leaned" toward a party or been a "pure" independent. Most Americans develop a preference for either the Republican or the Democratic Party. Very few identify with any third party. The rest are mostly independents who, according to this classic view, are not only unattached to a party but also relatively unattached to politics in general. They are less interested, less informed, and less active than those who identify with a party.

Partisan identification in this view becomes an attachment or loyalty similar to that between the individual and other groups or organizations in society such as a religious body, a social class, or even a favorite sports team. As we will see partisanship attachments in this polarized era have heightened in such a fashion that some scholars see them as a part of one's political identity. This "third" view of partisanship was developed by Donald Green et al. and serves as Christopher Achen and Larry Bartels's conclusion.[4] We will return to this topic shortly. The major point, though, is that as with loyalties to many racial, ethnic, or religious groups, partisan affiliation often begins early and lasts perhaps over the life cycle. One of the first political attitudes children develop is partisan identification, and it develops well before they acquire policy preferences and many other political orientations. Furthermore, as with other group loyalties, once an attachment to a party develops, it tends to endure.[5] Some people do switch parties, of course, but they usually do so only if their social situation changes dramatically, if there is an issue of overriding concern that sways their loyalties, or if the political parties themselves change substantially.

Party identification, then, stands as a base or core orientation to electoral politics. Once formed, this core orientation, predicated on a general evaluation of the two parties, affects many other specific orientations. Democratic loyalists tend to rate Democratic candidates and officeholders more highly than Republican candidates and officeholders and vice versa. In effect, one is predisposed to evaluate the promises and performance of one's party leaders relatively more favorably. It follows, therefore, that Democrats are more likely to vote for Democratic candidates than are Republicans and vice versa.

## PARTY IDENTIFICATION AS RETROSPECTIVE EVALUATION: A SECOND VIEW

In *The Responsible Electorate*, V. O. Key argued that party loyalties contributed to electoral inertia and that many partisans voted as "standpatters" from election to election.[6] In other words, in the absence of any information to the contrary, or if the attractions and disadvantages of the candidates are fairly evenly balanced, partisans are expected to vote for the candidate of their party. This "rule" is one of voters' having a "standing decision" to vote along party lines until and unless they are given good reasons not to follow that rule. This finding led scholars to reexamine the bases of such behavior.

In this second view citizens who consider themselves Democrats have a standing decision to vote for the Democratic nominee because of the past positions of the Democrats and the Republicans and because of the parties' comparative past performances while in office. In short this view of partisan identification presumes that it is a "running tally" of past experiences (mostly in terms of policy and performance), a sort of summary expression of political memory, according to Morris P. Fiorina.[7]

Furthermore, when in doubt about how, for example, a Democratic candidate is likely to handle a civil rights issue in comparison with the Republican opponent, voters can reasonably assume that the Democrat will be more liberal than the Republican—until and unless the candidates indicate otherwise. Political parties tend to be consistent with their basic historical policy cleavages for long periods of time, changing in any fundamental ways only rarely. Naturally, therefore, summary judgments of parties and their typical candidates do not change radically or often.[8] As a result a citizen's running tally serves as a good first approximation, changes rarely, and can be an excellent device for saving time and effort that would be spent gathering information in the absence of this "memory."

Many of the major findings used in support of the original interpretation of party identification are completely consistent with this more policy-oriented view.[9] Indeed the two interpretations are not mutually exclusive. Moreover, they share the important conclusion that party identification plays a central role in shaping voters' decisions and make many of the same predictions. Equally clearly they connote quite different aspects of a political attribute. The original emphasizes affective evaluations and loyalty, the second view is more substantively based in the cognition of politics and in adjusting political views to the world one experiences. We will discuss strong empirical findings in this chapter but will be unable to resolve fully just which view is correct. In part this is because of the confluence of two newer forces in American politics: polarization of political elites and the development of a better understanding of how identity politics works and how it may have spread to include partisanship.

## PARTY IDENTIFICATION, POLARIZATION, AND IDENTITY: A SYNTHESIS?

These two views are still widely studied today. The two views sometimes seem irreconcilable, but they make many similar empirical claims. We propose here a way to think about how the two might be related in concepts to match their empirical similarity.

Robert S. Erikson, Michael B. MacKuen, and James A. Stimson argued that an updated version of the Key-Downs-Fiorina view of partisanship is one of the central concepts for understanding what they call the "macro polity"—that is, an explanation of how political leaders, institutions, and policy respond to changes in aggregate public opinion.[10] They argue that partisanship in the electorate changes, as do macro-level conditions such as inflation and unemployment rates, akin to the Key-Downs-Fiorina view. In turn political elites react to changes in this "macro-partisanship," among other aspects of public opinion and beliefs. On the other side, Donald Green, Bradley Palmquist, and Eric Schickler developed an equally elegant account of the affective base of partisan identification and its stability over time.[11] This view is therefore the modern version of the original account by Campbell et al. And, as their exchanges have shown, the two sets of authors differ substantially in their interpretations of what partisanship means, but empirical differences are slighter.[12]

Both views agree that partisan identifications are long-term forces in politics. Both agree that for most people, such identifications are formed early in life; children often develop a partisan loyalty, which they usually learn from their parents, although these loyalties are seldom explicitly taught. Both views recognize that partisan loyalties contribute to voter participation, as we demonstrated in Chapter 4. Partisan choices also are often closely associated with social forces, as discussed in Chapter 5, especially when a social group is actively engaged in partisan politics. An important illustration of this point is the affiliation of evangelical and other religious groups on the right with the Republican Party today, reinforcing the tendency of those who share such religious beliefs to identify with the Republican Party, much as members of labor and civil rights groups have long affiliated with the Democrats. Finally both views agree that partisanship is closely associated with more immediate evaluations, including assessments of candidates and their traits and both prospective and retrospective evaluations of the issues and candidates, as analyzed in Chapters 6 and 7.

The two views may not disagree, however, if viewed in a larger perspective. We pose a way to think about party identification in this partisan-polarized era. To be sure, the hard work of actual synthesis is yet to come, but we pose this as a way forward. Partisan polarization is taken firstly to mean that the two parties present—and act in government—by taking relatively homogenous views on issues within each party with very different and thus heterogeneous views on issues between the two. But polarization means not only differentiation between the two parties on issues but on an increasingly broad and diverse array of political matters, from social groups that align with only one party (e.g., religious conservatives with Republicans or civil rights groups with Democrats) to a wider and wider array of affective and evaluative judgments that distinguish a Republican from a Democrat. If Fiorina is right and the variety of experiences (no longer policy experiences alone but social and cultural experiences) that differentiate the two parties increase, then we would expect to find heightened affective support for one party (if one is close to them on policy, economic, social, and cultural dimensions) and negative feelings toward the more distant party (distant on nearly all matters). Still, if the standing decision really is a "running tally" such that this increasingly wide array of matters all go together into the calculation of which party is more like the individual than the other party, then Fiorina would be right: those pieces of evidence that push the citizen one way or the other are included but then set aside from memory and forgotten, with only the tally and perhaps a few of the most memorable pieces held in mind—those individual pieces often being those that arouse the most affect, that is, emotional reactions.

The key point, however, is that partisan polarization of elites is not just over policy—it is that to be sure and very importantly—but it is a set of political, social, cultural, and economic differentiations that have grown from the 1980s to today and that make partisanship a retrospective judgement, an affective loyalty, and an all-around guide to understanding politics and especially the political choices the voter faces. Is it policy choice? Yes. It is a loyalty? Yes. Is it part of one's political identity? Yes. All of these reinforce one another. In the jargon of politics, partisan polarization is the result of a large number of political cleavages that have grown over recent decades and that reinforce one another.[13] This makes them unlike the partisan politics of the 1950s to 1980s, when cleavages cross-cut one another, some pushing along lines of partisan cleavages but many cutting across them. Every reinforcing cleavage today adds one more dimension on which the parties polarize. As it grows across increasingly diverse arrays of topics, that reinforcement is nearly multiplicative in that it not only reinforces but adds both cognitive differentiation and increasingly emotive differentiation between the two parties. The stakes in having one party or the other in power simply increase with each reinforcing cleavage.

## PARTY IDENTIFICATION IN THE ELECTORATE

If partisan identification is a fundamental orientation for most citizens, then the distribution of partisan loyalties is crucial. The ANES surveys have monitored the party loyalties of the American electorate since 1952. In Table 8-1, we show the basic distributions of partisan loyalties in presidential election years from 1980 to 2016, and the results for 1952 to 1976 (and every election thereafter) can be found in Table A8-1 in the appendix. As the table shows most Americans identify with a political party. In 2016, 63 percent claimed to think of themselves as a Democrat or as a Republican, and another 22 percent, who initially said they were independent or had no partisan preference, nevertheless said they felt closer to one of the major parties than to the other.[14] One in seven was purely independent of party. One of the biggest changes in partisanship in the electorate began in the mid-1960s, when more people claimed to be independents.[15] This growth stopped, however, in the late 1970s and early 1980s. There was very little change in partisan loyalties between the 1984 and 1992 surveys.

There were signs in 1996 of reversals of the trends in party identification toward greater independence. All partisan groups increased slightly in 1996 compared with 1992, and the percentage of "pure" independents (i.e., those with no partisan leanings)

**Table 8-1 Party Identification in Presidential Years, Pre-election Surveys, 1980–2016 (Percent)**

| Party Identification | 1980 | 1984 | 1988 | 1992 | 1996 | 2000 | 2004 | 2008 | 2012 | 2016 |
|---|---|---|---|---|---|---|---|---|---|---|
| Strong Democrat | 18 | 17 | 18 | 17 | 18 | 19 | 17 | 19 | 17 | 21 |
| Weak Democrat | 24 | 20 | 18 | 18 | 20 | 15 | 16 | 15 | 12 | 14 |
| Independent, leans Democratic | 12 | 11 | 12 | 14 | 14 | 15 | 17 | 17 | 16 | 11 |
| Independent, no partisan leanings | 13 | 11 | 11 | 12 | 8 | 12 | 10 | 11 | 10 | 15 |
| Independent, leans Republican | 10 | 13 | 14 | 13 | 12 | 13 | 12 | 12 | 19 | 11 |
| Weak Republican | 14 | 15 | 14 | 15 | 16 | 12 | 12 | 13 | 12 | 12 |
| Strong Republican | 9 | 13 | 14 | 11 | 13 | 12 | 17 | 13 | 14 | 16 |
| Total | 100 | 100 | 101 | 100 | 101 | 98 | 101 | 100 | 100 | 100 |
| (*N*) | (1,577) | (2,198) | (1,999) | (2,450) | (1,696) | (1,777) | (1,193) | (2,301) | (1,804) | (4,244) |
| Apolitical | 2 | 2 | 2 | 1 | 1 | 1 | a | a | b | b |
| (*N*) | (35) | (38) | (33) | (23) | (14) | (21) | (3) | (2) | b | b |

*Source:* Authors' analysis of ANES surveys.

*Note:* Numbers are weighted.

[a]Less than 1 percent.

[b]The ANES survey did not use the apolitical category in 2012 and 2016.

at its lowest level, 8 percent, since 1968. That dip in independence stopped, however, so that the percentages of independents in 2004, 2008, and 2012 were at about the same levels as during the 1980s. There was, however, a substantial increase in (pure) independence in 2016 to go along with a growth of partisanship, both coming at the expense of independent leaners.

Table 8-1 also shows that people are rather evenly divided between the two parties but less evenly so in 2016 than 2012. Whereas a few more in 2012 claimed to be Democrat, when "leaners" are included, the two parties have exactly the same percentage of the public, 45 percent each. Over the last forty years, the balance between the two parties had favored the Democrats by a range of about 55/45 to about 60/40. The results from the last six presidential election years before 2012 still fell within that range, although more often at the lower part of the range. From 1984 to 2000, there was a clear shift toward the Republicans. In 1980, 35 percent of partisans were Republicans; in 2000 Republicans accounted for 42 percent. The inclusion of independents who leaned toward a party would increase the percentage of Republicans to 38 percent in 1980 and 43 percent in 2000. The high point was 47 percent in 1988. In 2004 the (strong and weak) Democrats led comparable Republicans in the ANES survey with 33 percent to 29 percent (or 54/46). The Democratic advantage increased in 2008, as the percentage of Republicans declined, while there was a one-point increase on the Democratic side. These two small differences nevertheless brought the ratio of Democrats to Republicans to 57/43. The percentage of independents who leaned toward a party remained the same as in 2004, and as a result, including them maintained the Democrats' edge over Republicans at 57/43, keeping the partisan balance within the historical range of a noticeable Democratic lead. By 2012, however, that edge was gone.

The 2016 election brought back that edge. The Democratic advantage among strong and weak partisans returned to 55 percent, with the number of strong Democrats reaching its highest point since 1964. Of course the edge Democrats recovered in 2016 was still at the lower end of the heretofore usual range, and it is softened somewhat more by the ordinarily higher turnout of Republicans compared to Democrats (see Chapter 4).

Gary C. Jacobson has provided two excellent analyses of the shift in party loyalties away from the Republican Party from a high watermark in 2003 to a low watermark in 2009.[16] His analyses strongly suggest that the decline was driven largely by the decline in approval of George W. Bush's performance as president. Jacobson relies mainly on Gallup data, which probably capture more short-term variation than the standard Michigan Survey Research Center (SRC) question.[17]

The earlier shift toward the Republican Party was concentrated among white Americans.[18] As described in Chapter 5, the sharpest social division in U.S. electoral politics is race, and this division has been reflected in partisan loyalties for decades. Moreover, the racial gap has appeared to be widening, with a sharp increase in 2004.

Although the distribution of partisanship in the electorate as a whole has changed only somewhat since 1984, this stability masks the growth in Republican identification among whites through 2004 and the compensating growth of already strong Democratic loyalties among African Americans and other minorities. In Tables 8-2 and 8-3 we report the party identification of whites and blacks, respectively, between 1980 and 2016. In Tables A8-2 and A8-3 in the appendix, we report the party identification

## Table 8-2 Party Identification among Whites in Presidential Years, Pre-election Surveys, 1980–2016 (Percent)

| Party Identification | 1980 | 1984 | 1988 | 1992 | 1996 | 2000 | 2004 | 2008 | 2012 | 2016 |
|---|---|---|---|---|---|---|---|---|---|---|
| Strong Democrat | 14 | 15 | 14 | 14 | 15 | 15 | 13 | 14 | 13 | 16 |
| Weak Democrat | 23 | 18 | 16 | 17 | 19 | 14 | 12 | 14 | 10 | 12 |
| Independent, leans Democratic | 12 | 11 | 10 | 14 | 13 | 15 | 17 | 17 | 15 | 11 |
| Independent, no partisan leanings | 14 | 11 | 12 | 12 | 8 | 13 | 8 | 12 | 10 | 14 |
| Independent, leans Republican | 11 | 13 | 15 | 14 | 12 | 14 | 13 | 17 | 22 | 13 |
| Weak Republican | 16 | 17 | 15 | 16 | 17 | 14 | 15 | 13 | 13 | 14 |
| Strong Republican | 9 | 14 | 16 | 12 | 15 | 14 | 21 | 15 | 17 | 21 |
| Apolitical | 2 | 2 | 1 | 1 | 1 | 1 | a | 16 | b | b |
| Total | 101 | 101 | 99 | 100 | 100 | 100 | 99 | 101 | 100 | 101 |
| (*N*) | (1,405) | (1,931) | (1,693) | (2,702) | (1,451) | (1,404) | (859) | (1,824) | (1,449) | 2,917 |

*Source:* Authors' analysis of ANES surveys.

*Note:* Numbers are weighted.

[a]The percentage supporting another party has not been presented: it is usually less than 1 percent and never totals more than 1 percent.

[b]The ANES survey did not use the apolitical category in 2012 and 2016.

**Table 8-3 Party Identification among Blacks in Presidential Years, Pre-election Surveys, 1980–2016 (Percent)**

| Party Identification | 1980 | 1984 | 1988 | 1992 | 1996 | 2000 | 2004 | 2008 | 2012 | 2016 |
|---|---|---|---|---|---|---|---|---|---|---|
| Strong Democrat | 45 | 32 | 39 | 40 | 43 | 47 | 30 | 47 | 53 | 52 |
| Weak Democrat | 27 | 31 | 24 | 24 | 22 | 21 | 30 | 23 | 17 | 19 |
| Independent, leans Democratic | 9 | 14 | 18 | 14 | 16 | 14 | 20 | 15 | 17 | 10 |
| Independent, no partisan leanings | 7 | 11 | 6 | 12 | 10 | 10 | 12 | 9 | 5 | 13 |
| Independent, leans Republican | 3 | 6 | 5 | 3 | 5 | 4 | 5 | 3 | 7 | 1 |
| Weak Republican | 2 | 1 | 5 | 3 | 3 | 3 | 2 | 1 | 0 | 2 |
| Strong Republican | 3 | 2 | 1 | 2 | 1 | 0 | 1 | 1 | 1 | 3 |
| Apolitical | 4 | 2 | 3 | 2 | 0 | 1 | 0 | 0 | [a] | [a] |
| Total | 100 | 99 | 101 | 100 | 100 | 100 | 100 | 99 | 100 | 100 |
| (*N*) | (187) | (247) | (267) | (317) | (200) | (225) | (193) | (281) | (124) | (460) |

*Source:* Authors' analysis of ANES surveys.

*Note:* The percentage supporting another party has not been presented: it is usually less than 1 percent and never totals more than 1 percent. Numbers are weighted.

[a]The ANES survey did not use the apolitical category in 2012 and 2016.

of whites and blacks between 1952 and 1978 (as well as through 2016). As these four tables show, black and white patterns in partisan loyalties were very different from 1952 to 2008. There was a sharp shift in black loyalties in the mid-1960s. Before then about 50 percent of African Americans were strong or weak Democrats. Since that time, 60 to 70 percent—and even higher—of blacks have considered themselves Democrats.

The party loyalties of whites have changed more slowly. Still, the percentage of self-professed Democrats among whites declined over the Reagan years, whereas the percentage of Republicans increased. In the five elections that followed, partisanship among whites changed. If independents who lean Republican are included, there was close to an even balance among whites between the two parties in 1984. By 1988 the numbers of strong and weak Democrats and strong and weak Republicans were virtually the same, with more strong Republicans than strong Democrats for the first time. Adding in the two groups of independent leaners gave Republicans a clear advantage in identification among whites. In 1992, however, there were slightly more strong and weak Democrats than strong and weak Republicans. In 1996 all four of the partisan categories were larger, by one to three points, than in 1992. The result was that the balance of Republicans to Democrats changed very slightly, and the near parity of identifiers with the two parties among whites remained. By 2000 the parity was even more striking. But 2002 revealed a substantial increase in Republican identification among whites, one that was constant in terms of the three Republican groups in 2004. Democratic identification declined slightly so that from 2000 to 2004, strong and weak Democrats fell by four points, partially balanced by a two-point gain among independent leaners. Pure independents declined sharply, to 8 percent, in both 2002 and 2004, a sign (along with the growth in strong Republicans) that the white electorate was polarizing somewhat on partisanship. As a result the three Republican groups constituted very nearly half of the white electorate and led Democrats by a 49 to 42 percent margin. That changed in 2008.[19] Democratic identification (over the three Democratic categories) increased three percentage points to 45 percent, whereas strong Republicans fell from 21 to 16 percent, dropping their three-category total to 44 percent. Thus in 2008 Democrats had at least regained parity with Republicans among white identifiers. And pure independents increased four points, to 12 percent, the highest level in over a decade. That changed again in 2012. The Democrats lost ground in all three categories in 2012 compared to 2008, and pure independents also declined somewhat. The strong and not-so-strong Republican categories changed only slightly, and as a result, the entire decline among Democrats and pure independents was concentrated in one spot—among independents who leaned toward the Republican Party. As a result the GOP held a seven-point advantage over Democrats in terms of strong and weak identifiers but a fourteen-point advantage if adding in those who lean toward a party.[20]

The 2016 survey reveals that Democrats continued to trail Republicans among whites, by the same seven points among strong and weak partisans, but only by nine points when leaners are included. That is real progress for Democrats but leaves a lot of work to return to parity with Republicans, as was true as recently as 2000. Of course standing among whites is different from standing among all voters, and indeed whites continue to decline as a proportion of the total population.

Party identification among blacks is very different. In 2016 there were very few black Republicans. Indeed, whereas the percentage of black Republicans increased in 2016 over 2012 (when the percentage of black Republicans fell to near trace levels, with only 4 percent choosing any Republican option and a mere 1 percent being strong and weak Republican), they nonetheless remained a very small percentage, with only 5 percent of strong and weak partisans and 6 percent including leaners. Because the Democrats were the first major party to choose an African American presidential candidate, we would expect this choice to exert a strong pull of blacks toward the party in 2008 and 2012, and that should continue into 2016 as the Obama administration was the basis of making retrospective evaluations. Indeed a majority of black respondents considered themselves strong Democrats, and greater than 70 percent were strong or weak Democrats, eight in ten when including those leaning toward the Democrats.

These racial differences in partisanship are long-standing, and they have increased over time. Between 1952 and 1962 blacks were primarily Democratic, but about one in seven supported the Republicans. Black partisanship shifted massively and abruptly even further toward the Democratic Party in 1964. In that year more than half of all black voters considered themselves strong Democrats. Since then well over half have identified with the Democratic Party. Black Republican identification fell to barely a trace in 1964 and edged up only slightly since then, only to fall back even further in recent years.

The abrupt change in black loyalties in 1964 reflects the two presidential nominees of that year: Democrat Lyndon Johnson and Republican Barry Goldwater. President Johnson's advocacy of civil rights legislation appealed directly to black voters, and his Great Society and War on Poverty programs made only slightly less direct appeals. Arizona senator Barry Goldwater voted against the 1964 Civil Rights Act, a vote criticized even by many of his Republican peers. In 1968 Republican nominee Richard Nixon began to pursue systematically what was called the "Southern strategy"—that is, an attempt to win votes and long-term loyalties among white southerners. This strategy unfolded slowly but consistently over the years, as Republicans, particularly Ronald Reagan, continued to pursue the southern strategy. Party stances have not changed appreciably since then.[21]

In 1964 the proportion of blacks considered apolitical dropped from the teens to very small proportions, similar to those among whites. This shift resulted from the civil rights movement, the contest between Johnson and Goldwater, and the passage of the Civil Rights Act. The civil rights movement stimulated many blacks, especially in the South, to become politically active. Furthermore, the 1965 Voting Rights Act enabled many of them to vote for the first time. Party and electoral politics suddenly were relevant, and blacks responded as all others by becoming engaged with the political—and party—system.

## HISPANIC PARTISANSHIP IN 2008, 2012, AND 2016

One of the most important changes in American society and its politics has been the growth of the Hispanic community. They are now the largest ethnic or racial minority in the United States. The outcome of the 2012 election spurred a vast commentary on the future of the Republican Party based on whether and how they might be able to appeal to the Hispanic vote or seek a majority in some other way, such as through voter identification laws. The discussion of the stance of the Republican Party toward both documented (i.e., legal) and undocumented Hispanic immigrants turned dramatically in 2016, especially due to Trump's candidacy, where "Build the Wall!" was a common response of his audience to his calls for an end to at least illegal if not nearly all immigration and the possible deportation of up to 19 million undocumented and mostly Hispanic immigrants living in the United States.

We have not been able to assess the attitudes and behavior of Hispanic citizens eligible to vote until recently due to the small numbers that appear in ANES and other survey opinion polls. Fortunately, in 2008 and 2012, the ANES included a supplemental sample of Hispanics so that we have access to sufficiently large numbers to support at least a modicum of analysis, whereas the large numbers involved in the ANES 2016 survey, considering both face-to-face and online surveys, provides sufficient numbers to analyze. Table 8-4 reports the distribution of partisan loyalties among Hispanics in Part A and their voting patterns in Part B, which we consider in our analyses. As can be seen there, Hispanic partisanship may not be as massively Democratic as that of African Americans, but Republicans do very poorly among Hispanics (fewer than one in four identify as a Republican, including "leaners"), whereas by 2016, the Democrat have secured the loyalties of very close to a majority of Hispanics, and three in five respond with one of the three Democratic categories. Recall that to be included in the ANES survey, respondents need to be citizens so that these results are relevant to vote-eligible Hispanics in 2008, 2012, and 2016, respectively. With large numbers of documented Hispanics in the United States, combined with many who were born in the United States and thus native-born Americans, the number of Hispanics eligible to vote will only increase, likely considerably faster than any other source of new voters in the United States. Hence the Republicans are currently choosing a path that will make it harder to keep their overall electoral support as high as in 2016, and they must find a way to attract new voters to their camp to compensate for the growth in the total number of Hispanic voters election after election who tilt disproportionately to the Democrats. As Trump demonstrated in 2016, compared to Romney in 2012, that is not an impossible task, but it will be an increasingly challenging one.

## PARTY IDENTIFICATION AND THE VOTE

As we saw in Chapter 4, partisanship is related to turnout. Strong supporters of either party are more likely to vote than weak supporters, and independents who lean toward a party are more likely to vote than independents without partisan leanings. Republicans are somewhat more likely to vote than Democrats. Although partisanship influences whether people vote, it is more strongly related to how people vote.

Table 8-5 reports the percentage of white major-party voters who voted for the Democratic candidate across all categories of partisanship since 1980 and Table A8-5 in the appendix reports the same for all ANES studies.[22] Clearly there is a strong relationship between partisan identification and choice of candidate. In every election

**Table 8-4 Party Identification among Latinos in Presidential Years, Pre-election Surveys, 2008–2016 (Percent)**

| **Part A: Party Identification** | | | |
|---|---|---|---|
| **Party Identification** | **2008** | **2012** | **2016** |
| Strong Democrat | 23 | 27 | 28 |
| Weak Democrat | 21 | 23 | 21 |
| Independent, leans Democratic | 17 | 16 | 11 |
| Independent, no partisan leanings | 16 | 15 | 18 |
| Independent, leans Republican | 9 | 7 | 7 |
| Weak Republican | 6 | 6 | 7 |
| Strong Republican | 7 | 5 | 8 |
| Total | 99 | 99 | 100 |
| (*N*) | (192) | (222) | (503) |
| **Part B: Vote for Democratic Candidate** | **2008** | **2012** | **2016** |
| Strong Democrat | 95 | 100 | 84 |
| Weak Democrat | 90 | 87 | 91 |
| Independent, leans Democratic | 94 | 99 | 100 |
| Independent, no partisan leanings | 61 | 82 | 69 |
| Independent, leans Republican | 35 | 39 | 32 |
| Weak Republican | 24 | 4 | 23 |
| Strong Republican | 20 | 1 | 5 |
| Total | 79 | 78 | 74 |
| (*N*) | (104) | (107) | (227) |

*Source:* Authors' analysis of ANES surveys.

*Note:* Numbers are weighted.

except 1972, the Democratic nominee has received more than 80 percent of the vote of strong Democrats and majority support from both weak Democratic partisans and independent Democratic leaners. In 1996 these figures were higher than in any other election in this period, with nine in ten white Democratic identifiers voting for their party's nominee. Although the figures fell somewhat in 2000, especially in the independent-leaning Democrat category, that reversed in 2004, with John Kerry holding onto very large majorities of those who identified with the Democratic Party, including nearly nine in ten independents who were leaning toward the Democratic Party. In 2008 this very high level of Democratic voting continued, with slight declines among strong Democrats balanced by comparable increases among weak Democrats. The 2012 election looked more similar to 1996 than any other in this regard, and was only slightly less solidly Democrat in voting than in that year. Perhaps in the absence of the pull of Obama's candidacy, Democratic partisans supported Clinton at "only" the levels they supported Kerry in 2004, but that still was at very high levels.

Since 1952 strong Republicans have given the Democratic candidate less than one vote in ten. In 1988 more of the weak Republicans and independents who leaned toward the Republican Party voted for Michael Dukakis than had voted for Walter Mondale in 1984, but even so, only about one in seven voted Democratic. In 1992 Clinton won an even larger percentage of the two-party vote from these Republicans, and he increased his support among Republicans again in 1996. In 2000 George W. Bush held essentially the same level of support among the three white Republican categories as his father had in 1988 and 1992 and if anything increased his support among Republicans in 2004. In 2008 more than 90 percent of the strong and weak Republicans voted for McCain, just as they did for Bush four years earlier. The 2012 data looked rather similar to 2008, with Romney doing a little worse in holding weak Republican votes but doing much better than McCain among Republican leaners. In 2016 Clinton gathered more support from weak Republicans than anyone since her husband but did quite poorly among those whites who lean toward the Republican Party.

The pure independent vote among whites, which fluctuates substantially, has been more Republican than Democratic in eleven of these sixteen elections and was strongly Democratic only in 1964. Clinton did well among major-party voters in 1992. John F. Kennedy won 50 percent of that vote in 1960, but Bill Clinton won nearly two-thirds of the pure independents' vote (between the two parties) in 1992. Kerry was able to win 54 percent of the pure independent vote. Obama, like Kennedy, won exactly half of the vote among whites who are pure independents in 2008. However, that 50-50 vote in 1960 was the same as the overall vote, whereas Obama won a higher proportion from the full electorate than from white pure independents. But, in 2012, he fell back significantly, winning only 42 percent of the "pure" independent vote among whites. Clinton did particularly poorly among whites who claimed to be "pure" independents, holding only as many of them as did Dukakis in 1988.

Thus, at least among major-party white voters, partisanship is very strongly related to the vote. In recent elections the Democrats have been better able to hold support among their partisans, perhaps because the loss of southern white support has made the party more homogeneous in its outlook. Their partisan base has become essentially as strong as the Republicans', which has been consistently strong except in the very best years for the Democrats. Partisanship, then, has become more polarized in its relationship to the vote. Obama won because he broke relatively even among independents and because he held his base well, about as well as Republicans held theirs.

Table 8-5 White Major-Party Voters Who Voted Democratic for President, by Party Identification, 1980–2016 (Percent)

| Party Identification | 1980 | 1984 | 1988 | 1992 | 1996 | 2000 | 2004 | 2008 | 2012 | 2016 |
|---|---|---|---|---|---|---|---|---|---|---|
| Strong Democrat | 87 | 88 | 93 | 96 | 98 | 96 | 97 | 92 | 98 | 95 |
| Weak Democrat | 59 | 63 | 68 | 80 | 88 | 81 | 78 | 83 | 82 | 75 |
| Independent, leans Democratic | 57 | 77 | 86 | 92 | 91 | 72 | 88 | 8 | 86 | 88 |
| Independent, no partisan leanings | 23 | 21 | 35 | 63 | 39 | 44 | 54 | 50 | 42 | 36 |
| Independent, leans Republican | 13 | 5 | 13 | 14 | 26 | 15 | 13 | 17 | 11 | 8 |
| Weak Republican | 5 | 6 | 16 | 18 | 21 | 16 | 10 | 10 | 14 | 17 |
| Strong Republican | 4 | 2 | 2 | 2 | 3 | 1 | 3 | 2 | 4 | 2 |

*Source:* Authors' analysis of ANES surveys.

Table 8-4B shows that there is a very powerful relationship between Hispanic party identification and their vote. Nearly all Democratic Hispanics voted for Obama in 2008 and 2012. Obama was able to hold about a quarter of the relatively small number of Hispanics who identified with the GOP in 2008, but Romney won nearly all of the by-now very small number of strong and weak Republican Hispanic votes in 2008. The pure independent vote broke strongly for Obama in 2008 but increased dramatically in 2012. Whereas Clinton's support among strong Democrats declined, the pattern looks similar to that of 2008. Our conclusion is that, whereas particular percentages are somewhat variable, presumably primarily due to the smaller numbers involved, the overall pattern is one in which Hispanic voting follows white voting in that partisanship is a very strong guide to voting. The big difference is that so many more Hispanics are Democrats that they are a solid and important part of the Democratic voting coalition, not as heavily pro-Democratic as blacks but certainly far more Democratic than Republican in their loyalties and their voting choices.

Although nearly all blacks vote Democratic regardless of their partisan affiliations (most are, however, Democratic identifiers), among Hispanics and whites partisanship leads to loyalty in voting. Between 1964 and 1980 the relationship between party identification and the vote was declining, but in 1984 the relationship between party identification and the presidential vote was higher than in any of the five elections from 1964 to 1980. The relationship remained strong in 1988 and continued to be quite strong in the two Clinton elections and the Gore-Bush election, at least among major-party voters. The question of whether the parties are gathering new strength at the presidential level could not be answered definitively from the 2000 election data, but the 2004 through 2016 election data now make it clear that these growing signs have become a strong trend, to the point that party identification is as strongly related to the presidential vote as it has been since the 1950s and early 1960s, and indeed may be stronger. The relationship between party identification and voting in general will be reconsidered in Chapter 10, when we assess its relationship to the congressional vote.[23]

Partisanship is related to the way people vote. The question, therefore, is why do partisans support their party's candidates? As we shall see party identification affects behavior because it helps structure (and, according to the understanding of partisanship as a running tally of experiences, is structured by) the way voters view both policies and performance.

## POLICY PREFERENCES AND PERFORMANCE EVALUATIONS

In their study of voting in the 1948 election, Bernard R. Berelson, Paul F. Lazarsfeld, and William N. McPhee discovered that Democratic voters attributed to their nominee, incumbent Harry S Truman, positions on key issues that were consistent with their beliefs—whether those beliefs were liberal, moderate, or conservative.[24] Similarly Republicans tended to see their nominee, Gov. Thomas E. Dewey of New York, as taking whatever positions they preferred. These tendencies toward "projection" (projecting one's own preferences onto what one thinks the favored candidate prefers) are discomforting for those who hope that in a democracy, issue preferences shape candidate assessment and voting choices rather than the other way around. These authors did find, however, that the more the voters knew, the less likely they were to project their preferences onto the candidates. Research since then has emphasized the role of party identification not only in projection but also in shaping the policy preferences in the public in the first place.[25] In this section we use four examples to illustrate the strong relationship between partisan affiliation and perceptions, preferences, and evaluations of candidates.

## Partisanship and Approval of President's Job Performance

Most partisans evaluate the job performance of a president from their party more highly than do independents and, especially, more highly than do those who identify with the other party. Figure 8-1A shows the percentage of each of the seven partisan groups that approves of the way the incumbent has handled his job as president (as a proportion of those approving or disapproving) in the last four presidential elections in which there was a Democratic president (1980, 1996, 2000, and 2012).

**Figure 8-1A Approval of Democratic Incumbents' Handling of Job, by Party Identification, 1980, 1996, 2000, 2012, and 2016**

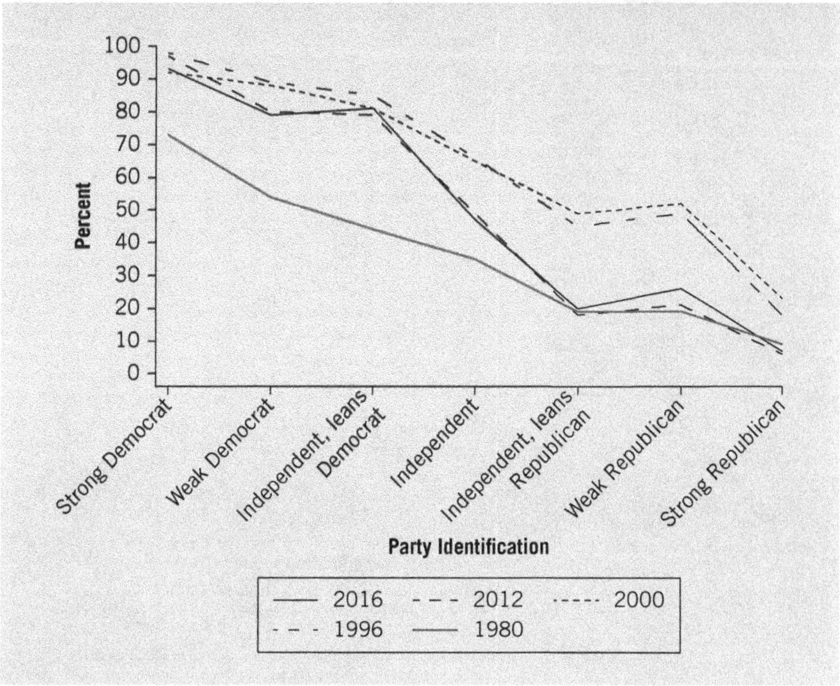

*Source:* Authors' analysis of the ANES surveys.

*Note:* Data are weighted.

Figure 8-1B presents similar results for the seven elections in which there was been a Republican incumbent (1972, 1976, 1984, 1988, 1992, 2004, and 2008).[26] Strong partisans of the incumbent's party typically give overwhelming approval to that incumbent. (Table A8-8 in the appendix presents the exact values for each year.) It is not guaranteed, however. In 1980 only 73 percent of strong Democrats approved of Jimmy Carter, which is just about the same percentage of strong Republicans who approved of Bush's job performance in 2008.

We can draw two conclusions about 2016 from the data in Figures 8-1A and 8-1B. First, just as in every election, there was a strong partisan cast to evaluations of the president in 2016. Democrats are very likely to approve of any Democratic incumbent and very unlikely to approve of any Republican incumbent and vice versa for Republicans. This fact was perhaps even truer in 2016 than in prior elections as the degree of partisan polarization of approval of Obama's handling of his job was more dramatic than any other. Virtually all strong Democrats approved; virtually no strong Republicans did. Even independent leaners were divided four to one in each party,

**Figure 8-1B Approval of Republican Incumbents' Handling of Job, by Party Identification, 1976, 1976, 1984, 1988, 1992, 2004, and 2008**

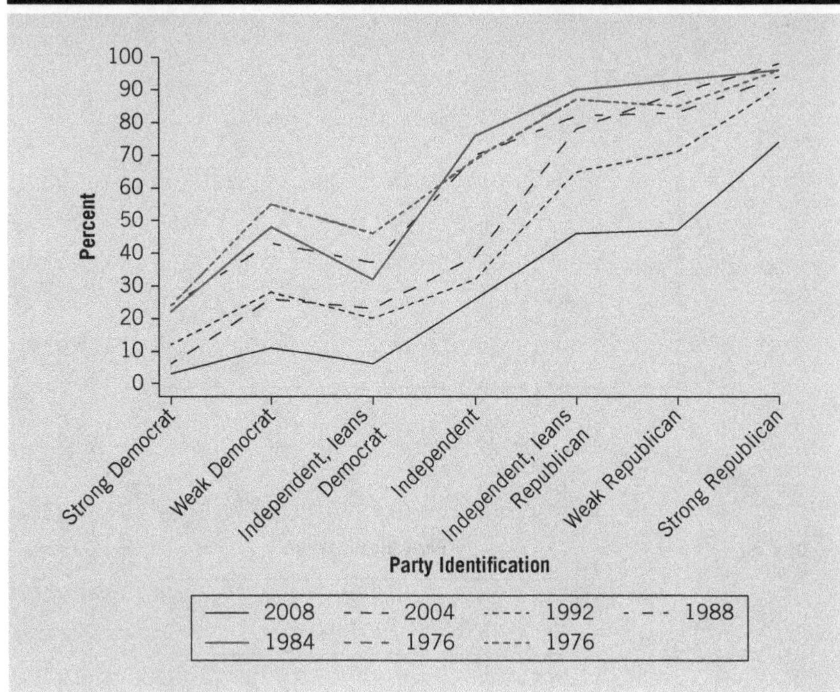


*Source:* Authors' analysis of the ANES surveys.

*Note:* Data are weighted.

with Democrats approving, Republicans disapproving, and pure independents falling directly in between.

## Partisanship and Approval of President's Handling the Economy

Our second illustration extends the connection we have drawn between partisanship and approval of the incumbent's job performance. In this case we examine the relationship between partisanship and approval of the incumbent's handling of the economy. Table 8-6 shows the relationship among all seven partisan categories and approval of incumbent presidents' handling of the economy from 2000 through 2012, whereas Table A8-6 in the appendix provides data back to 1984.[27]

In 1984 and 1988 more than three-quarters of each of the three Republican groups approved of Reagan's handling of the economy, whereas more than half—and often more than two-thirds—of the three Democratic groups disapproved. Independents generally approved of Reagan's economic efforts, albeit more strongly in 1984 than in 1988. The 1992 election was dramatically different, with overwhelming disapproval of George H. W. Bush's handling of the economy among the three Democratic groups and the pure independents. Even two-thirds of the weak and Republican-leaning independents disapproved. Only strong Republicans typically approved, and even then one in three did not. The relationship in 1996 is most like that of 1984. In 2000 the vast majority of Democrats and even three in four of the pure independents approved of Clinton's economic performance—by far the highest economic approval mark independents have given. But then most Republicans also approved. In 2004 the weak but improving economy meant that George W. Bush was approved by "only" nine in ten strong Republicans and about seven in ten weak and independent-leaning Republicans. Democratic disapproval reached very high levels, and once again pure independents did not favor Bush, only one in three approving of his handling of the economy. In 2008 the Wall Street meltdown occurred in the midst of the campaign, and its effects were devastating to President Bush's approval ratings. Only 18 percent of respondents approved of Bush's handling of the economy. Even though these ratings were lower than the overall approval ratings, they displayed a clear partisan effect. Strong Republicans still approved more than they disapproved, and one in four in the other two Republican categories approved. These are very low percentages to be sure, but they are higher than among pure independents and much higher than the mere trace levels of any type of Democrat, with about one in twenty approving. The relationship between partisanship and approval of Obama's handling of the economy in 2012 was very strong. Of the three Democrat categories of partisanship, nine in ten or more approved of Obama's performance. Nine in ten strong Republicans disapproved, but Obama was able to do marginally better among weak Republicans, being approved by two in ten of them, and even better among independents who lean Republican, being approved by a bit more than a third. And pure independents approved of Obama's performance by a two-to-one ratio. Thus, as in so many other cases we have examined, evaluations and voting in 2012 were quite polarized by party even in the electorate.

**Table 8-6 Approval of Incumbent's Handling of the Economy among Partisan Groups, 2016 (Percent)**

| | | Party Identification | | | | | | | |
|---|---|---|---|---|---|---|---|---|---|
| Year | Attitudes toward handling of the economy | Strong Democrat | Weak Democrat | Independent, leans Democrat | Independent | Independent, leans Republican | Weak Republican | Strong Republican | Total |
| 2016 | Approve | 93 | 75 | 79 | 44 | 21 | 29 | 10 | 53 |
| | Disapprove | 7 | 25 | 21 | 56 | 79 | 71 | 90 | 47 |
| | Total | 100 | 100 | 100 | 100 | 100 | 100 | 100 | 100 |
| | (*N*) | (896) | (582) | (460) | (606) | (470) | (499) | (691) | (4,221) |

*Source:* Authors' analysis of ANES surveys.

In 2016 the trend of highly polarized partisan evaluations continued to grow. There is an almost four-step linear pattern. Greater than nine of ten strong Democrats approved of Obama's handling of the economy; about three in four weak and leaning Democrats approved. Nine in twenty pure independents did so, circa one in four weak and leaning Republicans approved, whereas one in ten strong Republicans did.

## Prospective Issues

The third example of the impact of partisanship on attitudes and beliefs is its relationship to positions on policy issues. In Table 8-7 and Table A8-7, we report this relationship among the seven partisan categories and our balance-of-issues measure developed in Chapter 6, collapsed into three groupings: pro-Republican, neutral, pro-Democratic.[28] As we saw in Chapter 6, these issues favored the Republicans in 1972, 1976, and 1980, worked slightly to the Democratic advantage in 1984, 1988, and 1992, then once again favored the Republicans in the elections from 1996 to 2012 but barely doing so in 2016. In all cases the balance-of-issues measure had only moderately favored one party over the other, except in 2008, where the measure pointed to a clear favoring of the Republicans.[29]

As Table 8-7 and A8-7 show for 1976–2016, there has been a steady, clear, moderately strong relationship between partisanship and the balance-of-issues measure, and it is one that, by 2000, had strengthened considerably and continued to strengthen into 2008, with only modest weakening in 2012. In 2016, while "leaners" were more like strong than weak partisans, the relationship otherwise continued to strengthen. Until 1984 the relationship had been stronger among Republicans than among Democrats.

Prospective issues appear to be increasingly polarized by party, strikingly so by 2000. The data for the 2000 through 2016 elections are quite similar in that there is a strong relationship between party identification and the balance-of-issues measure. In 2016 more than three in five strong Democrats were closer to Clinton's position than to Trump's, whereas more than nine out of ten strong Republicans were closer to where the electorate placed Trump. Thus the degree of polarization on this measure continues to be quite strong in recent elections.

Partisan polarization characterizes not only prospective issues but also most other factors we have examined. In our balance-of-issues measure, "polarization" really means "consistency"—that is, partisans find their party's candidate closer to them than the opposing party's nominee on more and more issues. On these measures, then, what we observe as growing polarization stems from the increased differentiation and consistency of positions of the candidates and not as much from changes in the issue positions among the public. This is often called "sorting"—that is, sorting Democrats into the Democratic camp and Republican identifiers into their partisan camp.[30] It might also indicate partisan polarization—the two parties becoming more distant from each other—but we do not directly measure that.

## Retrospective Evaluations

Finally we find a strong relationship between party identification and our measure of retrospective evaluations in 2016. We cannot directly compare this measure

**Table 8-7 Balance-of-Issues Positions among Partisan Groups, 2016 (Percent)**

| | | Party Identification | | | | | | | |
|---|---|---|---|---|---|---|---|---|---|
| Year | Issue positions closer to . . . | Strong Democrat | Weak Democrat | Independent, leans Democrat | Independent | Independent, leans Republican | Weak Republican | Strong Republican | Total % |
| 2016 | Democratic candidate | 64 | 48 | 56 | 34 | 13 | 13 | 7 | 35 |
| | Neutral | 14 | 19 | 19 | 24 | 11 | 17 | 6 | 16 |
| | Republican candidate | 22 | 33 | 24 | 42 | 76 | 70 | 87 | 49 |
| | Total | 100 | 100 | 99 | 100 | 100 | 100 | 100 | 100 |
| | (*N*) | (902) | (587) | (462) | (620) | (472) | (501) | (696) | (4242) |

*Source:* Authors' analysis of ANES surveys.

*Note:* The Democratic category on the condensed balance-of-issues measures includes any respondent who is at least slightly Democratic; the Republican category includes any respondent who is at least slightly Republican. The neural category is the same as the neutral category on the seven-point issue scale (see Table 6-5). Numbers are weighted.

in the 2016 election with those for earlier elections because the questions that make up the summary retrospective measure in the last seven presidential elections differ from those available in 2004, and both differ from those available in 2008 and again in 2012 and 2016.[31] Still, it is worth noting that this measure was very strongly related to partisanship in those earlier elections. Table 8-8 shows the relationship in 2016, collapsing the summary retrospective measure into the three categories of pro-Democratic, neutral, and pro-Republican. The relationship is strong. Almost all strong Republicans had negative retrospective evaluations, for example, whereas nine in ten strong Democrats were moderately or strongly positive. We conclude that retrospective evaluations are invariably strongly related to partisanship, and if comparable measures were available, we suspect that 2016, like 2012, would be among the most strongly related to partisanship.[32]

Not only are party identification and retrospective evaluations consistently and strongly related to the vote, but these two measures also are strongly related to each other in every election. Do they both still contribute independently to the vote? As we learn from the data in Table 8-9 about the 2016 election, the answer is yes.[33] In Table 8-9, we examine the combined impact of party identification and retrospective evaluations on voting choices. To simplify the presentation, we use the three groupings of the summary retrospective evaluations, and we collapsed party identification into the three groups: strong and weak Republicans, all three independent categories, and strong and weak Democrats.

Table 8-9 shows the percentage of major-party voters who voted Democratic by both party identification and retrospective evaluations in 2016. Reading down the columns reveals that party identification is strongly related to the vote, regardless of the voter's retrospective evaluations, a pattern found in the nine elections before 2016. Not enough people assessed the Republicans positively on retrospective evaluations to say much about that column, but the other two columns illustrate a very strong relationship. Reading across each row reveals that in all elections, retrospective evaluations are related to the vote, regardless of the voter's party identification, and once again a pattern was discovered in all nine earlier elections. Moreover, as in all nine elections between 1976 and 2008, party identification and retrospective evaluations had a combined impact on how people voted in 2008. For example, in 2012 all Republicans with pro-Republican evaluations reported voting for Romney; among Democrats with pro-Democratic evaluations, 99 percent voted for Obama.

Finally partisanship and retrospective assessments appear to have roughly equal effects on the vote (although retrospective evaluations might, if anything, outweigh partisanship in 2016, as it appeared to do in 2012 as well), and certainly both are strongly related to the vote, even when both variables are examined together. For example, the effect of retrospective evaluations on the vote is not the result of partisans having positive retrospective assessments of their party's presidents and negative ones when the opposition holds the White House. Republicans who hold pro-Democratic retrospective judgments were much more supportive of Clinton than other Republicans (indeed three in four of those few voted for her, whereas only one in four Democrats with pro-Republican retrospective evaluations voted for Clinton). Overall, then, we can conclude that partisanship is a key component for understanding evaluations of the public and their votes, but the large changes in outcomes over time

**Table 8-8 Retrospective Evaluations among Partisan Groups, 2016 (Percent)**

| | Party Identification | | | | | | | |
|---|---|---|---|---|---|---|---|---|
| Summary measure of retrospective evaluations | Strong Democrat | Weak Democrat | Independent, leans Democrat | Independent | Independent, leans Republican | Weak Republican | Strong Republican | Total % |
| Pro-Democratic | 55 | 33 | 31 | 12 | 3 | 8 | 1 | 23 |
| Slightly supportive, opposed, or neutral | 41 | 50 | 54 | 38 | 19 | 25 | 8 | 34 |
| Pro-Republican | 3 | 18 | 14 | 49 | 78 | 68 | 91 | 43 |
| Total | 99 | 101 | 99 | 99 | 100 | 101 | 100 | 100 |
| (*N*) | (763) | (505) | (400) | (486) | (407) | (427) | (573) | (3560) |

*Source:* Authors' analysis of the 2016 ANES survey.

*Note:* The Democratic category on the condensed measure of retrospective evaluations includes any respondent who is at least moderately opposed to the incumbent's party; the Republican category includes any respondent who at least moderately supports the incumbent's party. The middle retrospective category is the same as the middle retrospective category in Table 7-10. Numbers are weighted.

**Table 8-9 Percentage of Major-Party Voters Who Voted for Clinton, by Party Identification and Summary Retrospective Evaluations, 2016**

| Party Identification | Summary Retrospective Evaluations | | | | | | | |
|---|---|---|---|---|---|---|---|---|
| | Pro-Democratic | | Neutral | | Pro-Republican | | Total | |
| | % | (N) | % | (N) | % | (N) | % | (*N*) |
| Democratic | 99 | (462) | 96 | (394) | 28 | (75) | 92 | (941) |
| Independent | 96 | (129) | 79 | (209) | 10 | (342) | 47 | (694) |
| Republican | 77 | (27) | 38 | (85) | 1 | (625) | 8 | (743) |
| Total | 26 | (618) | 29 | (688) | 44 | (1,042) | 99 | (2348) |

*Source:* Authors' analysis of the 2016 ANES survey.

*Note:* The Democratic category on the condensed measure of retrospective evaluations includes any respondent who is at least moderately opposed to the incumbent's party; the Republican category includes any respondent who at least moderately supports the incumbent's party. The middle retrospective category is the same as the middle retrospective category in Table 7-10. The numbers in parentheses are the totals on which the percentages are based. Numbers are weighted.

must be traced to retrospective and prospective evaluations simply because partisanship does not change substantially over time.

In summary partisanship appears to affect the way voters evaluate incumbents and their performances. Positions on issues have been a bit different. Although partisans in the 1970s and early 1980s were likely to be closer to their party's nominee on policy, the connection was less clear than between partisanship and retrospective evaluations. It is only recently that prospective evaluations have emerged as being nearly as important a set of influences on candidate choice as retrospective evaluations, and this appears to track closely the growing partisan polarization of members of Congress. Still, policy-related evaluations are influenced in part by history and political memory and in part by the candidates' campaign strategies. Partisan attachments, then, limit the ability of a candidate to control his or her fate in the electorate, but such attachments are not entirely rigid. Candidates have some flexibility in the support they receive from partisans, especially depending on the candidates' or their predecessors' performance in office and on the policy promises they make in the campaign.

## CONCLUSION

Party loyalties affect how people vote, how they evaluate issues, and how they judge the performance of the incumbent president and his party. In recent years research has suggested that party loyalties not only affect issue preferences, perceptions, and evaluations but that preferences, perceptions, and evaluations may also may affect those loyalties in turn. There is good reason to believe that the relationship between partisanship and these factors is more complex than any model that assumes a one-way relationship would suggest. Doubtless, evaluations of the incumbent's performance may also affect party loyalties.[34]

As we saw in this chapter, there was a substantial shift toward Republican loyalties over the 1980s; among whites, the clear advantage Democrats had enjoyed over the last four decades appeared to be gone. Although the 2008 election suggests that there was at least a chance that the Democrats would enjoy a resurgence, that advantage was at least temporarily stemmed in 2012, as the two parties were near parity. This parity turned back toward a Democratic advantage in 2016, which is somewhat unusual, not just because the Republicans won the Electoral College vote but also because Clinton won the popular vote by only a couple of percentage points—hardly a sweep toward the Democratic Party. To some extent the earlier shift in party loyalties in the 1980s must have reflected Reagan's appeal and his successful performance in office, as judged by the electorate. His successor, the senior Bush, lost much of the partisan appeal he inherited primarily because of negative assessments of his handling of the economy, and he was not able to hold onto the high approval ratings he had attained in 1991 after the success in the Persian Gulf War. In 1996 Clinton demonstrated that a president could rebound from a weak early performance as judged by the electorate and benefit from a growing economy.

The 1996 election stood as one comparable to the reelection campaigns of other recent, successful incumbents, although Clinton received marks as high as or higher than Nixon's in 1972 and Reagan's in 1984 for his overall performance and for his handling of the economy. With strong retrospective judgments the electorate basically decided that one good term deserved another.

The question for the 2000 campaign was why Vice President Al Gore was unable to do better than essentially tie George W. Bush in the election (whether counting by popular or electoral votes). We must remember, however, how closely balanced all other key indicators were. Partisanship among whites was essentially evenly split between the two parties, with a Republican advantage in turnout at least partially offsetting the Democratic partisanship of blacks. Prospective issues, as in most election years, only modestly favored one side or the other. Retrospective evaluations, however, provided Gore with a solid edge, as did approval ratings of Clinton on the economy. The failure, then, was in Gore's inability to translate that edge in retrospective assessments into a more substantial lead in the voting booth. Retrospective evaluations were almost as strongly related to the vote in 2000 as in other recent elections, but Gore failed to push beyond that slight popular vote plurality and turn a virtual tie into an outright win.

George W. Bush, it appears, learned some lessons from 2000 for his 2004 reelection. In 2004 he faced an electorate that, like its immediate predecessors, was almost evenly balanced in its partisanship, with a slight Democratic edge in numbers of identifiers balanced by their lower propensity to turn out than Republican identifiers. Meanwhile, because of the continuing decline in the proportion of pure independents, there were fewer opportunities to win over those not already predisposed to support one party or the other. Furthermore, although Bush held an edge in prospective evaluations, Kerry held an advantage on retrospective assessments, but in both cases the edges were small. Thus with fewer independents to woo and such an even balance, the contest became a race for both the remaining independents and the weakly attached and an effort to "strengthen the base"—by motivating supporters to, in turn, motivate the base to turn out. Perhaps for this reason we observed a strengthening of the affective component of partisan attachments—that is, a growth in strong partisans at the expense of the more weakly attached, at least during the campaign itself.

All of this was lost in 2008. Partisanship shifted toward the Democrats. The Bush administration was the least popular we have yet been able to measure. The public rejected his incumbency in general and his handling of the economy in particular. As a result John McCain faced an unusually steep uphill battle. It is no wonder that he and Sarah Palin emphasized their "maverick" status as independent of the Bush administration. They did not, however, cut themselves loose from their partisan base. McCain might have been able to do so, but his selection of Palin as running mate indicated that his administration would be distinct from Bush's administration but nevertheless just as Republican. In view of the edge he held on prospective issues, that was a plausible choice. But the financial meltdown in the fall of 2008 probably sealed his fate. The election came down to being a partisan one, on which the Democrats turned out to hold an increased advantage, and a retrospective one, on which the Democrats held an overwhelming advantage. These two factors translated into a comfortable victory for Obama—and many other Democrats.

Much changed between 2008 and 2012. The Democratic hold on the House and Senate was lost in a disastrous congressional election in 2010. The legislative victories of the Obama administration and Democrats in 2009 and early 2010 yielded controversy and what was originally a rather popular-based outpouring of protest that became the "Tea Party." This movement pushed Republican candidates and officeholders toward the right wing of their party, deepening polarization. The result was that voters increasingly saw and acted upon that partisan polarization among political elites. Public opinion on partisanship and evaluations of all kinds reflected the polarization they perceived, even if the public was more or less evenly balanced in their views and not evidently deeply polarized in their own issue opinions. When given a menu of polarized campaigns, the public responded with polarized choices, making partisanship and its relationship to evaluations and choices as strong an influence as ever.

Perhaps the most surprising thing about presidential voting in 2016 was how similar it was to other recent elections, perhaps most especially to 2012. A female headed a major party ticket for the first time. A non-politician lacking in any sort of governmental experience (political or military) was also a groundbreaker. Further, he had been a Democrat far longer than he had been a Republican, and he had long made public what had been his quite liberal policy preferences on many issues, some held right up to the 2016 campaign. He took on the Republican political establishment, and many of them took him on in return. And yet, the voting patterns, although not precisely identical from election to election, look much like those that preceded them. It appears that the voters saw not a populist, former Democrat, or one who held a number of liberal positions on important issues. Rather they saw a Republican, purely and simply.

There are a few ways in which voters saw Trump as different from other candidates, such as we saw in Chapter 6, where they were clear, for example, that he speaks his mind. But these differences, important as they may be, were concentrated primarily in evaluations of Trump the individual candidate. In virtually all other ways, the dominant story is that of voters assessing a highly (and highly charged) political world overwhelmingly understood by partisan polarization. In some ways the voter is polarized, but as we can see, especially with respect to prospective issues, that is not always true. Indeed the typical voter's policy stances in these terms have changed little since these measures first were used. But their evaluations of the candidates, incumbents, parties, and their performances increasingly reflect a mostly partisan electorate embedded in a world where political elites (whether establishment or populist or maverick) are polarized by party affiliation. The increasing strengthening of the various relationships in this chapter reflect a partisan voter world that is at least sorted. One big change, for example, was the slow transition of southern conservatives in the 1980s from Democratic to Republican partisanship as Republicans, for the first time there since before 1876, provided more and more conservative candidates running for more and more offices.[35] Given that most in the electorate have at least some partisan inclinations, and given that they are sorted into the same partisan groups as the parties' political candidates and officeholders, that means that even only moderately liberal Democrats will choose a partisan polarized, liberal Democrat for office after office, in election after election, over any conservative Republican. And, of course, the same works in reverse for even modestly conservative Republicans. Thus elections are dominated by the polarized parties at the elite level and the sorted parties at the voter level (and possibly polarized voters, too, at least in some dimensions). Elections look a lot like one another because the big picture is that they are like one another—conservative Republican candidates appealing to conservative Republican voters, liberal Democratic voters appealing to liberal Democrats.[36] Increasingly polarized parties mean that each election looks a lot like the preceding one, only a bit more so, election after election. And that there are reasonably similar number of Democrats at the voting booth as there are Republicans holds this all in balance.[37] That is, partisan polarization has nearly locked voting patterns into place, such that once the public observed this dramatic change, the electoral world is less change and much more continuity.

# PART THREE

# THE 2016 CONGRESSIONAL ELECTIONS

CHAPTER NINE

# CANDIDATES AND OUTCOMES IN 2016

In 1994 the Republicans unexpectedly won control of both chambers of Congress, the first time the GOP had won the House since 1952. (The only time they had controlled the Senate during that period was 1980–1986.) The electoral earthquake of 1994 shaped all subsequent Congressional contests. From 1996 on, there was at least some doubt about who would control the next Congress after the voters chose, which had not been in the case during the previous period of Democratic control. In the next five elections after 1994, the GOP retained control of the House, although they lost seats in the first three and gained in the next two. In the Senate the Republicans added to their majority in 1996, broke even in 1998, and then lost ground in 2000, leaving the chamber evenly divided. Then in 2002 the GOP made small gains to get a little breathing room, and in 2004 they gained a bit more. Going into the elections of 2006, the GOP still had control of Congress, but that year their luck ran out. The GOP suffered a crushing defeat, losing thirty seats in the House and six in the Senate, shifting control of both bodies to the Democrats, and in 2008 the Democrats achieved a second substantial gain in a row, adding twenty-one seats in the House and eight seats in the Senate.

In 2010 party fortunes reversed again. In the wake of the Great Recession, the Democrats lost the House, with the Republicans picking up a net gain of sixty-three seats. In the Senate the GOP fell short of control, but they did gain six seats. In 2012 the Republicans had hoped to continue to make gains, but that was not to be. Instead the Democrats regained some ground. In the House they won 201 seats to the Republicans' 234, a gain of eight seats. In the Senate the result was a fifty-three to forty-five division in favor of the Democrats, with two independents (both of whom sided with the Democrats on control),[1] which reflected a gain of two Senate seats. Two years later in 2014, the Republicans made a net gain of thirteen seats in the House, netting them their largest majority (247–188) since 1928. More significant, however, was the Republican's capture of the Senate—they picked up nine Democratic seats while losing none of their own to take a fifty-four to forty-six majority. Although the Republicans ended up losing six seats in the House and two in the Senate during the 2016 elections, they were able to maintain control of Congress, giving them unified control of the government for the first time since 2005–2006. This initially gave them considerable hope that they would be able to pass a Republican agenda, such as repealing and replacing the Affordable Care Act (ACA), among other initiatives. The smaller majority in the House, along with a moderately diverse party conference, and the small, two-vote majority in the Senate, gave them very little room to maneuver if they wanted to pass that agenda with only Republican votes.

In this chapter we examine the pattern of congressional outcomes for 2016 and see how it compares to previous years. We explain why the 2016 results took the shape they did—what factors affected the success of incumbents seeking to return and what permitted some challengers to run better than others. We also discuss the likely impact of the election results on the politics of the 115th Congress. Finally we consider the implications of the 2016 results for the 2018 midterm elections and for other subsequent elections.

## ELECTION OUTCOMES IN 2016

### Patterns of Incumbency Success

One of the most dependable generalizations about American politics is that most congressional races involve incumbents and most incumbents are reelected. Although this statement has been true for every set of congressional elections since World War II, the degree to which it has held varied from one election to another. Table 9-1 presents information on election outcomes for House and Senate races involving incumbents between 1954 and 2016.[2] During this period, an average of 93 percent of House incumbents and 85 percent of Senate incumbents who sought reelection were successful.

The proportion of representatives reelected in 2016 (about 96 percent) was three points above the sixty-two year average, whereas the 93 percent success rate for senators was eight points above the average for that chamber. As we discuss later in the chapter, the limited number of quality challengers running in 2016 significantly affected the results for the House. In the absence of a quality challenger, incumbents have a much easier time getting reelected.[3] In the Senate there were a disproportionate number of Republican seats up, and as we will see later, the Democrats performed substantially below expectations.

During the period covered by Table 9-1, House and Senate outcomes have sometimes been similar and in other instances have exhibited different patterns. For example, in most years between 1968 and 1988, House incumbents were substantially more successful than their Senate counterparts. In the three elections between 1976 and 1980, House incumbents' success averaged over 93 percent, whereas senators averaged only 62 percent. By contrast the success rates during the 1990s were fairly similar. More recently, in all but one of the nine elections beginning with 2000, we have again seen some divergence, with House incumbents being more successful.

These differences between the two bodies stem from at least two factors. The first is primarily statistical: House elections routinely involve around four hundred incumbents, whereas Senate contests usually have fewer than thirty. A smaller number of cases is more likely to produce volatile results over time. Thus the proportion

## Table 9-1 House and Senate Incumbents and Election Outcomes, 1954–2016

| Year | Incumbent Running | Primary Defeats | | General Election Defeats | | Reelected | |
|---|---|---|---|---|---|---|---|
| | (*N*) | % | (*N*) | % | (*N*) | % | (*N*) |
| **House** | | | | | | | |
| 1954 | (407) | 1.5 | (6) | 5.4 | (22) | 93.1 | (379) |
| 1956 | (410) | 1.5 | (6) | 3.7 | (15) | 94.9 | (389) |
| 1958 | (394) | 0.8 | (3) | 9.4 | (37) | 89.8 | (354) |
| 1960 | (405) | 1.2 | (5) | 6.2 | (25) | 92.6 | (375) |
| 1962 | (402) | 3.0 | (12) | 5.5 | (22) | 91.5 | (368) |
| 1964 | (397) | 2.0 | (8) | 11.3 | (45) | 86.6 | (344) |
| 1966 | (411) | 1.9 | (8) | 10.0 | (41) | 88.1 | (362) |
| 1968 | (409) | 1.0 | (4) | 2.2 | (9) | 96.8 | (396) |
| 1970 | (401) | 2.5 | (10) | 3.0 | (12) | 94.5 | (379) |
| 1972 | (392) | 3.3 | (13) | 3.3 | (13) | 93.4 | (366) |
| 1974 | (391) | 2.0 | (8) | 10.2 | (40) | 87.7 | (343) |
| 1976 | (383) | 0.8 | (3) | 3.1 | (12) | 96.1 | (368) |
| 1978 | (382) | 1.3 | (5) | 5.0 | (19) | 93.7 | (358) |
| 1980 | (398) | 1.5 | (6) | 7.8 | (31) | 90.7 | (361) |
| 1982 | (393) | 2.5 | (10) | 7.4 | (29) | 90.1 | (354) |
| 1984 | (411) | 0.7 | (3) | 3.9 | (16) | 95.4 | (392) |
| 1986 | (393) | 0.5 | (2) | 1.5 | (6) | 98.0 | (385) |
| 1988 | (409) | 0.2 | (1) | 1.5 | (6) | 98.3 | (402) |
| 1990 | (407) | 0.2 | (1) | 3.7 | (15) | 96.1 | (391) |
| 1992 | (368) | 5.4 | (20) | 6.3 | (23) | 88.3 | (325) |
| 1994 | (387) | 1.0 | (4) | 8.8 | (34) | 90.2 | (349) |
| 1996 | (384) | 0.5 | (2) | 5.5 | (21) | 94.0 | (361) |
| 1998 | (401) | 0.2 | (1) | 1.5 | (6) | 98.3 | (394) |
| 2000 | (403) | 0.7 | (3) | 1.5 | (6) | 97.8 | (394) |
| 2002 | (398) | 2.0 | (8) | 1.8 | (7) | 96.2 | (383) |
| 2004 | (404) | 0.5 | (2) | 1.7 | (7) | 97.8 | (395) |
| 2006 | (404) | 0.5 | (2) | 5.4 | (22) | 94.1 | (380) |
| 2008 | (403) | 0.9 | (4) | 4.7 | (19) | 94.2 | (380) |
| 2010 | (396) | 1.0 | (4) | 13.6 | (54) | 85.4 | (338) |
| 2012 | (391) | 4.6 | (18) | 5.6 | (22) | 89.8 | (351) |
| 2014 | (395) | 1.3 | (5) | 3.3 | (13) | 95.4 | (377) |
| 2016 | (393) | 1.5 | (6) | 2.0 | (8) | 96.4 | (379) |

*(Continued)*

**Table 9-1** (Continued)

| Year | Incumbent Running | Primary Defeats | | General Election Defeats | | Reelected | |
|---|---|---|---|---|---|---|---|
| | (*N*) | % | (*N*) | % | (*N*) | % | (*N*) |
| **Senate** | | | | | | | |
| 1954 | (27) | — | (0) | 15 | (4) | 85 | (23) |
| 1956 | (30) | — | (0) | 13 | (4) | 87 | (26) |
| 1958 | (26) | — | (0) | 35 | (9) | 65 | (17) |
| 1960 | (28) | — | (0) | 4 | (1) | 96 | (27) |
| 1962 | (30) | — | (0) | 10 | (3) | 90 | (27) |
| 1964 | (30) | — | (0) | 7 | (2) | 93 | (28) |
| 1966 | (29) | 7 | (2) | 3 | (1) | 90 | (26) |
| 1968 | (28) | 14 | (4) | 14 | (4) | 71 | (20) |
| 1970 | (28) | 4 | (1) | 11 | (3) | 86 | (24) |
| 1972 | (26) | 4 | (1) | 19 | (5) | 77 | (20) |
| 1974 | (26) | 4 | (1) | 8 | (2) | 88 | (23) |
| 1976 | (25) | — | (0) | 36 | (9) | 64 | (16) |
| 1978 | (22) | — | (1) | 27 | (6) | 68 | (15) |
| 1980 | (29) | — | (4) | 31 | (9) | 55 | (16) |
| 1982 | (30) | — | (0) | 7 | (2) | 93 | (28) |
| 1984 | (29) | — | (0) | 10 | (3) | 90 | (26) |
| 1986 | (27) | — | (0) | 22 | (6) | 78 | (21) |
| 1988 | (26) | — | (0) | 12 | (3) | 88 | (23) |
| 1990 | (30) | — | (0) | 3 | (1) | 97 | (29) |
| 1992 | (27) | 4 | (1) | 11 | (3) | 85 | (23) |
| 1994 | (26) | — | (0) | 8 | (2) | 92 | (24) |
| 1996 | (20) | — | (0) | 5 | (1) | 95 | (19) |
| 1998 | (29) | — | (0) | 10 | (3) | 90 | (26) |
| 2000 | (27) | — | (0) | 22 | (6) | 78 | (21) |
| 2002 | (26) | 4 | (1) | 8 | (2) | 88 | (23) |
| 2004 | (25) | — | (0) | 5 | (1) | 96 | (24) |
| 2006 | (28) | — | (0) | 21 | (6) | 79 | (22) |
| 2008 | (29) | — | (0) | 17 | (5) | 93 | (24) |
| 2010 | (25) | 12 | (3) | 8 | (2) | 84[a] | (21) |
| 2012 | (22) | 5 | (1) | 5 | (1) | 91 | (20) |
| 2014 | (28) | — | (0) | 18 | (5) | 82 | (23) |
| 2016 | (29) | — | (0) | 7 | (2) | 93 | (27) |

*Source:* Compiled by the authors.

[a] In 2010 Senator Lisa Murkowski (R-AK) was defeated in the primary and then won the general election as a write-in candidate. Thus she is counted both as a primary defeat and as reelected.

of successful Senate incumbents tends to vary more than for the House. In addition Senate races are more likely to be vigorously contested than House races, making incumbents more vulnerable. In many years a substantial number of representatives had no opponent at all or had one who was inexperienced, underfunded, or both. Senators, on the other hand, often had strong, well-financed opponents. Thus representatives were electorally advantaged relative to senators. In the early 1990s the competitiveness of House elections increased, reducing the relative advantage for representatives, although the election cycles since then still have seen competition in House contests confined to a narrower range of constituencies than Senate races.[4] We will consider this issue in more detail later in the chapter.

Having considered incumbency, we now consider political parties. Figure 9-1 shows the percentage of seats in the House and Senate held by the Democrats after each election since 1952. It graphically demonstrates how large a departure from the past the elections of 1994 through 2004 were. In House elections before 1994, the high percentage of incumbents running and the high rate of incumbent success led to fairly stable partisan control. Most importantly the Democrats won a majority in the House in every election since 1954 and had won twenty consecutive national elections. This was by far the longest period of dominance of the House by the same party in American history.[5] This winning streak was ended by the upheaval of 1994, when the GOP made a net gain of fifty-two representatives, winning 53 percent of the total seats. They held their majority in each subsequent election through 2004, although there were small shifts back to the Democrats in 1996, 1998, and 2000. Then in 2006 the Democrats took back the House and expanded their margin in 2008. The huge GOP success of 2010 restored their control, and 2012 returned them as the majority with a reduced margin. They picked up thirteen additional seats during the 2014 midterm before losing a net of six seats in 2016.

In the Senate previous Republican control was much more recent. They had taken the Senate in the Reagan victory of 1980 and retained it in 1982 and 1984. When the class of 1980 faced the voters again in 1986, however, the Democrats made significant gains and won back the majority. They held it until the GOP regained control in 1994, and then the Republicans expanded their margin in 1996. Then in 2000 fortune turned against them, resulting in the 50-50 division of the chamber. (This was followed a few months later by the decision of Senator James Jeffords of Vermont to become an independent, and to vote with the Democrats on organizing the chamber, shifting majority control to them until after the 2002 elections.) In 2004 the GOP gained four seats and again reached their high watermark of 55 percent. Finally the combined Democratic gain of fourteen seats in 2006 and 2008 restored solid control for that party, which they retained for the next few years despite the difficult election of 2010. In 2014 the Republicans captured nine additional Senate seats, giving them unified congressional control for the final two years of the Obama presidency. Despite defending more than two-thirds of the seats up for reelection in 2016, the Republicans only lost two Senate seats in that election, yielding a relatively slim majority control.

The combined effect of party and incumbency in the general election of 2016 is shown in Table 9-2. Overall the Democrats won 45 percent of the races for House seats and 48 percent of the Senate contests. Despite the sharp partisanship of both the presidential and congressional races, incumbents of both parties did well in their

**Figure 9-1 Democratic Share of Seats in the House and Senate, 1953–2017 (in Percentages)**

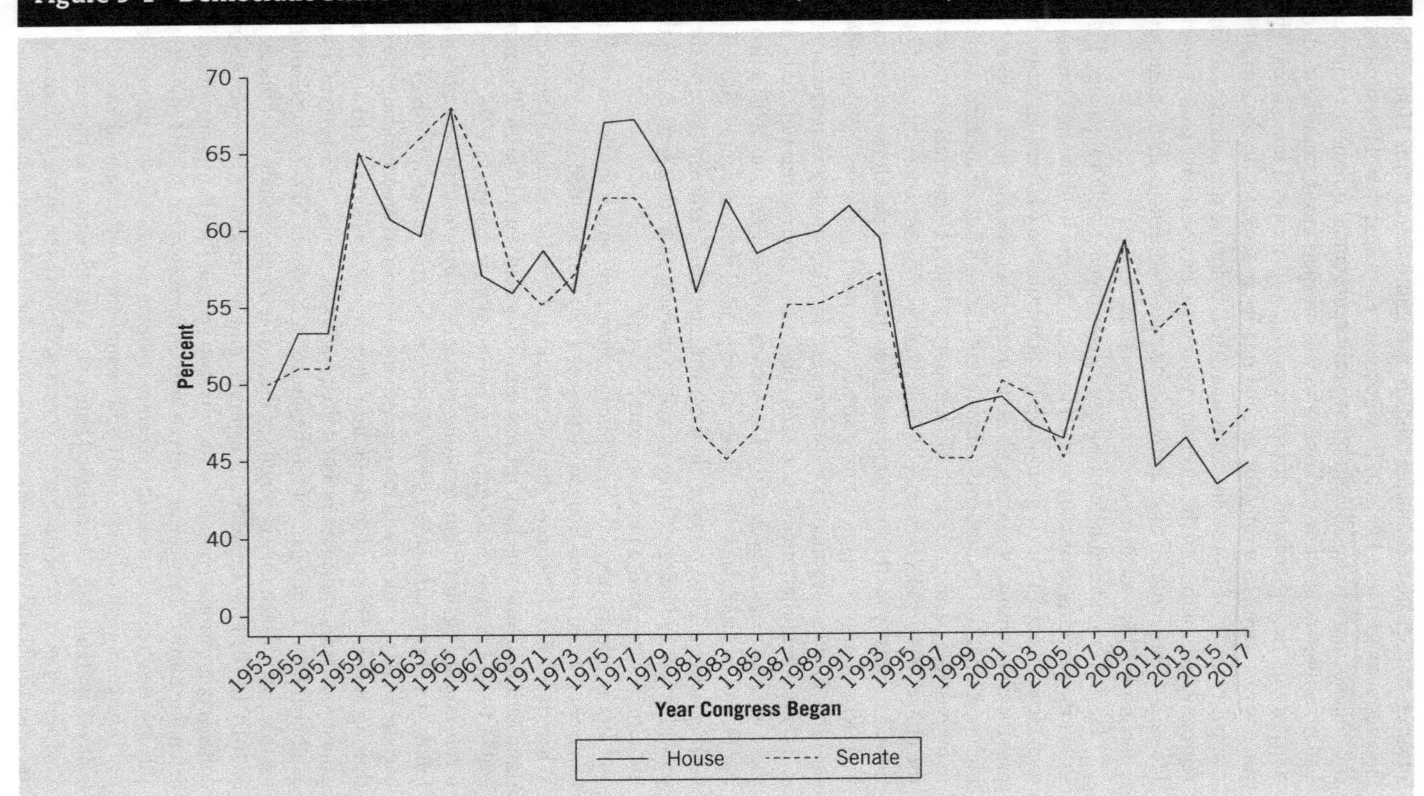


*Sources:* Data for the House are from History, Art & Archives, United States Representatives, http://history.house.gov/Institution/Party-Divisions/Party-Divisions/. Data for the Senate are from United States Senate, https://www.senate.gov/history/partydiv.htm.

**Table 9-2 House and Senate General Election Outcomes, by Party and Incumbency, 2016 (Percent)**

| | | No Incumbent | | | |
|---|---|---|---|---|---|
| | Democratic Incumbent | Democratic Seat | Republican Seat | Republican Incumbent | Total |
| **House** | | | | | |
| Democrats | 99 | 89 | 12 | 3 | 45 |
| Republicans | 1 | 11 | 88 | 97 | 55 |
| Total | 100 | 100 | 100 | 100 | 100 |
| (*N*) | 169 | 19 | 26 | 221 | 435 |
| **Senate** | | | | | |
| Democrats | 100 | 100 | 0 | 9 | 35 |
| Republicans | 0 | 0 | 100 | 91 | 65 |
| Total | 100 | 100 | 100 | 100 | 100 |
| (*N*) | 7 | 3 | 2 | 22 | 34 |

*Source:* Compiled by the authors.

House races. Ninety-nine percent of House Democratic incumbents in the general election won reelection, and 97 percent of House Republicans were successful. In the 2016 Senate races, all seven Democratic incumbents won, as did twenty-two of twenty-four GOP incumbents.

## Regional Bases of Power

The geographic pattern of 2016 outcomes in the House and Senate can be seen in the partisan breakdowns by region in Table 9-3.[6] For comparison we also present corresponding data for 1981 (after the Republicans took control of the Senate in Reagan's first election) and for 1953 (the last Congress before 1995 in which the Republicans controlled both chambers). This series of elections reveals the enormous shifts in the regional political balance that have occurred over the last six decades. In the House, comparing 2017 to 1981, we see that the GOP share declined in the East and West, whereas it increased in the Midwest, South, and the border states. The most pronounced shifts were in the West, the South, and the border states, with the Republican share decreasing by eleven percentage points in the first region while increasing by thirty-six points in the latter two. Overall the Republicans won a majority of House

**Table 9-3 Party Shares of Regional Delegations in the House and Senate, 1953, 1981, and 2017 (Percent)**

| | 1953 | | | 1981 | | | 2017 | | |
|---|---|---|---|---|---|---|---|---|---|
| | Dems | Reps | | Dems | Reps | | Dems | Reps | |
| Region | (%) | (%) | (N) | (%) | (%) | (N) | (%) | (%) | (N) |
| **House** | | | | | | | | | |
| East | 35 | 65 | (116) | 56 | 44 | (105) | 65 | 35 | (79) |
| Midwest | 23 | 76 | (118) | 47 | 53 | (111) | 36 | 64 | (86) |
| West | 33 | 67 | (57) | 51 | 49 | (76) | 62 | 38 | (102) |
| South | 94 | 6 | (106) | 64 | 36 | (108) | 28 | 72 | (138) |
| Border | 68 | 32 | (38) | 69 | 31 | (35) | 33 | 67 | (30) |
| Total | 49 | 51 | (435) | 56 | 44 | (435) | 45 | 55 | (435) |
| **Senate** | | | | | | | | | |
| East | 25 | 75 | (20) | 50 | 50 | (20) | 90 | 10 | (20) |
| Midwest | 14 | 86 | (22) | 41 | 59 | (22) | 45 | 55 | (22) |
| West | 45 | 55 | (22) | 35 | 65 | (26) | 50 | 50 | (26) |
| South | 100 | 0 | (22) | 55 | 45 | (22) | 14 | 86 | (22) |
| Border | 70 | 30 | (10) | 70 | 30 | (10) | 40 | 60 | (10) |
| Total | 49 | 51 | (96) | 47 | 53 | (100) | 48 | 52 | (100) |

*Source:* Compiled by the authors.

seats in all regions but the East and West in 2016. With the exception of the Midwest, the pattern is roughly similar in the Senate. Between 1981 and 2017 GOP gains were limited to two regions of the country (the South and border), while they lost ground in the East, Midwest, and West.

The 2017 election results are even more interesting when viewed from the longer historical perspective. In 1953 there were sharp regional differences in party representation in both houses. These differences diminished significantly by 1981, but new and substantial deviations developed subsequently. The most obvious changes occurred in the East and the South. In 1953 the Republicans held nearly two-thirds of the House seats in the East, but by 2017 their share had fallen to slightly more than one-third. Indeed, in New England, historically a bastion of Republican strength, the GOP managed to win only one of the twenty-one seats in 2016. The Republican decline in eastern Senate seats over the period was even greater, down from 75 percent to only 10 percent. In the South, on the other hand, the percentage of House seats held by Democrats declined from 94 percent in 1953 to 28 percent in 2017. In 1953 the Democrats held all twenty-two southern Senate seats, but in 2017 they controlled only three.

This change in the partisan share of the South's seats in Congress has had an important impact on that region's influence within the two parties. The South used to be the backbone of Democratic congressional representation. This, and the tendency of southern members to build up seniority, gave southerners disproportionate power within the Democratic Party in Congress. Because of declining Democratic electoral success in the region, the numerical strength of southern Democrats within their party in Congress has waned. In 1953, with the Republicans in control of both chambers, southerners accounted for around 45 percent of Democratic seats in the House and Senate. By the 1970s southern strength had declined, stabilizing at between 25 and 30 percent of Democratic seats. In 2017 southerners accounted for 20 percent of Democratic House seats and only 6 percent of Democratic senators.

The South's share of Republican congressional representation presents the reverse picture. Minuscule at the end of World War II, it steadily grew, reaching about 20 percent in the House after the 1980 elections and 41 percent after the 2016 election. As a consequence of these changes, southern influence has declined in the Democratic Party and grown in the GOP, to the point that southerners have often held a disproportionate share of the Republican leadership positions in both houses of Congress. Because southerners of both parties tend to be more conservative than their colleagues from other regions, these shifts in regional strength have tended to make the Democratic Party in Congress more liberal and the Republican Party more conservative.[7]

Other regional changes since 1953, although not as striking as those in the South and East, are also significant. In the 1953 House, the Republicans controlled the West by a two-to-one margin and the Midwest by three to one. In 2017 they were a 38 percent minority in the West and had a 64 percent share in the Midwest. The Senate also exhibited shifts away from substantial Republican strength in the West and Midwest. On the other hand, with the increased Republican control of the South and Democratic dominance in the East, regional differences in party shares are more prominent in 2017 than they were in 1981, and partisan representation is only a little more regionally homogeneous in the Congress of 2017 than it was in the Congress of 1953.

## National Forces in Congressional Elections

The patterns of outcomes discussed here were shaped by a variety of influences. As with most congressional elections, the most important among these were the resources available to individual candidates and how those resources were distributed between the parties in specific races. We will discuss those matters shortly, but first we consider potential and actual national-level influences particular to 2016.

The first national force to assess is whether there was a pattern in public opinion that advantaged one party or the other. Such "national tides" may occur in presidential years or in midterms, and they can have a profound impact on the outcomes of congressional elections. Often these tides flow from reaction to presidents or presidential candidates. For example, in 1964 the presidential landslide victory of Lyndon B. Johnson over Barry M. Goldwater carried over to major Democratic gains in both congressional chambers, and Ronald Reagan's ten-point margin over Jimmy Carter in 1980 helped Republicans achieve an unexpected majority in the Senate and major gains in the House. Similarly negative public reactions to events in the first two years of Bill Clinton's presidency played a major part in the Republicans' congressional victories in 1994, and dissatisfaction with President Bush significantly enhanced the Democrats' campaign to retake the House in 2006.

Clearly 2016 was an election without a significant national tide working in favor of either the Democrats or the Republicans. This is not surprising after three wave elections in a row in 2006–2010 as well as a modest one in 2014. We saw in Chapter 2 that the presidential race was close all year, despite the fact that Hillary Clinton had a small lead according to most polls. A modest number of House and Senate races were deemed "up for grabs," but the proportion of each party's seats that were projected as competitive remained similar. Moreover, unlike what would be usual for an election with a partisan wave, the number of seats that were classified as close remained fairly stable over the election cycle. Figure 9-2 presents the number of Democratic and Republican House seats that political analyst Charlie Cook estimated to be highly competitive at various points in the 2015–2016 period.[8] The total number of competitive seats only increased a small amount, from thirty-two to forty, between July of 2015 and November of 2016. Moreover, the ratio between the parties was also fairly constant: in August of 2015, 78 percent of the competitive seats were held by Republicans, while in November of the following year, it was 77.5 percent.

Another potential national influence is public reaction to the performance of Congress. In the 1996 presidential race, for example, Clinton and the Democrats tried to focus public attention on what they claimed was the extremism and excesses of the new GOP congressional majority, albeit with only very limited success.[9] In 2016 public opinion toward Congress had turned very negative. In almost every major survey taken during the year leading up to the election, approval of the job Congress was doing was between 15 and 20 percent.[10] According to a CNN/ORC poll conducted in late October, only 44 percent of registered voters indicated that their own member of Congress deserved to be reelected. Additionally "[t]hat figure is the lowest in CNN/ORC polling back to fall 2006—a window in which the House has changed hands twice. Just 29% say 'most members of Congress' deserve re-election, a touch higher than the share saying so at recent low-points in congressional approval during the 2013 partial government shutdown and 2011 near-shutdown (August 2011 and October 2013)."[11]

## Efforts of National Parties and Their Allies

One important national-level influence is the efforts of congressional party leaders and their allies to influence the races. Before the 1980s the activities of national parties in congressional elections were very limited. Individual candidates were mostly self-starters who were largely on their own in raising money and planning strategy. More recently this situation has changed substantially, and party leaders and

**Figure 9-2 Competitive House Districts, 2015–2016**

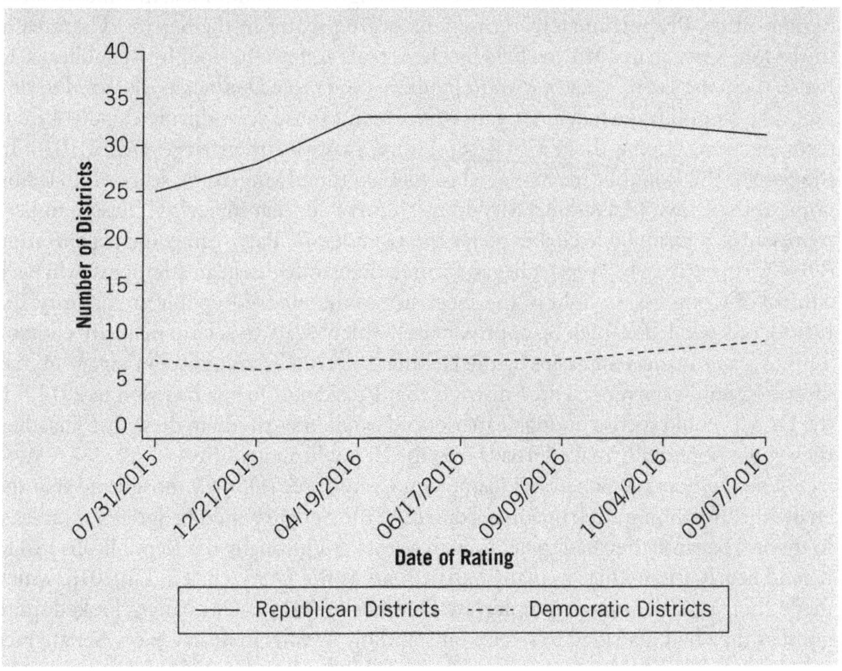


*Source:* Compiled by the authors from editions of *The Cook Political Report* on listed dates.

organizations are now heavily involved in recruiting and funding their candidates.[12] As we will see the quality of candidates and their level of funding are two of the central determinants of election outcomes. Thus both the short-term and long-term fates of the parties in Congress provided incentives for them to be active in efforts to improve their circumstances in these respects.

## Recruiting Candidates

National party organizations are now continually active in candidate recruiting and fund-raising. As soon as the voting in one election ends, activity for the next begins. Democrats' main concern after their electoral defeat in the 2014 midterms was that many of their senior members would become frustrated by their minority status (and the expectation that it would continue) and retire. The situation was exacerbated by the fact that the Republicans had shored up their majority in the House and picked up a narrow majority in the Senate during the 2014 elections. The plans of individual candidates were monitored and possible strategies for eventually taking back the majority were discussed by the Democrats. The perceived prospects of success were key elements of the strategic calculations of potential recruits. It is much easier for a party to persuade a prospect to run if that party's national prospects look bright.

In the end both parties were moderately successful in staving off House retirements, with only twenty-eight representatives (twenty Republicans and eight Democrats) opting to leave office entirely, although fifteen additional members sought higher office. Proportionately, retirements were greater in the Senate. There were thirty-four seats up in 2016, ten held by Democrats and twenty-four by Republicans. In five of these the sitting senator (two Republicans and three Democrats) declined to run.

The Republicans had a net gain of thirteen House seats during the 2014 midterm elections, giving them a 247–188 House majority, their largest since 1928. In the Senate the Republicans managed to pick up nine Democratic seats while losing none of their own to assume a fifty-four- to forty-six-seat majority. These numbers represented a formidable challenge for the Democratic Party campaign organization (DCCC) in early 2015, when it began formulating strategies in an attempt to win back control of Congress. In light of the sheer size of the House Republican majority, the Democrats needed to pick up approximately thirty seats to secure majority control. This task was made a bit easier by the fact that the DCCC recognized that twenty-six House Republicans represented districts that President Obama had won in 2012.[13] If the DCCC could recruit enough experienced candidates to run in these districts, then they could potentially make inroads into the Republican majority.

The Democratic Senatorial Campaign Committee (DSCC) recognized that the challenge of winning back majority control of the Senate would be far easier (at least in theory) because they had to net only five seats. Additionally the Republicans had to defend nearly three times as many Senate seats as the Democrats did in 2016, which made their task that much simpler. By October of 2015 their chances looked quite good as they had managed to secure outstanding recruits in nearly every Senate race they had targeted. "Aside from Hassan in New Hampshire, the DSCC secured strong candidates in Florida, Illinois, Missouri, Nevada, Ohio, Pennsylvania and Wisconsin. The DSCC also scored wins with Rep. Ann Kirkpatrick's decision to run for Senate in Arizona, as well as three Democratic senators from red states forgoing gubernatorial bids in 2016."[14]

For the Republicans the challenge leading up to the 2016 elections was twofold. First, the National Republican Campaign Committee (NRCC) wanted to minimize losses in the House, especially because the majority caucus had grown increasingly heterogeneous with the election of a number of fiscally conservative, Tea Party Republicans since 2010. With respect to the Senate, the National Republican Senatorial Committee (NRSC) had the more formidable challenge of trying to defend at least nine Republican incumbents, all of which were deemed vulnerable by *Roll Call* in November 2015 (compared with only one Democratic senator, Michael Bennet from Colorado). Among the most at-risk Republican senators leading up to the 2016 election were Mark Kirk (IL), Ron Johnson (WI), Pat Toomey (PA), Kelly Ayotte (NH), and Rob Portman (OH). Many considered Kirk to be among the most vulnerable because he had been elected in the Republican wave of 2010 by a narrow margin and represented a traditionally blue state. He was also heavily targeted by the DSCC and Emily's List, who were going all in on their support of his opponent, Rep. Tammy Duckworth.[15]

## Money and Other Aid

In addition to recruitment, party leaders have grown increasingly active in fund-raising, pursuing many different strategies. For example, top party leaders solicit donations to the congressional campaign committees like the NRCC and the DCCC, and they appear at fund-raisers for individual candidates in their districts. The amounts they raise are considerable. As of January 28, 2016, "House Minority Leader Nancy Pelosi raised more than $40.1 million in the 2016 cycle, her largest fundraising haul since joining Democratic leadership in 2002. That sum includes $30.4 million for the DCCC. Since 2002, Pelosi has raised $468.9 million."[16] Nevertheless, majority status is an asset for fund-raising, and Speaker Paul Ryan of Wisconsin did substantially better than Pelosi, amassing nearly $90 million in contributions for the Republicans, $40.6 of which was transferred to the NRCC to distribute across other House races.[17]

In both parties raising campaign funds for the party has become a prominent obligation for members who hold or want leadership posts and committee chairmanships, and the amounts they raise are a significant portion of money spent in campaigns. According to opensecrets.org, House Majority Leader Kevin McCarthy raised nearly $12 million for both the NRCC and the Republican Leadership PAC during the 2016 election cycle, the bulk of which was transferred to other Republican candidates for the House.[18] In recent years the parties have set contribution targets for their incumbents (which they term "dues"). Although many members would prefer to retain the money they raise for their own use, they have increasingly been pressured to share that money with other members. One interesting pattern that emerged in 2016 is that after Paul Ryan and Kevin McCarthy, the next five top earners among Republicans were all freshmen who had been elected in 2014—Martha McSally (AZ), Ryan Zinke (MT), Bob Dold (IL), Mia Love (UT), and Barbara Comstock (VA).[19]

Party leaders are able to do more to help candidates' reelection efforts than just raise or spend campaign money, at least for the House majority. Because the majority party has almost total control over the floor agenda and the content of bills, it can add or remove provisions in bills that will enhance their members' reelection chances or permit vulnerable colleagues to bring their popular bills to the floor, thus enhancing their reputations.

In addition to funding by the formal party organizations like the DCCC and the NRCC, the parties' congressional candidates are receiving increasing support from outside groups and super PACs.[20] During the 2016 election cycle, more than $630 million was spent by outside groups in Senate contests, 93 percent of which was allocated across nine Senate races—Pennsylvania, New Hampshire, Nevada, North Carolina, Ohio, Florida, Indiana, Missouri, and Wisconsin.[21] That was an increase of nearly 30 percent spent by outside groups during the same period in the 2014 contests.[22] Whereas the lion's share of outside spending went to Senate contests during 2016, nearly $315 million from those sources were spent on competitive House races.[23]

## CANDIDATES' RESOURCES AND ELECTION OUTCOMES

Seats in the House and Senate are highly valued posts for which candidates compete vigorously. In contests for these offices, candidates draw on every resource they have. To explain the results of congressional elections, we must consider the comparative advantages and disadvantages of the various candidates. In this section, we will discuss the most significant resources available to candidates and the impact those resources have on the outcomes of congressional elections.

### Candidate Quality

The personal abilities that foster electoral success can be a major political asset. Many constituencies today do not offer a certain victory for one of the two major parties, and for those that do strongly tilt to one party, there is often a contested primary, so election outcomes usually depend heavily on candidate quality. A strong, capable candidate is a significant asset for a party; a weak, inept one is a liability that is difficult to overcome. In his study of the activities of House members in their districts, Richard F. Fenno, Jr., described how members try to build support within their constituencies, establishing bonds of trust between constituents and their representatives.[24] Members attempt to convey to their constituents a sense that they are qualified for their job, that they identify with their constituents, and that they empathize with constituents and their problems. Challengers of incumbents and candidates for open seats must engage in similar activities to win support. The winner of a contested congressional election will usually be the candidate who is better able to establish these bonds of support among constituents and to convince them that he or she is the person for the job (or that the opponent is not).

One indicator of candidate quality is previous success at winning elective office. The more important the office a candidate has held, the more likely it is that he or she has overcome significant competition to obtain the office.[25] Moreover, the visibility and reputation for performance that usually accompany public office can also be a significant electoral asset. For example, state legislators running for House seats can claim that they have experience that has prepared them for congressional service. State legislators may also have built successful organizations that are useful in conducting congressional campaigns. Finally previous success in an electoral arena suggests that experienced candidates are more likely to be able to run strong campaigns than candidates without previous success or experience. Less adept candidates are likely to have been screened out at lower levels of office competition. For these and other reasons, an experienced candidate tends to have an electoral advantage over a candidate who has held no previous elected office.[26] Moreover, the higher the office previously held, the stronger the candidate will tend to be in the congressional contest.[27]

In Table 9-4, we present data showing which candidates were successful in 2016, controlling for office background, party, and incumbency.[28] In House contests the vast majority of candidates who challenged incumbents lost regardless of their office background or party, although those with previous elective experience did better than those who had none. The impact of candidate quality is stronger in races without incumbents. Here, candidates who had been state legislators were very successful, and those with other elective experience won at a higher rate than those without any elective office experience (except for Republicans). In Senate races, because there were only two incumbent losses, no pattern is visible there. For non-incumbent candidates those with stronger office backgrounds generally did better.

Given the importance of candidate quality, it is worth noting that there has been substantial variation in the proportion of experienced challengers over time. During the 1980s the proportion of House incumbents facing challengers who had previously won elective office declined. In 1980, 17.6 percent of incumbents faced such challenges; in 1984, 14.7 percent did; in 1988, only 10.5 percent did. In 1992, due largely to perceptions of incumbent vulnerability because of redistricting and scandal, the proportion rose to 23.5 percent, but in 1996, it was back down to 16.5 percent, and it

**Table 9-4 Success in House and Senate Elections, Controlling for Office Background, Party, and Incumbency, 2016 (Percent)**

| | Candidate Is Opponent of . . . | | No Incumbent in District | |
|---|---|---|---|---|
| | Democratic Incumbent % (N) | Republican Incumbent % (N) | Democratic Candidate % (N) | Republican Candidate % (N) |
| **House** | | | | |
| State Legislature/ U.S. House | 0 (6) | 17 (18) | 79 (14) | 88 (8) |
| Other elected | 0 (5) | 5 (18) | 55 (11) | 50 (10) |
| No elected | 1 (144) | 1 (170) | 23 (13) | 53 (17) |
| **Senate** | | | | |
| U.S. House | 0 (0) | 25 (4) | 50 (2) | 50 (2) |
| Statewide elected | 0 (0) | 25 (4) | 67 (3) | 100 (1) |
| Other elected | 0 (4) | 0 (3) | 0 (1) | 0 (1) |
| No elected | 0 (3) | 0 (11) | 0 (0) | 0 (0) |

*Source:* Data on office backgrounds were taken from issues of *The Cook Political Report* and the *Green Papers*. Compiled by the authors.

remained at that level in 2000.[29] In 2004, however, there was a substantial resurgence in the number of experienced candidates in both parties, with 22.4 percent of the total challengers having previously held elective office, followed by a decline again in 2008 to 14.8 percent. In 2012 the proportion rebounded again to 20 percent before declining again in both 2014 and 2016.[30]

Whether experienced politicians actually run for the House or Senate is not an accident. These are significant strategic decisions made by politicians, and they have much to lose if they make the wrong choice. The choices will be governed by factors related to the perceived chance of success, the potential value of the new office compared to what will be lost if the candidate fails, and the costs of running.[31] The chances of success of the two major parties vary from election to election, both locally and nationally. Therefore, each election offers a different mix of experienced and inexperienced candidates from the two parties for the House and Senate.

The most influential factor in whether a potential candidate will run is whether there is an incumbent in the race. High reelection rates tend to discourage potentially strong challengers from running, which in turn makes it even more likely that the incumbents will win. In addition to the general difficulty of challenging incumbents, factors related to specific election years (both nationally and in a particular district) will affect decisions to run. For example, the Republican Party had particular difficulty recruiting strong candidates during 1986 because of fears about a potential backlash from the Iran-Contra scandals. And the 2008 decline in quality candidates was likely a function of the Republicans having less success recruiting strong candidates in many districts because the electoral environment was perceived to be negative for their party. On the other hand some research indicates that potential House candidates are most strongly influenced in their decisions by their perceived chances of winning their party's nomination.[32] Moreover, the actions of incumbents may influence the choices of potential challengers. For example, building up a large reserve of campaign funds between elections may dissuade some possible opponents, although analysis of Senate contests (which usually involve experienced challengers) indicates that this factor does not have a systematic impact in those races.[33]

As we have seen most congressional races do not involve challengers who have previous office experience. Given their slight chance of winning, why do challengers without experience run at all? As Jeffrey S. Banks and D. Roderick Kiewiet point out, although the chances of success against incumbents may be small for such candidates, such a race may still be their best chance of ever winning a seat in Congress.[34] If inexperienced challengers were to put off their candidacies until a time when there is no incumbent, their opposition would likely include multiple experienced candidates from both parties. Moreover, as David Canon demonstrates, previous office experience is an imperfect indicator of candidate quality because some candidates without such experience can still have significant political assets and be formidable challengers.[35] For example, four former television journalists who had never previously held office won House seats in 1992, and three of them defeated incumbents. They were able to build on their substantial name recognition among voters to win nomination and election.[36] Moreover, consider two 2000 contests, one from each chamber. The Republican candidate for the House in Nebraska's third district was Tom Osborne, the extremely popular former head coach of the University of Nebraska's football team. Osborne was elected to an open seat with a phenomenal 82 percent of the vote. In the New York Senate race, the very visible (and ultimately successful) Democratic candidate was then First Lady Hillary Rodham Clinton. In many respects this win may have set her on the path to running for the presidency in 2008 and again in 2016.

## Incumbency

One reason most incumbents win is that incumbency itself is a significant resource. To be more precise, incumbency is not a single resource but rather a status that usually gives a candidate a variety of benefits. In some respects incumbency works to a candidate's advantage automatically. For example, incumbents tend to be more visible to voters than do challengers.[37] Less automatic, but very important, incumbents usually tend to be viewed more favorably than challengers. Moreover, at least a plurality of the electorate in most districts will identify with the incumbent's political party, and this pattern has become stronger over the last couple of decades. Incumbents can also use their status to gain advantages. Incumbents generally raise and spend more money than challengers, and they usually have a better developed and more experienced campaign organization. They also have assets, provided at public expense, such as a staff and franking privileges (free postage for mail to their constituents), that both help them perform their jobs and provide electoral benefits. Incumbents also have the opportunity to vote and perhaps work on bills favored by their constituents and to bring "pork" home to the district, when they think it will be advantageous to do so. Challengers, by contrast, lack such advantages.

## Increasing Electoral Margins

From the mid-1960s through the late 1980s, the margins by which incumbents were reelected increased (the pattern was less clear and more erratic in Senate elections than in House elections).[38] These changing patterns interested analysts primarily because they believed that the disappearance of marginal incumbents means less congressional turnover and a House that would be less responsive to the electorate.

Edward R. Tufte offered an early explanation for the increased incumbency margins by arguing that redistricting had protected incumbents of both parties.[39] This argument seemed plausible because the increase in margins occurred about the same time as the massive redistricting required by Supreme Court decisions of the mid-1960s. But other analysts showed that incumbents had won by larger margins both in states that had been redistricted and in those that had not as well as in Senate contests.[40] Thus redistricting was initially dismissed as the major reason for the change.

Another explanation offered for the increase in incumbents' margins was the growth in the perquisites of members and the greater complexity of government. Morris P. Fiorina notes that in the post-New Deal period, the level of federal services and the bureaucracy that administers them had grown tremendously.[41] A more complex government means that many people will encounter problems in receiving services, and people who have problems frequently contact their representatives to complain and seek help. Fiorina contends that in the mid-1960s, new members of Congress emphasized such constituency problem-solving more than their predecessors. This expanded constituency service developed into a reservoir of electoral support. Although analyses of the impact of constituency services have produced mixed conclusions, it is likely that the growth of these services offers a partial explanation for changing incumbent vote margins and for the incumbency advantage generally.[42]

The declining impact of party loyalties provided a third explanation for the growth in incumbent vote margins, either alone or in conjunction with other factors. Until the mid-1960s, there was a very strong linkage between party identification and congressional voting behavior. Most Americans identified with a political party, many identified strongly, and most voters supported the candidate of their chosen party. Subsequently, however, the impact of party identification decreased, as we will see in Chapter 10. John A. Ferejohn, drawing on data from the ANES, shows that the strength of party ties weakened and that within any given category of party identification, the tendency to support the candidate of one's party declined.[43] An analysis by Albert D. Cover shows that between 1958 and 1974, voters who did not identify with the party of a congressional incumbent were increasingly more likely to defect from their party and support the incumbent, although there had been no increase in defections from party identification by voters of the same party as incumbents.[44] Thus weakened party ties produced a substantial net benefit for incumbents,[45] although as we saw in Chapter 8 (and will discuss further in Chapter 10), party loyalties among the electorate have grown stronger in recent years.[46]

## The Trend Reversed

Whatever the relative importance of these factors (and the others we will discuss) in explaining the increase in incumbents' victory margins, the increase continued through the 1980s, as the data in Table 9-5 show, peaking at 68.4 percent in 1986. These data are only for races in which both parties ran candidates. Thus they exclude contests where an incumbent ran unopposed. Such races were also increasing in number over this period; therefore, the data actually understate the growth in incumbents' margins.

Then, in 1990, something changed. The average share of the vote for incumbents declined by nearly four percentage points. The decline was, moreover, not a result of a shift of voters toward one party, as with the decline from 1980 to 1982; both parties' incumbents suffered. Rather the shift in incumbents' electoral fortunes was apparently the result of what was called the "anti-incumbent mood" among the voters. Early in 1990 pollsters and commentators began to perceive stronger anti-Congress sentiments within the electorate.[47] For the first time analysts began to question whether incumbency remained the asset it used to be.

There was, of course, nothing new about Congress being unpopular; Congress had long suffered ups and downs in approval, just like the president. What changed in 1990 was that Congress's unpopularity appeared to be undermining the approval of individual members by their own constituents. Yet, as the data presented in Table 9-1 shows, even though there was a drop in the average percentage of the vote received by incumbents in 1990, the rate of reelection still reached 96 percent. The decline in vote margins was not great enough to produce a rash of defeats. Many observers wondered,

**Table 9-5 Average Vote Percentages of House Incumbents, 1974–2016**

| Year | Democrats | Republicans | All Incumbents |
|---|---|---|---|
| 1974 | 71.3 | 56.9 | 64.1 |
| 1976 | 67.0 | 63.8 | 65.8 |
| 1978 | 66.0 | 65.9 | 66.0 |
| 1980 | 64.4 | 68.7 | 66.0 |
| 1982 | 69.2 | 60.6 | 65.1 |
| 1984 | 64.4 | 68.9 | 66.2 |
| 1986 | 70.4 | 65.9 | 68.4 |
| 1988 | 68.8 | 67.7 | 68.3 |
| 1990 | 65.8 | 62.4 | 64.6 |
| 1992 | 63.7 | 63.4 | 63.6 |
| 1994 | 60.8 | 68.7 | 63.7 |
| 1996 | 68.5 | 62.2 | 64.9 |
| 1998 | 68.8 | 64.0 | 66.4 |
| 2000 | 69.7 | 65.1 | 67.5 |
| 2002 | 68.4 | 67.4 | 67.9 |
| 2004 | 69.2 | 64.7 | 66.8 |
| 2006 | 71.1 | 60.1 | 64.7 |
| 2008 | 69.8 | 61.2 | 66.0 |
| 2010 | 60.5 | 67.7 | 63.0 |
| 2012 | 69.1 | 61.2 | 64.6 |
| 2014 | 63.4 | 66.0 | 64.8 |
| 2016 | 67.5 | 64.6 | 65.9 |

*Source:* Compiled by the authors.

*Note:* These figures include only races where both major parties ran candidates. Thus they exclude contests in which an incumbent ran unopposed.

however, whether 1990 was the beginning of a new trend: would incumbents' electoral drawing power continue to decline?

In 1992 scandals damaged many representatives of both parties, and among the public, the evaluation of Congress was very low. Opponents of incumbents emphasized that they were "outsiders" and not "professional politicians" (even when they had substantial political experience). The results from 1992 show that incumbents' share of the vote dropped a bit more. Republicans rebounded a little from their bad 1990 showing, whereas Democrats fell more than two percentage points. Yet again, however, the casualty rate among incumbents who ran in the general election was lower than many expected: 93 percent were reelected. (It is important to note, however, that a substantial number of incumbents had already been defeated in the primaries, and many weak incumbents had retired.) Then, in 1994, although there was only a slight additional drop in incumbents' share of the vote overall, the drop was greater (and concentrated) for Democrats, and their casualty rate was high. The result was the loss of their majority. Next, in 1996, there was a slight rebound in incumbents' vote share, with Democrats increasing sharply, while the GOP fell. That vote shift translated into eighteen Republican incumbents defeated but only three Democrats. Finally the results from 2000 through 2016 fall in between the highs of the mid-1980s and the lows of 1994 and 1996. Indeed, during those years, the average incumbent vote percentage has been virtually identical each year, although the averages for the parties have varied with the electoral climate.

This discussion illustrates that incumbents' vote margins and incumbents' reelection success are related but distinct phenomena.[48] When—as was true in the 1980s—the average share of the vote received by incumbents is very high, they can lose a lot of ground before a large number of defeats occur. What appears to have occurred in 1990 is that many incumbents were subjected to vigorous contests for the first time in years. Such challenges were then repeated or extended to additional incumbents in 1992, 1994, and 1996. Potential candidates apparently looked at the political situation and concluded that incumbents who had previously looked unbeatable could now potentially be defeated, and there was a substantial increase in the number of candidates for Congress. These vigorous contests by challengers who were stronger than usual resulted in a decrease in the share of the vote received by many incumbents.

Jacobson, in his *Journal of Politics* article, offers a slightly different interpretation for the reversal of fortune among incumbents since the 1990s. He argues that the increasing nationalization of elections stemming from a resurgence in party voting among the electorate has actually contributed to a decline in the incumbency advantage during the past few decades. With more constituents basing their voting decisions on partisan criteria in light of increasing levels of polarization, it has become more difficult for incumbents to win districts that lean toward the other party as was once the case. This, in turn, has contributed to a decline in the personal incumbency advantage because members of the House can no longer rely on the resources of office to carry them to victory in polarized congressional districts.[49] The same general pattern holds for the U.S. Senate, although it was not quite as pronounced until 2016 when, "for the first time in history, every Senate contest was won by the party that won the state's electoral votes."[50]

## Campaign Spending

A third resource that strongly affects congressional elections is campaign spending. Campaign spending has received a great deal of attention in the last four decades because researchers gained access to more dependable data than had previously been available.[51] The data on spending have consistently shown that incumbents usually outspend their challengers, often by large margins, and that through the early 1990s, the disparity had increased.[52] (As we shall see shortly, more recent data show significant changes.)

Disparities in campaign spending are linked to the increase in incumbents' election margins. Beginning in the 1960s congressional campaigns relied more heavily on campaign techniques that cost money—for example, media time, campaign consulting, and direct mailing—and these became increasingly expensive. At the same time candidates were progressively less likely to have available pools of campaign workers from established party organizations or from interest groups. This made using expensive media and direct mail strategies relatively more important. Most challengers are unable to raise significant campaign funds. Neither individuals nor groups interested in the outcomes of congressional elections like to throw money away; before making contributions they usually need to be convinced that the candidate has a chance. Yet we have seen that in most election years, few incumbents have been beaten. Thus it is often difficult to convince potential contributors that their money will produce results, and contributions are often not forthcoming. Most challengers are thus at a strategic disadvantage, and they are unable to raise sufficient funds to wage a competitive campaign.[53]

It is the ability to compete, rather than the simple question of relative amounts of spending, that is at the core of the issue. We have noted that incumbents have many inherent advantages that the challenger must overcome if he or she hopes to win. But often the money is not there to overcome them. In 2016, for example, greater than 41 percent of challengers spent $25,000 or less, and slightly more than 60 percent spent $75,000 or less. With so little money available, challengers are unable to make themselves visible to the electorate or to convey a convincing message.[54] Under such circumstances, most voters—being unaware of the positions, or perhaps even the existence, of the challenger—vote for the incumbent.

Data from 2016 on campaign spending and election outcomes seem consistent with this argument, and they show patterns similar to those exhibited in other recent elections.[55] Linking spending to outcomes, Table 9-6 shows the relationship between the incumbent's share of the vote in the 2016 House elections and the amount of money spent by the challenger. Clearly there is a strong negative relationship between how much challengers spend and how well incumbents do. In races where challengers spent less than $26,000, 91 percent of the incumbents received 60 percent or more of the vote, the traditional cutoff for marginality. At the other end of the spectrum, in races where challengers spent $800,000 or more, 78 percent of the incumbents received less than 60 percent of the vote, and approximately 46 percent got less than 55 percent of the vote. These results are consistent with those in earlier House elections for which comparable data are available.[56]

**Table 9-6 Incumbents' Share of the Vote in the 2016 House Elections, by Challenger Campaign Spending (Percent)**

| Challenger Spending | Incumbents' Share of the Two-Party Vote | | | | | |
|---|---|---|---|---|---|---|
| | 70% or More | 60%–69% | 55%–59% | Less Than 55% | Total | *N* |
| $0–$25,000 | 50.7 | 40.7 | 7.1 | 1.4 | 100 | 140 |
| $26,000–$75,000 | 24.6 | 56.9 | 16.9 | 1.5 | 100 | 65 |
| $76,000–$199,000 | 13.6 | 52.3 | 34.1 | 0.0 | 100 | 44 |
| $200,000–$399,000 | 9.7 | 48.4 | 25.8 | 16.1 | 100 | 31 |
| $400,000–$799,000 | 0.0 | 55.0 | 40.0 | 5.0 | 100 | 20 |
| $800,000 and up | 2.7 | 18.9 | 32.4 | 45.9 | 100 | 37 |
| All | 28.8 | 44.5 | 19.0 | 7.7 | 100 | 337 |

*Source:* Federal Election Commission, http:www.fec.gov. Compiled by the authors.

*Note:* Races without a major party opponent are excluded, and challenger spending that is unavailable was coded in the $0–25,000 row.

These findings are reinforced by other research that shows that challenger spending has a greater influence on election outcomes than does incumbent spending.[57] This generalization has been questioned on methodological grounds,[58] but further research by Gary Jacobson reinforced his earlier findings. Using both aggregate and survey data, he found that "the amount spent by the challenger is far more important in accounting for voters' decisions than is the amount of spending by the incumbent."[59] More recently Jacobson emphasizes the importance of incumbent spending. Comparing successful House challengers to those who are unsuccessful, he notes that the successful candidates were more likely to be familiar to voters. He writes, "It is no mystery why winning challengers reached so many voters and were so much more familiar to them. They ran much better financed campaigns than did the losers."[60] In contrast, analysis of Senate elections has also resulted in somewhat more conflicting conclusions.[61]

Of course challengers who appear to have good prospects will find it easier to raise money than those whose chances seem slim. Thus, one might wonder whether these data simply reflect the fulfillment of expectations in which money flows to challengers who would have done well regardless of spending. Other research, however, indicates that is likely not the case. In an analysis of the 1972 and 1974 congressional elections, Jacobson concluded, "Our evidence is that campaign spending helps candidates, particularly non-incumbents, by bringing them to the attention of the voters; it is not the case that well-known candidates simply attract more money; rather money buys attention."[62] From this perspective adequate funding is a necessary but not sufficient condition for a closely fought contest, a perspective consistent with the data in Table 9-6. Heavily outspending one's opponent is not a guarantee of victory; the evidence does not indicate that elections can simply be bought because money does not literally buy votes. Indeed having to spend large sums of money in a prior race may signal to an astute challenger that the incumbent is vulnerable and likely to lose under the right circumstances. Even if an incumbent outspends the challenger, the incumbent can still lose if the challenger is adequately funded and runs a campaign that persuades the voters.[63]

The 2016 elections, for example, offer clear evidence of this. In four of the eight races in which incumbents faced a non-incumbent challenger and the incumbent lost, the loser outspent the winner.[64] The losing incumbent in each of these eight races spent an average of $2.8 million dollars on the unsuccessful reelection bid. The fact that incumbents in each of these races had to spend as much as they did is consistent with Jacobson's argument that spending large sums of money is no guarantee of electoral victory, especially when one factors in the fund-raising prowess of their opponents.

On the other hand a spending advantage is not a guarantee to a challenger. In an extreme example from 2000, losing Republican challenger Phil Sudan spent $3.25 million against incumbent Ken Bentsen of Texas, who spent $1.35 million. Despite being outspent over two to one, Bentsen won more than 60 percent of the vote. A somewhat less extreme case occurred in 2008, when Republican Sandy Treadwell spent more than $7 million compared to incumbent Democrat Kristen Gillibrand of New York's $4.49 million. The Democrat was reelected with more than 61 percent of the vote. Based on this analysis our view can be summarized as follows: if a challenger is to attain visibility and get his or her message across to the voters—neutralizing the incumbent's advantages in name recognition and perquisites of office—the challenger needs to be adequately funded. If both sides in a race are adequately funded, the outcome will tend to turn on factors other than just money, and the relative spending of the two candidates is unlikely to control the outcome.[65]

This argument carries us full circle back to our earlier discussion and leads us to bring together the three kinds of resources that we have considered—candidate experience, incumbency, and campaign spending. Table 9-7 presents data showing the impact of these three factors in the 2016 House elections. We categorize challenger experience as strong or weak depending on previous elective-office experience; challenger spending was classified as low or high depending on whether it was below or above $200,000.[66] The data show that each element exerts some independent effect, but the impact of spending seems to be more consequential in the most recent election cycle (as was also true in 2012). When challengers had weak experience and low spending (68 percent of the races), all incumbents won, and 85 percent won with more than 60 percent of the vote. In the opposite situation, where the challenger had both strong experience and substantial spending, 64 percent of the races were considered competitive. The combined results for the two intermediate categories fall between the extremes. In addition incumbent defeats occur with greater frequency in situations where the challenger is experienced and has strong spending. Yet it is important to note how few such races there were in 2016. Table 9-7 also reveals that 64 percent of

**Table 9-7 Percentage of Incumbents by Vote Share, Challenger Experience, and Spending in the 2016 House Elections**

| Challenger | Incumbents' Share of Two-Party Vote | | | | | |
|---|---|---|---|---|---|---|
| Experience/ Spending | 70% or More | 60%–69% | 55%–59% | Less Than 55% | Total | *N* |
| Weak/low | 39.91 (93) | 45.49 (106) | 13.73 (32) | 0.86 (2) | 100 | 233 |
| Strong/low | 0 (0) | 68.75 (11) | 25.00 (4) | 6.25 (1) | 100 | 16 |
| Weak/high | 15.15 (10) | 36.36 (24) | 25.75 (17) | 22.72 (15) | 100 | 66 |
| Strong/high | 3.57 (1) | 32.14 (9) | 39.29 (11) | 25.00 (7) | 100 | 28 |

*Source:* See Tables 9-4 and 9-6. Compiled by the authors.

*Note:* Percentages read across. Strong challengers have held a significant elected office (U.S. representative; statewide office; countywide or citywide office such as mayor, prosecutor, etc.). High-spending challengers spent more than $200,000. Races without a major-party opponent are excluded. Ns are in parentheses.

the challengers with previous experience were able to raise substantial funds (twenty-eight of forty-four), whereas only 36 percent of challengers with no elective experience were able to do so.

This combination of factors also helps explain the greater volatility of outcomes in Senate races discussed earlier. Previous analysis has shown that the effects of campaign spending in Senate contests are consistent with what we have found true for House races: if challenger spending is above some threshold, the election is often quite close; if it is below that level, the incumbent is likely to win by a large margin.[67] In Senate races, however, the mix of well-funded and poorly funded challengers is different. Senate challengers are more likely to be able to raise significant amounts of money than their House counterparts. Indeed, in recent elections, a number of challengers (and open-seat candidates) have been wealthy individuals who could provide a large share of their funding from their own resources. One of the most extreme examples comes from 2000, when Jon Corzine, the Democratic candidate for the open New Jersey Senate seat, spent more than $60 million of his own money to defeat his opponent. Corzine spent a total of $63 million; the Republican spent $6.4 million.[68] Nevertheless, Corzine was only elected by a three-percentage point margin. A more recent case comes from the 2016 Senate race in Pennsylvania, where Republican incumbent Pat Toomey received 48.8 percent of the vote compared to Katie McGinty's 47.3 percent. During the election, Toomey spent $30.8 million compared with $16.3 million spent by McGinty. However, outside spending in the race approached $120 million, bringing the total amount spent in the Pennsylvania Senate race to approximately $167 million.[69]

Senate challengers, moreover, are also more likely to possess prior elective experience. Thus, in Senate contests, incumbents often face well-funded and experienced challengers, and the stage is then set for their defeat if other circumstances work against them.

The lesson from the evidence presented here is captured by the words of David Johnson, the director of the Democratic Senatorial Campaign Committee, to Rep. Richard C. Shelby of Alabama, who was challenging Republican Senator Jeremiah Denton in 1986. Shelby, who eventually won, was concerned that he did not have enough campaign funds as Denton was outspending him two to one. Johnson responded: "You don't have as much money, but you're going to have enough—and enough is all it takes to win."[70]

## THE 2016 ELECTIONS: THE IMPACT ON CONGRESS

The elections of 1994 produced huge consequences for politics and governing, and each subsequent election over the next decade was seen in relation to whether GOP control would be strengthened or weakened. The GOP retained control in the next five elections. A significant electoral tide in 2006 gave the Democrats control of both chambers, which they improved on in 2008. That was followed by the Republican congressional landslide of 2010 and the return of divided government when the GOP took the House. Divided government was maintained in 2012, with modest Democratic gains in both chambers. During the 2014 midterms, the Republicans managed to gain a net thirteen House seats and nine Senate seats, giving them control of both chambers for the first time since 2006. Although the Republicans lost a net of six House seats and two Senate seats in 2016, they maintained control of both chambers, giving them unified party control of Congress coupled with a Republican president at the start of the 115th Congress in 2017.

The modest Democratic gains in both chambers in 2016 maintained roughly the same political balance as in the previous Congress, a close division in which moderate members were still important. This should be seen in the context of a long-term decline of such members in the Congress and an increase in the number of conservative Republicans and liberal Democrats. Forty years ago, there was considerable ideological "overlap" between the political parties. The Democrats had a substantial conservative contingent, mostly from the South, that was as conservative as the right wing of the Republican Party. Similarly the GOP had a contingent (primarily northeasterners) whose members were as liberal as northern Democrats. In addition each party had a significant number of moderate members. During the intervening years, however, because of changes in the electorate and in the Congress, this overlap between the parties began to disappear.[71] By the mid-1980s both parties in the House and Senate had become more politically homogeneous, and that homogeneity continued to increase in subsequent elections. In each chamber there was little departure from a complete ideological separation of the two parties.[72] Thus, in the 115th Congress that resulted from the 2016 elections, substantial majorities of each party had sharply different policy preferences from those in the other party, with a very small but potentially influential group of members in the middle.

### The Trump Administration and Unified Government

Following Donald Trump's election as president along with unified Republican control of Congress, the Republicans had their best chance in a decade to advance their political agenda. Throughout the 2016 presidential campaign, Trump had made a variety of promises including the repeal and replacement of the Affordable Health Care Act ("Obamacare"), temporarily banning Muslims from entering the United States, building a wall between the United States and Mexico, pushing for a $1 trillion infrastructure bill, adding a conservative justice to the Supreme Court to replace Antonin Scalia, and cutting taxes. Despite having Republican control of both chambers, Trump opted to issue a number of executive orders and memoranda in his first few days in office in an attempt to deliver on several of his campaign promises. His first executive order, issued on January 20 within hours of his inauguration, declared Trump's intention to repeal the ACA passed approximately seven years earlier. Three days later he issued a presidential memorandum signaling his intent to withdraw from the TPP, a trade deal designed to lower tariffs for a number of Pacific Rim countries. On the same day he issued another memorandum freezing all hiring in the executive branch, except for the military, in an attempt to cut government spending and "waste."[73]

Over the course of the next week, President Trump issued three presidential memoranda approving construction of the Dakota Access and the Keystone XL Pipelines, with the third one requiring all pipeline materials used be built within the United States. He also issued an executive order cutting funding for sanctuary cities. Although many of his previous directives were perceived as controversial, this one immediately gained national attention after the city of San Francisco announced that it was suing the president for withholding funding, arguing that the order was unconstitutional.[74] On January 27 Trump issued arguably his most controversial executive action yet when he temporarily barred Muslims from Iran, Libya, Somalia, Sudan, and Yemen from entering the country for 90 days and Syrians from entering indefinitely.[75] This order prompted immediate outrage because it stranded hundreds of individuals at airports around the country. Within days a federal judge in Seattle declared the order unconstitutional, leading the Trump administration to revise the order in early March. However, that travel ban was also later struck down in federal courts in both Hawaii and Maryland.[76]

Research on the U.S. presidency suggests that chief executives are more likely to utilize unilateral tools like executive orders during periods of unified government.[77] Part of the rationale for this behavior is that presidents have more flexibility in issuing executive orders when their party is in control of Congress, especially if Congress is unable or unwilling to act as a result of gridlock or such decisions are perceived as controversial. Nevertheless, it is curious that Trump chose to pursue a unilateral strategy so early after being sworn into office, particularly because Congress had not yet had a chance to act. One factor in his decision to utilize unilateral tools may have been his relatively low levels of presidential approval. During the first four months of his presidency, for instance, his approval averaged around 40 percent, which is at least twenty points less than the same point among all of his predecessors for which we have public opinion data.[78]

Trump has also made a number of controversial statements and decisions, including firing FBI Director James Comey in early May and sharing classified information with the Russian ambassador, which led to widespread calls for further investigation into his actions and even talk of impeachment.[79] Indeed, on May 17, Rod Rosenstein, the deputy attorney general, appointed former FBI Director Robert Mueller III to serve as special counsel to continue the ongoing investigation into the Russian government's efforts "to influence the 2016 presidential election and related matters."[80] As we discuss in what follows, these developments may have been a significant factor in why Congress appeared reluctant at times to take up Trump's major policy initiatives.

## The House: Testing Majority Party Control

Following the historic 1994 elections, the new Republican majority instituted major institutional changes in the 104th Congress that convened in 1995.[81] By comparison the changes in House organization for the 115th Congress were much more modest—although one proposed change proved rather controversial. On January 2, 2017, the House Republicans met in secret session and voted to eliminate the Office of Congressional Ethics, an independent body that had been created in 2008 to investigate scandals in the House. "House Republicans, led by Representative Robert W. Goodlatte of Virginia, had sought on Monday to prevent the office from pursuing investigations that might result in criminal charges. Instead, they wanted to allow lawmakers on the more powerful House Ethics Committee to shut down inquiries."[82] The party reversed course the following day, however, after legislators received thousands of phone calls condemning the action. Speaker Paul Ryan and House Majority Leader Kevin McCarthy also came out against the vote, recognizing that it sent the wrong message to the American people.

The inauspicious start to the 115th Congress was emblematic of a long string of conflicts between the Republican leadership and the party's rank and file during the past few years. The electoral landslide of 2010 had brought to the House a large Republican freshman class that was dominated by populist insurgents who identified with the Tea Party movement, many of which were still part of the Republican majority in the 115th Congress and who now identified with the Freedom Caucus. This group was suspicious of establishment Republicans and especially of former speaker John Boehner and the House leadership.[83] Throughout the 112th and subsequent Congresses, the leadership had significant difficulty in persuading the Tea Party wing to follow their lead, and this led to frequent problems with passing bills the leaders deemed necessary. The newly elected members wanted major changes in national policy (such as the complete repeal of "Obamacare"), and they were reluctant to compromise to get legislation passed. The GOP's internal conflicts brought the government close to a shutdown and a near default on the national debt, and these led to a temporary downgrade of the nation's debt rating.

Former Speaker Boehner struggled to maintain cohesion within the Republican caucus during his nearly 5 years as leader of the party. After repeatedly violating the "Hastert Rule" (named after the former GOP House Speaker Dennis Hastert of Illinois, which held the House should only take up bills that were backed by a majority of the majority party) during the 112th and 113th Congresses, Boehner sought to reassure the conservative wing of his party by saying that this was "not a practice that I would expect to continue long term."[84] Nevertheless, the Tea Party faction was not mollified, and some members proposed enshrining the Hastert Rule in the rules of the House Republican Conference.

At the start of the 113th Congress in 2013, several of the more conservative Republicans sought to deny Boehner the absolute majority of votes he needed for election to be speaker in light of his past behavior. The hope was that if a second ballot were forced, someone more acceptable might come forward to contest the election. And even if that did not happen, it would be a strong blow to Boehner's stature as leader. In the event, enough Republican members initially pledged not to vote for Boehner, but by the morning of the vote, a few members had changed their minds. As it was, twelve GOP members abstained or voted for others (as did all the Democrats), and Boehner narrowly won reelection.[85] Despite more internal partisan turmoil during the next two and half years, Boehner managed to hang onto the speakership until he announced his retirement on September 25, 2015, becoming the first speaker to voluntarily step down since Thomas "Tip" O'Neil did so in 1986. In discussing his decision to step down once a new speaker was named, Boehner explained, "My first job as speaker is to protect the institution [but] it had become clear to me that this prolonged leadership turmoil would do irreparable harm to the institution."[86]

Boehner had been grooming Eric Cantor, then majority leader, to take over his position as speaker until Cantor was defeated in a shocking primary upset in June 2014 by political amateur Dave Brat.[87] Kevin McCarthy succeeded Cantor as majority leader and was in line to become speaker once Boehner announced his impending departure. However, McCarthy's candidacy was damaged as a result of a remark made during an interview "in which he seemed to suggest that the Select Committee on Benghazi, the panel assembled by Republicans to investigate the 2012 attacks on U.S. facilities in Libya, was intended to damage Hillary Rodham Clinton's presidential poll numbers."[88] On October 8, 2015, McCarthy decided to withdraw his bid as a result of the fallout from this comment, leaving the party scrambling to find a replacement who could lead the fractious Republican Party. Several members of the conference immediately reached out to Paul Ryan (R-WI), chair of the House Ways and Means Committee and former vice-presidential nominee, asking him to consider running for the speakership. Although Ryan continued to insist that he was not interested in the job (as he had done for years), he eventually agreed to serve on the condition that the party unite behind him.[89] On Thursday, October 29, 2015, Paul Ryan was sworn in as the fifty-fourth speaker of the House of Representatives by a vote of 236–184.

Ryan's initial tenure as speaker was noticeably smoother than that of his predecessor, but tensions within the party began to emerge during the second session of the 114th Congress. Key members of the House Freedom Caucus had been critical of Ryan since he took over in fall 2015, but things began to escalate when then candidate Donald Trump refused to endorse Ryan during his primary campaign because Ryan had been critical of some of Trump's recent actions. After the tape was released in early October with Trump making lewd comments toward women, Ryan sought to further distance himself from the Republican nominee, much to the chagrin of some of the more conservative members of the caucus. Such controversy seemed to be short-lived once Trump tapped Reince Priebus to be his chief of staff, however. Priebus had previously served as the chair of the Republican National Committee and was a boyhood friend of Ryan.[90] With the announcement that one of the leaders of the Freedom Caucus, Mark Meadows (R-NC), would continue to support Ryan as speaker, any efforts to support someone else quickly dissipated.

Despite some early setbacks as noted, the 115th Congress represented a chance for the Republicans to advance their legislative agenda. Paul Ryan was sworn in again as speaker, and the Republicans had unified control of government for the first time since 2006. On the Democratic side, Nancy Pelosi (D-CA) continued as minority leader, and Steny Hoyer (D-MD) was reelected as minority whip. The first major bill considered in the 115th Congress was the repeal and replacement of the ACA ("Obamacare") with the American Health Care Act. This was a critical piece of legislation for President Trump and the Republicans in Congress because it had been such an important issue during the 2016 campaign. Trump had promised on more than one occasion that the ACA would be repealed, and Republicans had been eager to replace the legislation since it had first been passed. In the end, however, it proved to be more challenging than the Republicans initially expected.

Although members of the Republican conference were unanimous in their desire to repeal Obamacare, they recognized the need to replace it with something more acceptable to members of their party. Initially they conducted negotiations over the legislation in secret behind closed doors, and only key Republican members were privy to the specifics of the bill. Eventually, however, details about the bill began to emerge. "The Republican bill would have repealed tax penalties for people without health insurance, rolled back federal insurance standards, reduced subsidies for the purchase of private insurance and set new limits on spending for Medicaid, the federal-state program that covers more than 70 million low-income people."[91] Ryan claimed the bill included "huge conservative wins," but most members of the Freedom Caucus felt it did not go far enough with respect to eliminating what were perceived as imperfect provisions of the ACA. Additionally, the bill failed to attract support of more moderate Republican members "who were anxiously aware of the Congressional Budget Office's assessment that the bill would leave 24 million more Americans without insurance in 2024, compared with the number who would be uninsured under the current law."[92] Others feared that insurance premiums would increase under the Republican plan, and Americans approaching retirement would be hardest hit with the rising costs.

Despite mounting criticism of the bill, the Republicans managed to schedule a floor vote to repeal and replace Obamacare in late March 2017 that would have coincided with passage of the ACA seven years earlier. However, the attempt ultimately failed as a result of growing dissension within the Republican ranks. At least thirty members of the Republican conference, including key members of the Freedom Caucus, made it clear that they could not support the Republican plan. As a result Paul Ryan had no choice but to postpone and eventually cancel scheduled votes on March 23 and 24.[93] In his remarks later that Friday, Ryan proclaimed, "We're going to be living with Obamacare for the foreseeable future."[94] The failed attempt ultimately drew the ire of President Trump, who initially blamed Democrats for the bill's defeat. The failure later led him to suggest that he might have to reach out to Democrats to craft a new bill as well as campaign against members of the Freedom Caucus in retribution during the 2018 midterm elections.[95]

Following the failed attempt to repeal Obamacare, the Republicans met in a closed-door meeting the following week to try to bridge the divide between various factions in the party. Initially Ryan approached members of the Freedom Caucus in an attempt to assuage some of their concerns on health care reform. Although several members of the caucus indicated their willingness to work with the leadership, provisions of the bill that would remove protections for those who were insured, defund

Planned Parenthood, and cut subsidies for the elderly and low-income earners turned off some of the moderate Republicans.[96] Efforts to bring a modified version of the bill to the floor in early April failed because the Republicans lacked the votes needed to pass it in the House. After yet another setback to their agenda, some members of the caucus began to question the ability of the party to effectively govern despite unified control of government. In the words of Tom Cole (R-OK), "We've been dysfunctional for a while. We were able to stay relatively united against President Obama. But we have not been able to be united as a governing party, and that's got to be worked through."[97]

Republicans would eventually get another chance at repealing and replacing Obamacare, but first they had to avert a government shutdown. On April 28, the House approved a continuing resolution by a 382–30 bipartisan vote, and the Senate approved the measure by voice vote, that would maintain funding at current levels for another week. This gave Republicans more time to come up with a spending package that would fund the government through September 30 (the end of the fiscal year). The vote came just shy of Trump's hundredth day in office, when White House officials had hoped to have more significant legislative accomplishments to claim credit for. "House Republicans left the Capitol with their goal of voting to repeal the Affordable Care Act still eluding them—and eluding Mr. Trump, who will conclude his first 100 days on Saturday without a marquee legislative achievement."[98] Additionally, Mark Meadows (R-NC), chair of the House Freedom Caucus, remarked, "I would love to have had the vote in the first 100 days." However, in noting that it took much longer for the Democrats to initially pass the ACA in place initially, he added, "If it takes another couple of days, then so be it."[99]

Although Congress passed a $1.1 trillion spending bill the following week that would fund the government through the remainder of the fiscal year, it was not the version that House Republicans originally envisioned. On Wednesday, May 3, the House passed the bill 309–118, but the Republican conference split 132–103 on the final vote, arguing that the bill made too many concessions to the Democrats (who had supported the bill 178–15). The following day the Senate adopted the legislation by a 79–18 vote before sending it to Trump for his signature. With the potential threat of a filibuster in the Senate, the Democrats were able to achieve many of their objectives in the early stages of negotiation, such as denying funding for the wall on the U.S.-Mexico border and maintaining federal funding for Planned Parenthood. Even though the final version of the bill did include provisions for modest increases to military spending and border security, many Republicans in the House expressed their displeasure with the outcome.[100]

With the passage of the spending bill behind them, Republicans in the House were able to renew their attention on passing a revised health care bill. After nearly a month of negotiations, the Republicans narrowly approved legislation on Thursday, May 4, to repeal and replace the ACA. Among its various provisions, the updated bill would roll back expansion of Medicaid that had occurred under the ACA, eliminate tax penalties for persons who chose not to purchase health insurance, and replace government-subsidized insurance policies with varying tax credits based on a person's age. Although no Democrats voted in favor of the bill, and twenty Republicans opted to vote against it, the bill managed to pass the House by a vote of 217–213. President Trump immediately called a press conference to celebrate the legislative victory, even though the Senate had yet to consider the bill. Despite its passage, "[t]he House measure faces profound uncertainty in the Senate, where a handful of Republican senators immediately rejected it, signaling that they would start work on a new version of the bill virtually from scratch."[101] On top of that, the Congressional Budget Office announced in late May that the new bill would leave as many as 23 million people without health insurance by 2026, making it even more difficult for senators to embrace the House's version of the bill.[102]

## The Senate: How Effective Is Majority Control?

The surprising success of the Republicans in the 2016 Senate elections, despite the large number of Republican seats up for reelection, offered little pressure for a leadership change. At the start of the 115th Senate, Senators Mitch McConnell of Kentucky and John Cornyn of Texas were reelected as majority leader and majority whip, respectively, posts they have both held since January of 2015. On the Democratic side, Chuck Schumer of New York was elected as minority leader (replacing retiring Senator Harry Reid of Nevada), and Dick Durbin of Illinois continued as the Democratic whip, a position he has held since 2005.

The Senate has always been predominantly a men's club, but that has been gradually changing in recent decades. The Senate membership resulting from the 2016 elections varied significantly in gender diversity. The number of female Democrats remained the same at sixteen, whereas the number of female Republicans increased from four to five. As a result a record 21 percent of the senators serving in the 115th Congress were women, 33 percent of the Democrats and 10 percent of the Republicans. By comparison, eighty-three women were elected to the U.S. House in 2016, which constitutes 19.1 percent of the 435 members.[103]

The central organizational issue at the start of the 115th Congress was whether there would be a change in the rules regarding the Senate's distinctive practice of the filibuster for Supreme Court nominations. Also known as *extended debate*, the filibuster refers to an effort to prevent resolution of a measure under consideration in the Senate by refusing to end discussion of it. Unlike the House, where debate can be ended by a simple majority vote at any time, Senate consideration can only be terminated against the will of those who would continue by invoking "cloture." Under Senate rules, cloture requires sixty votes, except on a proposal to change Senate rules, when the support of two-thirds of those voting is needed.[104]

The incidence of filibusters and cloture efforts, and their relevance to the legislative process, has increased greatly over the last six decades. In the seven congresses from 1947 through 1960, motions to invoke cloture were filed only four times, and none were approved. Filibusters were rare and were almost always employed by southerners in an attempt to block civil rights bills. Then, gradually, as partisan polarization came to characterize the Senate, the scope of topics for filibusters broadened, and their frequency increased. In the five congresses from 2007 through 2016, for instance, 772 cloture motions were filed and were successfully invoked 413 times.[105]

The increased use of filibusters has made it more difficult and costly for the majority party to secure passage of the bills it favors. As a consequence some senators in the majority have sought to alter the Senate's rules to place limits on what could be filibustered or how many votes would be required to impose cloture. Of course members of the minority would be unlikely to support such efforts, and they would be likely to use the filibuster to block them. As noted, Senate rules specify that motions to invoke cloture on attempted rules changes require even more votes than such efforts on regular legislation. But some members and outside observers contend that the rule does not apply at the opening of a congress and that only the vote of a majority is then necessary to end debate and adopt an alternative rule. Whether such an interpretation (dubbed the "nuclear option" by participants) would be applied in a particular instance would depend on whether the presiding officer of the Senate, the vice president, so ruled and whether that ruling was upheld by a majority of senators. A significant proportion of the senators of both parties have accepted the view that a simple majority was sufficient to impose cloture on a rules change when they were in the minority (and the same people have often taken the opposite view when in the majority).

In 2005 the nuclear option in the Senate gained national attention when Majority Leader Bill Frist (R-TN) threatened to invoke it to put an end to Democratic filibusters of President George W. Bush's judicial nominees by a simple majority vote. When the Democrats promised to shut down the Senate and prevent any legislation from being considered if the practice was implemented, a group of seven Democratic and seven Republican senators (known as the Gang of 14) agreed in principle to oppose the nuclear option and the filibuster of judicial nominees.[106] After the GOP Senate gains of 2010, Democrats began talking about changing the cloture rules by a majority vote, but a confrontation was avoided by a "gentleman's agreement" between the two party leaders that purported to limit the scope of filibusters. Harry Reid and many Democrats were unhappy with the operation of that agreement, and after the 2012 elections, Democrats again raised the specter of a rules change. Indeed, in late November 2012, Reid flatly predicted that Senate Democrats would vote to limit Republican use of the filibuster in the new congress, although many observers questioned whether he actually had the votes to effect the change.[107]

When the new Senate convened in 2013, a confrontation over the nuclear option was initially avoided by negotiations between the party leaders and other members. However, by July of that year, the Senate Democratic majority came within hours of invoking the nuclear option in light of Republican opposition to several of President Obama's executive branch appointments. Although the president decided to withdraw two of the nominations at the last moment, thus preserving the minority's ability to filibuster nominations, the victory was short-lived. By late November 2013 Senator Reid decided that action finally had to be taken. On November 21, "the Senate approved the most fundamental alteration of its rules in more than a generation on Thursday, ending the minority party's ability to filibuster most presidential nominees in response to the partisan gridlock that has plagued Congress for much of the Obama administration."[108] As a result of the change, which passed by a narrow fifty-two to forty-eight vote, the Senate can effectively cut off debate on executive and judicial branch nominees with a simple majority rather than with sixty votes as had previously been necessary. However, the new rule did not apply to Supreme Court nominations or legislation under consideration in the Senate.[109]

Republicans were initially furious with Reid's decision to "go nuclear" and warned that the Democrats would regret their action if they lost control of the Senate in the future. In fact, when the Republicans won back control of the Senate in 2014 and maintained a majority in the 2016 elections, some Democrats began to lament the decision to trigger the nuclear option.[110] Indirectly this also shaped the discussion over potential Supreme Court vacancies, especially after Justice Scalia's unexpected death in February 2016. Although some Democrats privately wished the nuclear option had included appointments to the Supreme Court as a result of the vacancy caused by Scalia's death, it ended up being a moot point because Republicans controlled a majority of the seats in the 114th Senate and would have likely blocked any of President Obama's nominees. Indeed, even before the president nominated U.S. Court of Appeals Justice Merrick Garland on March 16, 2016, to fill Scalia's seat on the Court, Senate Majority Leader Mitch McConnell said that the Senate should not hold a vote on any Supreme Court nominee during the president's final year in office.[111] Democrats were understandably outraged by this statement, but it later came to light that then Senator Joe Biden had made a similar remark about filling Supreme Court appointments in 1992 during President Bush's last year in office.[112] In the end Scalia's seat remained vacant for the remainder of the year given the Republicans' reluctance to move forward with the Garland nomination.

Within days of being sworn in as the forty-fifth president of the United States, Donald Trump nominated Neil Gorsuch on January 31, 2017, to fill the vacant seat on the Supreme Court that was formerly held by Scalia. In late March the Senate held confirmation hearings for Gorsuch, which lasted for a total of four days. On April 3, the Judiciary Committee approved Gorsuch by an eleven to nine vote, and the nomination was sent to the Senate floor for consideration the following day. When the Democrats proceeded to filibuster Gorsuch's nomination, Mitch McConnell elected to fully extend the nuclear option that had been invoked back in November 2013 to now include Supreme Court nominees. As a result Gorsuch was confirmed on April 7, 2017, by a fifty-four to forty-five vote that included three Democrats joining all the Republicans in attendance and was sworn in as the 113th justice of the Supreme Court later that day.[113] As before none of the changes adopted affected the ability of senators to filibuster final passage votes on bills, so the strength of that tactic for blocking action remains in effect.

At the end of May, President Trump expressed frustration that the Senate had yet to take up the health care bill passed previously by the House as well as his tax reform legislation. At one point he urged the Republican Senate leadership to change the chamber rules to allow any legislation to pass by a simple majority vote as they had done with votes on Supreme Court nominees to expedite the passage of his key agenda items. Several commentators noted this was not really necessary because these bills could already be considered via reconciliation, which only requires approval by a majority of those in the Senate. Very few Republican senators seemed interested in Trump's proposal given that it would have enormous implications for their ability to object to legislation should they become the minority again in the future.[114]

In mid-June, Senate Republicans announced that they were close to scheduling a vote on their version of the health care bill to repeal and replace "Obamacare." Much of the discussion on the bill had occurred behind closed doors, but the bill's proponents initially argued that it sought to address many of the problems with the House version passed in May. Before the Senate had a chance to schedule a vote, however, the Congressional Budget Office announced that the Senate version of the bill would leave 22 million more people uninsured over the next 10 years.[115] As a result of this announcement, Senate leaders had no choice but to postpone a vote on the bill until after the July 4th recess because five Republican senators indicated they could not support this bill in light of the new estimates.[116] The vote on the Senate bill was again delayed in mid-July when Senator John McCain underwent surgery to remove a blood clot from behind his left eye as his vote was viewed as necessary to reach the fifty-vote threshold for passage.[117] Two days later Majority Leader Mitch McConnell announced that the Senate would no longer focus on trying to pass their own version of the health care bill in light of growing opposition to the plan among Republican senators. Instead they would now focus on dismantling the existing law.[118]

By late July the possibility of trying to dismantle the ACA seemed even less likely when at least three senators announced they would not support repealing existing law without some form of replacement.[119] On July 25, however, the Senate managed to schedule a motion to proceed on health care reform once John McCain flew back to Washington, DC, less than a week after being diagnosed with brain cancer. The motion ultimately passed by a vote of fifty-one to fifty (Vice President Mike Pence broke the 50-50 tie). Both Susan Collins (R-ME) and Lisa Murkowski (R-AK) defected on the motion and voted with the Democrats, thus necessitating the vice president's tie-breaking vote. Later that evening the Senate attempted to pass an initial amendment introduced to strip many of the provisions of the existing health care law, but it ultimately failed on a fifty-seven to forty-three vote including nine GOP defections.[120] In the early morning hours on July 28, the Senate sought to repeal portions of the ACA (the so-called slimmed-down version), but it failed when Republican Senators Susan Collins (ME), Lisa Murkowski (AK), and John McCain (AZ) along with all forty-eight Democrats voted against it.[121] As of December 2017, the status of the Republican health care bill remains uncertain despite considerable time and effort devoted to repealing the existing law.

## THE 2018 ELECTIONS AND BEYOND

Expectations about midterm elections are usually shaped by a strong historical pattern: The party of the president lost strength in the House in twenty-five of the twenty-nine midterm elections since the beginning of the twentieth century. The first column in Table 9-8 shows the magnitude of these losses in midterms since World War II. They average 25.2 seats for the president's party. There was, however, considerable variation in the outcomes, from the sixty-three-seat loss by the Democrats in 2010 to the six-seat Republican gain in 2002. When thinking about the concept of midterm loss, one needs to keep in mind how long the president has served in office. During the first midterm election of his tenure, for instance, the president may be able to make a plausible appeal that he has not had enough time to bring about substantial change or to solidify many achievements. Moreover, even if things are not going very well, voters may not be inclined to blame a president who has served for such a short time. But four years later (if the president is fortunate enough to face a second midterm), appeals of too little time are unlikely to be persuasive. After six years, if the economy

**Table 9-8 House Seat Losses by the President's Party in Midterm Elections, 1946–2014**

| Year | All Elections | First Term of Administration | Later Term of Administration |
|---|---|---|---|
| 1946 | 55 Democrats | | 55 Democrats |
| 1950 | 29 Democrats | | 29 Democrats |
| 1954 | 18 Republicans | 18 Republicans | |
| 1958 | 47 Republicans | | 47 Republicans |
| 1962 | 4 Democrats | 4 Democrats | |
| 1966 | 47 Democrats | | 47 Democrats |
| 1970 | 12 Republicans | 12 Republicans | |
| 1974 | 43 Republicans | | 43 Republicans |
| 1978 | 11 Democrats | 11 Democrats | |
| 1982 | 26 Republicans | 26 Republicans | |
| 1986 | 5 Republicans | | 5 Republicans |
| 1990 | 9 Republicans | 9 Republicans | |
| 1994 | 52 Democrats | 52 Democrats | |
| 1998 | (+5) Democrats | | (+5) Democrats |
| 2002 | (+6) Republicans | (+6) Republicans | |
| 2006 | 30 Republicans | | 30 Republicans |
| 2010 | 63 Democrats | 63 Democrats | |
| 2014 | 13 Democrats | | 13 Democrats |
| **Average Seat Loss** | | | |
| | 25.2 seats | 21.0 seats | 29.3 seats |

*Source:* Compiled by the authors.

or foreign policy is not going well, voters may seek a policy change by reducing the number of the president's partisans in Congress.

The second and third columns in Table 9-8 indicate that this is what has usually happened in the past. Losses by the president's party in the first midterm election of a presidency have tended to be much smaller than losses in subsequent midterms.[122]

Indeed, with the exception of the results in 1986, 1994, 1998, 2002, and 2010, the two categories yield two sets of outcomes that are sharply different from one another. In the six midterm elections besides 1994, 2002, and 2010 that took place during a first term, the president's party lost between four and twenty-six seats, with an average loss of thirteen. In the seven elections after the first term (excluding 1986 and 1998), the range of losses was between thirteen and fifty-five seats, with an average loss of thirty-eight. (We will discuss the atypical years later.)

## Models of House Elections

In the 1970s and 1980s, a number of political scientists constructed and tested models of congressional election outcomes, focusing especially on midterms, seeking to isolate the factors that most strongly influenced the results. The earliest models, constructed by Tufte and by Jacobson and Samuel Kernell, focused on two variables: presidential approval and a measure of the state of the economy.[123] Tufte hypothesized a direct influence by these forces on voter choice and election outcomes. The theory was that an unpopular president or a poor economy would cause the president's party to lose votes and, therefore, seats in the House. In essence the midterm elections were viewed as a referendum on the performance of the president and his party.

Jacobson and Kernell, on the other hand, saw more indirect effects of presidential approval and the economy. They argued that these forces affected election results by influencing the decisions of potential congressional candidates. If the president is unpopular and the economy is in bad shape, potential candidates will expect the president's party to perform poorly. As a consequence strong potential candidates of the president's party will be more inclined to forgo running until a better year, and strong candidates from the opposition party will be more inclined to run because they foresee good prospects for success. According to Jacobson and Kernell, this mix of weak candidates from the president's party and strong opposition candidates will lead to a poor election performance by the party occupying the White House. To measure this predicted relationship, their model related the partisan division of the vote to presidential approval and the economic situation early in the election year. This, they argued, is when decisions to run for office are being made, not at the time of the election, so it is not appropriate to focus on approval and the economy at that time. This view has come to be called the "strategic politicians hypothesis."[124]

Subsequent research built from this base. One model, developed by Alan I. Abramowitz, Albert D. Cover, and Helmut Norpoth, considered a new independent variable: short-term party evaluations.[125] They argued that voters' attitudes about the economic competence of the political parties affect the impact of presidential approval and economic conditions on voting decisions. If the electorate judges that the party holding the presidency is better able to deal with the problems voters regard as most serious, the negative impact of an unpopular president or a weak economy will be reduced. The authors concluded from their analysis of both aggregate votes and responses to surveys in midterm elections that there is evidence for their "party competence" hypothesis.

All of these models used the division of the popular vote as the variable to be predicted, and they focused only on midterm elections. Later work merged midterm results with those of presidential years, contending that there should be no conceptual distinction between them. These efforts sought to predict changes in seats without reference to the division of the vote. For example, a study by Bruce I. Oppenheimer, James A. Stimson, and Richard W. Waterman argued that the missing piece in the congressional election puzzle is the degree of "exposure" or "the excess or deficit number of seats a party holds measured against its long-term norm."[126] If a party wins more House seats than normal, those extra seats will be vulnerable in the next election, and the party is likely to suffer losses. Thus the party that wins a presidential election does not automatically benefit in House elections. But if the president's party does well in the House races, it will be more vulnerable in the subsequent midterm elections. Indeed the work by Oppenheimer and his colleagues predicted only small Republican losses for 1986 because Reagan's large 1984 victory was not accompanied by substantial congressional gains for his party. The actual result in 1986 was consistent with this prediction, for the GOP lost only five seats.

Another model of House elections was constructed by Robin F. Marra and Charles W. Ostrom, Jr.[127] They developed a "comprehensive referendum voting model" of both presidential year and midterm elections and included factors such as changes in the level of presidential approval, party identification, foreign policy crises, scandals, and unresolved policy disputes. The model also incorporated measures reflecting hypothesized relationships in the models we discussed earlier: the level of presidential approval, the state of the economy, the strategic politicians' hypothesis, exposure, and party competence. The model was tested on data from all congressional elections from 1950 through 1986.

The Marra-Ostrom analysis showed significant support for a majority of the predicted relationships. The results indicated that the most powerful influences affecting congressional seat changes were presidential approval (directly and through various events) and exposure. The model was striking in its statistical accuracy: the average error in the predicted change was only four seats. The average error varied little whether presidential or midterm years were predicted, and the analysis demonstrated that the usually greater losses for the president's party in second midterm years resulted from negative shifts in presidential approval, exposure, and scandals. However, when the empirical analysis was extended by Ostrom and Brian Newman to include the election years from 1988 through 1998, the accuracy of the model declined.[128] They produced a revised model that included some additional variables. In particular they found that the relative number of open seats held by the two parties was important in determining losses. Moreover, once that variable was taken into account, the importance of the exposure variable decreased. That is, the most important form of exposure was open seats; incumbents were less vulnerable.

Drawing on the insights of these various models, we can see how these factors may influence outcomes in the 2018 House elections. How well the economy is doing and what proportion of the voters approves of Trump's performance early in the year may encourage or discourage high-quality potential challengers. The same variables close to election time may lead voters to support or oppose Republican candidates based on their judgments of the job the Trump administration is doing. The usual midterm losses happen for predictable reasons; they are not part of the laws of nature. Therefore, if the usual reasons for such losses (such as a recession or an unpopular president) are not present in 2018, we should not expect the consequent losses to occur or at least not the magnitude of losses that history might lead us to expect. This is why the president's party gained seats in the midterms of 1998 and 2002. If, on the other hand, those reasons are present, the context will be quite different.

During the summer of 2017, Trump's approval remained low relative to other presidents at this early stage of the presidency. If his approval numbers do not improve throughout the year and into 2018, this could have significant consequences for the 2018 midterm elections. Trump has held steady at approximately 40 percent approval since mid-March, but his overall level of disapproval has fluctuated between 50 and 55 percent, which is much higher than normal for this early in a president's first year in office.[129] With respect to the economy, there was a very modest increase in early 2017, but growth was lower than during the last quarter of 2016. If the economy improves further and Trump's popularity begins to approach 50 percent, Republicans could be insulated from significant losses in the upcoming midterm elections. On the other hand recent scandals in the administration (the Comey firing and ongoing questions about Trump and his family's connection with Russia) may further undermine the president's approval rating. Additionally the models we discussed indicate that other considerations may be important. Republican exposure is relatively high due to the gains they made in 2010 and 2014, and to this point there appears to be a greater proportion of Republican departures or retirements from the House. This could create more opportunities for Democrats than normal if these trends persist.

With regard to quality candidates emerging to run, Democrats are at least as aware of the pattern of midterm losses as are political scientists, so potential candidates may regard the political landscape as encouraging. Given any potential backlash against Trump in 2018, that same landscape might make recruiting challengers a bit easier than usual despite the structural advantage Republicans have in the House in light of how rural seats are distributed.[130] In March 2017, for instance, "EMILY's List announced . . . that more than 10,000 women have reached out to the group since Hillary Clinton lost the presidential election to say they want to run for office, a record number in such a short time for the group."[131] Additionally the Democratic Party is seeking to recruit candidates with military backgrounds to run against Republican incumbents in 2018, with fifteen veterans already committed to launch House campaigns as of May 2017.[132] In addition to each of these considerations, the impact of events like crises and scandals in the Marra-Ostrom model reminds us that there are many unforeseeable events that may influence the 2018 congressional election results.

## Some Additional Considerations about House Races

A few further points related to the previous discussion are necessary to complete our analysis of the prospects for 2018 House races. The vulnerability of individual members varies between parties and across other attributes, and we should not expect those distributions to be similar from election to election. For example, in one year a party may have a relatively high percentage of freshmen or members who won by narrow margins in the preceding election, whereas in another year the party's proportion of such potentially vulnerable members may be low. As Table 9-9 shows, both parties have a roughly similar (and relatively small) number of members who won with less than 55 percent of the vote. Eleven Republicans and twenty-one Democrats fell into this category. There are fewer close races for each party than the number that resulted from the 2000 elections, and it is substantially fewer than the total of ninety-five after 1996 (also two years after a Republican landslide). It is in this type of district that strong challengers are most likely to come forward and where the challengers who do run are most able to raise adequate campaign funds. Thus, based solely on these election-margin figures, the political landscape does not present a very attractive prospect for challengers of either party.

As our earlier analysis indicates, the parties' respective success in recruiting strong candidates for open seats and to oppose the other party's incumbents can be expected to play a significant role in shaping outcomes for 2018. Both Democratic and Republican campaign organizations were actively pursuing recruits during 2017, with some early successes and some disappointments. The personal and financial costs of candidacies and the difficulty of defeating an incumbent often make recruitment difficult, and the unique circumstances of each party make the task harder. In late January 2017 the DCCC identified approximately sixty House seats they plan to target in 2018, including some congressional districts carried by President Trump in the 2016 elections.[133] Nevertheless, they still face an uphill battle to win back control of Congress. On the Republican side, the RNCC is seeking to mitigate potential losses as a result of departures and retirements from Congress. We will return to these issues at the end of this section.

Even when the party organizations do recruit strong challengers, this offers no guarantee of electoral success. For example, in a Kansas special House election in April 2017 (to replace Mike Pompeo, who Donald Trump appointed to be the new

**Table 9-9 Percentage of Vote Received by Winning House Candidates, by Party and Type of Race, 2016**

| | Republican | | | Democrat | | |
|---|---|---|---|---|---|---|
| | Reelected Incumbent | Successful Challenger | Open-Seat Winner | Reelected Incumbent | Successful Challenger | Open-Seat Winner |
| 55 or less | 8 | 1 | 2 | 11 | 6 | 4 |
| 55.1–60 | 37 | 0 | 7 | 26 | 0 | 5 |
| 60.1–70 | 98 | 0 | 8 | 53 | 0 | 4 |
| 70.1–100 | 72 | 0 | 8 | 78 | 0 | 7 |
| Total | 215 | 1 | 25 | 168 | 6 | 20 |

*Source:* Compiled by the authors.

*Note:* Table shows the number of districts that meet the criteria for each cell. Open seats include races in which an incumbent lost a primary.

CIA director), the GOP candidate, Ron Estes, was a state treasurer from the district. Moreover, a Republican had represented the district for over two decades, and Trump carried it by twenty-seven points in November. The Democrats nominated James Thompson, a Wichita civil rights lawyer with no experience in public office. Although Estes went on to win the special election, it turned out to be much closer than expected with a vote of 53 to 46 percent in the district. Many pundits regarded this race as a preview of what might occur in the 2018 elections, especially if voters viewed the midterm as a potential referendum against President Trump.[134]

Just over a week after the Kansas special election, a second critical test for Republicans came in the form of a special election in Georgia's sixth district. Tom Price resigned from the seat in early 2017 after being confirmed as the U.S. secretary of health and human services in the Trump administration. As a result several candidates emerged from both parties to vie for the April 18 primary election in the open seat—five Democrats and eleven Republicans. Although the Democrats quickly coalesced their support around Jon Ossoff, a former congressional aide, Republican leaders and voters had a much harder time deciding whom to support among the top five or six candidates in the pool, most of whom had previous elective experience. Given the symbolic nature of the race in light of the upcoming midterm elections, and the fact that Trump carried the district by a narrow margin, Democrats saw it as a real opportunity to win back a seat from the Republicans. As a result donations poured into the race in unprecedented amounts—Ossoff raised over $8 million prior to the April election, and $14 million in outside spending was used to fund a series of political commercials.

Jon Ossoff went on to earn slightly more than 48 percent in the primary, with Republican Karen Handel coming in second with nearly 20 percent of the vote. Under Georgia law, if no candidate receives a majority of votes in the special election, the first- and second-place finishers then go to a runoff election, which was held on June 20, 2017. Many Democrats viewed this as a potentially winnable race, although Republicans did everything in their power to keep the seat under Republican control, including having Paul Ryan campaign on Handel's behalf in May and Vice President Mike Pence visit the district the second week of June.[135] By the time the runoff election was held, nearly $60 million was spent on the race, making it the most expensive U.S. House election in history.[136] Karen Handel ultimately defeated Jon Ossoff 51.9 to 48.1 percent in the special election despite the enormous sum spent by both sides.[137]

On May 25, a third special election was held in Montana, following Representative Ryan Zinke's decision to vacate the seat in March to serve as Trump's interior secretary. Although Trump carried Montana by twenty points in the presidential election and Zinke won reelection by sixteen points, Democrats still were undeterred. Republicans fielded Greg Gianforte in the special election, who had lost Montana's gubernatorial election in fall 2016 by nearly four points. His opponent was Rob Quist, a small businessman and entrepreneur with no prior political experience. Given Gianforte's previous electoral defeat and partially due to what was happening in the Georgia sixth district race, the Congressional Leadership Fund (the super PAC endorsed by the House GOP leadership) invested $2.7 million, whereas the DCCC spent only about half a million dollars in the race. During a rally on the night before the election, Gianforte physically attacked a reporter who asked him a question about the Republican health care plan and was later cited for misdemeanor assault. Despite this considerable lapse in judgment—Gianforte later apologized during his victory speech—he went on to win the race by about six points.[138]

Also worth noting here is the continuing impact of term limits in the states. Although the term limits movement during the 1990s failed to impose restrictions on members of Congress, it succeeded in imposing them on state legislators in fifteen states, and those limits continue to have an impact. One potential outlet for a state legislator who is ineligible to run for reelection is to seek a congressional seat. This may lead to a greater number of strong challengers in House races than would otherwise be the case. For example, California limits state legislators to twelve years combined in the two chambers, and a number of legislators will have to leave their current positions next year. Some of them are contemplating races against Republican members of the U.S. House as a result of enhanced recruitment efforts on the part of the DCCC.[139]

As we have discussed, the potential number of open seats is also relevant to questions of candidate recruitment and district vulnerability. Our analysis shows that open seats are more likely to switch parties than are those with incumbents, and that both parties are more likely to field strong candidates. As of October 2017 there were eleven confirmed retirements in the House, nine of which were Republicans: Carol Shea-Porter of New Hampshire, Niki Tsongas of Massachusetts (both Democrats), Lynn Jenkins of Kansas, Dave Trott of Michigan, Charlie Dent of Pennsylvania, Tim Murphy of Pennsylvania, John Duncan, Jr., of Tennessee, Sam Johnson of Texas, Jason Chaffetz of Utah, Dave Reichert of Washington, and Ileana Ros-Lehtinen of Florida—the latter of which could be a winnable seat for the Democrats in light of past voting trends.[140] However, there were also concerns that a number of representatives will leave the House to seek Senate seats or governorships, and by October 2017 eighteen members (eight Democrats and ten Republicans) had already committed to such races.[141] When Chaffetz announced his retirement on April 19 (effective June 30), the chair of the House Oversight Committee told his supporters that he would not seek reelection to Congress, or any office, in 2018.[142] Some suspect that Chaffetz's decision might be a signal that he plans to run for governor in state of Utah in 2020.[143]

Finally one should remember that the rules that shape elections are subject to change and that such changes can have a substantial impact on the pattern of election outcomes. One source of such change is the courts. In 2013 the U.S. Supreme Court struck down a provision of the Voting Rights Act in *Shelby County v. Holder* requiring many state and local governments, mainly in the South, to seek permission from the U.S. Justice Department or a federal court before they can make changes to certain voting procedures. The provision, which had been reauthorized by Congress in 2006, had been challenged on the grounds that such restrictions on the rights of states were no longer required. Five justices joined in an opinion by Chief Justice John Roberts in which he said that Congress was able to impose federal restrictions on states where voting rights were at risk, but it must do so based on contemporary data on discrimination which was not true in this instance. Although the Court left it open for Congress to pass a new law, several attempts since 2013 have failed, most likely a function of the increased polarization and gridlock in Congress. This case is likely to have significant consequences moving forward because many Republican-controlled state governments have pushed for and adopted new voting regulations in the years following the Court's decision.[144] Indeed many viewed the Supreme Court's May 2017 decision not to overturn the Fourth Circuit Court of Appeal's ruling to strike down a controversial North Carolina voter ID law as a victory for voting right's activists.[145] At the same time several states may have to redraw their congressional district boundaries as a result of ongoing legal challenges (including North Carolina).

As a consequence of all of the factors we have discussed, Republicans may have more reason for concern than Democrats, especially in light of Trump's meager approval ratings to date.[146] Although the twenty-four net gain the Democratic party needs to win a majority is not inconsequential, in the eighteen midterm elections since World War II, the president's party has lost that many seats nine times. Yet our analysis also indicates that Democratic success is not certain. We have seen that it is possible for the historical pattern to be broken under certain conditions. Perhaps the most relevant one for 2018 relates to the Republican Party's reputation with voters. Poll data from the Pew Research Center (supported by similar analyses in other polls) shows that the party's ratings stand at the highest point in seven years, with 47 percent of respondents indicating that they have a favorable view of the GOP and 49 percent seeing it unfavorably.[147] Whether those more favorable numbers will hold leading up to the 2018 midterms is unclear.

## Senate Races in 2018

Because there are few Senate races and because they are relatively independent of one another, we have focused our discussion of 2018 on the House. We will now close with a few comments about the upper chamber's contests. Due to the six-year Senate terms, and the fact that these terms are staggered, the number of seats to be defended by each party varies from election to election. As was true in 2012, the Democrats hold most of the thirty-four seats that will be contested in 2018, with twenty-five seats—including independent senators Angus King (ME) and Bernie Sanders (VT)—compared to the Republicans' nine.[148] As a result, the GOP has more targets for gains, and some features of the landscape make the situation look even more attractive for them. As of October 2017, Bob Corker (R-TN) is the only senator to date to announce his retirement at the end of the 115th Congress. Nevertheless, "ten of the 25 Senate seats Democrats are defending are in states that voted for Donald Trump for president last year: Florida, Indiana, Michigan, Missouri, Montana, North Dakota, Ohio, Pennsylvania, West Virginia, and Wisconsin. Meanwhile, Republicans are defending just one seat in a state that Hillary Clinton won (Nevada)."[149] In light of the increasing nationalization of elections coupled with the fact that no state split their presidential and senatorial votes in 2016, this portends to be an uphill battle for the Democrats.

Although the numbers appear to favor the Republicans with respect to the 2018 Senate races at first glance, they only tell part of the story. If the Republicans successfully picked up most, if not all, of the vulnerable Democratic seats, they could have a filibuster-proof Senate in the 116th Congress assuming they held onto their own Republican seats in the process. However, one of the biggest challenges that the Republicans face is being able to recruit quality candidates to run against potentially vulnerable senators. We have seen that the kinds of candidates seeking office have a major influence on the outcome, and that parties, therefore, try to get the strongest candidates to come forward. In this cycle, however, some of the strongest potential challengers may decide 2018 does not represent the best set of circumstances to run for the Senate.

As of mid-summer, several high-profile Republicans have declined to challenge Democratic senators in some of the more competitive states, potentially because of President Trump's record-low approval levels. In Indiana, for instance, Representative Susan Brooks (R) has decided not to challenge Senator Joe Donnelly (D) in 2018, even though Trump carried the state by nineteen points and party officials believe she would be a formidable opponent. Still, early reports suggest that two other Republican House members might be considering running against Joe Donnelly—Luke Messer and Todd Rokia.[150] Although Representative Sean Duffy (R) briefly considered running against Senator Tammy Baldwin (D) in Wisconsin, he recently announced that he would forgo the bid for higher office, most likely due to the uphill nature of the battle—Trump only carried the state by one percentage point. "In Pennsylvania, four-term Rep. Patrick Meehan (R) was considering, then declined, to challenge Senator Bob Casey. Meehan would have been a bigger name than the two state lawmakers and one borough councilman who have jumped in so far to try to challenge Casey."[151]

As noted, the Democrats face formidable hurdles given the large number of Senate seats they must defend, particularly those in swing and Republican-leaning states previously carried by Trump. In West Virginia, for instance, Senator Joe Manchin III (D) is running for reelection in a state that Trump defeated Clinton by more than forty points.[152] In many ways this is an extreme example, but it illustrates the difficulties that Democrats face in trying to defend, let alone pick up, seats in the Senate. Even with Trump's relatively high levels of unpopularity in recent Gallup polls, Democrats need an ideal set of conditions going into the 2018 midterms to not fall further behind in the number of seats they control in the upper chamber. Although their prospects for picking up seats in the Senate will likely improve in 2020 when there are fewer Democratic seats up for reelection, the 2018 elections could represent an important symbolic victory if the Democrats can mitigate their potential losses.

To summarize, then, House election results are likely to depend heavily on the political context that exists both late in 2017 (when most candidate decisions are made) and in November of 2018. The context may also determine whether the historical pattern of midterm losses by the president's party occurs again or is broken as it was in both 1998 and 2002. For the Senate seats, on the other hand, the election results probably depend more on the circumstances in individual races, largely fought independently of one another.

## Beyond 2018: Polarization and the Struggle for Control of Congress

Just as every election has implications for those that follow, the elections of 2018 will have an impact on subsequent contests. We do not know those results, so we cannot yet describe the effects, but a few general considerations are likely to have an impact on future congressional contests. The national demographic changes we have touched on in Chapter 2, and that we will discuss further in Chapter 11, will continue to be important. Although these shifts slowed somewhat due to reduced immigration during the economic slump, the proportion of the population that is made up of Latinos and other minorities will continue to grow. The Democrats are currently advantaged among these groups, and they will pursue strategies that seek to retain that advantage and that improve the activation of those constituencies, as demonstrated by efforts to frame the debate over immigration in recent congresses. Republicans, on the other hand, may look for ways to improve their standing among minorities, particularly Latinos. Indeed they will have to succeed to a degree if they are to remain competitive as the population distribution changes in the coming years.

The impact of the shifting demographics will be shaped by the Democratic Party's efforts to improve its reputation. The soul-searching that followed the unexpected failures of 2016 led Democrats to scramble after Hillary Clinton's loss, as individuals began jockeying within the party over who would assume the reins of leadership. Shortly after the election, "the country's first Muslim lawmaker and a prominent liberal voice in the House, Rep. Keith Ellison (D-MN), announced that he would run for chair of the Democratic National Committee."[153] Former U.S. secretary of labor under President Obama, Thomas "Tom" Perez also announced his candidacy for chair of the DNC on December 15, 2016. When the election was held on February 25, 2017, Perez was elected chair on the second ballot, narrowly defeating Ellison for the position, which led to visible frustration and outrage among Ellison's supporters. Within minutes of the election, he immediately named Ellison as his deputy chair, signaling to Ellison's supporters that he hoped to find a middle ground between the factions within the Democratic Party.[154]

Despite the initial controversy over who would be chosen to chair the Democratic Party, many party insiders welcome Perez's selection and what it represented for greater unity among Democrats. "Mr. Perez, 55, the son of Dominican immigrants, is the first Latino chairman of the Democratic Party. He was reared in Buffalo and has held a series of state and federal government jobs, most recently as Mr. Obama's labor secretary."[155] Although Perez has limited experience in electoral politics, he has already signaled that more attention needs to be given to House and Senate races in future elections. "Addressing reporters with Mr. Ellison after the election, Mr. Perez vowed to shift the committee from its overriding focus on presidential politics."[156] In the interim Democrats plan to focus their attention on the upcoming special elections in four House races and recruiting strong candidates for the thirty-six gubernatorial races taking place in 2018, which has long-term implications for redistricting in House districts during the next decade.[157]

Even though the Republicans currently have unified control of government, the party has its own share of concerns, especially given Trump's low approval ratings, various administrative scandals that have precipitated talk of impeachment, the current state of the economy and its impact, and the lack of policy successes to date. As noted, they are in a reasonably good position with the 2018 Senate elections given they will be defending nine of the thirty-four seats, nearly all in solidly Republican states (whereas ten of the Democratic senators must compete in more competitive states as reflected by presidential vote in the 2016 election). However, the Republicans in the House may be in a more precarious situation if Trump's approval ratings do not improve, citizens react adversely to the vote on health care reform, and more

## Table A7-6 President's Handling of the Job and Major-Party Vote, 1972–2016

| Response | 1972 | 1976 | 1980 | 1984 | 1988 | 1992 | 1996 | 2000 | 2004 | 2008 | 2012 | 2016 |
|---|---|---|---|---|---|---|---|---|---|---|---|---|
| **Part A** | | | | | | | | | | | | |
| Approve | 71 | 63 | 41 | 63 | 60 | 43 | 68 | 67 | 51 | 27 | 50 | 53 |
| Disapprove | 29 | 37 | 59 | 37 | 40 | 57 | 32 | 33 | 49 | 73 | 50 | 47 |
| Total | 100 | 100 | 100 | 100 | 100 | 100 | 100 | 100 | 100 | 100 | 100 | 100 |
| (*N*) | (1,215) | (2,439) | (1,475) | (2,091) | (1,935) | (2,419) | (1,692) | (1,742) | (1,182) | (2,245) | (1,704) | (4,226) |
| **Part B** | | | | | | | | | | | | |
| Approve | 83 | 74 | 81 | 87 | 79 | 81 | 84 | 74 | 91 | 88 | 92 | 91 |
| (*N*) | (553) | (935) | (315) | (863) | (722) | (587) | (676) | (662) | (408) | (441) | (537) | (1,263) |
| Disapprove | 14 | 9 | 18 | 7 | 12 | 11 | 4 | 13 | 6 | 26 | 6 | 8 |
| (*N*) | (203) | (523) | (491) | (449) | (442) | (759) | (350) | (366) | (372) | (1,075) | (568) | (1,102) |

*Source:* Authors' analysis of ANES surveys.

*Note:* The numbers in parentheses in Part B are the totals on which percentages are based. Question was asked of a randomly selected half-sample in 1972. Numbers are weighted.

**Table A8-1 Party Identification in Presidential Years, Pre-election Surveys, 1952–1976 (Percent)**

| Party identification | 1952 | 1956 | 1960 | 1964 | 1968 | 1972 | 1976 | 1980 | 1984 | 1988 | 1992 | 1996 | 2000 | 2004 | 2008 | 2012 | 2016 |
|---|---|---|---|---|---|---|---|---|---|---|---|---|---|---|---|---|---|
| Strong Democrat | 23 | 22 | 24 | 27 | 20 | 15 | 15 | 18 | 17 | 18 | 17 | 18 | 19 | 17 | 19 | 17 | 21 |
| Weak Democrat | 26 | 24 | 25 | 25 | 26 | 25 | 24 | 24 | 20 | 18 | 18 | 20 | 15 | 16 | 15 | 12 | 14 |
| Independent, leans Democratic | 10 | 7 | 6 | 9 | 10 | 11 | 12 | 12 | 11 | 12 | 14 | 14 | 15 | 17 | 17 | 16 | 11 |
| Independent, no partisan leanings | 5 | 9 | 9 | 8 | 11 | 15 | 15 | 13 | 11 | 11 | 12 | 8 | 12 | 10 | 11 | 10 | 15 |
| Independent, leans Republican | 8 | 9 | 7 | 6 | 9 | 10 | 10 | 10 | 13 | 14 | 13 | 12 | 13 | 12 | 12 | 19 | 11 |
| Weak Republican | 14 | 14 | 14 | 14 | 15 | 13 | 14 | 14 | 15 | 14 | 15 | 16 | 12 | 12 | 13 | 12 | 12 |
| Strong Republican | 14 | 16 | 15 | 11 | 10 | 10 | 9 | 9 | 13 | 14 | 11 | 13 | 12 | 17 | 13 | 14 | 16 |
| Total | 100 | 101 | 100 | 100 | 101 | 99 | 99 | 100 | 100 | 101 | 100 | 101 | 98 | 101 | 100 | 100 | 100 |
| (*N*) | 1,689 | 1,690 | 1,132 | 1,536 | 1,531 | 2,695 | 2,218 | 1,577 | 2,198 | 1,999 | 2,450 | 1,696 | 1,777 | 1,193 | 2,301 | 1,804 | (4,244)[a] |
| Apolitical | | | | | | | | 2 | 2 | 2 | 1 | 1 | 1 | b | b | c | c |
| Apolitical N | | | | | | | | 35 | 38 | 33 | 23 | 14 | 21 | 3 | 2 | c | c |

*Source:* Authors' analysis of ANES surveys.

## Table A8-2 Party Identification among Whites, 1952–2016 (Percent)

| Party identification[a] | 1952 | 1954 | 1956 | 1958 | 1960 | 1962 | 1964 | 1966 | 1968 | 1970 | 1972 | 1974 | 1976 | 1978 | 1980 | 1982 | 1984 | 1986 | 1988 | 1990 | 1992 | 1994 | 1996 | 1998 | 2000 | 2002 | 2004 | 2008 | 2012 | 2016 |
|---|---|---|---|---|---|---|---|---|---|---|---|---|---|---|---|---|---|---|---|---|---|---|---|---|---|---|---|---|---|---|
| Strong Democrat | 21 | 22 | 20 | 26 | 20 | 22 | 24 | 17 | 16 | 17 | 12 | 15 | 13 | 12 | 14 | 16 | 15 | 14 | 14 | 17 | 14 | 12 | 15 | 15 | 15 | 12 | 13 | 14 | 13 | 16 |
| Weak Democrat | 25 | 25 | 23 | 22 | 25 | 23 | 25 | 27 | 25 | 22 | 25 | 20 | 23 | 24 | 23 | 24 | 18 | 21 | 16 | 19 | 17 | 19 | 19 | 18 | 14 | 16 | 12 | 14 | 10 | 12 |
| Independent, leans Democrat | 10 | 9 | 6 | 7 | 6 | 8 | 9 | 9 | 10 | 11 | 12 | 13 | 11 | 14 | 12 | 11 | 11 | 10 | 10 | 11 | 14 | 12 | 13 | 14 | 15 | 14 | 17 | 17 | 15 | 11 |
| Independent, no partisan leaning | 6 | 7 | 9 | 8 | 9 | 8 | 8 | 12 | 11 | 13 | 13 | 15 | 15 | 14 | 14 | 11 | 11 | 12 | 12 | 11 | 12 | 10 | 8 | 11 | 13 | 8 | 8 | 12 | 10 | 14 |
| Independent, leans Republican | 7 | 6 | 9 | 5 | 7 | 7 | 6 | 8 | 10 | 9 | 11 | 9 | 11 | 11 | 11 | 9 | 13 | 13 | 15 | 13 | 14 | 13 | 12 | 12 | 14 | 15 | 13 | 13 | 22 | 13 |
| Weak Republican | 14 | 15 | 14 | 17 | 14 | 17 | 14 | 16 | 16 | 16 | 14 | 15 | 16 | 14 | 16 | 16 | 17 | 17 | 15 | 16 | 16 | 16 | 17 | 18 | 14 | 17 | 15 | 15 | 13 | 14 |
| Strong Republican | 14 | 13 | 16 | 12 | 17 | 13 | 12 | 11 | 11 | 10 | 11 | 9 | 10 | 9 | 9 | 11 | 14 | 12 | 16 | 11 | 12 | 17 | 15 | 11 | 14 | 17 | 21 | 16 | 17 | 21 |
| Apolitical | 2 | 2 | 2 | 3 | 1 | 3 | 1 | 1 | 1 | 1 | 1 | 3 | 1 | 3 | 2 | 2 | 2 | 2 | 1 | 1 | 1 | 1 | 1 | 2 | 1 | 1 | a | a | b | b |
| Total | 99 | 99 | 99 | 100 | 99 | 101 | 99 | 101 | 100 | 99 | 99 | 99 | 100 | 101 | 101 | 100 | 101 | 101 | 99 | 99 | 100 | 100 | 100 | 101 | 100 | 100 | 99 | 101 | 100 | 101 |
| *N* | 1,615 | 1,015 | (1,610)[b] | (1,638)[b] | (1,739)[b] | 1,168 | (1,394)[b] | 1,131 | 1,131 | 1,387 | 1,395 | 2,397 | (2,246)[b] | (2,490)[b] | (1,405) | (1,248) | (1,931) | (1,798) | (1,693) | (1,663) | (2,702) | (1,510) | (1,451) | (1,091) | (1,404) | (1,129) | (859) | (1,824) | (1,449) | 2,917 |

*Source:* Authors' analysis of ANES surveys.

[a]The percentage supporting another party has not been presented; it usually totals less than 1 percent and never totals more than 1 percent.

[b]Numbers are weighted.

## Table A8-3 Party Identification among Blacks, 1952–2016 (Percent)

| Party identification[a] | 1952 | 1954 | 1956 | 1958 | 1960 | 1962 | 1964 | 1966 | 1968 | 1970 | 1972 | 1974 | 1976 | 1978 | 1980 | 1982 | 1984 | 1986 | 1988 | 1990 | 1992 | 1994 | 1996 | 1998 | 2000 | 2002 | 2004 | 2008 | 2012 | 2016 |
|---|---|---|---|---|---|---|---|---|---|---|---|---|---|---|---|---|---|---|---|---|---|---|---|---|---|---|---|---|---|---|
| Strong Democrat | 30% | 24% | 27% | 32% | 25% | 35% | 52% | 30% | 56% | 41% | 36% | 40% | 34% | 37% | 45 | 53 | 32 | 42 | 39 | 40 | 40 | 38 | 43 | 48 | 47 | 53 | 30 | 47 | 53 | 52 |
| Weak Democrat | 22 | 29 | 23 | 19 | 19 | 25 | 22 | 31 | 29 | 34 | 31 | 26 | 36 | 29 | 27 | 26 | 31 | 30 | 24 | 23 | 24 | 23 | 22 | 23 | 21 | 16 | 30 | 23 | 17 | 19 |
| Independent, leans Democratic | 10 | 6 | 5 | 7 | 7 | 4 | 8 | 11 | 7 | 7 | 8 | 15 | 14 | 15 | 9 | 12 | 14 | 12 | 18 | 16 | 14 | 20 | 16 | 12 | 14 | 17 | 20 | 15 | 17 | 10 |
| Independent, no partisan leaning | 4 | 5 | 7 | 4 | 16 | 6 | 6 | 14 | 3 | 12 | 12 | 12 | 8 | 9 | 7 | 5 | 11 | 7 | 6 | 8 | 12 | 8 | 10 | 7 | 10 | 6 | 12 | 9 | 5 | 13 |
| Independent, leans Republican | 4 | 6 | 1 | 4 | 4 | 2 | 1 | 2 | 1 | 1 | 3 | [a] | 1 | 2 | 3 | 1 | 6 | 2 | 5 | 7 | 3 | 4 | 5 | 3 | 4 | 2 | 5 | 3 | 7 | 1 |
| Weak Republican | 8 | 5 | 12 | 11 | 9 | 7 | 5 | 7 | 1 | 4 | 4 | [a] | 2 | 3 | 2 | 2 | 1 | 2 | 5 | 3 | 3 | 2 | 3 | 3 | 3 | 4 | 2 | 1 | 0 | 2 |
| Strong Republican | 5 | 11 | 7 | 7 | 7 | 6 | 2 | 2 | 1 | 0 | 4 | 3 | 2 | 3 | 3 | 0 | 2 | 2 | 1 | 2 | 2 | 3 | 1 | 1 | 0 | 2 | 1 | 1 | 1 | 3 |
| Apolitical | 17 | 15 | 18 | 16 | 14 | 15 | 4 | 3 | 3 | 1 | 2 | 4 | 1 | 2 | 4 | 1 | 2 | 2 | 3 | 2 | 2 | 3 | 0 | 2 | 1 | [a] | [a] | [a] | [b] | [b] |
| Total | 100% | 101% | 100% | 100% | 101% | 100% | 100% | 100% | 101% | 100% | 100% | 100% | 99% | 100% | 100 | 100 | 99 | 99 | 101 | 101 | 100 | 101 | 100 | 99 | 100 | 100 | 100 | 99 | 100 | 100 |
| *(N)* | 171 | 101 | 146 | (161)[b] | (171)[b] | 110 | 156 | 132 | 149 | 157 | 267 | (224)[b] | (290)[b] | 230 | (187) | (148) | (247) | (322) | (267) | (270) | (317) | (203) | (200) | (149) | (225) | (161) | (193) | (281) | (124) | (460) |

*Source:* Authors' analysis of ANES surveys.

*Note:* The percentage supporting another party has not been presented; it usually totals less than 1 percent and never totals more than 1 percent.

[a]Less than 1 percent.

[b]Numbers are weighted.

## Table A8-4 White Major-Party Voters Who Voted Democratic for President, by Party Identification, 1952–2016 (Percent)

| Party Identification | 1952 | 1956 | 1960 | 1964 | 1968 | 1972 | 1976 | 1980 | 1984 | 1988 | 1992 | 1996 | 2000 | 2004 | 2008 | 2012 | 2016 |
|---|---|---|---|---|---|---|---|---|---|---|---|---|---|---|---|---|---|
| Strong Democrat | 82 | 85 | 91 | 94 | 89 | 66 | 88 | 87 | 88 | 93 | 96 | 98 | 96 | 97 | 92 | 98 | 95 |
| Weak Democrat | 61 | 63 | 70 | 81 | 66 | 44 | 72 | 59 | 63 | 68 | 80 | 88 | 81 | 78 | 83 | 82 | 75 |
| Independent, leans Democratic | 60 | 65 | 89 | 89 | 62 | 58 | 73 | 57 | 77 | 86 | 92 | 91 | 72 | 88 | 8 | 86 | 88 |
| Independent, no partisan leanings | 18 | 15 | 50 | 75 | 28 | 26 | 41 | 23 | 21 | 35 | 63 | 39 | 44 | 54 | 50 | 42 | 36 |
| Independent, leans Republican | 7 | 6 | 13 | 25 | 5 | 11 | 15 | 13 | 5 | 13 | 14 | 26 | 15 | 13 | 17 | 11 | 8 |
| Weak Republican | 4 | 7 | 11 | 40 | 10 | 9 | 22 | 5 | 6 | 16 | 18 | 21 | 16 | 10 | 10 | 14 | 17 |
| Strong Republican | 2 | [a] | 2 | 9 | 3 | 2 | 3 | 4 | 2 | 2 | 2 | 3 | 1 | 3 | 2 | 4 | 2 |

*Source:* Authors' analysis of ANES surveys.

[a]Less than 1 percent.

**Table A8-5 Approval of Incumbent's Handling of the Economy among Partisan Groups, 1984–2016 (Percent)**

| Year | Attitudes toward handling of the economy | Strong Democrat | Weak Democrat | Independent, leans Democrat | Independent | Independent, leans Republican | Weak Republican | Strong Republican | Total |
|---|---|---|---|---|---|---|---|---|---|
| 1984 | Approve | 17 | 41 | 32 | 68 | 84 | 86 | 95 | 58 |
| | Disapprove | 83 | 59 | 68 | 32 | 16 | 14 | 5 | 42 |
| | Total | 100 | 100 | 100 | 100 | 100 | 100 | 100 | 100 |
| | (*N*) | 309 | 367 | 207 | 179 | 245 | 277 | 249 | 1,833 |
| 1988 | Approve | 19 | 35 | 32 | 57 | 76 | 79 | 92 | 54 |
| | Disapprove | 81 | 65 | 68 | 43 | 24 | 21 | 8 | 46 |
| | Total | 100 | 100 | 100 | 100 | 100 | 100 | 100 | 100 |
| | (*N*) | 337 | 332 | 229 | 185 | 262 | 262 | 269 | 1,876 |
| 1992 | Approve | 3 | 9 | 6 | 9 | 31 | 34 | 66 | 20 |
| | Disapprove | 97 | 91 | 94 | 91 | 69 | 66 | 34 | 80 |
| | Total | 100 | 100 | 100 | 100 | 100 | 100 | 100 | 100 |
| | (*N*) | 425 | 445 | 340 | 267 | 310 | 347 | 266 | 2,401 |
| 1996 | Approve | 96 | 82 | 76 | 58 | 46 | 49 | 30 | 66 |
| | Disapprove | 4 | 18 | 24 | 42 | 54 | 50 | 70 | 34 |
| | Total | 100 | 100 | 100 | 100 | 100 | 100 | 100 | 100 |
| | (*N*) | 310 | 325 | 228 | 131 | 188 | 263 | 209 | 1,655 |

| Year | Attitudes toward handling of the economy | Strong Democrat | Weak Democrat | Independent, leans Democrat | Independent | Independent, leans Republican | Weak Republican | Strong Republican | Total |
|---|---|---|---|---|---|---|---|---|---|
| 2000 | Approve | 95 | 90 | 84 | 73 | 60 | 70 | 47 | 77 |
| | Disapprove | 5 | 10 | 16 | 27 | 40 | 30 | 53 | 23 |
| | Total | 100 | 100 | 100 | 100 | 100 | 100 | 100 | 100 |
| | (*N*) | 342 | 265 | 264 | 198 | 206 | 184 | 200 | 1,659 |
| 2004 | Approve | 5 | 18 | 10 | 34 | 68 | 72 | 89 | 40 |
| | Disapprove | 95 | 82 | 90 | 66 | 32 | 28 | 11 | 60 |
| | Total | 100 | 100 | 100 | 100 | 100 | 100 | 100 | 100 |
| | (*N*) | 197 | 176 | 204 | 107 | 139 | 141 | 194 | 1,158 |
| 2008 | Approve | 4 | 7 | 5 | 16 | 27 | 25 | 58 | 18 |
| | Disapprove | 96 | 93 | 95 | 84 | 73 | 75 | 42 | 82 |
| | Total | 100 | 100 | 100 | 100 | 100 | 100 | 100 | 100 |
| | (*N*) | 428 | 338 | 381 | 240 | 255 | 274 | 291 | 2,208 |
| 2012 | Approve | 98 | 89 | 89 | 64 | 36 | 22 | 8 | 64 |
| | Disapprove | 2 | 11 | 11 | 36 | 64 | 78 | 92 | 36 |
| | Total | 100 | 100 | 100 | 100 | 100 | 100 | 100 | 100 |
| | (*N*) | 287 | 167 | 176 | 74 | 129 | 116 | 173 | 1,122 |
| 2016 | Approve | 93 | 75 | 79 | 44 | 21 | 29 | 10 | 53 |
| | Disapprove | 7 | 25 | 21 | 56 | 79 | 71 | 90 | 47 |
| | Total | 100 | 100 | 100 | 100 | 100 | 100 | 100 | 100 |
| | (*N*) | 896 | 582 | 460 | 606 | 470 | 499 | 691 | 4,221 |

*Source:* Authors' analysis of ANES surveys.

*Note:* Numbers are weighted.

**Table A8-6 Approval of Incumbent's Handling of the Economy among Partisan Groups, 1984–1996 (Percent)**

| | | Party Identification | | | | | | | |
|---|---|---|---|---|---|---|---|---|---|
| Year | Attitudes toward handling of the economy | Strong Democrat | Weak Democrat | Independent, leans Democrat | Independent | Independent, leans Republican | Weak Republican | Strong Republican | Total |
| 1984 | Approve | 17 | 41 | 32 | 68 | 84 | 86 | 95 | 58 |
| | Disapprove | 83 | 59 | 68 | 32 | 16 | 14 | 5 | 42 |
| | Total | 100 | 100 | 100 | 100 | 100 | 100 | 100 | 100 |
| | (*N*) | (309) | (367) | (207) | (179) | (245) | (277) | (249) | (1,833) |
| 1988 | Approve | 19 | 35 | 32 | 57 | 76 | 79 | 92 | 54 |
| | Disapprove | 81 | 65 | 68 | 43 | 24 | 21 | 8 | 46 |
| | Total | 100 | 100 | 100 | 100 | 100 | 100 | 100 | 100 |
| | (*N*) | (337) | (332) | (229) | 1(85) | (262) | (262) | (269) | (1,876) |
| 1992[a] | Approve | 3 | 9 | 6 | 9 | 31 | 34 | 66 | 20 |
| | Disapprove | 97 | 91 | 94 | 91 | 69 | 66 | 34 | 80 |
| | Total | 100 | 100 | 100 | 100 | 100 | 100 | 100 | 100 |
| | (*N*) | (425) | (445) | (340) | (267) | (310) | (347) | (266) | (2,401) |
| 1996[a] | Approve | 96 | 82 | 76 | 58 | 46 | 49 | 30 | 66 |
| | Disapprove | 4 | 18 | 24 | 42 | 54 | 50 | 70 | 34 |
| | Total | 100 | 100 | 100 | 100 | 100 | 100 | 100 | 100 |
| | (*N*) | (310) | (325) | (228) | (131) | (188) | (263) | (209) | (1,655) |

*Source:* Authors' analysis of ANES surveys.

[a]Numbers are weighted.

**Table A8-7 Balance-of-Issues Positions among Partisan Groups, 1976–2016 (Percent)**

| Year | Issue positions closer to . . . | Strong Democrat | Weak Democrat | Independent, leans Democrat | Independent | Independent, leans Republican | Weak Republican | Strong Republican | Total |
|---|---|---|---|---|---|---|---|---|---|
| 1976 | Democratic candidate | 28 | 27 | 22 | 15 | 12 | 9 | 3 | 18 |
| | Neutral | 32 | 26 | 37 | 29 | 27 | 23 | 27 | 29 |
| | Republican candidate | 39 | 47 | 40 | 55 | 61 | 67 | 69 | 53 |
| | Total | 99 | 100 | 99 | 99 | 100 | 99 | 99 | 100 |
| | (*N*) | (422) | (655) | (336) | (416) | (277) | (408) | (254) | (2,778) |
| 1980 | Democratic candidate | 26 | 23 | 27 | 20 | 12 | 10 | 9 | 19 |
| | Neutral | 81 | 65 | 68 | 43 | 40 | 43 | 31 | 37 |
| | Republican candidate | 40 | 40 | 40 | 37 | 48 | 48 | 60 | 43 |
| | Total | 100 | 100 | 100 | 100 | 100 | 101 | 100 | 99 |
| | (*N*) | (245) | (317) | (161) | (176) | (150) | (202) | (127) | (1,378) |
| 1984 | Democratic candidate | 57 | 49 | 59 | 35 | 23 | 29 | 14 | 39 |
| | Neutral | 32 | 37 | 28 | 48 | 46 | 40 | 39 | 38 |
| | Republican candidate | 11 | 14 | 13 | 17 | 32 | 32 | 47 | 23 |
| | Total | 100 | 100 | 100 | 100 | 101 | 101 | 100 | 100 |
| | (*N*) | 331 | 390 | (215) | 213 | 248 | 295 | 256 | 1,948 |

*(Continued)*

**Table A8-7** (Continued)

| Year | Issue positions closer to . . . | Strong Democrat | Weak Democrat | Independent, leans Democrat | Independent | Independent, leans Republican | Weak Republican | Strong Republican | Total |
|---|---|---|---|---|---|---|---|---|---|
| 1988 | Democratic candidate | 49 | 36 | 50 | 33 | 21 | 21 | 11 | 32 |
| | Neutral | 34 | 40 | 38 | 48 | 46 | 43 | 35 | 40 |
| | Republican candidate | 17 | 24 | 12 | 19 | 33 | 36 | 53 | 29 |
| | Total | 100 | 100 | 100 | 100 | 100 | 100 | 99 | 101 |
| | (*N*) | (355) | (359) | (240) | (215) | (270) | (281) | (279) | (1,999) |
| 1992 | Democratic candidate | 40 | 36 | 30 | 26 | 13 | 13 | 9 | 25 |
| | Neutral | 55 | 57 | 65 | 70 | 74 | 77 | 74 | 67 |
| | Republican candidate | 5 | 7 | 4 | 5 | 13 | 11 | 17 | 9 |
| | Total | 100 | 100 | 99 | 101 | 100 | 101 | 100 | 101 |
| | (*N*) | (380) | (389) | (313) | (235) | (283) | (335) | (238) | (2,192) |
| 1996 | Democratic candidate | 44 | 27 | 35 | 17 | 13 | 9 | 1 | 22 |
| | Neutral | 27 | 36 | 34 | 43 | 27 | 23 | 14 | 29 |
| | Republican candidate | 30 | 37 | 31 | 40 | 60 | 68 | 85 | 49 |
| | Total | 101 | 100 | 100 | 100 | 100 | 100 | 100 | 100 |
| | (*N*) | (313) | (333) | (229) | (140) | (195) | (268) | (217) | (2,696) |

| Year | Issue positions closer to . . . | Strong Democrat | Weak Democrat | Independent, leans Democrat | Independent | Independent, leans Republican | Weak Republican | Strong Republican | Total |
|---|---|---|---|---|---|---|---|---|---|
| 2000 | Democratic candidate | 30 | 26 | 25 | 20 | 8 | 10 | 2 | 19 |
| | Neutral | 47 | 48 | 46 | 49 | 40 | 33 | 25 | 43 |
| | Republican candidate | 23 | 25 | 29 | 31 | 51 | 57 | 73 | 38 |
| | Total | 100 | 101 | 100 | 100 | 99 | 100 | 100 | 100 |
| | (*N*) | (188) | (161) | (157) | (113) | (134) | (101) | (99) | (953) |
| 2004 | Democratic candidate | 72 | 55 | 57 | 40 | 19 | 21 | 9 | 40 |
| | Neutral | 8 | 11 | 9 | 10 | 9 | 6 | 5 | 8 |
| | Republican candidate | 21 | 33 | 34 | 50 | 73 | 73 | 86 | 52 |
| | Total | 100 | 99 | 101 | 100 | 100 | 99 | 100 | 100 |
| | (*N*) | (168) | (157) | (180) | (100) | (124) | (136) | (179) | (1,046) |
| 2008a | Democratic candidate | 60 | 46 | 47 | 28 | 16 | 14 | 8 | 34 |
| | Neutral | 6 | 9 | 14 | 10 | 17 | 9 | (2) | 9 |
| | Republican candidate | 34 | 45 | 40 | 63 | 67 | 77 | 90 | 56 |
| | Total | 100 | 100 | 101 | 101 | 100 | 100 | 99 | 99 |
| | (*N*) | (219) | (163) | (203) | (135) | (143) | (148) | (142) | (1,153) |

*(Continued)*

**Table A8-7** (Continued)

| Year | Issue positions closer to . . . | Strong Democrat | Weak Democrat | Independent, leans Democrat | Independent | Independent, leans Republican | Weak Republican | Strong Republican | Total |
|---|---|---|---|---|---|---|---|---|---|
| 2012 | Democratic candidate | 47 | 36 | 29 | 22 | 6 | 7 | 5 | 22 |
| | Neutral | 16 | 18 | 17 | 10 | 10 | 5 | 3 | 11 |
| | Republican candidate | 37 | 46 | 54 | 68 | 85 | 88 | 93 | 67 |
| | Total | 100 | 100 | 100 | 100 | 100 | 100 | 100 | 100 |
| | (*N*) | 307 | 214 | 282 | 182 | 342 | 210 | 258 | (1,795) |
| 2016 | Democratic candidate | 64 | 48 | 56 | 34 | 13 | 13 | 7 | 35 |
| | Neutral | 14 | 19 | 19 | 24 | 11 | 17 | 6 | 16 |
| | Republican candidate | 22 | 33 | 24 | 42 | 76 | 70 | 87 | 49 |
| | Total | 100 | 100 | 99 | 100 | 100 | 100 | 100 | 100 |
| | (*N*) | 902 | 587 | 462 | 620 | 472 | 501 | 696 | 4242 |

*Source:* Authors' analysis of ANES surveys.

*Note:* In the one instance in which the category included fewer than ten observations, we show the total number of people in that category in brackets.

[a]The Democratic category on the condensed balance-of-issues measure includes any respondent who is at least slightly Democratic; the Republican category includes any respondent who is at least slightly Republican. The neutral category is the same as the neutral category on the seven-point issue scale (see Table 6-5). In 2008 the issue questions that were used to form the balance-of-issues scale were asked of a randomly selected half-sample.

[b]Numbers are weighted.

## Table A8-8 Approval of Incumbent's Handling of Job, by Party Identification, 1972–2016 (Percent)

| | Party Identification | | | | | | |
|---|---|---|---|---|---|---|---|
| Year | Strong Democrat | Weak Democrat | Independent, Leans Democrat | Independent | Independent, Leans Republican | Weak Republican | Strong Republican |
| 2016 | 93 | 79 | 81 | 47 | 20 | 26 | 7 |
| 2012 | 97 | 80 | 79 | 49 | 18 | 21 | 6 |
| 2008 | 3 | 11 | 6 | 26 | 46 | 47 | 74 |
| 2004 | 6 | 26 | 23 | 39 | 78 | 89 | 98 |
| 2000 | 92 | 88 | 81 | 65 | 49 | 52 | 23 |
| 1996 | 98 | 89 | 85 | 66 | 45 | 49 | 18 |
| 1992 | 12 | 28 | 20 | 32 | 65 | 71 | 91 |
| 1988 | 24 | 43 | 37 | 70 | 82 | 83 | 94 |
| 1984 | 22 | 48 | 32 | 76 | 90 | 93 | 96 |
| 1980 | 73 | 54 | 44 | 35 | 19 | 19 | 9 |
| 1976 | 24 | 55 | 46 | 69 | 87 | 85 | 96 |
| 1972 | 38 | 65 | 52 | 73 | 87 | 92 | 94 |

*Source:* Authors' analysis of ANES surveys.

*Note:* To approximate the numbers upon which these percentages are based, see Tables 8-2, 8-3, A8-2, and A8-3.

# NOTES

## INTRODUCTION

1. For an analysis of the strategies in this election, see John H. Kessel, *The Goldwater Coalition: Republican Strategies in 1964* (Indianapolis: Bobbs-Merrill, 1968).
2. See, for example, Benjamin Ginsberg and Martin Shefter, *Politics by Other Means: The Importance of Elections in America* (New York: Basic Books, 1990); and Matthew A. Crenson and Benjamin Ginsberg, *Downsizing Democracy: How America Sidelined Its Citizens and Privatized Its Public* (Baltimore: Johns Hopkins University Press, 2002).
3. U.S. Department of Commerce, Bureau of Economic Analysis, "Gross Domestic Product: Percent Change from Preceding Period," July 28, 2017, https://www.bea.gov/national/xls/gdpchg.xls.
4. For information about corporate profits, see the Bureau of Economic Analysis's National Economic Accounts, https://www.bea.gov/national. For Historical Dow Jones Industrial Average data, see the Federal Reserve Bank of St. Louis, Economic Research, https://fred.stlouisfed.org/series/DJIA.
5. The Federal Reserve Bank of St. Louis, Economic Research provides data on the civilian unemployment rate, https://fred.stlouisfed.org/series/UNRATE, the long-term unemployment rate, https://fred.stlouisfed.org/series/LNU03025703, and labor force participation, https://fred.stlouisfed.org/graph/?graph_id=109599&category_id=.
6. See Thomas Piketty and Emmanuel Saez, "Income Inequality in the United States, 1913–1998, *Quarterly Journal of Economics*, 118 (2003): 1-39, and http://eml.berkeley.edu/~saez/TabFig2015prel.xls for updated data.
7. Silvio Berlusconi served as Italian prime minister in four governments between 1994 and 2011. He was later convicted of tax fraud. Once estimated by *Forbes* to be the 169th richest person in the world, Berlusconi had built his fortune as an Italian media mogul and would later own one of soccer's most successful teams, A.C. Milan. See "Silvio Berlusconi and Family," *Forbes*, https://www.forbes.com/profile/silvio-berlusconi/. For a recent treatment of populism, see Jan-Werner Müller, *What Is Populism?* (Philadelphia, Pa.: University of Pennsylvania Press, 2016).
8. Quoted from a June 28, 2016, speech in Monessen, Pennsylvania, in "Clinton vs. Trump: Where They Stand on Economic Policy Issues," *The Wall Street Journal*, http://graphics.wsj.com/elections/2016/donald-trump-hillary-clinton-on-the-economy/.
9. Whereas the Republican Party of Abraham Lincoln in the 1860s and William McKinley in the 1890s supported protectionism in the form of higher tariffs, the Republican Party of Ronald Reagan and George H. W. Bush in the 1980s espoused free trade; see Michael Wilson, "The North American Free Trade Agreement: Ronald Reagan's Vision Realized," *The Heritage Foundation*, November 23, 1993, http://www.heritage.org/trade/report/the-north-american-free-trade-agreement-ronald-reagans-vision-realized, and Daniel Griswold, "Reagan Embraced Free Trade and Immigration," *The Cato Institute*, June 24, 2004,

https://www.cato.org/publications/commentary/reagan-embraced-free-trade-immigration. Passed during the administration of President Bill Clinton, a Democrat, The North American Free Trade Agreement (NAFTA) was passed through Congress with more Republican than Democratic votes. "In the House, NAFTA passed 234-200; 132 Republicans and 102 Democrats voted in favor of it. The Senate approved NAFTA 61-38, with the backing of 34 Republicans and 27 Democrats," according to Glenn Kessler, "History Lesson: More Republicans than Democrats Supported NAFTA," *Washington Post*, May 9, 2016, https://www.washingtonpost.com/news/fact-checker/wp/2016/05/09/history-lesson-more-republicans-than-democrats-supported-nafta/?utm_term=.6f3f9575b725.

10. Aaron Blake, "Trump Warns GOP on Immigration: 'They're Taking Your Jobs,'" *Washington Post*, March 6, 2014, https://www.washingtonpost.com/news/post-politics/wp/2014/03/06/trump-warns-gop-on-immigration-theyre-taking-your-jobs/?utm_term=.669d7a102ecf.
11. "Full Text: Donald Trump Announces a Presidential Bid," *Washington Post*, June 16, 2015, https://www.washingtonpost.com/news/post-politics/wp/2015/06/16/full-text-donald-trump-announces-a-presidential-bid/?utm_term=.5870ba9cf2f7. Trump's desire to build a wall on the Mexican border elicited unusually pointed criticism from Pope Francis, who said "a person who thinks only about building walls, wherever they may be, and not building bridges, is not Christian." In turn Trump called the Pope's comments "disgraceful." See Ben Jacobs, "Donald Trump Calls Pope Francis 'Disgraceful' for Questioning his Faith," *The Guardian*, February 18, 2016, https://www.theguardian.com/us-news/2016/feb/18/donald-trump-pope-francis-christian-wall-mexico-border. As we will see in Chapter 5, this exchange did not appear to affect Trump's level of support from white Catholics.
12. Quoted from a January 11, 2016, speech in Des Moines, Iowa, in "Clinton vs. Trump: Where They Stand on Economic Policy Issues."
13. Nick Timiraos, "Hillary Clinton Lays Out Economic Plan, while Criticizing Donald Trump's," *Wall Street Journal*, August 11, 2016, https://www.wsj.com/articles/clinton-to-criticize-trumps-economic-plan-as-self-serving-1470913205.
14. Louise Liu, "Here's Where Hillary Clinton and Donald Trump Stand on Immigration," *Business Insider*, September 25, 2016, http://www.businessinsider.com/hillary-clinton-and-donald-trump-immigration-2016-9.
15. Alison Kodjak, "Platform Check: Trump and Clinton on Health Care," *NPR*, November 2, 2016, http://www.npr.org/2016/11/02/500371785/platform-check-trump-and-clinton-on-health-care.
16. "Trump and Clinton Finish with Historically Poor Images," *Gallup*, November 8, 2016, http://www.gallup.com/poll/197231/trump-clinton-finish-historically-poor-images.aspx.
17. Tessa Berenson, "Reminder: The House Voted to Repeal Obamacare More than 50 Times," *Time*, March 24, 2017, http://time.com/4712725/ahca-house-repeal-votes-obamacare/.
18. Erin Kelly, Eliza Collins, and Deirdre Shesgreen, "Republicans Give Up on Obamacare Repeal Bill, Move on to Other Issues," *USA Today*, March 24, 2017, https://www.usatoday.com/story/news/politics/2017/03/24/house-obamacare-repeal-vote/99573690/.
19. Austin Ramzy, "McCain's Vote Provides Dramatic Moment in 7-Year Battle Over Obamacare," *New York Times*, July 28, 2017, https://www.nytimes.com/2017/07/28/us/politics/john-mccain-vote-trump-obamacare.html. Jenna Johnson, "Trump's Grand Promises to 'Very, Very Quickly' Repeal Obamacare Run into Reality," *Washington Post*, July 18, 2017, https://www.washingtonpost.com/politics/trumps-grand-promises-to-very-very-quickly-repeal-obamacare-run-into-reality/2017/07/18/91b5f220-6bd3-11e7-9c15-177740635e83_story.html?utm_term=.69b8ea32b9be.
20. Although the repeal and possible replacement of "Obamacare" was operating under a special provision in the Senate that required only a simple majority to pass (and hence fifty

votes and the vice president's tie-breaking vote at minimum), most other legislation in the Senate needs a sixty-vote supermajority to end any proposed filibuster to pass.

21. See, for one example, Lee Drutman, "Donald Trump Will Dramatically Realign America's Political Parties," *Foreign Policy*, November 11, 2016, http://foreignpolicy.com/2016/11/11/why-democrats-should-abandon-angry-working-class-whites/.
22. Lanny J. Davis, "The Obama Realignment," *Wall Street Journal*, November 6, 2008, A19.
23. Paul R. Abramson, John H. Aldrich, and David W. Rohde, *Change and Continuity in the 2008 and 2010 Elections* (Washington, D.C.: CQ Press, 2012), 284.
24. Kevin P. Phillips, *The Emerging Republican Majority* (New Rochelle, N.Y.: Arlington House, 1969).
25. Phil Gailey, "Republicans Start to Worry about Signs of Slippage," *New York Times*, August 25, 1988, E5.
26. For a discussion of the history of this concept, see Theodore Rosenof, *Realignment: The Theory that Changed the Way We Think about American Politics* (Lanham, Md.: Rowman and Littlefield, 2003).
27. V. O. Key, Jr., "A Theory of Critical Elections," *Journal of Politics* 17 (February 1955): 3–18.
28. V. O. Key, Jr., "Secular Realignment and the Party System," *Journal of Politics* 21 (May 1959): 198–210.
29. These states were, and still are, the most heavily Democratic states. Both voted Republican in seventeen of the eighteen presidential elections between 1856 and 1924, voting Democratic only when the Republican Party was split in 1912 by Theodore Roosevelt's Progressive Party candidacy. For a discussion of partisan change in the New England states, see Chapter 3.
30. V. O. Key, Jr., *Parties, Politics, and Pressure Groups*, 5th ed. (New York: Thomas Y. Crowell, 1964), 186.
31. In addition to the eleven states that formed the Confederacy (Alabama, Arkansas, Florida, Georgia, Louisiana, Mississippi, North Carolina, South Carolina, Tennessee, Texas, and Virginia), Delaware, Kentucky, Maryland, and Missouri were slave states. The fifteen free states in 1848 were Connecticut, Illinois, Indiana, Iowa, Maine, Massachusetts, Michigan, New Hampshire, New Jersey, New York, Ohio, Pennsylvania, Rhode Island, Vermont, and Wisconsin. By 1860 three additional free states—California, Minnesota, and Oregon—had been admitted to the Union.
32. John H. Aldrich, *Why Parties? A Second Look* (Chicago: University of Chicago Press, 2011), 282–287.
33. Thomas G. Hansford and Brad T. Gomez, "Estimating the Electoral Effects of Voter Turnout," *American Political Science Review* 104 (May 2010): 268–288.
34. Byron E. Shafer, ed., *The End of Realignment? Interpreting American Electoral Eras* (Madison: University of Wisconsin Press, 1991). See, for example, Joel H. Silbey, "Beyond Realignment and Realignment Theory," 3–23; Everett Carll Ladd, "Like Waiting for Godot: The Uselessness of 'Realignment' for Studying Change in Contemporary American Politics," 24–36; and Byron E. Shafer, "The Notion of an Electoral Order: The Structure of Electoral Politics at the Accession of George Bush," 37–84. Shafer's book also contains an excellent bibliographical essay: Harry F. Bass, "Background to Debate: Reader's Guide and Bibliography," 141–178.
35. David R. Mayhew, *Electoral Realignments: A Critique of an American Genre* (New Haven, Conn.: Yale University Press, 2002).
36. Edward G. Carmines and James A. Stimson, *Issue Evolution: Race and the Transformation of American Politics* (Princeton, N.J.: Princeton University Press, 1989), 12–13.

37. Carmines and Stimson, *Issue Evolution*, 13.
38. Key, "Secular Realignment and the Party System," 198–199.
39. The theory of punctuated equilibrium was first developed by the evolutionary biologists and paleontologists Niles Eldredge and Stephen Jay Gould. See Niles Eldredge and Stephen Jay Gould, "Punctuated Equilibria: An Alternative to Phyletic Gradualism" in Thomas J. M. Schropf, ed., *Models of Paleobiology* (San Francisco: Freeman, Cooper and Company, 1972).
40. Carmines and Stimson, *Issue Evolution*, 13.
41. John H. Aldrich argues that the decline of local party machines, technological innovations—particularly, the advent of television—and the rise of a policy-motivated activist class allowed ambitious politicians to bypass the party organization and create "candidate-centered" campaigns. The result was the demise of the traditional "mass political party" (i.e., the party as organization), and in its place followed a new type of party, one that provides services (e.g., expertise and financial and in-kind resources) to its candidates. The emergent activist class also pressured the parties to democratize their presidential nomination systems. Reforms, such as the Democratic Party's McGovern-Fraser Commission, resulted in the proliferation of primaries as the main vehicle by which party nominees are chosen. See Aldrich, *Why Parties: A Second Look*, 255–292.
42. Aldrich, *Why Parties: A Second Look*, 263.
43. See Russell J. Dalton, Paul Allen Beck, and Scott C. Flanagan, "Electoral Change in Advanced Industrial Democracies," in *Electoral Change in Advanced Industrial Democracies: Realignment or Dealignment?* eds. Russell J. Dalton, Scott C. Flanagan, and Paul Allen Beck (Princeton, N.J.: Princeton University Press, 1984), 14.
44. Ronald Inglehart and Avram Hochstein, "Alignment and Dealignment of the Electorate in France and the United States," *Comparative Political Studies* 5 (October 1972): 343–372.
45. We estimated the distribution of major-party identifiers (i.e., excluding pure independents) in both the general public and among voters. In both cases we estimate approximately 53 percent identify with the Democratic Party.
46. Mark Hugo Lopez, Ana Gonzalez-Barrerra, Jens Manuel Krogstad, and Gustavo López, "Democrats Maintain Edge as Party 'More Concerned' for Latinos, but Views Similar to 2012," *Pew Hispanic Center*, October 11, 2016, http://www.pewhispanic.org/2016/10/11/democrats-maintain-edge-as-party-more-concerned-for-latinos-but-views-similar-to-2012/.
47. According to Michael P. McDonald, 230,585,915 Americans were eligible to vote. See McDonald, "2016 General Election Turnout Rates," United States Election Project, http://www.electproject.org/home/voter-turnout/voter-turnout-data. We say "on or before" November 8 because in 2016 about 38 percent of voters voted before election day.
48. Voters may also be influenced by random factors as well, but by their very nature, these random factors cannot be systematically explained.
49. For two excellent summaries of research on voting behavior, see Russell J. Dalton and Martin P. Wattenberg, "The Not So Simple Act of Voting," in *Political Science: The State of the Discipline II*, ed. Ada W. Finifter (Washington, D.C.: American Political Science Association, 1993), 193–218; and Morris P. Fiorina, "Parties, Participation, and Representation in America: Old Theories Face New Realities," in *Political Science: The State of the Discipline*, eds. Ira Katznelson and Helen V. Milner (New York: Norton, 2002), 511–541.
50. For a more extensive discussion of our arguments, see Paul R. Abramson, John H. Aldrich, and David W. Rohde, "Studying American Elections," in *The Oxford Handbook of American Elections and Political Behavior*, ed. Jan E. Leighley (New York: Oxford University Press, 2010), 700–715.

51. Paul F. Lazarsfeld, Bernard R. Berelson, and Hazel Gaudet, *The People's Choice: How the Voter Makes Up His Mind in a Presidential Campaign* (New York: Duell, Sloan, and Pearce, 1944), 27. See also Bernard R. Berelson, Paul F. Lazarsfeld, and William McPhee, *Voting: A Study of Opinion Formation in a Presidential Campaign* (Chicago: University of Chicago Press, 1954).
52. See Robert R. Alford, *Party and Society: The Anglo-American Democracies* (Chicago: Rand McNally, 1963); Richard F. Hamilton, *Class and Politics in the United States* (New York: Wiley, 1972); and Seymour Martin Lipset, *Political Man: The Social Bases of Politics*, exp. ed. (Baltimore: Johns Hopkins University Press, 1981). For a more recent book using the perspective, see Jeff Manza and Clem Brooks, *Social Cleavages and Political Change: Voter Alignments in U.S. Party Coalitions* (Oxford: Oxford University Press, 1999).
53. Angus Campbell et al., *The American Voter* (New York: Wiley, 1960). For a recent assessment of the contribution of *The American Voter*, see William G. Jacoby, "The American Voter," in Leighley, *Oxford Handbook of American Elections and Political Behavior*, 262–277.
54. The Michigan model conceptualizes party identification as the individual's enduring attachment to a political party. The theory contends that party identification is socialized early in life and remains stable throughout adulthood. Dissatisfied with this static view of party loyalties, Morris P. Fiorina reconceptualized party identification as "a running tally of retrospective evaluations of party promises and performance." Fiorina, *Retrospective Voting in American National Elections* (New Haven, Conn.: Yale University Press, 1981), 84. For a counterargument to Fiorina, see Larry M. Bartels, "Beyond the Running Tally: Partisan Bias in Political Perceptions," *Political Behavior* 24 (June 2002): 117–150.
55. Anthony Downs, *An Economic Theory of Democracy* (New York: Harper and Row, 1957); William H. Riker, *A Theory of Political Coalitions* (New Haven, Conn.: Yale University Press, 1962).
56. See, for example, William H. Riker and Peter C. Ordeshook, "A Theory of the Calculus of Voting," *American Political Science Review* 62 (March 1968): 25–32; John A. Ferejohn and Morris P. Fiorina, "The Paradox of Not Voting: A Decision Theocratic Analysis," *American Political Science Review* 68 (June 1974): 525–536; and Fiorina, *Retrospective Voting in American National Elections*. For an excellent introduction to American voting behavior that relies on a rational choice perspective, see Rebecca B. Morton, *Analyzing Elections* (New York: Norton, 2006).
57. For a more extensive discussion of the merits and limitations of these approaches, see Paul R. Abramson, John H. Aldrich, and David W. Rohde, "Studying American Elections," in Jan E. Leighley, ed. *The Oxford Handbook of American Elections and Political Behavior* (New York: Oxford University Press, 2010), 700–715.
58. Most of the respondents were interviewed before *and* after the election. Many of the questions we are interested in, such as whether people voted, how they voted for president, and how they voted for Congress, were asked in the survey conducted after the election.

    For this volume we elected to use both the face-to-face and web-based interviews, that is, the "full sample." We did not do this following the 2012 election. This decision was driven by evidence demonstrating that the full sample estimates in 2016 were not affected significantly by differences in "survey mode." Put differently, estimates based on the face-to-face and web-based interviews—at least with regard to the variables that most interest us—do not differ significantly from one another. By electing to use the full sample, we more than double our sample size, allowing us to make more precise contrasts between variables (about which, more later).
59. The 2002 midterm survey was conducted by telephone. The ANES has not conducted a midterm survey since then.

60. For an overview of how the ANES is currently constructed and its recent innovations in measurement, see the collection of essays found in John H. Aldrich and Kathleen M. McGraw, eds., *Improving Public Opinion Surveys: Interdisciplinary Innovation and the American National Election Studies* (Princeton, N.J.: Princeton University Press, 2012).
61. For a brief nontechnical introduction to polling, see Herbert Asher, *Polling and the Public: What Every Citizen Should Know*, 7th ed. (Washington, D.C.: CQ Press, 2007). For a more advanced discussion, see Herbert F. Weisberg, *The Total Survey Error Approach: A Guide to the New Science of Survey Research* (Chicago: University of Chicago Press, 2005).
62. For a brief discussion of the procedures used by the Survey Research Center, which conducted the surveys from 1952 to 2004, to carry out its sampling for in-person interviews, see Paul R. Abramson, *Political Attitudes in America: Formation and Change* (San Francisco: W. H. Freeman, 1983), 18–23. For a more detailed description of the design and implementation of the 2016 ANES election study, see http://www.electionstudies.org/studypages/anes_timeseries_2016/anes_timeseries_2016_ userguidecodebook.pdf.
63. For an excellent table that allows us to evaluate differences between two groups, see Leslie Kish, *Survey Sampling* (New York: Wiley, 1965), 580. Kish defines differences between two groups to be significant if the results are more than two standard errors apart.
64. For 2016—as well as for 1958, 1960, 1974, 1976, 1992, 1994, 1996, 1998, 2000, 2002, 2004, 2008, and 2012—a weighting procedure is necessary to obtain a representative result, and so we report the "weighted" number of cases.
65. There also were numerous state-level ballot measures—initiatives, referenda, and state constitutional amendments—for which to vote. Voters in California, Massachusetts, and Nevada voted to legalize marijuana for recreational use, and several other states, including Arkansas, Florida, and North Dakota, passed medical marijuana provisions.

## CHAPTER 1

1. Note that many states that have presidential primaries also hold primary elections for many other offices. Most of these primaries, such as for the U.S. House and Senate, select the actual nominees of the two parties for those offices. Thus the party leadership plays no direct role at all in selecting the party's candidates.
2. They have ceded control to the substantial majority of potential voters who are eligible to vote in primary elections. They have ceded effective control to the substantial minority who actually participate in those elections.
3. George H. W. Bush in 1992 faced one challenger, Patrick Buchanan, who did have an impact on the race, although Bush defeated him rather easily.
4. Gov. Jerry Brown (then, as in 2016, governor of California) did run as a third Democrat in 1980. Although obviously a formidable politician over a long career, and even though he was also a very serious threat for the Democratic nomination in 1976, he was much less formidable in 1980, picking up the nickname "Governor Moonbeam."
5. The five who had declared their candidacy, participated in at least one presidential "debate" in 2015, and withdrew in 2015 were: former Governor Rick Perry (Texas, and presidential candidate in 2012), who withdrew on September 11, 2015; Governor Scott Walker (Wisconsin), who withdrew on September 21; Governor Bobby Jindal (Louisiana), who withdrew on November 17; Senator Lindsey Graham (South Carolina), who withdrew on December 21; and former Governor George Pataki (New York), who withdrew on December 29.

6. Three others declared and dropped out in 2015: former Senator James Webb (Virginia), October 20; former Governor Lincoln Chafee (Rhode Island), October 23; and Lawrence Lessing (professor), November 2.
7. There are parallels among the approximately seventeen Republican candidate field in 2015 and the seventeen Democratic field in 1976. For analysis of the 1976 race in these terms, see John H. Aldrich, *Before the Convention: Strategies and Choices in Presidential Nomination Campaigns* (Chicago: University of Chicago Press, 1980). A *Politico* story from 2015 makes the direct comparison, between the 1972 and 2016 races: http://www.politico.com/magazine/story/2015/09/2016-election-1976-democratic-primary-213125.
8. She of course had been a U.S. senator (New York) before Obama appointed her to his cabinet as well as First Lady even earlier. She resigned as secretary of state to prepare to run for the presidency.
9. Joseph A. Schlesinger, *Ambition and Politics: Political Careers in the United States* (Chicago: Rand McNally, 1966); Joseph A. Schlesinger, *Political Parties and the Winning of Office* (Ann Arbor: University of Michigan Press, 1991).
10. Obama was of course constitutionally ineligible to run for a third term. Although Vice President Joe Biden could have run for president, and indeed considered it carefully, he eventually made an agonizing personal decision not to run in part due to the recent death of his son.
11. Unlike Hillary Clinton this year, many of the early cabinet members who became major candidates and, in a number of cases, presidential nominees (and even presidents) had not held major elective office previously.
12. Florida law, unlike that in some states, prohibits running for two offices in the same election. Florida, like a number of states, holds separate primaries for president and all other offices. Doing so allows the state legislature to choose what they perceive to be the most favorable date for selecting presidential delegates (which is usually early in the year, see the following) and then hold primary elections at a more timely date (usually much later) for other offices. The main cost to this strategy is the cost of running two primary elections.
13. In addition to the fifty states, also included are events for the District of Columbia, various territories, and for the Democrats, even Americans Living Abroad.
14. The Democratic Party requires some form of proportionality for all of its states. Florida and Ohio on the GOP side employed the state-wide plurality version of WTA. Perhaps not coincidentally each had a candidate from the state (in Florida's case there were two at the outset of campaign, but Bush withdrew, leaving Rubio as the Florida candidate; Kasich ran from a base in Ohio), and both had a large number of delegates, so WTA could make a very large impact on the race. Of course the candidate potentially advantaged under the rules would actually have to win the state to get that reward.
15. The Democrats have long prohibited WTA primaries, although the rules often fall well short of being truly proportional.
16. Theodore H. White, *The Making of the President, 1968* (New York: Pocket Books, 1970).
17. Ibid., 153.
18. He was helped in this effort by the fact that one-third of the delegates had been chosen in 1967, before Johnson's renomination faced serious opposition.
19. Zeke Miller, "*Time* Guide to Official Republican Nomination Calendar," October 2, 2015, http://time.com/4059030/republican-primary-calendar-2016-nomination-convention/.
20. Clinton actually held a majority of the delegates in light of the DC primary on June 14. However, superdelegates had begun to publicly declare, mostly for her, giving her assurances of a majority a few days in advance of the DC primary.

21. To be sure there were calls from supporters of Sanders in 2016, as of Clinton in 2008, to maintain their candidacies. Both the Clinton and Sanders campaigns, however, chose to slowly wind down the level of competition and effectively accept defeat. Sanders formally endorsed Clinton as nominee on July 12. For a discussion of the importance of superdelegates in 1984 and 2008, see Paul R. Abramson, John H. Aldrich, and David W. Rohde, *Change and Continuity in the 1984 Elections*, rev. ed. (Washington, D.C.: CQ Press, 1987), 25; Abramson, Aldrich, and Rohde, *Change and Continuity in the 2008 and 2010 Elections*, 30–33.

    Note that the Democratic National Committee passed a rule intended to apply in 2020 that balanced between the Clinton and Sanders camps, keeping the superdelegates more or less intact and thereby ensuring that the convention includes experienced party leadership but requiring that two-thirds of them vote in accordance with their state's primary or caucus results, thus binding them. The first aspect favored Clinton's position, the second Sanders's, although this outcome was the first choice of neither candidate. The Republican Party does have its own superdelegates, but it limits them to the Republican National Committee membership, per se, which is a much smaller proportion of the total convention delegations.
22. Phil Paolino, "Candidate Name Recognition and the Dynamics of the Pre-Primary Period of the Presidential Nomination Process" (PhD diss., Duke University, 1995).
23. In addition a second primary for other offices often attracts very few voters, especially in the absence of a hotly contested gubernatorial or senatorial contest.
24. John Aldrich, "The Invisible Primary and Its Effects on Democratic Choice," *PS: Political Science and Politics* 42 (2009): 33–38.
25. See Paul R. Abramson, John H. Aldrich, and David W. Rohde, *Change and Continuity in the 2000 and 2002 Elections* (Washington, D.C.: CQ Press, 2003), chap. 1, for more details on the nomination campaigns in 2000.
26. His now infamous post-Iowa victory "scream" is often attributed for this, but we think it more likely that his quite liberal standing was hurting him as more moderate Democrats, in the coming states, learned about him.
27. In retrospect asking candidates to share chances and even delegates to defeat a frontrunner before necessarily turning on one another to secure the single prize of presidential nomination may work in parlor games such as Risk but seems implausible in the case of seeking the most powerful office in the world.
28. John H. Aldrich, *Before the Convention: Strategies and Choices in Presidential Nomination Campaigns* (Chicago: University of Chicago Press, 1980); Larry M. Bartels, *Presidential Primaries and the Dynamics of Public Choice* (Princeton, N.J.: Princeton University Press, 1988).
29. EMILY's List, a group that supports female candidates, draws its name from an acronym of this observation.
30. Thomas E. Mann, "Money in the 2008 Elections: Bad News or Good?," July 1, 2008, https://www.brookings.edu/opinions/money-in-the-2008-elections-bad-news-or-good/.
31. Michael Muskal and Dan Morain, "Obama Raises $55 Million in February; Clinton Reports Surge in Funds," *Los Angeles Times*, March 7, 2008, http://articles.latimes.com/2008/mar/07/nation/na-money.
32. U.S. Court of Appeals for the District of Columbia Circuit, *Speechnow.org v. Federal Election Commission*, March 26, 2010.
33. Center for Responsive Politics, "What Are Independent Expenditures and Communications Costs?," January 29, 2014, http://www.opensecrets.org/pacs/indexpend.php?strID=C00490045&cycle=2012.

34. See, e.g., Christopher Hare and Keith T. Poole, "The Polarization of Contemporary American Politics," *Polity* 46, no. 3 (July 2014).
35. Morris P. Fiorina and Samuel J. Abrams, "Political Polarization in the American Public," *Annual Review of Political Science* 11 (2008): 563–588; Morris P. Fiorina and S. J. Abrams, *Disconnect: The Breakdown of Representation in American Politics*, vol. 11 (Norman: University of Oklahoma Press, 2012). See also our data in Chapter 6.
36. Alan I. Abramowitz and Kyle L. Saunders, "Is Polarization a Myth?" *Journal of Politics* 70, no. 2 (2008): 542–555.
37. Marc J. Hetherington, *Why Trust Matters: Declining Political Trust and the Demise of American Liberalism* (Princeton, N.J.: Princeton University Press, 2005); Marc J. Hetherington and Jason A. Husser, "How Trust Matters: The Changing Political Relevance of Political Trust," *American Journal of Political Science* 56, no. 2 (2012): 312–325; Shanto Iyengar, Gaurav Sood, and Yphtach Lelkes, "Affect, Not Ideology: A Social Identity Perspective on Polarization," *Public Opinion Quarterly* 76, no. 3 (2012): 405–431.
38. Gary C. Jacobson, "Partisan Polarization in Presidential Support: The Electoral Connection," *Congress and the Presidency: A Journal of Capital Studies* 30, no. 1 (2003): 1–36. See also Christopher Hare, David A. Armstrong, Ryan Bakker, Royce Carroll, and Keith T. Poole, "Using Bayesian Aldrich-McKelvey Scaling to Study Citizens' Ideological Preferences and Perceptions," *American Journal of Political Science* 59 (2015): 759–774, doi:10.1111/ajps.12151.
39. The ANES conducted a four-wave panel beginning in January 1980, and here we use wave 1: Interview P1 (wave 1) January 22–February 25; personal interview; 1,008 completed cases. We also use the 2016 ANES pilot study: Data collection was conducted between January 22 and January 28, 2016. The sample consisted of 1,200 individuals who were part of an opt-in Internet panel.
40. Chapter 6 includes reports and more details about candidate thermometer measures.
41. Democrat and Republican here are those who answered the first question in the standard battery of questions about partisan identification used by the ANES as "Democrat" or as "Republican," with other responses including "independent" and so on. See Chapter 8 and note these are equivalent to using "strong" and "weak" Democratic and Republican responses. The differences are in absolute value, thus measuring the size of the gap between the two sets of partisans' responses.
42. Abramson, Aldrich, and Rohde, *Change and Continuity in the 2000 and 2002 Elections*.
43. We will let mature audiences look that up.
44. Jeremy Diamond, "Trump: I Could 'Shoot Somebody and I Wouldn't Lose Voters'" *CNN Politics*, January 24, 2016, http://www.cnn.com/2016/01/23/politics/donald-trump-shoot-somebody-support/.
45. Most states impose such constraints only for one ballot or have some other short-run obligation, after which delegates are freed from such laws to vote as they please. However, no nomination has taken more than one ballot since 1952 and thus within the new nomination system of 1972. So, in that sense, delegate votes have indeed been so constrained. Of course Republicans have a small number and Democrats a larger number of superdelegates who are free to vote as they choose.
46. Although there are sometimes nominations serving as protests to the party, the last time there was an open vote for vice president was in the 1956 Democratic Convention, when nominee Adlai Stevenson (Gov., IL) threw the choice to the delegates, who were choosing between Estes Kefauver (Sen., TN) and John Kennedy (Sen., MA).
47. The party holding the presidency, by tradition, holds its convention second.

# CHAPTER 2

1. Until 2008 neither Maine nor Nebraska had divided their electoral vote under these systems, but in that year Obama succeeded in carrying one of Nebraska's congressional districts, thus gaining one of the state's votes. In 2016 Donald Trump won the second congressional district in Maine, giving him one of the state's electoral votes.
2. The thirteen states were Colorado, Florida, Iowa, Michigan, Minnesota, Nevada, New Hampshire, New Mexico, North Carolina, Ohio, Pennsylvania, Virginia, and Wisconsin. On this point, see https://www.washingtonpost.com/politics/clinton-holds-clear-advantage-in-new-battleground-polls/2016/10/18/2885e3a0-94a6-11e6-bc79-af1cd3d2984b_story.html?utm_term=.acca4a5580e8. Some accounts had Georgia and Utah listed as battleground states as well.
3. For a discussion of electoral-vote strategies, see Daron R. Shaw, "The Methods Behind the Madness: Presidential Electoral-College Strategies, 1988–1996," *Journal of Politics* 61 (November 1999), 893–913.
4. Bill Allison, Mira Rojanasakul, Brittany Harris, and Cedric Sam, "Tracking the 2016 Presidential Money Race," *Bloomberg Politics*, December 9, 2016, https://www.bloomberg.com/politics/graphics/2016-presidential-campaign-fundraising/.
5. Ibid.
6. Nicholas Confessore and Karen Yourish, "Measuring Donald Trump's Mammoth Advantage in Free Media, *New York Times* (March 16, 2016).
7. Maggie Haberman, Alexander Burns, and Ashley Parker, "Donald Trump Fires Corey Lewandowski, His Campaign Manager," *New York Times*, June 20, 2016, https://www.nytimes.com/2016/06/21/us/politics/corey-lewandowski-donald-trump.html?_r=0.
8. Sean Sullivan, "Trump Hires ex-Cruz Super PAC Strategist Kellyanne Conway," *Washington Post*, July 1, 2016, https://www.washingtonpost.com/news/post-politics/wp/2016/07/01/trump-hires-ex-cruz-super-pac-strategist-kellyanne-conway/?utm_term=.9f43bbaf9b1b.
9. Jonathan Martin, Jim Rutenberg, and Maggie Haberman, "Donald Trump Appoints Media Firebrand to Run Campaign," *New York Times*, August 17, 2016, https://www.nytimes.com/2016/08/18/us/politics/donald-trump-stephen-bannon-paul-manafort.html.
10. Michael Schmidt, "Hillary Clinton Used Personal Email Account at State Dept., Possibly Breaking Rules," *New York Times*, March 2, 2015, https://www.nytimes.com/2015/03/03/us/politics/hillary-clintons-use-of-private-email-at-state-department-raises-flags.html.
11. Steven Lee Myers and Eric Lichtblau, "Hillary Clinton Is Criticized for Private Emails in State Dept. Review," *New York Times*, May 25, 2016, https://www.nytimes.com/2016/05/26/us/politics/state-department-hillary-clinton-emails.html.
12. Mark Landler and Eric Lichtblau, "F.B.I. Director James Comey Recommends No Charges for Hillary Clinton on Email," *New York Times*, July 5, 2016, https://www.nytimes.com/2016/07/06/us/politics/hillary-clinton-fbi-email-comey.html.
13. Emily Schultheis, "Donald Trump: FBI Decision on Clinton Emails a 'Total Miscarriage in Justice,'" *CBS News*, July 5, 2016, http://www.cbsnews.com/news/donald-trump-fbi-decision-on-clinton-emails-a-total-miscarriage-in-justice/.
14. For a discussion of factors that presidents consider when selecting their vice presidential nominees, see Mark Hiller and Douglas Kriner, "Institutional Change and the Dynamics of Vice Presidential Selection," *Presidential Studies Quarterly* 38 (Issue 3, 2008): 401–421.
15. Jonathan Swan, "Rankings: Trump's Top 10 VP Picks," *The Hill*, May 31, 2016, http://thehill.com/blogs/ballot-box/presidential-races/281527-power-rankings-trumps-top-10-vp-picks.

16. Eric Bradner, Dana Bash, and M. J. Lee, "Donald Trump Selects Mike Pence as VP," *CNN*, July 16, 2016, http://www.cnn.com/2016/07/14/politics/donald-trump-vice-presidential-choice/. The Koch brothers referenced here are Charles and David, who regularly contribute to conservative and libertarian causes.
17. Jeff Zeleny, "5 People to Watch in Hillary Clinton's Veepstakes," *CNN*, July 15, 2016, http://www.cnn.com/2016/07/14/politics/hillary-clinton-vice-president-choice/.
18. Jeff Zeleny, Ryan Nobles, and M. J. Lee, "Hillary Clinton Selects Tim Kaine as Her Running Mate," *CNN*, July 23, 2016, http://www.cnn.com/2016/07/22/politics/hillary-clinton-vp-pick/.
19. John Wagner, "Sanders Says He Would Have Preferred Warren as Clinton's VP Pick," *Washington Post*, July 24, 2016, https://www.washingtonpost.com/news/post-politics/wp/2016/07/24/sanders-says-he-would-have-preferred-warren-as-clintons-vp-pick/?utm_term=.895aaf7d5a00.
20. Michael Heaney, "Why Are the Protests at the Republican Convention So Small?" *Washington Post*, July 21, 2016, https://www.washingtonpost.com/news/monkey-cage/wp/2016/07/21/why-are-protests-at-the-republican-convention-so-small/?utm_term=.6222125c8341.
21. Tribune News Service, "After Earlier Turmoil, Republicans Seek to Mend Party Divisions on RNC's Opening Night," *Chicago Tribune*, July 19, 2016, http://www.chicagotribune.com/news/nationworld/politics/ct-republican-national-convention-cleveland-20160718-story.html.
22. Ryan Beckwith, "Watch Ted Cruz Fail to Endorse Trump at the Republican Convention," *Time*, July 20, 2016, http://time.com/4416396/republican-convention-ted-cruz-donald-trump-endorsement-speech-transcript-video/.
23. Shane Goldmacher, Katie Glueck, and Matthew Nussbaum, "Cruz Burns Trump: In a Stunning Convention Moment, the Texas Senator Told Republicans to Vote Their Conscience—and Refused to Endorse the Nominee," *Politico*, July 21, 2016, http://www.politico.com/story/2016/07/rnc-2016-donald-trump-unity-225915.
24. Patrick Healy and Jonathan Martin, "His Tone Dark, Donald Trump Takes G.O.P. Mantle," *New York Times*, July 21, 2016, https://www.nytimes.com/2016/07/22/us/politics/donald-trump-rnc-speech.html.
25. "Transcript: Donald Trump at the G.O.P. Convention," *New York Times*, July 22, 2016, https://www.nytimes.com/2016/07/22/us/politics/trump-transcript-rnc-address.html.
26. Marc Caputo and Daniel Strauss, "Wasserman Schultz Steps Down as DNC Chair," *Politico*, July 24, 2016, http://www.politico.com/story/2016/07/wasserman-schultz-wont-preside-over-dnc-convention-226088.
27. "Transcript: Read Michelle Obama's Full Speech from the 2016 DNC," *Washington Post*, July 26, 2016, https://www.washingtonpost.com/news/post-politics/wp/2016/07/26/transcript-read-michelle-obamas-full-speech-from-the-2016-dnc/?utm_term=.5c46598c493b.
28. "Full Text: Hillary Clinton's DNC Speech," *Politico*, July 28, 2016, http://www.politico.com/story/2016/07/full-text-hillary-clintons-dnc-speech-226410.
29. Michael O'Connell, "TV Ratings: Hillary Clinton's DNC Speech Falls Just Shy of Trump's With 33 Million Viewers," *Hollywood Reporter*, July 29, 2016, http://www.hollywoodreporter.com/live-feed/tv-ratings-hillary-clintons-dnc-915706.
30. Jennifer Agiesta, "Donald Trump Bounces into the Lead," *CNN*, July 25, 2016, http://www.cnn.com/2016/07/25/politics/donald-trump-hillary-clinton-poll/.
31. Hannah Hartig, John Lapinski, and Stephanie Psyllos, "Poll: Clinton Support Spikes Following Democratic Convention," *NBC News*, August 2, 2016, http://www.nbcnews.com/storyline/data-points/poll-clinton-support-spikes-following-democratic-convention-n621071.

32. Gregory Krieg, "Donald Trump's 27-Day Spiral: From Convention Bounce to Campaign Overhaul," *CNN*, August 18, 2016, http://www.cnn.com/2016/08/17/politics/donald-trump-post-convention-controversy-polls-shakeup/.
33. Ibid.
34. Philip Rucker, "Trump Refuses to Endorse Paul Ryan in GOP Primary: 'I'm Just Not Quite There Yet,'" *Washington Post*, August 2, 2016, https://www.washingtonpost.com/politics/trump-refuses-to-endorse-paul-ryan-in-gop-primary-im-just-not-quite-there-yet/2016/08/02/1449f028-58e9-11e6-831d-0324760ca856_story.html?hpid=hp_no-name_no-name%3Apage%2Fbreaking-news-bar&tid=a_breakingnews&utm_term=.5d955c9bc396.
35. Ibid.
36. David Wright, "Poll: Clinton Leads Trump in Red State Georgia," *CNN*, August 6, 2016, http://www.cnn.com/2016/08/05/politics/clinton-leads-trump-georgia-poll/index.html.
37. Nick Corasaniti and Maggie Haberman, "Donald Trump Suggests 'Second Amendment People' Could Act Against Hillary Clinton," *New York Times*, August 9, 2016, https://www.nytimes.com/2016/08/10/us/politics/donald-trump-hillary-clinton.html.
38. Ibid.
39. Gregory Krieg, "Donald Trump's 27-Day Spiral: From Convention Bounce to Campaign Overhaul," *CNN*, August 18, 2016, http://www.cnn.com/2016/08/17/politics/donald-trump-post-convention-controversy-polls-shakeup/.
40. Ivan Levingston, "Trump: If I Lose, I'll Have a 'Nice Long Vacation.'" *CNBC*, August 22, 2016, http://www.cnbc.com/2016/08/11/trump-if-i-lose-ill-have-a-nice-long-vacation.html.
41. Jonathan Martin, Jim Rutenberg, and Maggie Haberman, "Donald Trump Appoints Media Firebrand to Run Campaign," *New York Times*, August 17, 2016, https://www.nytimes.com/2016/08/18/us/politics/donald-trump-stephen-bannon-paul-manafort.html.
42. Abby Phillip, "Clinton: Half of Trump's Supporters Fit in 'Basket of Deplorables,'" *Washington Post*, September 9, 2016, https://www.washingtonpost.com/news/post-politics/wp/2016/09/09/clinton-half-of-trumps-supporters-fit-in-basket-of-deplorables/?utm_term=.fcb12bb30260.
43. Jonathan Martin and Amy Chozick, "Hillary Clinton's Doctor Says Pneumonia Led to Abrupt Exit from 9/11 Event," *New York Times*, September 11, 2016, https://www.nytimes.com/2016/09/12/us/politics/hillary-clinton-campaign-pneumonia.html.
44. Colleen McCain Nelson and Laura Meckler, "Hillary Clinton Prepping for Two Trumps at Debate," *Wall Street Journal*, September 20, 2016, https://www.wsj.com/articles/hillary-clinton-prepping-for-two-trumps-at-debate-1474415274.
45. Meg Anderson, "How Clinton and Trump Are Preparing for the First Presidential Debate," *NPR*, September 22, 2016, http://www.npr.org/2016/09/22/494901644/how-clinton-and-trump-are-preparing-for-the-first-presidential-debate.
46. Duane Patterson, "Hugh and Donald Trump Talk 2016," *Hugh Hewitt*, June 23, 2016, http://www.hughhewitt.com/hugh-donald-trump-talk-2016/.
47. Meg Anderson, "How Clinton and Trump Are Preparing for the First Presidential Debate."
48. "The First Trump-Clinton Presidential Debate Transcript, Annotated," *Washington Post*, September 26, 2016, https://www.washingtonpost.com/news/the-fix/wp/2016/09/26/the-first-trump-clinton-presidential-debate-transcript-annotated/?utm_term=.ae00ba1531ea.
49. Alex Burns and Matt Flegenheimer, "Did You Miss the Presidential Debate? Here Are the Highlights," *New York Times*, September 26, 2016, https://www.nytimes.com/2016/09/26/us/politics/presidential-debate.html.
50. Ibid.

51. Brian Stelter, "Debate Breaks Record as Most-Watched in U.S. History," *CNN*, September 27, 2016, http://money.cnn.com/2016/09/27/media/debate-ratings-record-viewership/.
52. Reena Flores, "Gallup: Clinton Beats Trump in First Debate by a Large Margin," *CBS News*, September 30, 2016, http://www.cbsnews.com/news/poll-hillary-clinton-beats-donald-trump-in-first-debate-by-a-large-margin/.
53. Ibid.
54. Eric Bradner, "5 Takeaways from the Vice Presidential Debate," *CNN*, October 5, 2016, http://www.cnn.com/2016/10/05/politics/vp-debate-takeaways/.
55. Ibid.
56. Nicolas Confessore and Matt Flegenheimer, "Vice-Presidential Debate: What You Missed," *New York Times*, October 4, 2016, https://www.nytimes.com/2016/10/04/us/politics/vice-presidential-debate.html.
57. Shane Goldmacher, Annie Karni, and Nolan McCaskill, "Trump Caught on Tape Making Crude, Sexually Aggressive Comments about Women," *Politico*, October 8, 2016, http://www.politico.com/story/2016/10/trump-wapo-229299.
58. Ruth Marcus, "Donald Trump's Remarkably Gross Comments about Women," *Washington Post*, October 7, 2016, https://www.washingtonpost.com/blogs/post-partisan/wp/2016/10/07/donald-trumps-remarkably-gross-comments-about-women/?utm_term=.5d3be1e6c085.
59. Aaron Blake, "Three Dozen Republicans Have Now Called for Donald Trump to Drop Out," *Washington Post*, October 9, 2016, https://www.washingtonpost.com/news/the-fix/wp/2016/10/07/the-gops-brutal-responses-to-the-new-trump-video-broken-down/?utm_term=.2dda7f621f26.
60. Maggie Haberman, "Donald Trump's Apology That Wasn't," *New York Times*, October 8, 2016, https://www.nytimes.com/2016/10/08/us/politics/donald-trump-apology.html.
61. Irin Carmon, "The Allegations Women Have Made against Donald Trump," *NBC News*, October 27, 2016, http://www.nbcnews.com/politics/2016-election/allegations-women-have-made-against-donald-trump-n665731.
62. Donald J. Trump, *Twitter*, October 8, 2016, https://twitter.com/realdonaldtrump/status/784840992734064641?lang=en.
63. "He Said, She Said: Highlights from the Second Trump-Clinton Presidential Debate of 2016," *Washington Post*, October 10, 2016, https://www.washingtonpost.com/graphics/politics/2016-election/hesaid-shesaid-second-debate/.
64. Ibid.
65. "He Said, She Said: Highlights from the Third Trump-Clinton Presidential Debate of 2016," *Washington Post*, October 19, 2016, https://www.washingtonpost.com/graphics/politics/2016-election/highlights-trump-clinton-third-debate/.
66. "Trump Calls Clinton a 'Nasty Woman' during Final Debate," *The Guardian*, October 20, 2016, https://www.theguardian.com/us-news/video/2016/oct/20/donald-trump-calls-hillary-clinton-a-nasty-woman-during-final-debate-video.
67. Jennifer Agiesta, "Hillary Clinton Wins Third Presidential Debate, According to CNN/ORC Poll," *CNN*, October 20, 2016, http://www.cnn.com/2016/10/19/politics/hillary-clinton-wins-third-presidential-debate-according-to-cnn-orc-poll/.
68. See Robert S. Erikson and Christopher Wlezien, *The Timeline of Presidential Elections* (Chicago: University of Chicago Press, 2012), 79–81, and the references cited therein. Also see John Sides, "Do Presidential Debates Really Matter?," *Washington Monthly*, September/October 2012, 19–21.
69. See Sides, "Do Presidential Debates Really Matter?"
70. Ibid.

71. "General Election: Trump vs. Clinton vs. Johnson vs. Stein," *Real Clear Politics*, https://www.realclearpolitics.com/epolls/2016/president/us/general_election_trump_vs_clinton_vs_johnson_vs_stein-5952.html.
72. Adam Edelman, "Clinton Has Major Lead over Trump in Poll Taken Days after Final Debate," *Daily News*, October 23, 2016, http://www.nydailynews.com/news/politics/clinton-major-lead-trump-final-debate-poll-article-1.2841984.
73. Ibid.
74. Josh Gerstein, "FBI Reviewing New Evidence in Clinton Email Probe," *Politico*, October 28, 2016, http://www.politico.com/story/2016/10/fbi-reopens-clinton-email-server-investigation-230454.
75. Ibid.
76. Adam Goldman and Alan Rappeport, "Emails in Anthony Weiner Inquiry Jolt Hillary Clinton's Campaign," *New York Times*, October 28, 2016, https://www.nytimes.com/2016/10/29/us/politics/fbi-hillary-clinton-email.html?smid=tw-nytimes&smtyp=cur&_r=0&mtrref=undefined&gwh=E2C883CDD6AA230DA807D264DDC41875&gwt=pay.
77. Josh Gerstein, "FBI Reviewing New Evidence in Clinton Email Probe," *Politico*, October 28, 2016, http://www.politico.com/story/2016/10/fbi-reopens-clinton-email-server-investigation-230454.
78. Ibid.
79. Ibid.
80. Lisa Mascaro, "Trump Welcomes FBI Probe: 'Clinton's Corruption Is on a Scale We Have Never Seen,'" *Los Angeles Times*, October 28, 2016, http://www.latimes.com/nation/politics/trailguide/la-na-trailguide-updates-trump-welcomes-new-fbi-probe-clinton-s-1477677693-htmlstory.html.
81. Ibid.
82. "General Election: Trump vs. Clinton," *Real Clear Politics*, http://www.realclearpolitics.com/epolls/2016/president/us/general_election_trump_vs_clinton-5491.html.
83. Julie Pace, Lisa Lerer, and Jill Colvin, "FBI Won't Recommend Charges against Clinton Based on New Emails, Comey Says," *Press Herald*, November 6, 2016, http://www.pressherald.com/2016/11/06/fbi-wont-recommend-charges-against-clinton-based-on-new-emails-comey-says/. President Trump would later catch many by surprise when he announced on May 9, 2017, that he was firing FBI Director James Comey for his mishandling of the email investigation of Clinton. See Niall Stanage, "The Memo: Trump Ignites Firestorm," *The Hill*, May 9, 2017, http://thehill.com/homenews/administration/332667-the-memo-trump-ignites-firestorm.
84. The data are from Michael McDonald's website: http://www.electproject.org/national-1789-present.
85. See Paul R. Abramson, John H. Aldrich, Brad T. Gomez, and David W. Rohde, *Change and Continuity in the 2012 Elections* (Washington, D.C.: CQ Press, 2015), Chapter 2.
86. Quoted in Michael Scherer, "Inside the Secret World of Quants and Data Crunchers Who Helped Obama Win," *Time*, November 19, 2012, 58.
87. Ibid.
88. Lee Drutman, "How Turnout-Only Politics Gave Us the 2016 Campaign—And a Historic Polling Upset," *Politico*, November 15, 2016, http://www.politico.com/magazine/story/2016/11/mobilization-only-politics-2016-214456. Many of the details in this section are drawn from this article.
89. Ibid.
90. Ibid.

91. Jeremy Peters, Amy Chozick, and Lizette Alvarez, "Fear of Donald Trump Helps Democrats Mobilize Hispanics," *New York Times*, November 6, 2016, https://www.nytimes.com/2016/11/07/us/fear-of-donald-trump-helps-democrats-mobilize-hispanics.html.
92. Ibid.
93. Republicans made a concerted effort to increase the number of field offices after Labor Day, when the traditional fall campaign begins. See Nikita Vladimirov, "RNC to Open 98 Field Offices in Effort to Boost Trump, GOP," *The Hill*, September 2, 2016, http://thehill.com/blogs/ballot-box/presidential-races/294260-gop-to-open-98-field-offices-in-effort-to-boost-trump.
94. Leign Ann Caldwell, "Clinton and Democrats Have Major Fundraising Advantage over Trump," *NBC News*, October 15, 2016, http://www.nbcnews.com/politics/2016-election/clinton-democrats-have-major-fundraising-advantage-over-trump-n667031.
95. Jason Le Miere, "Did the Media Help Donald Trump Win? $5 Billion in Free Advertising Given to President-Elect," *International Business Times*, November 9, 2016, http://www.ibtimes.com/did-media-help-donald-trump-win-5-billion-free-advertising-given-president-elect-2444115.
96. Jonathan Martin and Alan Rappeport, "Presidential Election: A Closing Act, with Clinton, Trump, and a Tiny 'Future Construction Worker,'" *New York Times*, November 4, 2016, https://www.nytimes.com/2016/11/05/us/politics/presidential-election.html.
97. Anthony Brooks, "In Final Weekend Before Election Day, Trump and Clinton Fiercely Campaign in New Hampshire," *Politicker*, November 7, 2016, http://www.wbur.org/politicker/2016/11/07/trump-clinton-nh-final-days.
98. Ibid.
99. Ibid.
100. There has been a lot of interesting research in recent years on the impact of presidential campaigns on outcomes. In addition to the Erikson and Wlezien volume already cited, see Lynn Vavreck, *The Message Matters* (Princeton, N.J.: Princeton University Press, 2009); Thomas H. Holbrook, *Do Campaigns Matter?* (Thousand Oaks, Calif.: Sage Publications, 1996); James E. Campbell, *The American Campaign* (College Station: Texas A&M University Press, 2000); and Darron R. Shaw, "A Study of Presidential Campaign Effects from 1956 to 1992," *Journal of Politics* 61 (May 1999): 387–422.
101. Lee Drutman, "How Turnout-Only Politics Gave Us the 2016 Campaign."
102. Chris Cillizza, "The 13 Most Amazing Findings in the 2016 Exit Poll," *Washington Post*, November 10, 2016, https://www.washingtonpost.com/news/the-fix/wp/2016/11/10/the-13-most-amazing-things-in-the-2016-exit-poll/?utm_term=.c93d4297b5db.
103. The figure used here is the Voting Eligible Population Highest Office Turnout Rate. The data are from the United States Elections Project: http://www.electproject.org/.
104. Carl Bialik, "Voter Turnout Fell, Especially in States That Clinton Won," *FiveThirtyEight*, November 11, 2016, https://fivethirtyeight.com/features/voter-turnout-fell-especially-in-states-that-clinton-won/.
105. Ray Long, "Why Did Hillary Clinton Lose? Simple. She Ran a Bad Campaign," *Chicago Tribune*, November 14, 2016, http://www.chicagotribune.com/news/opinion/commentary/ct-hillary-clinton-lost-bad-campaign-perspec-20161114-story.html.
106. Ibid.
107. Philip Bump, "Of Course Bernie Sanders Could Have Beaten Donald Trump," *Washington Post*, November 13, 2016, https://www.washingtonpost.com/news/the-fix/wp/2016/11/13/of-course-bernie-sanders-could-have-beaten-donald-trump/?utm_term=.c457152b5620.

108. Ibid.

109. Marcus Johnson, "No, Bernie Sanders Would Not Have Beaten Trump," *Huffington Post*, December 16, 2016, http://www.huffingtonpost.com/entry/bernie-sanders-was-on-the-2016-ballotand-he-underperformed_us_5852fbbce4b06ae7ec2a3cb7.

110. Gary C. Jacobson, "The Triumph of Polarized Partisanship in 2016: Donald Trump's Improbable Victory," *Political Science Quarterly* 132 (Spring 2017): 9–41.

## CHAPTER 3

1. Jeremy W. Peters and Matt Flegenheimer, "Early Turnout Tilts toward Democrats in Swing States," *New York Times*, October 31, 2016, A1; Byron Tau, "Early Voting Data Shows Who's Turning Out," wsj.com, November 4, 2016.
2. Ibid.
3. Real Clear Politics, "General Election: Trump vs. Clinton," https://www.realclearpolitics.com/epolls/2016/president/us/ general_election_trump_vs_clinton-5491.html.
4. For an approach that combines information from statistical forecasting models and weights their past performance to make future predictions, we recommend Jacob M. Montgomery, Florian M. Hollenbach, and Michael D. Ward, "Improving Predictions Using Ensemble Bayesian Model Averaging," *Political Analysis* 20 (Summer 2012): 271–291.
5. James E. Campbell, "Forecasting the 2016 American National Elections," *PS: Political Science and Politics* 49 (October 2016): 649–654. The forecasts begin on p. 655. Opinion polls offer a snapshot of the electorate at the time of the survey and thus vary with the ebbs and flows of the campaign. Statistical forecast models are based on "fundamentals," factors that have been shown to be predictive across many elections. Most of these fundamentals, such as leading economic indicators, war fatalities during past presidential term, and presidential approval, to name a few, are often known and measured before the general election campaign even begins.
6. Hillary Clinton was born in Chicago, Illinois, and spent much of her adult life in Arkansas before becoming First Lady of the United States in 1992. Clinton and her husband, former President Bill Clinton, moved to New York State after his presidency, where she was later elected twice to the United States Senate. Donald Trump was born in Queens, New York City, and maintained his primary residence in Manhattan. The 2016 election marks the fifth time in U.S. history that both of the major party candidates were from the same state. In 1860 Abraham Lincoln (R) and Stephen Douglas (D) were from Illinois. In 1904 Theodore Roosevelt (R) and Alton Parker (D) were from New York. In 1920 Warren G. Harding (R) and James M. Cox (D) were from Ohio. In 1944 Thomas Dewey (R) and Franklin D. Roosevelt (D) were from New York.
7. Real-Time Staff, "Hillary Clinton Rallying in Philadelphia with the Obamas, Springsteen, Bon Jovi," *Philly.com.*, November 7, 2016, http://www.philly.com/philly/blogs/real-time/Hillary-Clinton-to-hold-Nov-7-2016-rally-in-Philadelphia.html.
8. Lynn Bonner and Rachel Chason, "Lady Gaga Helps Draw Crowd to N.C. State Rally for Clinton before Polls Open," *News and Observer*, November 8, 2016, http://www.newsobserver.com/news/politics-government/state-politics/article113198468.html.
9. Ashley Parker, "Donald Trump Soaks in the Adulation in Improvised Final Stop," *New York Times*, November 8, 2016, https://www.nytimes.com/2016/11/08/us/politics/trump-rally.html

10. Donald Trump was seventy years old at the time of the election, and Hillary Clinton was sixty-nine. Although older candidates have run for the presidency (e.g., Ronald Reagan was seventy-three when he ran for reelection in 1984, and Robert Dole was seventy-three when he was the Republican nominee in 1996), they typically have faced much younger opponents. For a discussion of the role that the candidates' ages played in the campaign, see Jena McGregor, "Clinton and Trump Are the Oldest Candidates Ever. No One Seems to Care," *Washington Post*, July 14, 2016, https://www.washingtonpost.com/news/on-leadership/wp/2016/07/14/clinton-and-trump-are-the-oldest-candidates-ever-no-one-seems-to-care/?utm_term=.a2bf3d67a9ae.
11. Morgan Winsor, "Presidential Candidates Cast Votes on Election Day," *ABC News*, November 8, 2016, abcnews.go.com/Politics/presidential-candidates-cast-votes-election-day/story?id=43381482.
12. Ibid.
13. Bloomberg Businessweek, "Inside Election Night at the Trump and Clinton Parties," November 9, 2016, https://www.bloomberg.com/features/2016-clinton-trump-election-parties/; M. J. Lee, "Tears and Shock at Clinton's Election Night Party," *CNN*, November, 9, 2016, http://www.cnn.com/2016/11/09/politics/hillary-clinton-shock-election-party/index.html.
14. For two examples of pre-election forecasts of the Electoral College, see Chris Cillizza, "Yes, Donald Trump Can Win. Here Are 4 Maps That Prove It," *Washington Post*, November 2, 2016, https://www.washingtonpost.com/news/the-fix/wp/2016/11/02/4-electoral-maps-where-donald-trump-wins/?utm_term=.41f99b4604f0; and Nate Silver, "Election Update: The State of the States," *FiveThirtyEight*, November 7, 2016, https://fivethirtyeight.com/features/election-update-the-state-of-the-states/.
15. For a timeline of election night events, see David Leip's *Atlas of U.S. Presidential Elections*, "2016 Election Night Events Timeline," http://uselectionatlas.org/INFORMATION/ARTICLES/ElectionNight2016/pe2016elecnighttime.php. Leip notes that all "call times are from NBC News and are approximate."
16. Lee, "Tears and Shock."
17. The other presidential candidates to win the Electoral College while losing the popular vote were Republican Rutherford B. Hayes in 1876 (Democrat Samuel J. Tilden won 50.9 percent of the popular vote), Republican Benjamin Harrison in 1888 (Democrat and incumbent President Grover Cleveland won a 48.6 percent plurality of the popular vote), and George W. Bush in 2000 (Democrat Al Gore won a 48.4 percent plurality of the popular vote).
18. Both Johnson and Stein ran for the presidency in 2012, and each had far less appeal. In 2012 Johnson won 0.99 percent of national popular vote, and Stein won 0.36 percent.
19. As noted in Chapter 2, since 1972, Maine has used a system in which the statewide plurality-vote winner receives two electoral votes, and the plurality winner in each of the state's congressional districts receives that district's single electoral vote. Nebraska has used a similar system to allocate its Electoral College votes since the 1992 election. In our previous books we have not always reported these district-level results, but we do so here because in the 2016 election Trump won one Electoral College vote from Maine's Second Congressional District.
20. In 2012 Obama won twenty-six states and the District of Columbia. For a state-by-state reporting of the official presidential election returns for 2012, see Paul R. Abramson, John H. Aldrich, Brad T. Gomez, and David W. Rohde, *Change and Continuity in the 2012 Elections* (Los Angeles: Sage/CQ Press, 2015), Table 3-1.

21. Electors from the Electoral College officially gathered in their respective state capitals to cast ballots for president and vice president on December 19, 2016. For more on the workings of the Electoral College, visit the Office of the Federal Registrar website, http://www.archives.gov/federal-register/electoral-college/index.html.
22. The U.S. Constitution does not require that electors cast ballots in accordance with the popular vote in their states; however twenty-nine states and the District of Columbia bind their electors by law. Faithless electors are uncommon in American electoral history, and indeed, it is rare to see an Electoral College vote with more than one faithless ballot being cast. In 2016 three Democratic electors from the State of Washington cast ballots for former Secretary of State Colin Powell, a Republican, and another elector from the state voted for Faith Spotted Eagle, an activist from the Yankton Sioux Nation (this marks the first time a Native American has received an electoral vote). A Democratic Party elector from Hawaii cast a ballot for Bernie Sanders. On the Republican side two electors from Texas were faithless—one voted for John Kasich and the other for Ron Paul. The previous record for the number of faithless electors was established in the 1808 election, when six Democratic-Republican Party electors from New York cast ballots for New York Governor George Clinton, the party's vice presidential nominee, instead of James Madison. For a brief history of faithless electors, see Nina Agrawal, "All the Times in U.S. History that Members of the Electoral College Voted Their Own Way," *Los Angeles Times,* December 20, 2016, http://www.latimes.com/nation/la-na-faithless-electors-2016-story.html.
23. For a cross-national comparison of U.S. presidential selection rules, see Matthew Soberg Shugart, "The American Process of Selecting a President: A Comparative Perspective," *Presidential Studies Quarterly* 34 (September 2004): 632–655.
24. The respective plurality winners of the popular vote were Andrew Jackson in 1824, Samuel J. Tilden in 1876, incumbent President Grover Cleveland in 1888, and Al Gore in 2000. In 1824 no candidate won a majority of the electoral vote, so the election was thrown to the House of Representatives, where Adams was elected. In 1824 more than a fourth of the electors were chosen by state legislatures.
25. Jonathan Mahler and Steve Eder, "Many Call the Electoral College Outmoded. So Why Has it Endured?," *New York Times*, November 11, 2016, P8. Interestingly public support for or opposition to the Electoral College is likely biased by whether one sides with the winning or losing candidate; see Art Swift, "Americans' Support for Electoral College Rises Sharply," *Gallup*, December 2, 2016, http://www.gallup.com/poll/198917/americans-support-electoral-college-rises-sharply.aspx; see also John H. Aldrich, Jason Reifler, and Michael C. Munger, "Sophisticated *and* Myopic? Citizens Preferences for Electoral College Reform," *Public Choice* 158 (March 2014): 541–558.
26. These fourteen winners were James K. Polk (Democrat) in 1844, with 49.5 percent of the popular vote; Zachary Taylor (Whig) in 1848, with 47.3 percent; James Buchanan (Democrat) in 1856, with 45.3 percent; Abraham Lincoln (Republican) in 1860 with 39.9 percent; James A. Garfield (Republican) in 1880, with 48.3 percent; Grover Cleveland (Democrat) in 1884, with 48.9 percent; Cleveland in 1892, with 46.0 percent; Woodrow Wilson (Democrat) in 1912, with 41.8 percent; Wilson in 1916, with 49.2 percent; Harry S. Truman (Democrat) in 1948, with 49.5 percent; John F. Kennedy (Democrat) in 1960, with 49.7 percent; Richard M. Nixon (Republican) in 1968, with 43.4 percent; Bill Clinton (Democrat) in 1992, with 43.0 percent; and Clinton in 1996, with 49.2 percent. The results for Kennedy can be questioned, however, mainly because voters in Alabama voted for individual electors, and one can argue that Nixon won more popular votes than Kennedy.

27. Maurice Duverger, *Political Parties: Their Organization and Activity in the Modern State*, trans. Barbara North and Robert North (New York: Wiley, 1963), 217. In the original Duverger's proposition is "*le scrutin majoritaire à un seul tour tend au dualisme des partis.*" Duverger, *Les partis politiques* (Paris: Armand Colin, 1958), 247. For a discussion see William H. Riker, "The Two-party System and Duverger's Law: An Essay on the History of Political Science," *American Political Science Review* 76 (December 1982): 753–766. For a more recent statement by Duverger, see "Duverger's Law Forty Years Later," in *Electoral Laws and Their Political Consequences*, eds. Bernard Grofman and Arend Lijphart (New York: Agathan Press, 1986), 69–84. For more general discussions of the effects of electoral laws, see Rein Taagepera and Matthew Shugart, *Seats and Votes: The Effects and Determinants of Electoral Systems* (New Haven, Conn.: Yale University Press, 1989); and Gary W. Cox, *Making Votes Count: Strategic Coordination of the World's Electoral Systems* (Cambridge, U.K.: Cambridge University Press, 1997). See also John H. Aldrich and Daniel J. Lee, "Why Two Parties? Ambition, Policy, and the Presidency," *Political Science Research and Methods* 2 (May 2016): 275–292.
28. Duverger's inclusion of "a single ballot" in his formulation is redundant because, in a plurality vote win system, there would be no need for second ballots or runoffs unless needed to break ties. With a large electorate, ties will be extremely rare.
29. Duverger, *Political Parties*, 218.
30. William H. Riker, *The Art of Political Manipulation* (New Haven, Conn.: Yale University Press, 1986), 79.
31. For the most extensive evidence for the 1968, 1980, and 1992 elections, see Paul R. Abramson et al., "Third-Party and Independent Candidates in American Politics: Wallace, Anderson, and Perot," *Political Science Quarterly* 110 (Fall 1997): 349–367. For the 1996 and 2000 elections, see Paul R. Abramson, John H. Aldrich, and David W. Rohde, *Change and Continuity in the 1996 and 1998 Elections* (Washington, D.C.: CQ Press, 1999), 118–120; and Paul R. Abramson, John H. Aldrich, and David W. Rohde, *Change and Continuity in the 2000 and 2002 Elections* (Washington, D.C.: CQ Press, 2003), 124–126.
32. Britain provides an excellent example of the effects of plurality-vote win systems on third parties. In Britain, as in the United States, candidates for the national legislature run in single-member districts, and in all British parliamentary districts the plurality-vote winner is elected. In all nineteen general elections since World War II ended in Europe, the Liberal Party (and more recently the Alliance and the Liberal Democratic Parties) has received a smaller percentage of seats in the House of Commons than its percentage of the popular vote. For example, in the June 2017 election, the Liberal Democrats won 7.4 percent of the popular vote but won only 1.8 percent of the seats in the House of Commons.
33. Third-party candidates are not always underrepresented in the Electoral College. In 1948 J. Strom Thurmond, the States' Rights Democrat, won only 2.4 percent of the popular vote but won 7.3 percent of the electoral vote. Thurmond won 55 percent of the popular votes in the four states he carried (Alabama, Louisiana, Mississippi, and South Carolina), all of which had low turnout. He received no popular vote at all in thirty-one of the forty-eight states.
34. See George C. Edwards III, *Why the Electoral College is Bad for America*, 2nd ed. (New Haven, Conn.: Yale University Press, 2011).
35. Edwards argues that "[a] constitutional amendment is not a pipe dream," noting that a constitutional amendment to establish direct election of the president passed the House on a bipartisan vote in 1969. The amendment, which was publicly endorsed by President Nixon, was filibustered in the Senate, however, by southern senators. See Edwards, *Why the Electoral College Is Bad for America*, 203.

36. For the most extensive argument in favor of this reform, see John R. Koza et al., *Every Vote Equal: A State-Based Plan for Electing the President by National Popular Vote*, 4th ed. (Los Altos, Calif.: National Popular Vote Press, 2013).
37. Adoption of the district system would likely increase the incentive for state legislatures to gerrymander given that presidential electors would now be at stake.
38. David Wasserman, "Introducing the 2017 Cook Political Report Partisan Voting Index," *The Cook Political Report*, April 7, 2017, http://cookpolitical.com/file/Cook_Political_Report_Partisan_Voter_Index_.pdf.

    One should always be cautious when constructing counterfactuals such as this. Had the election taken place under these rules, the candidates most certainly would have campaigned using different strategies, and voter participation would have changed in all likelihood in response to varying levels of electoral competition across districts.
39. A. C. Thomas and colleagues offer a systematic study of alternative elector apportionment proposals using data from 1956 to 2004. They conclude that both the current Electoral College and the direct popular vote are substantially less biased than the district method. See A. C. Thomas, Andrew Gelman, Gary King, and Jonathan N. Katz, "Estimating Partisan Bias of the Electoral College Under Proposed Changes in Elector Apportionment," *Statistics, Politics, and Policy* 4 (Issue 1, 2013): 1–13.
40. Stuart Rothenberg, "The Unusual, Unexpected, Strange, Weird, and Now Bizarre Presidential Election, *Washington Post*, October 5, 2016, https://www.washingtonpost.com/news/powerpost/wp/2016/10/05/the-unusual-unexpected-strange-weird-and-now-bizarre-presidential-election/?utm_term=.6a2d48a5e054.
41. Daniel Gans views much of presidential election history as what statisticians call a "random walk," meaning that party success from one election to the next is essentially random. See Daniel J. Gans, "Persistence of Party Success in American Presidential Elections," *Journal of Interdisciplinary History* 2 (Winter 1986), 221–237.
42. Walter Dean Burnham, *Critical Elections and the Mainsprings of American Politics* (New York: Norton, 1970).
43. Stanley Kelley, Jr., establishes three criteria to classify an election as a landslide: if the winning candidate wins 53 percent of the popular vote *or* wins 80 percent of the electoral vote *or* wins 80 percent of the states. This definition may be too generous, but Reagan's 1984 victory, which met all three of Kelley's criteria, was most certainly a landslide. See Stanley Kelley, Jr., *Interpreting Elections* (Princeton, N.J., Princeton University Press, 1983).
44. Two other incumbents during this period had lower popular vote totals when they stood for reelection (Jimmy Carter in 1980 and George H.W. Bush in 1992); both lost.
45. For two studies of the Whig Party, see Michael F. Holt, *The Rise and Fall of the Whig Party: Jacksonian Politics and the Onset of the Civil War* (New York: Oxford University Press, 1999); and Daniel Walker Howe, *The Political Culture of the American Whigs* (Chicago: University of Chicago Press, 1979).
46. Former Whigs founded the Constitutional Union Party in 1860. Its candidate, John Bell, won 12.6 percent of the popular vote and thirty-nine of the 303 electoral votes.
47. For a discussion of agenda-setting during this period, see William H. Riker, *Liberalism against Populism: A Confrontation between the Theory of Democracy and the Theory of Social Choice* (San Francisco: W. H. Freeman, 1982), 213–232; and John H. Aldrich, *Why Parties? A Second Look* (Chicago: University of Chicago Press, 2011), 130–162.
48. Not all scholars agree with this assessment. The most important dissent is found in David R. Mayhew, *Electoral Realignments: A Critique of an American Genre* (New Haven, Conn.: Yale University Press, 2002), 43–69.

49. The election of 1912 is the last in which a party other than the Democrats and Republicans finished among the top-two vote getters. Former Republican president Theodore Roosevelt, running as the nominee of the Progressive Party (the "Bull Moose Party") finished second in both the popular and Electoral College votes.
50. After the 2000 election, the Republicans and Democrats each had fifty senators, and the Republicans held control of the Senate by virtue of Vice President Dick Cheney's tie-breaking vote. When Senator James M. Jeffords of Vermont left the Republican Party to become an independent and to vote with the Democrats on the organization of the Senate, the Democrats took control of the Senate from June 2001 until January 2003.
51. See David R. Mayhew, "Incumbency Advantage in U.S. Presidential Elections: The Historical Record," *Political Science Quarterly* 123 (Summer 2008): 201–228. An individual-level study of survey responses from the 1952 through 2000 American National Election Studies suggests that incumbent presidential candidates—controlling for a variety of other factors—enjoy a six percentage point advantage over their challengers in the popular vote; see Herbert F. Weisberg, "Partisanship and Incumbency in Presidential Elections," *Political Behavior* 24 (December 2002): 339–360.
52. Jodi Enda, "When Republicans Were Blue and Democrats Were Red: The Era of Color-coded Political Parties Is More Recent than You Might Think," November 1, 2012, smithsonian.com. The association of Republicans with the color red is actually a bit curious, given the color's historical association with revolution and socialism. For example, the song "The Red Flag," composed by James Connell in 1889, became the official song of the British Labour Party. As for flags specifically, the flag of the Soviet Union featured a solid red field with a gold hammer and sickle. Fear of the Soviet Union and the spread of communism in America, particularly during the 1950s, was called the "Red Scare."
53. Since ratification of the Twenty-third Amendment in 1961, the District of Columbia has had three electoral votes, which it first cast in the 1964 election.
54. The *National Journal* hosts a website that tracks all reported campaign visits by the presidential candidates, including those who ran during the primaries: "2016 Travel Tracker," *National Journal*, http://traveltracker.nationaljournal.com/. During the general election the vice presidential candidates also stayed away from California and Texas. Republican Vice Presidential Nominee Mike Pence visited California once, and Democratic Vice Presidential Nominee Tim Kaine visited Texas twice.
55. These counts were tabulated by the authors based on data reported by "2016 Travel Tracker," *National Journal*, http://traveltracker.nationaljournal.com/. We only count candidates' public appearances held after the party conventions.
56. This is not to say that campaigns view larger states alone as important to their electoral strategy. New Hampshire, for example, only has four electoral votes, but it was a battleground state in 2016. Trump made twelve general election campaign visits to New Hampshire, and Clinton made three. Despite Trump's efforts, Clinton narrowly won the Granite State by 0.3 percentage points.
57. U.S. Department of Commerce, *Statistical Abstract of the United States*, 101st ed. (Washington, D.C.: Government Printing Office, 1980), 514.
58. Edward Alden, "The Biggest Issue That Carried Trump to Victory," *Fortune*, November 10, 2016, http://fortune.com/2016 /11/10/trump-voters-free-trade-globalization/.
59. Maxwell Tani, "Democrats Think Trump Won on Economic Issues—But Exit Polls Offer a More Complicated Story," *Business Insider*, December 24, 2016, http://www.businessinsider .com/democrats-trump-econmic-issues-polls-2016-12.

60. See Morris P. Fiorina, with Samuel J. Abrams and Jeremy C. Pope, *Culture War? The Myth of a Polarized America*, 3rd ed. (New York: Pearson/Longman, 2010); and Andrew Gelman et al., *Red State, Blue State, Rich State, Poor State: Why Americans Vote the Way They Do* (Princeton, N.J.: Princeton University Press, 2008).
61. We use the Census Bureau's definition of the Northeast, which includes Connecticut, Maine, Massachusetts, New Hampshire, New Jersey, New York, Pennsylvania, Rhode Island, and Vermont.
62. From 1992 to 2012, the only northeastern state to cast its electoral votes for a Republican was New Hampshire in 2000, giving George W. Bush four electors. In the three elections preceding Clinton's victory in 1992, the Republicans fared quite well in the Northeast. The region was solidly pro-Reagan in 1980 (losing only Rhode Island) and 1984, and George H. W. Bush won six of the region's nine states in 1988.
63. Edward M. Burmila, "The Electoral College after Census 2010 and 2020: The Political Impact of Population Growth and Redistribution," *Perspectives on Politics* 7 (December 2009): 837–847.
64. Javier Panzar, "It's Official: Latinos Now Outnumber Whites in California," *Los Angeles Times*, July 8, 2015, http://www.latimes.com/local/california/la-me-census-latinos-20150708-story.html. Gustavo Lopez and Renee Stepler, "Latinos in the 2016 Election: California," *Pew Research Center*, January 19, 2016, http://www.pewhispanic.org/fact-sheet/latinos-in-the-2016-election-california/.
65. Mark Baldassare, *A California State of Mind: The Conflicted Voter in a Changing World* (Berkeley: University of California Press, 2002), 159.
66. CNN Election 2016, November 9, 2016, http://www.cnn.com/election/results/exit-polls/california/president.
67. Trump's largest victories—in terms of two-party differential (see Table 3-1)—were, in order, Texas, Tennessee, Alabama, Kentucky, Oklahoma, Indiana, and Missouri. In these states combined, Trump won 4.2 million more votes than Clinton.
68. Donald Trump did not willingly accept his popular vote loss. On November 27, 2016, Trump (@realDonaldTrump) tweeted, "In addition to winning the Electoral College in a landslide, I won the popular vote if you deduct the millions of people who vote illegally." We would not characterize Trump's Electoral College margin as a "landslide." In fact, Trump's electoral vote margin ranks as the forty-sixth-largest out of fifty-eight presidential elections and, based on the definition we established earlier, did not approach a landslide. And, to date, there is no systematic evidence that would suggest that more than 2.8 million ballots were cast illegally.
69. For more on the founders' view of the Electoral College, see *The Federalist Papers*, No. 68.
70. In 2012 Republican Nominee Mitt Romney won these states by an average margin of 20.9 percentage points.
71. Joseph A. Schlesinger, *Political Parties and the Winning of Office* (Ann Arbor: University of Michigan Press, 1991).
72. See Schlesinger, *Political Parties and the Winning of Office*, Figure 5-1, 112. Schlesinger does not report the exact values, but he provided them to us in a personal communication. Including the District of Columbia, which has voted for president since 1964, increases the standard deviation because the District always votes more Democratic than the most Democratic state. We report Schlesinger's results for states, not for his alternative results that include D.C. Likewise our updated results are for the fifty states.
73. The state-by-state deviation of 11.96 in the 1964 contest between Johnson and Goldwater is the highest deviation of any postwar election.

74. Since 1988, the last election reported by Schlesinger, state-by-state variation in party competition has increased slightly: 1988 (5.60), 1992 (5.96), 1996 (6.70), 2000 (8.51), 2004 (8.39), 2008 (9.54), 2012 (10.29), and 2016 (10.35), with standard deviations in parentheses.
75. See Aldrich, *Why Parties? A Second Look*, Part 3.
76. Burmila, "Electoral College," 843.
77. V. O. Key, Jr., *Southern Politics in State and Nation* (New York: Knopf, 1949), 5.
78. There have been many excellent studies of the postwar South. For three recent excellent volumes examining the political transformation of the South, see Eric Schickler, *Racial Realignment: The Transformation of American Liberalism, 1932–1965* (Princeton, N.J.: Princeton University Press, 2016); Robert Mickey, *Paths Out of Dixie: The Democratization of Authoritarian Enclaves in America's Deep South, 1944–1972* (Princeton, N.J.: Princeton University Press, 2015); and John H. Aldrich and John D. Griffin, *Why Parties Matter: Political Competition and Democracy in the American South* (Chicago: University of Chicago Press, 2018).
79. South Carolina was the most solidly Democratic, with an average Democratic vote share of 91.4 percent; Tennessee had the lowest with 56.7 percent of the vote going to the Democrats. Estimates calculated by the authors.
80. See Nancy J. Weiss, *Farewell to the Party of Lincoln: Black Politics in the Age of FDR* (Princeton, N.J.: Princeton University Press, 1983).
81. Earlier that month, southern Democrats suffered a defeat at the Democratic presidential nominating convention. Their attempts to weaken the national party's civil rights platform were defeated. At the same time, Hubert Humphrey, then mayor of Minneapolis, argued that the platform was too weak and offered an amendment for a stronger statement. Humphrey's amendment passed by a vote of 651½–582½. That victory led the southern delegations to walk out and thus led to the States' Rights Democratic Party, better known as the Dixiecrat Party.
82. Kennedy made a symbolic gesture that may have helped him with African Americans. Three weeks before the election, Martin Luther King, Jr., was arrested in Atlanta for taking part in a sit-in demonstration. Although all the other demonstrators were released, King was held on a technicality and sent to the Georgia State Penitentiary. Kennedy telephoned King's wife to express his concern, and his brother Robert F. Kennedy, Jr., acting as a private citizen, made a direct appeal to a Georgia judge that led to King's release on bail. This incident received little notice in the press, but it had a great effect on the African American community. See Theodore H. White, *The Making of the President, 1960* (New York: Atheneum, 1961), 321–323.
83. Alabama, Georgia, Louisiana, Mississippi, and South Carolina are considered the five Deep South states. They are also five of the six states with the highest percentage of African Americans.
84. When Congressman Tom Price joined the Trump administration as secretary of health and human services, a special election was held to fill his suburban Atlanta congressional seat. Hoping to capitalize on demographic trends in the area and the fact that Trump won the district by only 1.5 percentage points, the Democrats launched a significant campaign to capture the traditionally Republican seat once held by former Republican Speaker of the House Newt Gingrich. The Democratic candidate, Jon Ossoff, raised slightly more than $30 million, and overall spending by outside groups topped $50 million. Despite these efforts, Republican Karen Handel won the special election with 51.9 percent of the vote. See Robert Costa, Paul Kane, and Elise Viebeck, "Republican Karen Handel Defeats Democrat Jon Ossoff in Georgia's 6th Congressional District," *Washington Post*, June 21,

2017, https://www.washingtonpost.com/powerpost/trumps-agenda-on-the-line-in-hard-fought-georgia-house-race/2017/06/20/0d0e7086-559b-11e7-b38e-35fd8e0c288f_story.html?utm_term=.583337867faf. For Ossoff's final campaign finance report to the FEC, see https://www.fec.gov/data/committee/C00630426/.

85. John B. Judis and Ruy Teixeira, *The Emerging Democratic Majority* (New York: A Lisa Drew Book/Scribner, 2002). See also Ruy Teixeira, "The Emerging Democratic Majority Turns 10," theatlantic.com, November 9, 2012.
86. Pew Hispanic Center, "An Awakened Giant: The Hispanic Electorate Is Likely to Double by 2030," November 14, 2012, http://www.pewhispanic.org/2012/11/14/an-awakened-giant-the-hispanic-electorate-is-likely-to-double-by-2030/.
87. U.S. Census Bureau, "American Community Survey," http://www.census.gov/acs/www/.
88. Scholars have already noted the electoral consequences of Hispanic population growth. Alan Abramowitz argues that since 2000, increases in the Hispanic vote have transitioned New Mexico from a swing state to a safe Democratic state and caused the formerly Republican-leaning states of Colorado and Nevada to become Democratic-leaning. See Alan Abramowitz, "The Emerging Democratic Presidential Majority: Lessons of Obama's Victory," paper presented at the Annual Meeting of the American Political Science Association, Chicago, Illinois, August 31, 2013. See also Charles S. Bullock, III and M. V. Hood III, "A Mile-Wide Gap: The Evolution of Hispanic Political Emergence in the Deep South," *Social Science Quarterly* 87 (December 2006): 1117–1135, which shows the growing electoral strength of Hispanics in three southern states: Georgia, North Carolina, and South Carolina.
89. See, for instance, Paul R. Abramson, John H. Aldrich, and David W. Rohde, *Change and Continuity in the 1984 Elections*, rev. ed. (Washington, D.C.: CQ Press, 1987), 70–75.
90. According to Marjorie Randon Hershey, the Republicans had a "clear and continuing advantage" in presidential elections. See Marjorie Randon Hershey, "The Campaign and the Media," in *The Election of 1988: Reports and Interpretations*, ed. Gerald M. Pomper et al. (Chatham, N.J.: Chatham House, 1989), 74.
91. Jens Manuel Krogstad, "Key Facts about the Latino Vote in 2016," *Pew Research Center*, October 14, 2016, http://www.pewresearch.org/fact-tank/2016/10/14/key-facts-about-the-latino-vote-in-2016/.
92. Estimates for the size of the Latino electorate in Florida and Texas are taken from exit polls: CNN Election 2016, http://www.cnn.com/election/results/exit-polls.
93. See Jens Manuel Krogstad and Antonio Flores, "Unlike Other Latinos, about Half of Cuban Voters in Florida Backed Trump," *Pew Research Center*, November 15, 2016, http://www.pewresearch.org/fact-tank/2016/11/15/unlike-other-latinos-about-half-of-cuban-voters-in-florida-backed-trump/. The Cuban American community's enthusiasm toward Trump may in part represent a repudiation of President Obama's decision to resume diplomatic relations with Cuba. Keeping a campaign pledge, on June 17, 2017, President Trump partially reversed that policy, restricting commerce between the United States and Cuba and strictly limiting travel to the island nation.
94. Arian Campo-Flores, "Cuban-Americans Move Left," *Wall Street Journal*, November 8, 2012, http://online.wsj.com/ news/articles/SB1000142412788732407350457810741279540 5272.
95. Andrew Gelman, Jonathan N. Katz, and Gary King, "Empirically Evaluating the Electoral College," in *Rethinking the Vote: The Politics and Prospects of Electoral Reform*, eds. Ann N. Crigler, Marion R. Just, and Edward J. McCaffrey (New York: Oxford University Press, 2004), 75–88.

96. For a figure demonstrating the Republican dominance between 1972 and 1988, see Abramson, Aldrich, and Rohde, *Change and Continuity in the 1992 Elections*, rev. ed., 47.
97. See Daron R. Shaw, *The Race to 270: The Electoral College and the Campaign Strategies of 2000* (Chicago: University of Chicago Press, 2006).
98. We elected to start our measure in 1988, which reports the electoral balance following the 1972, 1976, 1980, 1984, and 1988 elections to eliminate observations that would have to use the 1968 presidential election, in which electoral votes were cast for a third-party candidate.
99. An admitted weakness of this measure is that it does not account for the average vote share within a state over time. Thus a state that consistently sided with the same party by narrow margins is equivalent to a state that consistently sided with the same party by large margins—both are categorized as "uncompetitive."

## CHAPTER 4

1. Michael McDonald reports that the voting-eligible population in 2016 was 230,585,915. This number is calculated by subtracting from the voting-age population those who are ineligible to vote, such as noncitizens, citizens living abroad, and when state law applies, felons and those judged mentally incompetent. McDonald estimates that nearly 19.5 million voting-age people living in the United States are ineligible to vote. McDonald, "2016 General Election Turnout Rates," United States Election Project, http://www.electproject.org/2016g. Our numerator, the total number of votes cast in the presidential election, comes from the Federal Election Commission's "Official 2016 Presidential General Election Results," https://transition.fec.gov/pubrec/fe2016/2016presgeresults.pdf.
2. The turnout measure for the United States divides the number of voters by the voting-age population. The International Voter Turnout Database measures turnout for the other countries by the dividing the number of voters by the number of people registered. In most democracies, voter registration is the responsibility of government, which maintains the voter rolls and automatically registers all eligible citizens for voting. Registration in the United States, however, is an individual responsibility. The U.S. Census estimates that 70.3 percent of American adult citizens are registered to vote. See U.S. Census Bureau, "Voting and Registration in the Election of November 2016, https://census.gov/data/tables/time-series/demo/voting-and-registration/p20-580.html.
3. For a comprehensive discussion of turnout change in comparative perspective, see Mark N. Franklin, *Voter Turnout and the Dynamics of Electoral Competition in Established Democracies Since 1945* (New York: Cambridge University Press, 2004).
4. In Australia, nonvoters may be subject to a small fine. In Belgium, which first adopted compulsory voting in 1892, nonvoters may suffer from future disenfranchisement and may find it difficult to obtain a public sector job. For more on the effect of compulsory voting on voter turnout, see Pippa Norris, *Election Engineering: Voting Rules and Political Behavior* (New York: Cambridge University Press, 2002); and Anthony Fowler, "Electoral and Policy Consequences of Voter Turnout: Evidence from Compulsory Voting in Australia," *Quarterly Journal of Political Science* 8 (2013): 159–182.
5. See André Blais and Kees Aarts, "Electoral Systems and Turnout," *Acta Politica*, 41 (2006): 180–196 for a review.
6. Of the remaining eight democracies in our sample, seven have experienced no significant changes in turnout rates, and only one, Malta, has experienced a significant increase in the postwar period. Much of the increase in Maltese voter turnout was experienced after the

archipelago nation achieved colonial independence from Great Britain. Elections in Malta are held via a proportional representation system using the single transferable vote.

7. This chapter focuses on one form of political participation, voting. For a major study of other forms of political participation, see Sidney Verba, Kay Lehman Schlozman, and Henry E. Brady, *Voice and Equality: Civic Voluntarism in American Politics* (Cambridge, Mass.: Harvard University Press, 1995). For a collection of essays on voting as well as other forms of political participation, see Russell J. Dalton and Hans-Dieter Klingemann, eds., *The Oxford Handbook of Political Behavior* (New York: Oxford University Press, 2007).
8. Alexander Keyssar, *The Right to Vote: The Contested History of Democracy in the United States*, rev. ed. (New York: Basic Books, 2000), 2. Keyssar's book is arguably the definitive account of the legal and political history of suffrage in the United States.
9. The Seventeenth Amendment to the United States Constitution, ratified in 1913, established direct election of United States senators by popular vote.
10. In 1790 ten of the thirteen states had property requirements for voting, and three of the thirteen limited suffrage to white males only. By 1820 property requirements were in effect in nine of the twenty-three states, and fourteen of the twenty-three states had race exclusions. See Keyssar, *The Right to Vote*, Table A.3 and Table A.5.
11. For a useful summary of the history of turnout in the United States, see Michael P. McDonald, "American Voter Turnout in Historical Perspective," in *The Oxford Handbook of American Elections and Political Behavior*, ed. Jan E. Leighley (New York: Oxford University Press, 2010), 125–143.
12. It is difficult to calculate the exact number of voters who turn out for an election. It is common to use the total number of ballots cast for the presidency as a substitute for the number of voters because in most elections more people vote for president than for any other office.
13. Women's suffrage was adopted in many of the western territories of the United States as a way of attracting female settlers. Wyoming, Utah, Washington, and Montana enfranchised women decades before they joined the union. Wyoming officially became the first state to give women the right to vote in 1890, when it obtained statehood.
14. At the outset of the Civil War, only five states—all in New England—granted blacks the right to vote. A sixth state, New York, allowed blacks who met a property requirement to vote. The Fifteenth Amendment was ratified in 1870. See Keyssar, *The Right to Vote*, 69–83.
15. See Martin J. Kousser, *The Shaping of Southern Politics: Suffrage Restrictions and the Establishment of the One-Party South, 1880–1910* (New Haven, Conn.: Yale University Press, 1974); and John H. Aldrich and John D. Griffin, *Why Parties Matter: Political Competition and Democracy in the American South* (Chicago: University of Chicago Press, 2018). For a more general discussion, see Paul Kleppner, *Who Voted? The Dynamics of Electoral Turnout, 1870–1980* (New York: Praeger, 1982), 55–82.
16. There has been a great deal of disagreement about the reasons for and the consequences of registration requirements. For some of the more interesting arguments, see Walter Dean Burnham, "The Changing Shape of the American Political Universe," *American Political Science Review* 59 (March 1965): 7–28; Philip E. Converse, "Change in the American Electorate," in *The Human Meaning of Social Change*, eds. Angus Campbell and Philip E. Converse (New York: Russell Sage, 1972), 266–301; and Walter Dean Burnham, "Theory and Voting Research: Some Reflections on Converse's 'Change in the American Electorate,'" *American Political Science Review* 68 (September 1974): 1002–1023. For two other perspectives, see Frances Fox Piven and Richard A. Cloward, *Why Americans Still Don't Vote and Why Politicians Want It That Way* (Boston: Beacon Press, 2000); and

Matthew A. Crenson and Benjamin Ginsberg, *Downsizing America: How America Sidelined Its Citizens and Privatized Its Public* (Baltimore, Md.: Johns Hopkins University Press, 2002).

17. This term originates from the fact that in 1856, two Australian colonies (now states) adopted a secret ballot to be printed and administered by the government.
18. For a rich source of information on the introduction of the Australian ballot and its effects, see Jerrold G. Rusk, "The Effect of the Australian Ballot on Split-Ticket Voting, 1876–1908," *American Political Science Review* 64 (December 1970): 1220–1238.
19. The secret ballot, like a few of the other "good government" electoral reforms of the Progressive Era, such as literacy tests, often had unintended consequences or were used in the South to disenfranchise African Americans. An analysis by Jac C. Heckelman estimates that the introduction of the secret ballot lowered voter turnout in U.S. gubernatorial elections by seven percentage points. See Jac C. Heckelman, "The Effect of the Secret Ballot on Voter Turnout Rates," *Public Choice* 82 (No. 1/2, 1995): 107–124.
20. Keyssar, *The Right to Vote*, 115.
21. Burnham presents estimates of turnout among the "politically-eligible population" between 1789 and 1984 in "The Turnout Problem," in *Elections American Style*, ed. James A. Reichley (Washington, D.C.: Brookings, 1987), 113–114. In a series of personal communications, Burnham provided us with estimates of turnout among the "voting-eligible population" between 1988 and 2004: 52.7 percent in 1988, 56.9 percent in 1992, 50.8 percent in 1996, 54.9 percent in 2000, and 60.7 percent in 2004. McDonald and Popkin's estimates of turnout between 1948 and 2000 are available in Michael P. McDonald and Samuel L. Popkin, "The Myth of the Vanishing Voter," *American Political Science Review* 95 (December 2001): 996. McDonald's estimates for the 2004, 2008, 2012, and 2016 elections are available on his United States Elections Project website, http://www.electproject.org/home/voter-turnout/voter-turnout-data.
22. Only Maine and Vermont allow prisoners to vote, and in nine states felons are permanently disenfranchised unless voting rights are restored by gubernatorial or court action. In 2015 Wyoming passed a law restoring voting rights to nonviolent felons who have completed their sentences.
23. McDonald's estimates of the eligible population do not account for the number of permanently disenfranchised felons "since time-series statistics on recidivism, deaths, and migration of felons are largely unavailable." See McDonald, "How Is the Ineligible Felon Population Estimated," http://www.electproject.org/home/voter-turnout/faq/felons.
24. McDonald, "2016 General Election Turnout Rates," http://www.electproject.org/2016g.
25. Thomas E. Patterson, *The Vanishing Voter: Public Involvement in an Age of Uncertainty* (New York: Knopf, 2002). See also Pippa Norris, *Democratic Participation Worldwide* (Cambridge, U.K.: Cambridge University Press, 2002).
26. See note 21.
27. Burnham estimated turnout in 1960 at 65.4 percent, and McDonald and Popkin estimated it at 63.8 percent. See Burnham, "Turnout Problem," 114; and McDonald and Popkin, "Myth of the Vanishing Voter," 966.
28. See Glenn Firebaugh and Kevin Chen, "Vote Turnout among Nineteenth Amendment Women: The Enduring Effects of Disfranchisement," *American Journal of Sociology* 100 (January 1995): 972–996.
29. For estimates of this reform on turnout, see Raymond E. Wolfinger and Jonathan Hoffman, "Registering and Voting with Motor Voter," *PS: Political Science and Politics* 34 (March 2001): 86–92. David Hill argues that whereas motor voter legislation has made the election rolls

more representative, it has had little effect on turnout. See David Hill, *American Voter Turnout: An Institutional Perspective* (Boulder, Colo.: Westview Press, 2006), 49–52, 55.

30. We follow Paul Gronke's usage of early voting as "a blanket term used to describe any system where voters can cast their ballots before the official election day . . . [including] in-person early voting, no-excuse absentee balloting, and vote-by-mail." See Paul Gronke, "Early Voting Reforms and American Elections," *William and Mary Bill of Rights Journal* 17 (Issue 2, 2008): 423–451.
31. Theory suggests that easing the "cost" of voting by making it more convenient should increase voting turnout. Yet scholarly research on the effect of early voting on turnout is mixed with some showing the effect to be quite small and others showing the increase to be as large as 10 percent. See Paul Gronke, Eva Galanes-Rosenbaum, and Peter A. Miller, "Early Voting and Turnout," *PS: Political Science and Politics* 40 (October 2007): 639–645, for a review.
32. National Conference of State Legislatures, "Absentee and Early Voting," http://www.ncsl.org/research/elections-and-campaigns/absentee-and-early-voting.aspx.
33. The 2016 Current Population Survey (CPS) is based on more than 131,000 respondent households nationally with sizable (and representative) samples drawn for each state. The CPS is commonly used in studies of turnout, although the Census Bureau only measures voting behavior along with demographic variables (federal law does not allow the Census Bureau to measure individual's political attitudes). The most important study to use the CPS remains Raymond E. Wolfinger and Steven J. Rosenstone, *Who Votes?* (New Haven, Conn.: Yale University Press, 1980).
34. Conventional political wisdom held that early voting laws would decrease the costs of voting, increase turnout, and disproportionately benefit Democratic candidates. A recent empirical study examining the effects of various state election laws on voter turnout suggests that early voting may actually benefit Republican candidates on average, although the effects are likely highly contingent on contextual factors. See Barry C. Burden, David T. Canon, Kenneth R. Mayer, and Donald P. Moynihan, "The Complicated Partisan Effects of State Election Laws," *Political Research Quarterly* 70 (2017): 564–576.
35. As Wolfinger and Rosenstone demonstrate, about one-fifth of this decline resulted from the enfranchisement of eighteen-, nineteen-, and twenty-year-olds. Their nationwide enfranchisement stemmed from the 1971 ratification of the Twenty-sixth Amendment, which made it possible for more people to vote, but because these youth have low levels of voting, overall levels of turnout declined. See Wolfinger and Rosenstone, *Who Votes?*, 58.
36. For our analysis of the reasons for the increase in turnout in 1992, see Paul R. Abramson, John H. Aldrich, and David W. Rohde, *Change and Continuity in the 1992 Elections*, rev. ed. (Washington, D.C.: CQ Press, 1995), 120–123. As we point out it is difficult to demonstrate empirically that Perot's candidacy made an important contribution to the increase in turnout. For additional analyses, see Stephen M. Nichols and Paul Allen Beck, "Reversing the Decline: Voter Turnout in 1992," in *Democracy's Feast: Elections in America*, ed. Herbert F. Weisberg (Chatham, N.J.: Chatham House, 1995), 62–65.
37. When appropriate we also rely on estimates from the 2016 Current Population Survey (CPS) and exit poll data. The Census Bureau published a detailed report of its 2016 survey in May 2017. See U.S. Census Bureau, "Voting in America: A Look at the 2016 Presidential Election," https://census.gov/newsroom/blogs/random-samplings/2017/05/voting_in_america.html. Interested readers can access data from the 2016 CPS, November Supplement (as well as other Census Bureau studies), using the Census Bureau's DataFerrett website, https://dataferrett.census.gov/.

Exit polls were conducted by Edison Research of Somerville, New Jersey, for the "National Election Pool," a consortium of ABC News, CBS News, CNN, Fox News, and NBC News. The exit polls are not a representative sample of the nation. Instead polls were conducted in twenty-eight states. Precincts in each state were selected by a stratified-probability sample, and every *n*th voter in the precinct was given a questionnaire to complete. In states with significant early and/or absentee voting, a supplemental telephone survey was conducted.

38. Respondents to the postelection survey of the ANES are asked: In talking to people about elections, we often find that a lot of people were not able to vote because they weren't registered, they were sick, or they just didn't have time. Which of the following statements best describes you?

    One, I did not vote (in the election this November);

    Two, I thought about voting this time, but didn't;

    Three, I usually vote, but didn't this time;

    Four, I am sure I voted.

    We classified respondents as voters if they were sure that they voted.

39. These studies suggest, however, that African Americans are more likely to falsely claim to have voted than whites. As a result racial differences are always greater when turnout is measured by the vote validation studies. Unfortunately we have no way of knowing whether this difference between the races has changed as African American turnout has increased with time. For results for the 1964, 1976, 1978, 1980, 1984, 1986, and 1988 elections, see Paul R. Abramson and William Claggett, "Racial Differences in Self-Reported and Validated Voting in the 1988 Presidential Election," *Journal of Politics* 53 (February 1991): 186–187. For a discussion of the factors that contribute to false reports of voting, see Brian D. Silver, Barbara A. Anderson, and Paul R. Abramson, "Who Overreports Voting?" *American Political Science Review* 80 (June 1986): 613–624. For a more recent study that argues that biases in reported turnout are more severe than Silver, Anderson, and Abramson claim, see Robert Bernstein, Anita Chadha, and Robert Montjoy, "Overreporting Voting: Why It Happens and Why It Matters," *Public Opinion Quarterly* 65 (Spring 2001): 22–44.

40. Barry Burden reports that the overreporting of voter turnout in the ANES increased with time. He attributes this to declining response rates for the ANES rather than question wording changes or other problems with the survey. See Barry C. Burden, "Voter Turnout and the National Election Studies," *Political Analysis* 8 (July 2000): 389–398. See Michael P. McDonald, "On the Overreport Bias of the National Election Study Turnout Rate," *Political Analysis* (May 2003): 180–186; and Michael D. Martinez, "Comment on 'Voter Turnout and the National Election Studies,'" *Political Analysis* (May 2003): 187–192 for counterarguments to Burden.

    In an analysis of the 2008 vote validation study, the ANES staff and principal investigators found a surprisingly high level of accuracy in self-reported turnout when compared with official turnout records, suggesting that overreporting comes from sources other than respondents simply saying they voted when they did not. See Matthew K. Berent, Jon A. Krosnick, and Arthur Lupia, "The Quality of Government Records and 'Over-estimation' of Registration and Turnout in Surveys: Lessons from the 2008 ANES Panel Study's Registration and Turnout Validation Exercises," American National Election Studies, Working Paper no. nes012554, August 2011, http://www.electionstudies.org/resources/papers/nes012554.pdf.

41. The response rate for the 2016 ANES is an improvement over the 2012 ANES, for which the response rate was a record low 38 percent.

42. Sidney Verba and Norman H. Nie, *Participation in America: Political Democracy and Social Equality* (New York: Cambridge University Press, 1972).
43. See Henry E. Brady, Sidney Verba, and Kay Lehman Schlozman, "Beyond SES: A Resource Model of Political Participation," *American Political Science Review* 89 (June, 1995): 271–294; and Sidney Verba, Kay Lehman Schlozman, and Henry E. Brady, *Voice and Equality: Civic Voluntarism in American Politics* (Cambridge, Mass.: Harvard University Press, 1995).
44. Nicholas Confessore, "For Whites Sensing Decline, Donald Trump Unleashes Words of Resistance," *New York Times*, July 14, 2016, A1; and Emma Green, "It Was Cultural Anxiety that Drove White, Working-Class Voters to Trump," *The Atlantic*, May 9, 2017, https://www.theatlantic.com/politics/archive/2017/05/white-working-class-trump-cultural-anxiety/525771/.
45. Respondents were classified by the interviewer into one of the following categories: white; black/African American; white and black; other race; white and another race; black and another race; and white, black, and another race. We classified only respondents who were white as whites; except for Asians, respondents in the other categories were classified as blacks.
46. For 1964 see U.S. Census Bureau, "Voting Participation in the National Election: November 1964," Table 1, http://www.census.gov/hhes/www/socdemo/voting/publications/p20/1964/tab01.pdf. For 2004 see U.S. Census Bureau, "Voting and Registration in the Election of November 2004," http://www.census.gov/prod/2006pubs/p20-556.pdf, Table B.
47. The church has been demonstrated to be an important mobilizer of black political participation; see Frederick C. Harris, *Something Within: Religion in African-American Political Activism* (New York: Oxford University Press, 1999). In past studies we too have shown that African Americans who regularly attend church ("once a week") are more likely to vote than those who never attend. In 2016, however, we do not see evidence of a statistically significant difference in turnout between blacks who attend church regularly and those who do not.
48. Benjamin Highton and Arthur L. Burris, "New Perspectives on Latino Voter Turnout in the United States," *American Politics Research* 30 (May 2002): 285–306 utilize CPS data to investigate socioeconomic, ethnic, and place-of-birth differences among Latinos. These authors find that native-born Latinos are more likely to turn out. Matt Barreto, however, using data from California, finds that Latino immigrants were more likely to vote than were native-born Latinos. Clearly this warrants further investigation. See Matt A. Barreto, "Latino Immigrants at the Polls: Foreign-born Voter Turnout in the 2002 Election," *Political Research Quarterly* 58 (March 2005): 79–86.
49. Abramson, Aldrich, and Rohde, *Change and Continuity in the 2008 Elections*, 98.
50. For an early example of this work, see M. Kent Jennings, "Another Look at the Life Cycle and Political Participation," *American Journal of Political Science* 23 (November 1979): 755–771.
51. See Benjamin Highton and Raymond E. Wolfinger, "The First Seven Years of the Political Life Cycle," *American Journal of Political Science* 45 (January 2001): 202–209.
52. Aaron Blake, "More Young People Voted for Bernie Sanders than Trump and Clinton Combined—By a Lot," *Washington Post*, June 20, 2016, https://www.washingtonpost.com/news/the-fix/wp/2016/06/20/more-young-people-voted-for-bernie-sanders-than-trump-and-clinton-combined-by-a-lot/?utm_term=.7f57570ea2c9.
53. Millennials are usually defined as those born between 1982 and 2000.
54. Jan E. Leighley and Jonathan Nagler, "Socioeconomic Class Bias in Turnout, 1972–1988: The Voters Remain the Same," *American Political Science Review* 86 (September 1992): 725–736.

55. See Warren E. Miller, Arthur H. Miller, and Edward J. Schneider, *American National Studies Data Sourcebook, 1952–1978* (Cambridge, Mass.: Harvard University Press, 1980), Table 5.23, 317.
56. For example, Robert D. Putnam and David E. Campbell, *American Grace: How Religion Divides and Unites Us* (New York: Simon and Schuster, 2012).
57. See the Pew Religion and Public Life Project, "U.S. Public Becoming Less Religious," http://assets.pewresearch.org/wp-content/uploads/sites/11/2015/11/201.11.03_RLS_II_full_report.pdf. When asked "how important is religion in your life?" 53.2 percent of Americans say "very important," 24.5 percent say "somewhat important," whereas 21.6 percent say religion is "not at all important" in their lives. Nearly 40 percent report attending religious services weekly or more and 15 "once or twice a month." Close to 50 percent of Americans say they attend religious services a few times a year or less.
58. See Dietram A. Scheufele, Matthew C. Nisbet, Dominque Brossard, and Erik C. Nisbet, "Social Structure and Citizenship: Examining the Impacts of Social Setting, Network Heterogeneity, and Informational Variables on Political Participation," *Political Communication* 21 (2004): 315–338.
59. For general treatments, see Clyde Wilcox and Lee Sigelman, "Political Mobilization in the Pews: Religious Contacting and Electoral Turnout," *Social Science Quarterly* 82 (September, 2001): 524–535; and David E. Campbell, "Acts of Faith: Churches and Political Engagement," *Political Behavior* 26 (June 2004): 155–180. For an examination of the mobilizing role of churches in the African American community, see Fredrick C. Harris, "Something Within: Religion as a Mobilizer of African-American Political Activism, *Journal of Politics* 56 (February 1994): 42–68.
60. Federal law prohibits the Census Bureau from measuring religious preferences on the CPS.
61. Miller, Miller, and Schneider, *American National Data Sourcebook*, Table 5.23, 317. Between 1952 and 1976 Catholics were on average 8.0 percentage points more likely to vote in presidential elections, and between 1958 and 1988 they were 10.8 points more likely to vote in midterm elections.
62. As noted earlier, exit polls were not conducted in all states but instead were used in states that were deemed most competitive. This may have affected the estimates of the religious composition of the electorate. Consider the fact that several states with the largest Catholic populations (e.g., Louisiana, Massachusetts, and Maryland) were not included in the 2016 exit polls. Nationally aggregated responses to the exit poll are also unweighted, so the exit poll results for religion may differ from those produced by a nationally representative probability sample, such as that used by the ANES.
63. For a study of Conservative Christian mobilization in a recent U.S. election, see J. Quin Monson and J. Baxter Oliphant, "Microtargeting and the Instrumental Mobilization of Religious Conservatives" in David E. Campbell, ed. *A Matter of Faith: Religion in the 2004 Presidential Election* (Washington, D.C.: Brookings Institution, 2007).
64. Respondents were asked, "Would you call yourself a born-again Christian, that is, have you personally had a conversion experience related to Jesus Christ?"
65. Pew Research Center, "Religious Landscape Survey," http://www.pewforum.org/religious-landscape-study/.
66. Due to data availability issues, we were unable to construct this measure in 2012. Our measure for 2016, which does not include an indicator of the respondent's frequency of prayer, differs slightly from that used in 2008 and earlier. For details regarding the construction of the religious commitment measure in earlier studies, see Abramson, Aldrich, and Rohde, *Change and Continuity in the 2008 Elections*, Chapter 4, note 49.

67. Kenneth D. Wald, *Religion and Politics in the United States*, 4th ed. (Lanham, Md.: Rowman and Littlefield, 2003), 161.
68. R. Stephen Warner, *New Wine in Old Wineskins: Evangelicals and Liberals in a Small-Town Church* (Berkeley: University of California Press, 1977), 173.
69. The branching questions used to classify respondents into specific denominational categories were changed in 2008, and therefore it is not possible to replicate our analyses of the 1992, 1996, 2000, and 2004 categories. In creating these new classifications, we relied largely on the Pew Forum on Religion and Public Life, *U.S. Religious Landscape Survey: Religious Affiliation, Diverse and Dynamic* (Washington, D.C.: Pew Forum on Religion and Public Life, 2008), 12. In addition, we were assisted by Corwin D. Smidt.

    Our classification for 2016 used the following procedures. We used the variable V161248 in the 2016 ANES survey to determine the respondent's denomination. Codes 2, 3, 4, 6, 9, 13, 14, 17, and 20 for this variable were classified as mainline; codes 1, 8, 12, 15, 16, 18, and 19 were classified as evangelical.
70. Wolfinger and Rosenstone, *Who Votes?*, 102.
71. For the effect of education on political knowledge and political awareness, see Michael X. Delli Carpini, and Scott Keeter, *What Americans Know about Politics and Why It Matters* (New Haven, Conn.: Yale University Press, 1996); and John R. Zaller, *The Nature and Origins of Mass Opinion* (New York: Cambridge University Press, 1992), respectively. Henry E. Brady, Sidney Verba, and Kay Lehman Schlozman, "Beyond SES: A Resource Model of Political Participation," *American Political Science Review* 89 (June 1995): 271–294, discuss how education enhances both political engagement and civic skills.
72. Richard A. Brody, "The Puzzle of Political Participation in America," in *The New American Political System*, ed. Anthony King (Washington, D.C.: American Enterprise Institute, 1978), 287–324.
73. U.S. Census Bureau, *Statistical Abstract of the United States, 1962* (Washington, D.C.: Government Printing Office, 1962), Tables 1 and 129; and U.S. Department of Justice, "Corrections in the United States," https://www.census.gov/ newsroom/cspan/incarceration/20120504_incarceration_bjs-slides.pdf.
74. Ruy A. Teixeira, *The Disappearing American Voter* (Washington, D.C.: American Enterprise Institute, 1992).
75. The Gallup Poll provides the best evidence regarding church attendance over the past six decades. Although church attendance has declined on average, Catholics appear to be driving the decline. Since 1955 weekly church attendance among Catholics has dropped by nearly 30 percent. Weekly church attendance among Protestants has been stable throughout the period. Interestingly the percentage of Catholics attending church weekly is now roughly equal to the rate among Protestants. See Lydia Saad, "Churchgoing among U.S. Catholics Slides to Tie Protestants," gallup.com, April 9, 2009, http://www.gallup.com/poll/117382/church-going-among-catholics-slides-tie-protestants.aspx.
76. Robert D. Putnam makes a similar argument, claiming that political disengagement was largely the result of the baby boom generation and that generational succession reduced other forms of civic activity as well. Putnam writes: "The declines in church attendance, voting, political interest, campaign activities, associational membership and social trusts are attributable almost entirely to generational succession." See Robert D. Putnam, *Bowling Along: The Collapse and Revival of American Community* (New York: Simon and Schuster, 2000), 265.
77. Steven J. Rosenstone and John Mark Hansen, *Mobilization, Participation, and Democracy in America* (New York: Macmillan, 1993), 214–215.

78. George I. Balch, "Multiple Indicators in Survey Research: The Concept 'Sense of Political Efficacy,'" *Political Methodology* 1 (Spring 1974): 1–43. For an extensive discussion of feelings of political efficacy, see Paul R. Abramson, *Political Attitudes in America: Formation and Change* (San Francisco: W. H. Freeman, 1983): 135–189.
79. Ruy A. Teixeira, *Why Americans Don't Vote: Turnout Decline in the United States, 1960–1964* (New York: Greenwood Press, 1987). In his more recent study, *The Disappearing American Voter*, Teixeira develops a measure of party-related characteristics that includes strength of party identification, concern about the electoral outcome, perceived difference between the parties, and knowledge about the parties and the candidates. See also Rosenstone and Hansen, *Mobilization, Participation, and Democracy.*
80. Our first analysis studied the decline of turnout between 1960 and 1980. See Paul R. Abramson, John H. Aldrich, and David W. Rohde, *Change and Continuity in the 1980 Elections*, rev. ed. (Washington, D.C.: CQ Press, 1983), 85–87. For a more detailed analysis using probability procedures, see Paul R. Abramson and John H. Aldrich, "The Decline of Electoral Participation in America," *American Political Science Review* 76 (September 1982): 502–521. For our analyses from 1984 through 2008, see Abramson, Aldrich, and Rohde, *Change and Continuity in the 2008 Elections*, 105–108 and Chapter 4, note 73.
81. ANES respondents are asked, "Generally speaking, do you usually think of yourself as a Republican, a Democrat, an Independent, or what?" Persons who call themselves Republicans are asked, "Would you call yourself a strong Republican or a not very strong Republican?" Those who call themselves Democrats are asked, "Would you call yourself a strong Democrat or a not very strong Democrat?" Those who called themselves independents, named another party, or who had no preference were asked, "Do you think of yourself as closer to the Republican party or to the Democratic party?"
82. The seminal work on party identification is Angus Campbell, Philip E. Converse, Warren E. Miller, and Donald E. Stokes, *The American Voter* (New York: Wiley, 1960), 120–167.
83. See Morris P. Fiorina, "The Voting Decision: Instrumental and Expressive Aspects," *Journal of Politics* 38 (May 1976): 390–413; and John H. Aldrich, "Rational Choice and Turnout," *American Journal of Political Science* 37 (February 1993): 246–278.
84. For a detailed discussion of party identification from 1952 to 2016, along with tables showing the distribution of party identification among whites and blacks during these years, see Chapter 8 in this volume as well as the appendix.
85. As Steven E. Finkel notes, the relationship between political efficacy and political participation is likely reciprocal. Not only do feelings of efficacy increase the likelihood of participation, participation increases individuals' feelings of efficacy. See Steven E. Finkel, "Reciprocal Effects of Participation and Political Efficacy: A Panel Analysis," *American Journal of Political Science* 29 (November 1985): 891–913.
86. Our measure of external efficacy is based on the responses to two statements: "Public officials don't care much what people like me think" and "People like me don't have any say about what the government does." Respondents who disagreed with both of these statements were scored as high in feelings of effectiveness; those who agreed with one statement and disagreed with the other were scored as medium; and those who agreed with both statements were scored as low. Respondents who scored "don't know" or "not ascertained" to one statement were scored high or low according to their answer on the other statement. Those with "don't know" or "not ascertained" responses to both statements were excluded from the analysis. Since 1988 ANES respondents have been asked whether they "strongly agreed," "agreed," "disagreed," or "strongly disagreed" with the statements. We classified respondents who "neither agreed nor disagreed," with

both statements as medium on our measure. This decision has little effect on the results because few respondents "neither agree nor disagree" to both statements, typically less than 5 percent. In 2008 and 2012 this standard measure of feelings of "external" political efficacy was asked of only half of the sample. In 2016 all respondents were asked the political efficacy questions.

87. See Abramson and Aldrich, "The Decline of Electoral Participation in America," 515.
88. The procedure uses the 1960 distribution of partisans by levels of efficacy as our base, thus assuming that levels of turnout for each subgroup (e.g., strong partisan/high efficacy and strong partisan/medium efficacy) would have remained the same if partisanship and efficacy had not declined. We multiply the size of each subgroup (set at 1960 levels) times the proportion of the whites who reported voting in each subgroups in the 2016 election. We then sum the products and divide by the sum of the subgroup sizes. The procedure is detailed in Abramson, *Political Attitudes in America: Formation and Change*, 296.
89. For a discussion of political trust, see Abramson, *Political Attitudes in America*, 193–238. For a more recent discussion, see Marc J. Hetherington, *Why Trust Matters: Declining Political Trust and the Demise of American Liberalism* (Princeton, N.J.: Princeton University Press, 2005).

    Russell J. Dalton reports a decline in confidence in politicians and government in fifteen of sixteen democracies. Although many of the trends are not statistically significant, the overall decline is impressive. Dalton's report includes results from the ANES, where the trend toward declining confidence is unlikely to occur by chance on two of the three questions. See Russell J. Dalton, *Democratic Challenges, Democratic Choices: The Erosion of Political Support in Advanced Industrial Democracies* (Oxford: Oxford University Press, 2004), 28–32.
90. Respondents were asked, "How much of the time do you think you can trust the government in Washington to do what is right—just about always, most of the time, or only some of the time?"
91. This question was asked of a randomly selected half-sample in 2008.
92. See Brad T. Gomez, Thomas G. Hansford, and George A. Krause, "The Republicans Should Pray for Rain: Weather, Turnout, and Voting in U.S. Presidential Elections," *Journal of Politics* 69 (August 2007): 649–663.
93. The recent proliferation in electoral laws allowing early voting is likely to diminish the chances that bad weather on election day will reduce voter turnout. Laws that allow citizens to vote by mail, such as those found in Colorado, Oregon, and Washington, make election day weather inconsequential.
94. In the past half century, a handful of elections could be classified—based upon pre-election polling—as "dead heats" going into election day. Recall from Chapter 3, for example, that the average of nine pre-election polls in 2012 showed a virtual tie between Obama and Romney. By contrast, in 1964, the final Gallup Poll before the election predicted a twenty-eight-point victory in the popular vote for Lyndon Johnson over Barry Goldwater.
95. See Anthony Downs, *An Economic Theory of Democracy* (New York: Harper and Row, 1957); and William H. Riker and Peter C. Ordeshook, "A Theory of the Calculus of Voting," *American Political Science Review* 72 (March 1968): 25–42.
96. These are Colorado, Florida, Iowa, Michigan, Minnesota, Nevada, New Hampshire, New Mexico, North Carolina, Ohio, Pennsylvania, Virginia, and Wisconsin.
97. Rosenstone and Hansen, *Mobilization, Participation, and Democracy in America*, 181–182.

98. The use of randomized field experiments in political science predates the work of Gerber and Green, although these authors are certainly responsible for the revived interest in the research design in the discipline. In the 1920s Harold Gosnell sent postcards to randomly assigned nonvoters emphasizing the importance of voter registration before the 1924 presidential election. Gosnell found a significant increase in voter registration among those who received the postcard treatment compared to those in his control group who received nothing. In the 1950s Samuel Eldersveld used random assignment to test the effectiveness of mail, phone, and in-person canvassing in a local mayoral race. It would be decades before another field experiment design was published in the academic journals of political science. See Harold F. Gosnell, *Getting Out the Vote* (Chicago: University of Chicago Press, 1927); and Samuel J. Eldersveld, "Experimental Propaganda Techniques and Voting Behavior," *American Political Science Review* 50 (March 1956): 154–165.
99. See Alan S. Gerber and Donald P. Green, *Field Experiments: Design, Analysis, and Interpretation* (New York: Norton, 2012), for an introduction to field experimentation in the social sciences.
100. See Donald P. Green and Alan S. Gerber, *Get Out the Vote: How to Increase Voter Turnout*, 2nd ed. (Washington, D.C.: Brookings Institution Press, 2008), for a summary of findings in this research program.
101. This is not to say that it is impossible to make causal inferences from survey data. Panel designs, where survey respondents are interviewed repeatedly at multiple time periods, can establish causal (temporal) order. Paul R. Abramson and William Claggett, for instance, use ANES panel data from 1990 and 1992 to show the effects of party contact on voter turnout persist even after one takes into account that the political elites are more likely to contact people who have participated in the past. See Paul R. Abramson and William Claggett, "Recruitment and Political Participation," *Political Research Quarterly* 54 (December 2001): 905–916.
102. Respondents were asked, "The political parties try to talk to as many people as they can to get them to vote for their candidate. Did anyone from the political parties call or come around to talk with you about the campaign this year?"
103. Lisa Desjardins and Daniel Bush, "The Trump Campaign Has a Ground-Game Problem," *PBS Newshour*, August 30, 2016, http://www.pbs.org/newshour/updates/trump-campaign-has-ground-game-problem/; Chris Cillizz, "No, Donald Trump—You Still Don't Have a Ground Game," *Washington Post*, September 2, 2016, https://www.washingtonpost.com/news/the-fix/wp/2016/09/01/donald-trump-has-1-field-office-open-in-all-of-florida-thats-a-total-disaster/?utm_term=.13b710ba1cc7; and Susan Milligan, "The Fight on the Ground," *US News and World Report*, October 14, 2016, https://www.usnews.com/news/the-report/articles/2016-10-14/donald-trump-abandons-the-ground-game.
104. Seymour Martin Lipset, *Political Man: The Social Bases of Politics*, exp. ed. (Baltimore: Johns Hopkins University Press, 1981), 226–229.
105. See James DeNardo, "Turnout and the Vote: The Joke's on the Democrats," *American Political Science Review* 74 (December 1980): 406–420; and Thomas G. Hansford and Brad T. Gomez, "Estimating the Electoral Effects of Voter Turnout," *American Political Science Review* 104 (May 2010): 268–288.
106. In addition to the partisan effect of high turnout, Hansford and Gomez argue that incumbents from both parties lose vote share as turnout becomes higher, suggesting that peripheral voters, that is, those who vote irregularly, are less supportive of incumbents than dedicated voters.

107. As reported by the National Conference of State Legislatures, see http://www.ncsl.org/legislatures-elections/elections/voter-id.aspx.
108. In 2013 the U.S. Supreme Court, in a 5–4 vote, struck down provisions—Sections 4(b) and 5—of the 1965 Voting Rights Act (VRA) that required several states with histories of racial discrimination in voting (mostly southern states, including North Carolina) to obtain "preclearance" from the federal government before changing their voting laws or practices. See *Shelby County v. Holder*, 570 U.S. 2 (2013). Following this decision, several states—Alabama, Arizona, Arkansas, North Carolina, Ohio, Wisconsin, and Texas—once covered by the VRA's preclearance requirements moved swiftly to alter their election laws. All of these states are governed by Republicans.
109. Robert Barnes and Ann E. Marimow, "Appeals Court Strikes Down North Carolina's Voter-ID Law," *Washington Post*, July 29, 2016, https://www.washingtonpost.com/local/public-safety/appeals-court-strikes-down-north-carolinas-voter-id-law/2016/07/29/810b5844-4f72-11e6-aa14-e0c1087f7583_story.html?utm_term=.0431a0552c6a.
110. "Supreme Court Rejects Appeal to Reinstate North Carolina Voter ID Law," *Fox News*, May 15, 2017, http://www.foxnews.com/politics/2017/05/15/supreme-court-rejects-appeal-over-nc-voter-id-law.html.
111. Abramson, Aldrich, and Rohde, *Change and Continuity in the 1980 Elections*, 88–92; *Change and Continuity in the 1984 Elections*, 119–124; and *Change and Continuity in the 1988 Elections*, 108–112.
112. Abramson, Aldrich, and Rohde, *Change and Continuity in the 1992 Elections*, 124–128.
113. Abramson, Aldrich, and Rohde, *Change and Continuity in the 1996 and 1998 Elections*, 86–89.
114. Paul R. Abramson, John H. Aldrich, and David W. Rohde, "The 2004 Presidential Election: The Emergence of a Permanent Majority," *Political Science Quarterly* 120 (Spring 2005): 43.
115. Abramson, Aldrich, and Rohde, *Change and Continuity in the 1992 Elections*, 110–112.
116. See Campbell, Converse, Miller, and Stokes, *The American Voter*, 96–115.
117. The kind and number of issues used varied from election to election. We used only issues on which respondents were asked to state their own positions and where they thought the major-party candidates were located. See Table 6-4 for the number of issues used in each election between 1980 and 2008.
118. Our issue scale differs slightly from the one used in our 2008 analysis, which included seven items. Since 2012 the ANES no longer asks respondents' opinions regarding the role of women in society. Consequently this item has been removed from our scale.
119. In their county-level analysis of the electoral effect of voter turnout in the 1944 through 2000 presidential elections, Hansford and Gomez use simulations from their statistical model to demonstrate that a 4 percent swing in turnout (from 2 percent below to 2 percent above actual turnout) leads to an average change in Democratic vote share at the national level of just under one percentage point. However, small changes are not necessarily trivial. The authors go on to show that varying turnout from two points above and below observed values causes an average change of approximately twenty Electoral College votes per presidential election in nonsouthern states. See Hansford and Gomez, "Estimating the Electoral Effects of Voter Turnout," 284.
120. For the most influential statement of this argument, see Wolfinger and Rosenstone, *Who Votes?*, 108–114.
121. Frances Fox Piven and Richard A. Cloward, *Why Americans Don't Vote* (New York: Pantheon Books, 1988), 21. See also Piven and Cloward, *Why Americans Still Don't Vote*.

## CHAPTER 5

1. For a classic treatment of the subject, see M. Kent Jennings and Richard G. Niemi, *Generations and Politics: A Panel Study of Young Adults and their Parents* (Princeton, N.J.: Princeton University Press, 1981).
2. See Larry M. Bartels, "What's the Matter with *What's the Matter with Kansas?*" *Quarterly Journal of Political Science* 1 (2006): 201–226.
3. See Paul R. Abramson, John H. Aldrich, and David W. Rohde, *Change and Continuity in the 2008 and 2010 Elections* (Washington, D.C.: CQ Press, 2012), 116–141.
4. The social characteristics used in this chapter are the same as those used in Chapter 4. The variables are described in the notes to that chapter.
5. In 2016 the National Election Pool consortium was composed of ABC News, Associated Press, CBS News, CNN, Fox News, and NBC News.
6. As noted in Chapter 4, note 37, the exit polls are not a representative sample of the nation. The exit polls were conducted separately in twenty-eight states. Precincts in each state were selected by a stratified-probability sample, and every *n*th voter in the precinct was offered a questionnaire to complete. In states with significant early and/or absentee voting, the sample was supplemented with a telephone survey.

   We draw on 2016 exit poll reports from Fox News (http://www.foxnews.com/politics/elections/2016/exit-polls), *New York Times* (https://www.nytimes.com/interactive/2016/11/08/us/politics/election-exit-polls.html), CNN (http://www.cnn.com/election/results/exit-polls/national/president), and *Washington Post* (https://www.washingtonpost.com/graphics/politics/2016-election/exit-polls/). For a discussion of the 2012 exit polls, see Abramson, Aldrich, Gomez, and Rohde, *Change and Continuity in the 2012 Elections*, 116–142.

   Exit polls have three main advantages: (1) they are less expensive to conduct than the multistage probability samples conducted by the American National Election Studies; (2) because of their lower cost, a large number of people can be sampled; and (3) because persons are selected to be interviewed as they leave the polling stations, the vast majority of respondents have actually voted. But these surveys also have four disadvantages: (1) organizations that conduct exit polls must now take into account the growing number of voters who vote early—about a third of all voters in 2008; (2) the self-administered polls used for respondents leaving the polls must be relatively brief; (3) it is difficult to supervise the fieldwork to ensure that interviewers are using the proper procedures to select respondents; and (4) these studies are of relatively little use in studying turnout because persons who do not vote are not sampled. For a discussion of the procedures used to conduct exit polls and their limitations, see Albert H. Cantril, *The Opinion Connection: Polling, Politics, and the Press* (Washington, D.C.: CQ Press, 1991), 142–144, 216–218.
7. This brief discussion cannot do justice to the complexities of black electoral participation. For an important study based on the 1984 ANES survey of blacks, see Patricia Gurin, Shirley Hatchett, and James S. Jackson, *Hope and Independence: Blacks' Response to Electoral and Party Politics* (New York: Russell Sage Foundation, 1989). For two important studies that use this survey, see Michael C. Dawson, *Behind the Mule: Race and Class in African American Politics* (Princeton, N.J.: Princeton University Press, 1994); and Katherine Tate, *From Politics to Protest: The New Black Voter in American Elections* (Cambridge, Mass.: Harvard University Press, 1994). For a summary of recent research on race and politics, see Michael C. Dawson and Cathy Cohen, "Problems in the Politics of Race," in *Political Science: The State of the Discipline*, eds. Ira Katznelson and Helen V. Milner (New York: Norton, 2002), 488–510.

8. The estimate of the black electorate in 2012 comes from exit poll data. Unfortunately we cannot compare the size of Trump's black electorate to Mitt Romney's in 2012 using the ANES. Even with an oversample of black respondents, the weighted ANES data shows only three black respondents who voted for Romney, a number that is too small to create reliable estimates. The 2012 exit poll suggests that 7 percent of blacks voted for Romney.
9. For a review of research on Latinos as well as African Americans, see Paula McClain and John D. Garcia, "Expanding Disciplinary Boundaries: Black, Latino, and Racial Minority Groups in Political Science," in *Political Science: The State of the Discipline II*, ed. Ada W. Finifter (Washington, D.C.: American Political Science Association, 1993), 247–279. For analyses of Latino voting in the 2008 and 2012 elections with an eye toward the future of Latino politics, see Matt Barreto and Gary Segura, *Latino America: How America's Most Dynamic Population Is Poised to Transform the Politics of the Nation* (New York: Public Affairs Books, 2014). For a review, see John D. Garcia, "Latinos and Political Behavior: Defining Community to Examine Critical Complexities," in *The Oxford Handbook of American Elections and Political Behavior*, ed. Jan E. Leighley (New York: Oxford University Press, 2010), 397–414.
10. Trump's comments about Mexican immigrants came on June 16, 2015, during the announcement of his presidential candidacy. For a transcript of his full remarks, see https://www.washingtonpost.com/news/post-politics/wp/2015/06/16/full-text-donald-trump-announces-a-presidential-bid/?utm_term=.826619831a93.
11. For three reviews of research on women in politics, see Susan J. Carroll and Linda M. Zerelli, "Feminist Challenges to Political Science," in Finifter, *Political Science: The State of the Discipline II*, 55–76; Nancy Burns, "Gender: Public Opinion and Political Action," in Katznelson and Milner, *Political Science: The State of the Discipline*, 462–487; and Kira Sanbonmastu, "Organizing American Politics, Organizing Gender," in Leighley, *Oxford Handbook of American Elections and Political Behavior*, 415–432.
12. The gender gap in 1980, coupled with Ronald Reagan's opposition to abortion rights and the Equal Rights Amendment, led the former president of the National Organization for Women, Eleanor Smeal, to write a report for the Democratic National Committee detailing how Democrats could take back the White House if the party placed a woman on the ticket in the next election. In 1984 Democratic Congresswoman Geraldine Ferraro became the first female vice presidential nominee in U.S. history. Reagan won reelection in a landslide.
13. See Abramson, Aldrich, and Rohde, *Change and Continuity in the 1980 and 1982 Elections* (Washington, D.C.: CQ Press, 1983), 290.
14. The ANES survey reports six types of marital status: married, divorced, separated, widowed, never married, and partners who are not married.
15. See Sheryl Gay Stolberg, "Obama Signs Away 'Don't Ask, Don't Tell,'" *New York Times*, December 22, 2010, http://www.nytimes.com/2010/12/23/us/politics/23military.html; and Jackie Calmes and Peter Baker, "Obama Says Same-Sex Marriage Should Be Legal," *New York Times*, May 10, 2012, A1.
16. Exit polls ask voters to cast a "secret ballot" after they have left the polling station. They are handed a short form that records the respondent's behavior, political views, and demographic information. Use of this procedure reduces the pressure for the respondent to answer in a socially "acceptable" way. The ANES also uses a private procedure for asking "sensitive" questions such as sexual orientation (and which also include income and other "standard" questions long asked face-to-face). At the end of the survey, respondents are

handed the tablet computer, and the interviewer leaves the room so that the respondent can answer sensitive questions in private.

17. Respondents were asked, "Do you consider yourself to be heterosexual or straight, homosexual or gay (lesbian), or bisexual?" This question was asked during a computer-assisted self-interview (CASI) portion of the face-to-face interview in which the respondent enters his or her response into a tablet computer.
18. Abramson, Aldrich, and Rohde, *Change and Continuity in the 2004 and 2006 Elections* (Washington, D.C.: CQ Press, 2007), 124–127. For cross-national evidence, see Ronald Inglehart, *Modernization and Postmodernization: Cultural, Economic, and Political Change in 43 Societies* (Princeton, N.J.: Princeton University Press, 1997), 255; and Russell J. Dalton, *Citizen Politics: Public Opinion and Political Parties in Advanced Industrial Democracies*, 5th ed. (Washington, D.C.: CQ Press, 2008), 145–152.
19. "America's Urban-Rural Divides," *The Economist*, July 1, 2017, https://www.economist.com/news/special-report/21724129-mutual-incomprehension-between-urban-and-rural-america-can-border-malice-americas.
20. Jeffrey M. Stonecash, *Class and Party in American Politics* (Boulder, Colo.: Westview Press, 2000), 87–121; Larry M. Bartels, *Unequal Democracy: The Political Economy of the New Gilded Age* (New York: Russell Sage Foundation, 2008), 64–126.
21. Rich Yeselson, "Can Trump Break the Democrats' Grip on the Union Movement?" *Politico*, http://www.politico.com/magazine/story/2017/02/trump-building-trades-unions-labor-support-history-republicans-214752.
22. For the single best summary, see Kenneth D. Wald and Allison Calhoun-Brown, *Religion and Politics in the United States*, 6th ed. (Lanham, Md.: Rowman and Littlefield, 2011). For a discussion of religion and politics in a comparative context, see Pippa Norris and Ronald Inglehart, *Sacred and Secular: Religion and Politics Worldwide* (Cambridge, U.K.: Cambridge University Press, 2004).
23. David E. Campbell, ed. *A Matter of Faith: Religion in the 2004 Presidential Election* (Washington, D.C.: The Brookings Institution), 1.
24. The exception to this generalization is religious devotion among African Americans, who overwhelmingly support the Democratic Party. Among non-Christian denominations, Jewish voters remain decidedly loyal to the Democrats.
25. See Robert D. Putnam and David E. Campbell, *American Grace: How Religion Divides and Unites Us* (New York: Simon and Schuster, 2010).
26. The Catholic Church had an uneasy relationship with the Obama administration. During the debate over health care reform in 2009, for instance, the U.S. Conference of Catholic Bishops supported the president's efforts to reform the health care system but threatened to oppose any bill that provided public funding for abortion or contraception. The Catholic Church had actually lobbied for decades for the adoption of a universal health care system, a more "liberal" system than what was eventually adopted under the Affordable Care Act, and a system that was supported by Hillary Clinton in the 1990. Nevertheless, the candidate and the Church were very much at odds with regard to the issue of abortion and women's rights, generally. And, in October 2016, when a set of emails from within the Clinton campaign staff was publicly released via WikiLeaks, they appeared to show a campaign at odds with Catholic leadership. See, for example, Sarah Pulliam Bailey, "WikiLeaks Emails Appear to Show Clinton Spokeswoman Joking about Catholics and Evangelicals," *Washington Post*, October 13, 2016, https://www.washingtonpost.com/news/acts-of-faith/wp/2016/10/12/wikileaks-emails-show-clinton-spokeswoman-joking-about-catholics-and-evangelicals/?utm_term=.3ee4fa742389.

27. Pew Research's Religious Landscape Study estimates that only 3 percent of American Catholics are African American. Thus Latinos are the main contributor to nonwhite support among Catholics. See http://www.pewforum.org/religious-landscape-study/religious-tradition/catholic/.
28. The question, which was asked to all Christians, was "Would you call yourself a born-again Christian; that is, have you personally had a conversion experience related to Jesus Christ?" This question was not asked in the 2004 ANES survey.
29. Lyman A. Kellstedt, "An Agenda for Future Research," in *Rediscovering the Religious Factor in American Politics*, ed. David C. Leege and Lyman A. Kellstedt (Armonk, N.Y.: M. E. Sharpe, 1993), 293–299.
30. Morris P. Fiorina and his colleagues have pointed out that ANES surveys suggest that the relationship between church attendance and the tendency to vote Republican was substantially higher in 1992 than in 1972, although the relationship leveled off or declined slightly between 1992 and 2004. See Morris P. Fiorina, with Samuel J. Abrams and Jeremy C. Pope, *Culture War? The Myth of a Polarized America*, 2nd ed. (New York: Pearson/Longman, 2006), 134.
31. Note, in comparing white Catholics, we do not reference those with "very high" religious commitment levels. This is because only 15 white Catholics in our sample fit into this category, a sample size that is too small from which to draw inferences.
32. Robert Axelrod, "Where the Votes Come From: An Analysis of Electoral Coalitions, *American Political Science Review* 66 (March 1972): 11–20. Axelrod updates his results through the 1984 elections. For his most recent estimate, including results from 1952 to 1980, see Robert Axelrod, "Presidential Coalitions in 1984," *American Political Science Review* 80 (March 1986): 281–284. Using Axelrod's categories, Nelson W. Polsby estimates the social composition of the Democratic and Republican presidential coalitions between 1952 and 2000. See Nelson W. Polsby and Aaron Wildavsky, *Presidential Elections: Strategies and Structures of American Politics*, 11th ed. (Lanham, Md.: Rowman and Littlefield, 2004), 32. For an update through 2004, see Nelson W. Polsby, Aaron Wildavsky, with David A. Hopkins, *Presidential Elections: Strategies and Structures in American Politics*, 12th ed. (Lanham, Md.: Rowman and Littlefield, 2008), 28.
33. John R. Petrocik, *Party Coalitions: Realignment and the Decline of the New Deal Party System* (Chicago: University of Chicago Press, 1981).
34. Harold W. Stanley, William T. Bianco, and Richard G. Niemi, "Partisanship and Group Support over Time: A Multivariate Analysis," *American Political Science Review* 80 (September 1986): 969–976. Stanley and his colleagues assess the independent contribution that group membership makes toward Democratic loyalties after controls are introduced for membership in other pro-Democratic groups. For an update and an extension through 2004, see Harold W. Stanley and Richard G. Niemi, "Partisanship, Party Coalitions, and Group Support, 1952–2004," *Presidential Studies Quarterly* 36 (June 2006): 172–188. For an alternative approach, see Robert S. Erikson, Thomas D. Lancaster, and David W. Romero, "Group Components of the Presidential Vote, 1952–1984," *Journal of Politics* 51 (May 1989): 337–346.
35. See Axelrod, "Where the Votes Come From."
36. The NORC survey, based on 2,564 civilians, used a quota sample that does not follow the probability procedures used by the ANES. Following the procedures used at the time, southern blacks were not sampled. Because the NORC survey overrepresented upper-income groups and the middle and upper-middle classes, it cannot be used to estimate the contribution of social groups to the Democratic and Republican presidential coalitions.

37. Abramson, *Generational Change in American Politics*, 65–68.
38. As Figure 5-1 shows, Bill Clinton did win a majority of the white major-party vote in 1992 and 1996.
39. Racial voting, as well as our other measures of social cleavage, is affected by including Wallace voters with Nixon voters in 1968, Anderson voters with Reagan voters in 1980, Perot voters with Bush voters in 1992, and Perot voters with Dole voters in 1996. For the effects of including these independent or third-party candidates, see Abramson, Aldrich, and Rohde, *Change and Continuity in the 1996 and 1998 Elections* (Washington, D.C.: CQ Press, 1999), 102, 104–106, 108, and 111.
40. The statements about low turnout in 1996 are true regardless of whether one measures turnout based on the voting-age population or the voting-eligible population. Turnout among the voting-eligible population fell about nine percentage points between 1960 and 1996. And even though black turnout fell in 1996, it was still well above its levels before the Voting Rights Act of 1965.
41. As we explain in Chapter 3, we consider the South to include the eleven states of the old Confederacy. Because the 1944 NORC survey and the 1948 University of Michigan Survey Research Center survey did not record the respondents' states of residence, we cannot include these years in our analysis of regional differences among the white electorate.
42. George H. W. Bush was born in Massachusetts and raised in Connecticut. As an adult Bush moved to Texas and was elected to the U.S. House from there.
43. Cheney had served as the U.S. representative from Wyoming from 1979 to 1989. When he became the chief executive officer of an oilfield services corporation in 1995, he established his residence in Texas. Being a resident of Texas would have complicated running on the same ticket as Bush because the Twelfth Amendment specifies that electors "vote by ballot for President and Vice-President, one of whom, at least, shall not be an inhabitant of the same state with themselves."
44. See, for example, Chapter 3, where we compare Kennedy's black support in the South in 1960 with Carter's in 1976.
45. Officially known as the Labor-Management Relations Act, this legislation, passed in 1947, qualified or amended much of the National Labor Relations Act of 1935 (known as the Wagner Act). Union leaders argued that the Taft-Hartley Act placed unwarranted restrictions on organized labor. This act was passed by the Republican-controlled Eightieth Congress, vetoed by Truman, and passed over his veto.
46. The Bureau of Labor Statistics estimates that in 2016, 10.7 percent of wage and salary workers are members of union, down from four years earlier. African American workers have a higher rate of union membership (13.0 percent) than white workers (10.5 percent). See Bureau of Labor Statistics, "Economic News Release: Union Members Summary," January 26, 2017, https://www.bls.gov/news.release/union2.nr0.htm.
47. This percentage may well be too low. According to the 2008 pool poll, Obama received 53 percent of the vote. Members of union households made up 21 percent of the electorate, and 50 percent voted for Obama. These numbers thus suggest that 23 percent of Obama's vote in 2008 came from members of union households. Even if one takes into account that not all these union voters were white, these numbers suggest that about one in five of Obama's votes in 2008 came from union households.
48. See Robert R. Alford, *Party and Society: The Anglo-American Democracies* (Chicago: Rand McNally, 1963); Seymour Martin Lipset, *Political Man: The Social Bases of Politics*, exp. ed. (Baltimore: Johns Hopkins University Press, 1981); and Inglehart, *Modernization and Postmodernization.*

49. The variation in class voting is smaller if one focuses on class differences in the congressional vote, but the data clearly show a decline in class voting between 1952 and 2008. See Dalton, *Citizen Politics,* 6th ed., 161.
50. Readers should bear in mind that in 2000, 2004, and 2008, there was no measure of the head of household's occupation or of the spouse's occupation, but our analysis of the 1996 data suggests that this limitation probably does not account for the negative level of class voting in the 2000 contest. Bartels discusses our attempts to maintain comparability in measuring social class in the face of changing survey measurement in *Unequal Democracy*, 70–71.
51. As we point out in *Change and Continuity in the 2000 and 2002 Elections*, when we define social class according to the respondent's own occupation, the overall size of the working class falls, and the overall size of the middle class grows. Because the relatively small size of the working class in 2000, 2004, and 2008, results mainly from a redefinition of the way our measure of social class is constructed, we assumed that the sizes of the working and the middle class in 2000, 2004, and 2008 were the same as they were in the 1996 ANES. See Abramson, Aldrich, and Rohde, *Change and Continuity in the 2000 and 2002 Elections*, chap. 4, 313n26.
52. See Anat Shenker-Osorio, "Why Americans All Believe They Are 'Middle Class,'" *Atlantic*, www.theatlantic.com, August 1, 2013 http://www.theatlantic.com/politics/archive/2013/08/why-americans-all-believe-they-are-middle-class/278240/.
53. See Mark N. Franklin, "The Decline of Cleavage Politics," in *Electoral Change: Responses to Evolving Social and Attitudinal Structures in Western Countries*, eds. Mark N. Franklin, Thomas T. Mackie, and Henry Valen, with others (Cambridge, U.K.: Cambridge University Press, 1992), 383–405. See also Inglehart, *Modernization and Postmodernization,* 237–266.
54. Jeff Manza and Clem Brooks, *Social Cleavages and Political Change: Voter Alignments and U.S. Party Coalitions* (New York: Oxford University Press, 1999).
55. Exit polls conducted between 1972 and 2016 show the same pattern. In all twelve elections Jews have been more likely to vote Democratic than white Catholics, and white Catholics have been more likely to vote Democratic than white Protestants.
56. For a discussion of the impact of religion on the 1960 election, see Philip E. Converse, "Religion and Politics: The 1960 Election," in *Elections and the Political Order*, ed. Angus Campbell et al. (New York: Wiley, 1967), 96–124.
57. The 1976 Democratic Party Platform can be found at http://www.presidency.ucsb.edu/ws/?pid=29606.
58. In our sample, 58.5 percent of Latinos identify themselves as Catholic.
59. According to the 2012 *Statistical Abstract of the United States,* as of 2010, 2.1 percent of the U.S. population was Jewish and, according to the Pew Forum on Religion and Public Life, only 1.9 percent. The *Statistical Abstract* results are based mainly on information provided by Jewish organizations, whereas the Pew results are based on a representative survey of 35,000 Americans from all 50 states. The Pew survey is presented in Pew Forum on Religion and Public Life, *U.S. Religious Landscape Survey*, http://www.pewforum.org/religious-landscape-study. For the *Statistical Abstract,* see U.S. Census Bureau, *The 2012 Statistical Abstract of the United States,* Table 77, https://www.census.gov/prod/2011pubs/12statab/pop.pdf.
60. States are listed in descending order according to their estimated number of Jews.
61. Since 1860 the Democrats have won the presidency only twice without winning New York: 1916, when Woodrow Wilson narrowly defeated Charles Evans Hughes by a margin of twenty-three electoral votes, and 1948, when Harry Truman defeated Thomas Dewey. Dewey, the governor of New York, won 46.0 percent of the popular vote in his home state, and Truman won 45.0 percent. Henry A. Wallace, the Progressive candidate in 1948, won 8.2 percent of the New York vote, substantially better than his share in any other state.

62. For an expanded treatment of the Catholic vote in 1960 and 2004, see J. Matthew Wilson, "The Changing Catholic Voter: Comparing Responses to John Kennedy in 1960 and John Kerry in 2004" in *A Matter of Faith*, ed., David E. Campbell (Washington, D.C.: Brookings Institution Press, 2007).
63. Robert Huckfeldt and Carol Weitzel Kohfeld provide strong evidence that Democratic appeals to blacks weakened the party's support among working-class whites. See their *Race and the Decline of Class in American Politics* (Urbana: University of Illinois Press, 1989).
64. For evidence on this point, see Paul R. Abramson, *Political Attitudes in America: Formation and Change* (San Francisco: W. H. Freeman, 1983), 65–68.
65. Edward G. Carmines and James A. Stimson, *Issue Evolution: Race and the Transformation of American Politics* (Princeton, N.J.: Princeton University Press, 1999). For a critique of their thesis, see Alan I. Abramowitz, "Issue Evolution Reconsidered: Racial Attitudes and Partisanship among the American Electorate," *American Journal of Political Science* 38 (February 1994): 1–24.

## CHAPTER 6

1. This set of attitudes was first formulated and tested extensively in Angus Campbell et al., *The American Voter* (New York: Wiley, 1960), using data from what are now called the ANES surveys. The authors based their conclusions primarily on data from a survey of the 1956 presidential election, a rematch between Democrat Adlai Stevenson and Republican (and this time the incumbent) Dwight Eisenhower. Recently Michael S. Lewis-Beck, William G. Jacoby, Helmut Norpoth, and Herbert F. Weisberg applied similar methods to data from 2000 and 2004. See their *The American Voter Revisited* (Ann Arbor: University of Michigan Press, 2008).
2. Campbell et al., *American Voter*. This was their next-to-the-lowest form of "issue"-related responses to what people said they liked or disliked about the parties and candidates. The "levels of conceptualization" had the category of ideological conceptualization at the top, followed by "near ideology," and then "group benefits." Only "no issue content" was lower than the nature of the times category.
3. Anthony Downs, *An Economic Theory of Voting* (New York: Harper and Row, 1957); V. O. Key, Jr., *The Responsible Electorate* (Cambridge, Mass.: Belknap Press of Harvard University Press, 1966).
4. Morris P. Fiorina, *Retrospective Voting in American National Elections* (New Haven, Conn.: Yale University Press, 1981).
5. Christopher H. Achen and Larry M. Bartels, *Democracy for Realists: Why Elections Do Not Produce Responsive Government* (Princeton, N.J.: Princeton University Press, 2016). Their signature example were shark attacks in 1916 that cut into incumbent Woodrow Wilson's votes in 1916, although it was, of course, a very small number of votes in the context of a presidential election and ones that therefore had no appreciable effect on the outcome. It is, however, certainly an eye-catching example.
6. Donald P. Green, Bradley Palmquist, and Eric Schickler, *Partisan Hearts and Minds: Political Parties and the Social Identities of Voters* (New Haven, Conn.: Yale University Press, 2002).
7. See, for example, Wendy M. Rahn et al., "A Social-Cognitive Model of Candidate Appraisal," in *Information and Democratic Processes*, ed. John A. Ferejohn and James H. Kuklinski (Urbana: University of Illinois Press, 1990), 136–159, and sources cited therein.

8. For the most extensive explication of the theory and tests in various electoral settings, see Gary W. Cox, *Making Votes Count: Strategic Coordination in the World's Electoral Systems* (New York: Cambridge University Press, 1997). For an examination in the American context, see Paul R. Abramson et al., "Third-Party and Independent Candidates in American Politics: Wallace, Anderson, and Perot," *Political Science Quarterly* 110 (Fall 1995): 349–367.
9. Or, at least, that is the conventional scholarly assumption about the causal ordering of influences, rather than, say, attitudes toward Trump leading the respondent to change their policy beliefs. Obviously, the latter is a possibility that needs to be taken seriously.
10. Ballotpedia (https://ballotpedia.org/Presidential_candidates,_2016) reports that 1,780 candidates filed a "Statement of Candidacy" with the Federal Election Commission, with eight candidates listed on at least 15 percent of the ballots nationwide. In addition to those discussed in the text, the other four are Darrell Lane Castle (Constitution Party), Rocky De La Fuente (Reform Party), Evan McMullin (Independent), and Gloria Estela La Riva (Party for Socialism and Liberation).
11. Such multicandidate elections are discussed in Paul R. Abramson, John H. Aldrich, and David W. Rohde, *Change and Continuity in the 1980 Elections*, rev. ed. (Washington, D.C.: CQ Press, 1983); Abramson, Aldrich, and Rohde, *Change and Continuity in the 1992 Elections*, rev. ed. (Washington, D.C.: CQ Press, 1995); Abramson, Aldrich, and Rohde, *Change and Continuity in the 1996 and 1998 Elections* (Washington, D.C.: CQ Press, 1999); and Abramson, Aldrich, and Rohde, *Change and Continuity in the 2000 and 2002 Elections* (Washington, D.C.: CQ Press, 2003).
12. We reproduced the feeling thermometer most recently in Abramson, Aldrich, and Rohde, *Change and Continuity in the 2000 and 2002 Elections*, 123.
13. Note that this percentage lead for Clinton in the ANES thermometer ratings reflects the percentage lead she won in the election exactly. A relatively smaller proportion than usual, 6 percent of respondents, rated the two candidates equally, suggesting how clearly the electorate distinguished the two candidates in 2016.
14. Two of these six ("speaks mind" and "even-tempered") are new to the ANES in 2016, reflecting uniquely relevant aspects of the 2016 contest, albeit reducing comparability to prior campaigns. These two replaced "moral" and "intelligent."
15. For what limited comparisons are possible to earlier surveys, see Abramson, Aldrich, and Rohde, *Change and Continuity in the 2008 and 2010 Elections*, Table 62-A, 146; and Abramson, Aldrich, and Rohde, *Change and Continuity in the 2012 and 2014 Elections*, Table 62-A, 149.
16. There is the single exception of responding that honesty describes her slightly well.
17. One might suggest that there is some rationalization here (those who like the candidate find reason to justify their support through positive evaluations of these traits). The distributions of responses here suggest that there is something more than mere rationalization to these responses overall (e.g., many who voted against Trump thought he spoke his mind in the campaign), and the vote pattern of even-tempered strongly suggests something other than mere rationalization is at work, although rationalization there well may be.
18. This was usually called a "pooled poll" in 2012, although typically referred to simply as an exit poll in 2016.
19. Concerns about foreign policy were also low in 1976, during the Cold War, although that occurred at a particularly low point of "détente" in it, and it was also the first election held after the withdrawal of the last American troops from Vietnam (and also of the defeat of our erstwhile allies there, the Republic of Vietnam).
20. Two such scales were used for the first time in 1968, and their popularity led to the larger and more diverse set of scales used thereafter. See Richard A. Brody and Benjamin I. Page,

"Comment: The Assessment of Policy Voting," *American Political Science Review* 66 (Issue 2, 1972): 450–458; Benjamin I. Page and Richard A. Brody, "Policy Voting and the Electoral Process: The Vietnam War Issue," *American Political Science Review* 66 (Issue 3, 1972): 979–995; and John H. Aldrich, "Candidate Support Functions in the 1968 Election," *Public Choice* 22 (Issue 1, 1975): 1–22.

21. See Abramson et al., *Change and Continuity in the 2008 and 2010 Elections*, for data and discussions about the 2008 data.
22. The only consistent exception since 1972 has been a women's rights scale, for which public opinion had become so favorable to the liberal end of the issue scale that it was dropped from the survey in 2012 due to lack of variation in opinion.
23. On government services the difference was actually 2.9 points, whereas on defense spending it was 1.9.
24. This theme is also a major claim in Achen and Bartels, *Democracy for Realists*, which is to say that one of the great recurring concerns in studying public opinion and voter behavior is the understanding of how much (or little) people know and how accurate what they claim to know actually is.
25. To maintain comparability with previous election surveys, for surveys from 1996 through 2012, we have excluded respondents who did not place themselves on an issue scale from columns II, III, and IV of Table 6-4. Because we do not know the preferences of these respondents on the issue, we have no way to measure the ways in which their issue preferences may have affected their votes.
26. For details, see Abramson, Aldrich, and Rohde, *Change and Continuity in the 1980 Elections*, Table 6-3, 130; Abramson, Aldrich, and Rohde, *Change and Continuity in the 1984 Elections*, rev. ed. (Washington, D.C.: CQ Press, 1987), Table 6-2, 174; Abramson, Aldrich, and Rohde, *Change and Continuity in the 1988 Elections*, rev. ed. (Washington, D.C.: CQ Press, 1991), Table 6-2, 165; Abramson, Aldrich, and Rohde, *Change and Continuity in the 1992 Elections*, Table 6-6, 186; Abramson, Aldrich, and Rohde, *Change and Continuity in the 1996 and 1998 Elections*, Table 6-6, 135; Abramson, Aldrich, and Rohde, *Change and Continuity in the 2000 and 2002 Elections*, Table 6-4, 137; Abramson, Aldrich, and Rohde, *Change and Continuity in the 2004 and 2006 Elections*, Table 6-4, 152; and Abramson, Aldrich, and Rohde, *Change and Continuity in the 2008 and 2010 Elections*, Table 6-4, 158.
27. Although this is evidence that most people claim to have issue preferences, it does not demonstrate that they do. For example, evidence indicates that some use the midpoint of the scale (point 4) as a means of answering the question even if they have ill-formed preferences. See John H. Aldrich et al., "The Measurement of Public Opinion about Public Policy: A Report on Some New Issue Question Formats," *American Journal of Political Science* 26 (May 1982): 391–414.
28. We use "apparent issue voting" to emphasize several points. First, voting involves too many factors to infer that closeness to a candidate on any one issue was the cause of the voter's choice. The issue similarity may have been purely coincidental, or it may have been only one of many reasons the voter supported that candidate. Second, we use the median perception of the candidates' positions rather than the voter's own perception. Third, the relationship between issues and the vote may be caused by rationalization. Voters may have decided to support a candidate for other reasons and also may have altered their own issue preferences or misperceived the positions of the candidates to align themselves more closely with their already favored candidate. See Richard A. Brody and Benjamin I. Page, "Comment: The Assessment of Policy Voting," *American Political Science Review* 66 (June 1972): 450–458.

29. Many individuals, of course, placed the candidates at different positions than did the public on average. Using average perceptions, however, reduces the effect of individuals rationalizing their perceptions of candidates to be consistent with their own vote rather than voting for the candidate whose views are actually closer to their own.
30. Of course, as we have seen, there were fewer in 2016 who failed to meet these conditions than in earlier elections. Still, it is a reminder that there may be other effects of the high levels of partisan polarization at the elite level than only making the informational demands for issue voting easier to satisfy.
31. Clinton's personal position has long been clear (and in line with that of her party). Trump's position has changed a great deal over the years, and it was really only in this campaign that he adopted the now-standard pro-life position of his party.

## CHAPTER 7

1. This is not to say that they did not dispute facts, nor did they stick to the facts on the performance of the economy.
2. Here we treat retrospective evaluations as directly related to attitudes, opinions, and choices. The alternative view is that these are not directly implicated in voting. Rather, they are simply bits of evidence as people make judgements about what the candidates and parties will do in the future.
3. V. O. Key, Jr., *Politics, Parties, and Pressure Groups*, 5th ed. (New York: Thomas Y. Crowell, 1964); V. O. Key, Jr., *The Responsible Electorate* (Cambridge, Mass.: Belknap Press of Harvard University Press, 1966).
4. Anthony Downs, *An Economic Theory of Democracy* (New York: Harper and Row, 1957).
5. Morris P. Fiorina, "An Outline for a Model of Party Choice," *American Journal of Political Science* 21 (August 1977): 601–625; Morris P. Fiorina, *Retrospective Voting in American National Elections* (New Haven, Conn.: Yale University Press, 1981).
6. Angus Campbell et al., *The American Voter* (New York: Wiley, 1960).
7. Fiorina, *Retrospective Voting in American National Elections*, 83.
8. We also return to the account of Christopher H. Achen and Larry M. Bartels, *Democracy for Realists: Why Elections Do Not Produce Responsive Government* (Princeton, N.J.: Princeton University Press, 2016), in which they demonstrate a great deal of additional data in favor of this Downs-Fiorina version of retrospective voting, except that they also show that many voters rely on the most recent evidence they heard, and it is therefore not very "retrospective," not necessarily based on evaluations of outcomes over which the president could reasonably be said to have any influence over, nor a very sound basis for building a democracy that relies on independent assessments of voters to shape elite choices. Here, we focus on just those things that presidents often claim to have at least significant degrees of influence over outcomes, notably war and peace and economic outcomes.
9. Indeed one thing that made 2012 and 2016 unusual was that economic conditions, although improving, were still a mixture of good and bad results, and thus voters might differ from one another in whether they thought the economy was sufficiently better than in 2008. Perhaps this was truer in 2012 than 2016, but the 2016 economy was sound, growing, a long run of positive results, but still leaving people behind.
10. See Benjamin I. Page, *Choices and Echoes in Presidential Elections: Rational Man and Electoral Democracy* (Chicago: University of Chicago Press, 1978). He argues that "party cleavages"

distinguish the party at the candidate and mass levels. This proved to be a forecast of the partisan polarization that began in earnest only a few years later.

11. See, e.g., Arthur H. Miller and Martin P. Wattenberg, "Throwing the Rascals Out: Policy and Performance Evaluations of Presidential Candidates, 1952–1980," *American Political Science Review* 79 (Issue 2, 1985): 359–372.
12. Note that this question is quite different from the questions we analyzed in election studies prior to 2012. These were questions asking the respondent about the government's handling of the most important problems facing the country. This question does not specifically ask about the government, nor does it ask about the most important problem per se. It is more general in its coverage and only by inference is attributable to the government.
13. Each respondent assesses government performance on the problem he or she considers the most important. In the seven surveys from 1976 to 2000, respondents were asked, "How good a job is the government doing in dealing with this problem—a good job, only fair, or a poor job?" In 1972 respondents were asked a different but related question (see the note to Table A7-1 in the appendix). In 2004 respondents were asked another question (see Chapter 6, note 9) and were given four options for assessing the government's performance: "very good job," "good job," "bad job," and "very bad job."
14. "Polls: Direction of Country," *Real Clear Politics*, https://www.realclearpolitics.com/epolls/other/direction_of_country-902.html.
15. Note that whereas perceptions of wrong versus right track began to narrow when Trump took office, they began to diverge again in March 2017 and have returned to relatively typical post-2009 levels, as of this writing.
16. See Gerald H. Kramer, "Short-Term Fluctuations in U.S. Voting Behavior, 1896–1964," *The American Political Science Review* 65 (Issue 1, 1971): 131–143, doi:10.2307/1955049; Fiorina, *Retrospective Voting in American National Elections*; M. Stephen Weatherford, "Economic Conditions and Electoral Outcomes: Class Differences in the Political Response to Recession," *American Journal of Political Science* 22 (November 1978): 917; D. Roderick Kiewiet and Douglas Rivers, "A Retrospective on Retrospective Voting," *Political Behavior* 6 (Issue 4, 1984): 369–393; D. Roderick Kiewiet, *Macroeconomics and Micropolitics: The Electoral Effects of Economic Issues* (Chicago: University of Chicago Press, 1983); Michael S. Lewis-Beck, *Economics and Elections: The Major Western Democracies* (Ann Arbor: University of Michigan Press, 1988); Alberto Alesina, John Londregan, and Howard Rosenthal, *A Model of the Political Economy of the United States* (Cambridge, Mass.: National Bureau of Economic Research, 1991); Michael B. MacKuen, Robert S. Erikson, and James A. Stimson, "Peasants or Bankers? The American Electorate and the U.S. Economy," *American Political Science Review* 86 (September 1992): 597–611; Robert S. Erikson, Michael B. MacKuen, and James A. Stimson, *The Macro Polity* (Cambridge, U.K.: Cambridge University Press, 2002).
17. John Mueller, *War, Presidents and Public Opinion* (New York: Wiley, 1973).
18. The appendix provides the full set of data from the entire set of ANES surveys.
19. We assume that people respond reasonably accurately and factually when talking about their personal situations. However, we are also assuming that they perceive that presidential (or governmental) performance is one of the reasons for their personal situation, which may well be a stretch. The overall view of the economy is, of course, a belief but one that is presumed to be grounded in real conditions, which are typically easily conveyed facts ("conveyed" does not mean "believed" or even remembered). And, in this case, lots of political actors are seeking to acclaim the successes or lament the failures of the incumbent and his or her party in achieving those outcomes.

20. Fiorina, *Retrospective Voting in American National Elections.*
21. Surveys have a very high degree of external validity. That is not only the strength of the survey method, but they are almost the only means by which one can make scientifically sound inferences about the voting public. Surveys are, however, weaker on internal reliability, that is, the ability to make a causal inference about "what causes what." Experiments (including perhaps the ultimate, the survey-embedded experiment) are one way to deal with the issue of causation. In a straight survey like (almost always) the ANES, it is difficult to say whether one approves of the job the president is doing because the president has done well in the respondent's eyes or whether the voter simply likes the president and therefore approves of whatever he or she does (at least up to some apparently very generous limits).
22. In the 1984 and 1988 surveys, this question was asked in both the pre-election and the postelection waves of the survey. Because attitudes held by the public before the election are what count in influencing its choices, we use the first question. In both surveys, approval of Reagan's performance was more positive in the postelection interview: 66 percent approved of his performance in 1984, and 68 percent approved in 1988.
23. Gary C. Jacobson, "Party Polarization in National Politics: The Electoral Connection," in *Polarized Politics: Congress and the President in a Partisan Era*, vol. 5 (Washington, D.C.: CQ Press, 2000), 17–18, demonstrates that evaluations of presidential performance have become much more sharply related to party identification in recent years compared to the earlier years of the ANES studies.
24. A summary measure of retrospective evaluations could not be constructed using either the 1972 or the 2004 ANES data. We were able to construct an alternative measure for 2004. See Abramson, Aldrich, and Rohde, *Change and Continuity in the 2004 and 2006 Elections*, chap. 7, Tables 7-9 and 7-10, 178–180, and 371n18. For procedures we used to construct this measure between 1976 and 2000, see Paul R. Abramson, John H. Aldrich, and David W. Rohde, *Change and Continuity in the 2000 and 2002 Elections* (Washington, D.C.: CQ Press, 2003), chap. 7, 328n13). A combined index of retrospective evaluations was created to allow an overall assessment of retrospective voting in 2016. To construct the summary measure of retrospective evaluations, we used the following procedures. First, we awarded respondents four points if they approved of the president's performance, two if they had no opinion, and zero if they disapproved. Second, respondents received four points if they thought the country was on the right track, zero if they thought the nation was on the wrong track, and two if they had no opinion. Finally, respondents received four points if they thought the incumbent president's party would do a better job handling the most important problem, zero points if they thought the challenger's party would do a better job, and two points if they thought there was no difference between the parties, neither party would do well, both parties would do the same, another party would do the better job, or they had no opinion. For all three questions "don't know" and "not ascertained" responses were scored as two, but respondents with more than one such response were excluded from the analysis. Scores on our measure were the sum of the individual values for the three questions and thus ranged from a low of zero (strongly against the incumbent's party) to twelve (strongly for the incumbent's party). These values were then grouped to create a seven-point scale corresponding to the seven categories in Table 7-9.
25. This measure is different in 2012 and 2016 than in prior elections due to our use of the "right track/wrong track" question. Other election years are also not always comparable, although they are more similar to each than to 2012. See Paul R. Abramson, John H. Aldrich, and David W. Rohde, *Change and Continuity in the 1996 and 1998 Elections* (Washington, D.C.: CQ Press, 1999), 158–159, for data on our (different) summary measure from 1972 to 1996;

Abramson, Aldrich, and Rohde, *Change and Continuity in the 2000 and 2002 Elections*, 164–165; Abramson, Aldrich, and Rohde, *Change and Continuity in the 2004 and 2006 Elections*, 178–180, 187–191, for analyses of those elections, respectively, in these terms.

26. The characterization of earlier elections is taken from Abramson, Aldrich, and David Rohde, *Change and Continuity in the 2000 and 2002 Elections*, 164.
27. For data from the 1976 and 1980 elections, see Abramson, Aldrich, and Rohde, *Change and Continuity in the 1980 and 1982 Elections* (Washington, D.C.: CQ Press, 1983), Table 7-8, 155–157; from the 1984 election, see Paul R. Abramson, John H. Aldrich, and David W. Rohde, *Change and Continuity in the 1984 Elections*, rev. ed. (Washington, D.C.: CQ Press, 1987), Table 7-8, 203–204; from the 1988 election, see Paul R. Abramson and Charles W. Ostrom, Jr., "Macropartisanship: An Empirical Reassessment," *American Political Science Review* 86 (March 1991): 181–192, Table 7-7, 195–198; from the 1996 election, see Abramson, Aldrich, and Rohde, *Change and Continuity in the 1996 and 1998 Elections*, 159–161; from the 2000 election, see Abramson, Aldrich, and Rohde, *Change and Continuity in the 2000 and 2002 Elections*, 165–166; and from the 2004 election, see Abramson, Aldrich, and Rohde, *Change and Continuity in the 2004 and 2006 Elections*, 178–180. The 2008 election is reported in Paul R., Abramson, John H. Aldrich, and David W. Rohde, *Change and Continuity in the 2008 and 2010 Elections* (Washington, D.C.: CQ Press, 2011), 188–191; and for 2012, see Paul R. Abramson, John H. Aldrich, Brad T. Gomez, and David W. Rohde, *Change and Continuity in the 2012 Elections* (Washington, D.C.: CQ Press, 2015), 188–191. The small number of seven-point issue scales included in the ANES survey precluded performing this analysis with 1992 data.

## CHAPTER 8

1. Angus Campbell et al., *The American Voter* (New York: Wiley, 1960); Warren E. Miller, "Party Identification, Realignment, and Party Voting: Back to the Basics," *American Political Science Review* 85 (June 1991): 557–568; Warren E. Miller and J. Merrill Shanks, *The New American Voter* (Cambridge, Mass.: Harvard University Press, 1996).
2. Campbell et al., *The American Voter*, 121.
3. For the full wording of the party identification questions, see Chapter 4, note 82. Note how simple this scientific advance was. They took a long-running question originally developed for the Gallup Poll survey and added the questions about "strength" of partisans and "party leanings" of independents. A simple measure of a rich theoretical concept can make a major difference.
4. Donald P. Green, Bradley Palmquist, and Eric Schickler, *Partisan Hearts and Minds: Political Parties and the Social Identities of Voters* (New Haven, Conn.: Yale University Press, 2002); Christopher H. Achen and Larry M. Bartels, *Democracy for Realists: Why Elections Do Not Produce Responsive Government* (Princeton, N.J.: Princeton University Press, 2016).
5. For evidence of the relatively high level of partisan stability among individuals from 1965 to 1982, see M. Kent Jennings and Gregory B. Markus, "Partisan Orientations over the Long Haul: Results from the Three-Wave Political Socialization Panel Study," *American Political Science Review* 78 (December 1984): 1000–1018, and see Laura Stoker and M. Kent Jennings, "Of Time and the Development of Partisan Polarization," *American Journal of Political Science* 52 (July 2008): 619–635, which cover 1965 to 1997.
6. V. O. Key, Jr., *The Responsible Electorate* (Cambridge, Mass.: Belknap Press of Harvard University Press, 1966).